*From Counter-Reformation
to Glorious Revolution*

BY HUGH TREVOR-ROPER

Archbishop Laud (1940; 2nd edition 1962;
3rd edition 1988)
The Last Days of Hitler
(1947; 5th edition 1978; 6th edition 1987)
The Gentry 1540–1640 (1953)
Historical Essays (1957)
The Rise of Christian Europe (1965)
Religion, the Reformation and Social Change
(1967; 3rd edition 1984)
The Philby Affair (1968)
The Plunder of the Arts in the Seventeenth Century (1970)
Princes and Artists (1976)
Hermit of Peking: The Hidden Life of Sir Edmund Backhouse
(1986. First published as *A Hidden Life:
The Enigma of Sir Edmund Backhouse* 1976)
Renaissance Essays (1985)
*Catholics, Anglicans and Puritans:
Seventeenth-Century Essays* (1987)

EDITED BY HUGH TREVOR-ROPER

Hitler's Table Talk 1941–4 (1953)
The Bormann Letters (1954)
The Poems of Richard Corbett
(with J. A. W. Bennett) (1955)
Hitler's Political Testament (1960)
The Great Histories: Edward Gibbon (1963)
*Essays in British History,
presented to Sir Keith Feiling* (1964)
Hitler's War Directives 1939–45 (1964)
The Age of Expansion (1968)
The Great Histories: Macaulay (1968)

From
Counter-Reformation
to
Glorious Revolution

Hugh Trevor-Roper

The University of Chicago Press
Chicago

The University of Chicago Press, Chicago 60637

© 1992 by Hugh Trevor-Roper

All rights reserved. Published 1992

Printed in England by Clays Ltd, St Ives plc

92 93 94 95 96 97 98 99 00 01   6 5 4 3 2 1

ISBN: 0–226–81230–8 (cloth)

First published in Great Britain in 1992
by Martin Secker & Warburg Limited

This book is printed on acid-free paper

CIP data are available from the Library of Congress

Phototypeset by Wilmaset Ltd, Birkenhead, Wirral
Printed by
Clays Ltd, St Ives plc

Contents

The sources of these essays are as follows:

1 'A Spiritual Conquest?': *New York Review of Books*, 13 June 1985.
2 'Sustaining an Empire': *New York Review of Books*, 27 September 1984.
3 'Medicine at the Early Stuart Court': Lecture at an international conference celebrating the 400th anniversary of the birth of William Harvey, in the Royal College of Physicians, London. Published in *Developments in Cardiovascular Medicine*, ed. C. J. Dickinson and J. Marks (MTP Press 1978).
4 'Hugo Grotius and England': Paper to the 11th Anglo-Dutch Historical Conference 1991. Now first published.
5 'The Church of England and the Greek Church': Lecture to the Ecclesiastical History Society. Published in *Studies in Church History*, ed. Derek Baker, vol. 15 (1978).
6 'The Plunder of the Arts in the Seventeenth Century': 2nd Walter Neurath Lecture. Published separately by Thames & Hudson (1970).
7 'Archbishop Laud in Retrospect': Lecture to Friends of Lambeth Palace Library. Published in *Annual Bulletin of the Friends of Lambeth Palace Library* (1978).
8 'Little Pope Regulus': Neil Lecture at Pembroke College, Cambridge, 1985. Printed in *The Pembroke Gazette* (1978).
9 'Edward Hyde, Earl of Clarendon': Commemorative (tercentenary) lecture at Oxford, 1974. Published separately by Clarendon Press (1975).
10 'Prince Rupert, the Cavalier': Lecture in Munich. Published (in German) in *Das Haus Wittelsbach und die Europäische Dynastien* (*Zeitschrift für Bayerische Landesgeschichte, Band 44, Heft 1*, Munich 1981).
11 'The Continuity of the English Revolution': Lecture to the Royal Historical Society, 1990. Published in *Transactions of the Royal Historical Society* (1990).
12 'The Glorious Revolution of 1688': Lecture at a historical conference on the subject in the British Academy, April 1989. Published in *The Anglo-Dutch Moment: Essays on the Glorious Revolution and its World Impact*, ed. Jonathan Israel (Cambridge 1990).

Introduction

A century is not much longer than a single human life-span, but it is a long time in history. How different is the world today from the world in the 1890s! And how different, in spite of the slower pace of life, between 1600 and 1700! In 1600 the Catholic Church, re-animated by the Council of Trent and the Counter-Reformation, had moved from conciliation to defiance of Protestantism, and the greatest secular power in the world, the Spanish empire, having absorbed Portugal with its empire in Brazil and the East, both provided that Church with material and drew from it spiritual strength. In the first thirty years of the seventeenth century the formidable combination of Habsburg power and papal influence, after some temporary rebuffs in Europe, reasserted itself. Having already subjected Italy and Flanders, it proceeded to take over Bohemia and the Rhineland. There seemed no end to its expansion. Spanish friars were conquering the souls, while Spanish colonists exploited the bodies, of the American Indians, and Italian Jesuits, under Portuguese and Spanish protection, had insinuated them-selves into the heart of the Mogul and Ming empires of India and China, the Shogunate of Japan.

Against this spectacular advance, what resistance was possible? Where could it begin? The rulers of the major Western monarchies, even Protestant monarchies, were dazzled, and sometimes seduced, by the spectacle of such success. They saw the model of an ordered monarchy, socially and spiritually guaranteed by an infallible Church. German Lutheranism offered now no challenge. For fifty years it had been quiescent, and the Habsburgs of Vienna, faced by

Ottoman power, and lacking the resources of their Spanish cousins,
had not sought to disturb it. But now Ottoman power was in retreat
and both Holy Roman Empire and Holy Catholic Church were
pressing eastward too. The Greek Orthodox Church would feel the
pressure: it would be undermined at its centre in Constantinople;
part of it would be taken over in Ruthenia and the Ukraine; and
after Bohemia, Poland, hitherto the model of religious toleration,
would succumb to the Jesuit missionaries.

Perhaps fortunately, every system creates its own antithesis:
against a world empire, nationalism; against a universal Catholic
Church, particular Protestant Churches. But how could such
disparate forces be mobilized for action? In the early years of the
new century, the most radical and determined articulators of
opposition, the antithesis of the Jesuits, were the Calvinists, and,
among them, especially, their original hard core, the French
Huguenots. It was they who had preached the doctrine of revolt in
the sixteenth century, they who inspired the resistance of the
Scottish Lords of the Congregation against Mary Stuart, of William
of Orange against Philip II, of Geneva against Savoy, of the Electors
Palatine – the permanent trouble-makers in the Empire – against
the Habsburgs of Vienna. It was the Huguenots who forced the
Bourbon dynasty on France – although here too, as so often, the
seduction of the Spanish model would periodically undermine the
spirit of resistance. It was a Huguenot, Pierre Asselineau, who
mobilized support for Venice against the power of the Papacy and
Spain. It was a Calvinist from Geneva, Jean Diodati, who would
animate the abortive international coalition against Spanish domination in the West in 1610, and another, Antoine Léger, who would
seduce the Patriarch of Constantinople and persuade him to carry
the Greek Orthodox Church to the Protestant side in the 1620s.
Another triumph of Huguenot diplomacy had even more dramatic
consequences. This was the marriage, in 1613, of the King of
England's daughter to the young Elector Palatine: a marriage which
was planned by the Elector's Huguenot uncle, the machiavellian
Duc de Bouillon, and whose sequel, the Calvinist usurpation of the
throne of Bohemia, would threaten to subvert the whole Habsburg–
Catholic system.

A brilliant coup in the short run; but alas, there are no short cuts
in politics. How often has a perfectly calculated *Blitzkrieg* led to a
long and uncalculated war, disastrous to the calculators! The Thirty

Years War, which was precipitated by that daring coup, has long
enjoyed a reputation – till it lost it in our century – as the most brutal
and destructive war in modern times. Its consequences – political,
religious, intellectual – were enormous. By the time it was over, the
balance of power in Europe had been transformed. The Catholic–
Habsburg combine, which had triumphed so easily in the first years,
ended defeated. France extended its frontiers permanently in the
West, Sweden, less permanently, in the East. In the course of the
struggle a whole philosophy, the philosophy of the Renaissance, was
dissolved. So was much of its cultural deposit: libraries looted,
monuments defaced, picture-galleries sold up by bankrupt
monarchies or pillaged by conquering armies. The one monument
of human thought produced directly by the war was in protest
against its barbarity: Hugo Grotius' *De Jure Belli ac Pacis*, the
philosophical foundation of international law.

From this terrible continental struggle one major European
power stood aloof – but only to founder in an internal revolution. In
the 1630s England was an island of peace. Though English
Protestants pressed for intervention in the holy war, Charles I,
having tasted the effects of such intervention in the 1620s, decided
firmly to keep out. Of course he would like to see his sister and her
family restored, not indeed to their usurped throne in Prague, but to
their electoral court and castle in Heidelberg; but not by war; rather
by appeasement: he would beg or buy this favour from those who
had the power to grant it. That meant, effectively, from Spain.
Besides, to an aesthete king who wished to keep a splendid and
cultured court, the Spanish model was so seductive. Like the French
court in the years between Henri IV and Richelieu, the court of
Charles I was being quietly sapped by the subtle, tempting narcotic
of revived Catholic devotion.

And yet not entirely: for was there not a middle way, an Anglican
via media, continuous with the English past, which would have all the
secular and aesthetic advantages of Roman Catholicism without its
much-publicized abuses and intolerable claims? To the king of a
Protestant country this was a tempting option; and not only to an
English king and his bishops and councillors, for there were other
men in Europe, idealists who saw such a Church as the perfect
model for a restored universal Church, the true remedy for the
schism of the Reformation and the horrible wars which it had
caused or inflamed. Such men were, or included, the intellectual

élite of the time: Grotius himself was one of them; but after the outbreak of the great war, and the religious polarization which it caused, the mirage receded. Only in England, its natural home, and in alliance with the English Crown, which drew strength from it, could it be turned into reality, and that only under the protection of peace: the peace which was secured – indeed needed – by the 'personal government' of Charles I and Archbishop Laud.

Perhaps, if the peace had been preserved a little longer, that government would have taken root. A new synthesis of a national semi-Catholic anti-Roman Church and an institutionalized, legalized royal 'absolutism' might then have been established and become traditional, to be accepted as an unquestioned inheritance by the next generation. Something similar was happening in contemporary France where Cardinal Richelieu, at the end of his life, was seeking to set up an anti-Roman national 'patriarchate' as an ideological prop for despotic royal power. The patriarchate did not outlast him but the power did. But such a victory had to be won by ruthless methods. Richelieu did not shrink from such methods. He was prepared to fight a civil war, to wear down, divide and absorb the powerful Huguenot nobility, to break, ruin and murder his domestic enemies. Charles I was not ruthless, or at least not ruthless enough; and his peace did not last. When his domestic enemies forced him into a frontier war, he lost the initiative. Richelieu would never do that.

By the summer of 1641 the English nobility and gentry who were determined to stop the drive to such 'absolutism' believed that they had succeeded. By a brilliant and dangerous strategy they had trapped their king, thrown out his chief ministers, almost usurped his kingdom, which they would then politely offer back to him on their own terms. It was like the masterly coup of the Calvinist international in 1618. But like those precursors they soon found that they had miscalculated. Once again, there was no such short cut. Soon they would be fighting a bloody civil war in the course of which their philosophy too, the philosophy of the 'Elizabethan compromise', would go down.

The mid-seventeenth century is a great watershed in European history, especially in intellectual history; but history has its continuities as well as its breaches: continuities contained within the experience of generations. Those who exercise power and determine policy are generally men whose minds have been formed by events twenty or thirty years before: thus the lessons of one crisis may be applied, or misapplied, in another, twenty or thirty years later. There is such a continuity between Europe in 1618–20 and England in 1641–2 and again between England in 1641 and England in 1688. In 1620 the Palatine family had been evicted from their usurped throne in Prague, and afterwards, in 1622, from their inherited electorate. In 1641–2 they re-surfaced in England to seek advantage in that crisis. The widowed Queen of Bohemia – still accorded that title by her supporters – and her eldest son, the Elector, cautiously backed the Parliament; her younger son, Prince Rupert, already a veteran of the Thirty Years War, would fight for the King. In 1618 utopian enthusiasts from Germany, Hungary, Bohemia, had converged in Prague to proclaim the coming of the prophet Elijah 'to make all things new'; in 1641 they reappear in London, preaching the same message. In 1618 the Dutch 'Arminians' had been routed and the Calvinist hard-liners had taken over in the Netherlands, in preparation for war; in 1640–1 the same reversal of fortune recurs in England. Then Oldenbarnevelt, now Strafford is judicially murdered; then Grotius, now Laud is thrown into prison. The Englishmen of 1641 had been young in 1618: now they re-enacted at home what then they had seen abroad. And similarly the men who were young in the 1640s and had seen the disastrous consequences of an English revolution which had failed, repeated that bold and dangerous adventure with more skill, or perhaps more luck, but certainly more success, in 1688.

There is, or recently was, a school of historians to whom the origins of the English revolution of 1641 are to be sought in the latent political or social tensions of the reign of Queen Elizabeth. It is a respectable view, with a long pedigree, going back to the Civil War itself. I do not share it, because I do not believe that any events are so predetermined: it is the historians who, retrospectively and sometimes arbitrarily, provide the link between cause and effect and presuppose the necessity. There is also now another school which, perhaps by over-reaction, sees great events as the effect, almost exclusively, of 'high politics': that is (I presume) politics abstracted from long, or wide, or deep historical considerations. I cannot accept this interpretation either, but I will not argue the matter here. I will only say that to separate any particular revolution from its long context in time – i.e. from the accumulated direct experience of those who made it – and from its wide context in space – i.e. from the events which were then unfolding in neighbouring countries – and to reduce it to cabinet politics, enclosed, like academic politics, in a small circle, argues, to me, a jejune view of history. To understand the politics of the past we must recapture the memories and the experience of a generation. The Englishmen who, in the 1670s and 1680s, mounted the revolution of 1688 remembered the 1630s and 1640s. They also looked abroad to France and Holland. And in Holland William of Orange also looked both abroad and back: abroad to France, and back to 1672, to the great crisis which had brought him to power in his own country.

Our 'Glorious Revolution' of 1688 was not an isolated event. What long memories lay behind it, what family traditions going back to the 1640s and beyond: from Charles II and James II to their father, Charles I, from the Hyde brothers to their father, the great Earl of Clarendon, from whig nobles, Russells and Sidneys, to their 'Puritan', and beyond them to their Elizabethan ancestors! But it was not a mere aristocratic coup, nor a mere English, or even, like the revolution of the 1640s, a mere British event. It transformed Britain, but it also transformed Europe, as that earlier revolution did not. How remote the old political configuration of Europe must have seemed in 1700, even though the English Revolution was seen to be, and indeed was, a conservative revolution! But then all English revolutions are conservative in intent, though not always in effect. Once again, consequences are rarely foreseen.

The lines of continuity are visible. One of them is still supplied by the Huguenot international: that old overflow from sixteenth-century France now dramatically reinforced by the brutal expulsion of 1685. The Edict of Nantes of 1598 had secured, for the Huguenots, if not equality of rights in a Catholic State, at least practical toleration. Its revocation, in 1685, was vivid in 1687–8: who can measure its psychological force, both in England and in the Netherlands? In the course of our revolution, the old Huguenot manifestos of the 1570s are republished in England as topical pamphlets, the old Huguenot interpretation of French history is given a new 'whig' application to English history in the immensely popular work of the Huguenot Rapin. The ideology indeed is not the same. Calvinist theology has been drained out of it. Toleration and rationalism, the distinguishing doctrines of 'Socinianism', so hateful to orthodox Calvinism, have crept in. The age of Enlightenment has begun.

*

The great Swiss historian Jacob Burckhardt, faced by the mountainous monographs of his German contemporaries, exclaimed, 'They forget the shortness of human life!' – the life of their readers, especially their non-specialist readers. His own aim, he wrote, was to encourage his pupils to find a personal interest in history, 'or at least not to sicken them of it', and his method was to make '*Querdurchschnitte*' – oblique cuts – through it, 'and those in as many directions as possible'. Fortified by so distinguished an example, I offer my *Querdurchschnitte* into the crowded period of history which I have summarized in my title. I may even add, with Burckhardt, that 'I know well that such an aim may be criticized as fostering amateurism', but 'at my advanced age that does not trouble me overmuch,' although, as a sop to the critics, I have taken my usual precaution of including one essay of rebarbative pedantry, which I shall not specify in advance.

The general theme of the essays has been sketched in this introduction. The first two, which were originally printed as reviews, touch on the 'imperial over-stretch' of the Counter-Reformation Church and Habsburg Spain: the former in China, the latter in Europe. All the others began as special lectures and all but one of them have been published either separately or in the appropriate journals, 'bulletins', 'proceedings', etc., which I have listed in the proper place. I have revised and extended some of them for publication here. In them I seek to describe and interpret, in brief compass, some of the side-effects of the Thirty Years War: the destruction and removal of art-treasures and manuscripts in Europe and the Levant, the competitive pressure of the rival Western Churches on the unfortunate, enslaved Greek Church, the ecumenical aspirations of Grotius, their insular application and ultimate repudiation by the Anglican Church on which they were centred, and their survival in the 'Socinianism' of Falkland and Hyde and in the religious toleration secured, *de facto* though not *de jure*, in the compromise of the Glorious Revolution. I have also considered the breaches and continuities of our two revolutions, and the interaction, throughout the period, of English with European history, intellectual as well as political: Grotius and the English Church, Rupert of the Rhine in the English Civil War, and the constant presence of the émigré Huguenots, from the Huguenot physician who overshadowed the greater Dr Harvey at the court of James I and Charles I to the Huguenot soldier of William III who would offer the first classic whig interpretation of English history: an interpretation which, by repetition, competition, refinement and reaction, has dominated our view of the seventeenth century in England, directly or indirectly, ever since.

A Spiritual Conquest? Matteo Ricci in China

In 1583 two Italian Jesuits established themselves in Chao-ch'ing near Canton. They had come thither from Macao on the unexpected invitation of the Governor of Canton and the Viceroy of the province, who offered them land on which to build a church, a promise of protection, and freedom to travel. One of them was Michele Ruggieri, a Neapolitan from Salerno, who had already, but briefly, set foot in China. His companion was Matteo Ricci, a native of Macerata in the Papal State. Ruggieri would remain in China for several years; then he would return to Europe in an abortive attempt to stimulate a papal embassy to the court of Peking. Ricci would stay for twenty-seven years, establishing Jesuit houses first at Chao-ch'ing, then at Nan-ch'ang, the capital of Kiangsi province, at Nanking, the southern capital of China, and finally in Peking. It was the beginning of an astonishing adventure: the Jesuit penetration of the Chinese court, begun by them under the Ming dynasty and brought, through fierce controversy, to its climax under their successors, the Manchu Emperors, the Ch'ing.

Merely to have entered China at that time was an achievement, for China under the Ming was a closed country. Three centuries before, under the conquering Mongol Yüan dynasty, it had been relatively open. It was then that Marco Polo had visited the court of Kublai Khan at Peking and that Franciscan friars had waited on his successor at Karakorum in Outer Mongolia. China was then part of an even vaster empire, open to the West. But the Ming Emperors, having restored the independence of China, were jealous protectors of it. Under their rule foreigners were not allowed into the country except as tributary delegations, licensed traders, or admiring visitors admitted by personal favour and then forbidden ever to leave. The Celestial Empire (it was agreed) had no need of foreigners or their wares. Was it not the centre of the world, self-sufficient in all things, the only source of civilization, science and rhubarb? It did not even need the tribute that was brought by its vassals and neighbours, and was indifferent whether it was paid or not – rationally so, since 'the dignity of so great a prince' as the Emperor required that such tribute be acknowledged with far costlier gifts in return, so that these ritual exchanges ended in an adverse balance of barter.

How then did the Jesuits not only continue to enter this closed empire but also establish themselves firmly in its capital? The story of that achievement is told by Ricci himself in the *History of the Introduction of Christianity into China* which he wrote, on the orders of the Jesuit General Claudio Acquaviva, in his last years in Peking. It is a classic of cultural history and a fascinating story in itself; but what Ricci so attractively describes needs also to be explained. The explanation lies not only in the extraordinary dynamism of the Italian Counter-Reformation but also in the mechanics of the no less extraordinary Portuguese commercial empire in the Far East.

By 1550 that empire was well established and, as yet, unchallenged by any European power. The Portuguese had a viceroyalty of India at Goa, which they had acquired in 1502; having secured control of the Strait of Malacca, they had then entered the South China Sea; and there they had discovered vast opportunities of wealth if only they could force their trade on both China and Japan. After attempting to break into China at Canton and Ningpo, and thereby still further increasing Chinese xenophobia, they finally secured trading facilities at Macao in 1557, which soon became, effectively, a Portuguese colony, as it would long remain. Meanwhile they had forged links with the warring feudatories of Japan. So a system was built up which brought in fabulous profits. From Macao, European manufactures reached the licensed bi-annual fairs of Canton. At Canton they were exchanged for Chinese silk. Chinese silk and European firearms were then carried, in the annual 'Great Ship', from Macao to Japan; and the same ship returned to Macao with a cargo of Japanese silver to refuel the system. By the 1570s this system was firmly established. Macao, Canton and

Nagasaki were the focal points of a hugely profitable triangular system of international trade.

With trade went religion. Already in the 1540s, Francis Xavier, the Jesuit apostle of the East, had been to Japan; but having discovered that Japan was a cultural colony of China, he had decided that, in religion as in trade the key lay in China. However, his three attempts to reach China – first by attaching himself to embassies from Goa and Siam, then by finding his own way into Canton – proved abortive, and in 1552 he had died in the offshore island of Shang-ch'uan, the first base of the Portuguese, before they obtained Macao. As Ricci afterwards put it, 'the holy man was not as yet acquainted with the conditions prevailing in China'. He had not done his political homework. Later Jesuits would not make that mistake.

In the thirty years after Francis Xavier's death, various attempts were made, by Augustinian, Dominican and Franciscan friars, to penetrate the closed empire; but it was not till 1582 that a breach was made. By now the objective situation had changed; the triangular trade-system of Macao, Canton and Nagasaki was in full swing; and since the Jesuits were established at Macao and Nagasaki, it was logical to plant them, if possible, in Canton too. In that year Ruggieri contrived to make two visits to Canton. The first was exploratory. On the second, thanks to the favour of the Governor, he thought that he had secured a firm base; but then there was a sudden change: he was ordered out by the Viceroy of the province and reprisals were threatened against the Chinese interpreters in Macao who had taught him their language. However, he had left behind him certain objects which gradually weakened the Viceroy's resistance: in particular, a watch – 'a beautiful little machine made of brass which struck the hours without anyone touching it', and several triangular glass prisms 'in which objects were reflected in beautiful multi-coloured tints'. Such watches were 'unheard of by the Chinese, something new and to them quite mystifying', and the glass prisms were assumed to be 'a kind of precious stone of wonderful value'. They were to prove powerful engines for the spiritual conquest of China. Immediately they caused the Viceroy to relent, and so, in 1583, the Jesuits were invited back. This time they came for good – or at least for two hundred years.

Thus the Jesuit missions to China and to Japan were complementary. Both were sent out from Macao, and financed by the profits of the Great Ship. Both were directed by the Jesuit college at Macao, 'the seminary', as Ricci called it, 'of the two great missions of Japan and China'. And behind both stood the same great organizer, the man whom Ricci would describe as 'the first author of this mission', 'the founding father of the undertaking of China': Alessandro Valignano. He too was an Italian – like Ruggieri, he came from the kingdom of Naples – and he had been Rector of the college of Macerata where Ricci had studied. Now he was Visitor – that is Superior – of all the Jesuit missions in the Far East. It was he who had devised the contract with the Portuguese capitalists which made the mission in Japan so successful, and it was he who had fetched Ruggieri and Ricci from Goa to Macao and told them to learn Chinese. In 1582 he had been in Macao himself, with four converted Japanese princes whom he was dispatching to Rome, and had personally organized the mission to China. He had also laid down the policy and the long-term strategy for the future. For this enterprise was to be very different from the heroic individual apostolate of Francis Xavier.

What characterized these Jesuit pioneers was their keen political nose. While the unsophisticated Portuguese friars laboured inconspicuously among the poor, the Jesuits, wherever they went, studied the society around them and set out scientifically to woo the ruling élite. This entailed tactics which varied from country to country. In India they went straight to the top: they sent a mission to the Mogul conqueror Akbar, and hoped, through him, to convert his whole empire. In anarchical Japan, where the Emperor was a cypher, they courted the feudal warlords, presenting themselves as soldiers of Christ, a disciplined military order with high notions of aristocratic honour: the *samurai* of the Church. In settled, peaceful China, where feudalism had been extinct for 1,800 years, and military men were at the bottom of the social hierarchy, their policy must be different: there they must appear as urbane scholars, fit to sip tea with the ruling literati and discuss philosophy with them in perfect Mandarin Chinese.

At first, naturally enough, they made mistakes. For instance, they called each other, and were called by their servants, by their own names. 'To the Chinese', they soon found, 'this was, to put it mildly, quite unrefined'. So they swallowed their Christian humility and assumed 'honour names'. Another mistake was more serious. At first they imitated the Buddhist monks and went about on foot, clean-shaven with cropped hair. Rather belatedly, they discovered that Buddhist monks were considered very low-class, so they changed their style: they grew their beards and hair, wore high hats and long robes of purple silk, and were carried in sedan chairs on the shoulders of porters, with servants in attendance. 'If these customs were neglected', Ricci explained, 'one would not be known as learned': a terrible fate in a society ruled by scholars. Thus they separated themselves from the vulgar herd and ensured that they could move freely, and find protectors, in high official circles. As they put it, when they turned down the offer of a delightful place of residence among pleasant hills and neat orchards, it was 'too far from the town and from the educated classes, among whom, as their equals, they were accustomed to live'.

What did these Jesuits discuss when drinking tea with the local mandarins? Science, literature, ethics certainly; for this was what interested their hosts. But on one subject, at first, they were deliberately reticent. They were careful never to make 'any mention of Christianity', or to divulge, even indirectly, their secret purpose in entering China, the spiritual conquest of the country. 'The one thing necessary', they reckoned, was 'to remain within the kingdom', and until that was guaranteed – that is, until they had got to Peking and acquired an irreversible permit of residence from the Emperor – they would take no risks. They admitted, of course, that they were Christian priests; but they insisted that they were not evangelists. They had been drawn to China, they said, merely by the fame of the Empire, and they wanted no more than to practise their religion in private. All that they asked was 'a small plot of land to build a house, and also a church in honour of the King of Heaven'.

'The King of Heaven' – what a simple, and yet what an artful phrase! For this was the name which the Confucians of China gave to their remote, abstract deity, and by using it the Jesuits suggested that the religion which they wished to practise so privately in China hardly differed from the official religion of the Confucian literati: that it too was a kind of gentlemanly deism, free from vulgar mysteries and 'the odious name of sacrifices'. And indeed, when they touched on the subject, they constantly emphasized the similarities and attenuated the differences between the two systems of belief. With such a Christianity, they argued, Confucianism, being also 'in perfect accord with the light of conscience and with the Natural

Law', was entirely compatible. It only needed the top-dressing of the immortality of the soul (on which the Confucians were open-minded) in order to be identical. How different from the other religions of China: the 'disorderly ravings' of the Taoists, 'a low and dishonest class' of enthusiasts who believed in saints, miracles, 'a trinity of gods', and other such follies, or of vulgar Buddhist 'idol-worshippers' whose doctrines were fit only for 'women, eunuchs and the common herd'! The Grand Master of a Buddhist temple did indeed venture to remonstrate, explaining that 'idols as such were not worthy of any honour' but were necessary to preserve religion among ordinary people. However, this sound Catholic reasoning, which the Jesuits themselves would use in Europe, did not satisfy them in China.

Ricci and his companions spent much time refuting Taoist and Buddhist 'idolaters' and identifying with courtly Confucian mandarins, even if this obliged them to disown some inconvenient aspects of their Christianity. Thus they thought it prudent to remove a picture of the Virgin Mary from above the altar of their church in Chao-ch'ing lest the Chinese should think 'that we adored a woman as our God'; and when Ricci felt secure enough to print a Christian catechism in Chinese, he adjusted the emphasis to suit the readers: he dwelt upon 'such points of doctrine as appeared to be drawn only from the Natural Law', but contrived not to mention the story of the crucifixion, which a Chinese gentleman would have found unedifying. Even so, he afterwards felt that he had gone too far, and in a revised edition, written as if by 'men of letters' for other men of letters, he saw to it that all references to sacrifice or religious cult were cut out; after which the printing forms of the first edition were destroyed. In this way Christianity was made to conform completely with 'the natural law, as developed by their prince of philosophers, Confucius, and adopted by the sect of the literati'. How successfully this was done appears from the gratifying comment of an eminent Confucian scholar. 'In your teachings concerning the Lord of Heaven', he wrote to Ricci, 'there seems no difference from what our sages have taught'.

Ricci justified his tactical modifications of Christian doctrine by citing the claim of St Paul, who had made himself 'all things to all men for the winning of souls to Christ'. He could do so safely, because he and his little band of fellow Jesuits had a complete monopoly of Christianity in China. The Franciscans and Dominicans who were now spoiling the Jesuit game in Japan were bottled up in Macao. Had they been allowed to enter China, no doubt they would have reminded their rivals of that other Pauline claim: 'I am determined not to know anything among you save Jesus Christ, and him crucified'. In the next century, when they got into China, they did.

A religion of natural law, a religion without mystery or sacrifice, Christianity without the crucifixion, Christianity as an extension of Confucianism, obeisance only to an undefined King of Heaven – in other words deism – this was the religion which the Jesuits, by their own account, quietly avowed at Chao-ch'ing, at Shao-chou, and later at Nan-ch'ang, Nanking and Peking. Of course, in their eyes, it was a stage only, a tactical necessity while they were feeling their way. Ultimately Ricci looked forward to a very different situation. Just as he had foreseen the conversion of Akbar leading to 'nothing less than the conversion of all India', so he envisaged himself being received by the Emperor of China, converting the Emperor of China, being appointed confessor to the Emperor of China; and then, of course, all the literati of China, and, through them the teeming, docile population of that whole vast empire, would solemnly repudiate Confucianism and embrace Counter-Reformation Catholicism, which, by then, would have recovered its central but hitherto suppressed features: trinity of gods, the mystery of the Incarnation, the sacrifice of the mass, saints, miracles, images . . .

So the Jesuits sought friends and protectors among the mandarins of China. They needed such protection, because there were many Chinese who suspected that they were up to no good – indeed that they portended 'some great calamity' for the country. For who could deny that the new invaders from the West – the Portuguese in Macao, the Spaniards in Manila (and Portugal and Spain were now ruled by the same King) – were predators in the China Sea? Their power, and their will to use it ruthlessly, were evident. What, then, it was asked, were these innocent-seeming travellers doing in the closed empire? Were they not spies, searching out the land? Since Spanish and Portuguese agents were in fact often recommending the conquest of China, which they insisted would be easy,[1] these suspicions were not unreasonable, and of course they were spread with particular zeal by those whom the Jesuits called 'the idolatrous emissaries of Satan', the hated Buddhist priests.

The predicament of these remarkable missionaries – their loneliness, their vast ambition, and their necessary secretiveness – is illustrated by a little episode which occurred in 1595. Expelled from Nanking, weary, frustrated and perplexed, Ricci dreamed that he met 'a strange wayfaring man', who said to him, 'Is this the way you wander about this vast kingdom, imagining that you can uproot an age-old religion and replace it with a new one?' 'Now it so happened', Ricci comments, 'that from the time of his entrance into China' – that is, throughout the last twelve years – 'he had always kept his ultimate design as an utter secret'. So he answered, 'You must be either God or the Devil, to know what I have never revealed to anyone'. The stranger declared that he was God, and Ricci thereupon protested to Him that He did not give him much help in his missionary efforts; whereupon God encouraged him to persevere, promising ultimate success. Ricci persevered; and by perseverance, combined with courtesy, tact, modesty and his remarkable gifts, he would at last find his way to Peking.

Particularly by his gifts: gifts both material and intellectual. The most acceptable material gifts were the clocks, watches and prisms which had already seduced the Viceroy of Kwangtung, but there were also astronomical spheres and globes, astrolabes, maps, sundials, musical instruments; and occasionally a religious picture was slipped in. The Chinese were delighted with these marvels of Western technology, especially the clocks – mechanical striking clocks driven by wheels and springs, such as they had never known – and the Jesuits used them to the full. They fetched a clockmaker from Macao to make a clock for the Governor of Canton. They put up a large clock outside their house in Chao-ch'ing whose chimes were audible to all. Another clock, presented to a royal prince in Nan-ch'ang, showed the hours of sunrise and sunset, the varying length of day and night, and the signs of the zodiac cut in black China marble. But the grandest of all was one specially sent by the Jesuit General, Acquaviva, as a gift for the Emperor. It 'struck all the Chinese dumb with astonishment', we are told, for it not only kept perfect time and announced the hours without being touched, 'but also sounded the half-hours and the quarters in triple chimes'. Such a clock, says Ricci, had never been seen, or heard, or even imagined, in Chinese history.

The Chinese officials might be seduced and delighted by the clocks and other instruments, but even more impressive to them was the science which lay behind them. Their own science had been in decline since the end of the Mongol dynasty, the nationalist reaction, and the reinforced Confucian orthodoxy of the Ming; and now, having forgotten their own achievements, they were dazzled by the European science of which Ricci himself, a true Renaissance man, seemed to be master: by his knowledge of mathematics (he had studied the subject in Rome under Christopher Clavius, 'prince of mathematicians of his day', the deviser of the Gregorian calendar); of music (he brought a clavichord for the imperial palace); of cosmography (his maps of the world, based on those of the great Flemish cartographer Ortelius, but tactfully placing China in the centre, were a great success in Canton and afterwards in Peking); of chronometry (he would be employed to reform the Chinese calendar); of mnemonics (of which more hereafter); even – so the Chinese thought – of alchemy: for how, they asked, could these wandering priests pay their way and sustain their mandarin life-style? Surely they must have mastered the secret of transmuting base metals into gold. The innocent Chinese did not understand the mysterious economy of the Portuguese Great Ship. All this was a great help to the Jesuits. Their clocks and prisms might, in Ricci's phrase, 'oil the wheels of social progress' – that is, of their own upward social mobility – but their scientific brilliance had a far more profound effect. It convinced the Chinese that Europeans were not merely the predatory buccaneers whom they had known at Canton and Ningpo, and that even the Celestial Empire might have something to learn from the West.

Ricci and his little party – one other Jesuit and two lay brothers – finally arrived in Peking in September 1598. They came by canal, in the Viceroy of Nanking's fast boat. But this first visit was a failure: after waiting two months, they were obliged to return to Nanking. They had not been received by the Emperor. It was in fact an ill-chosen moment. The Empire was then at war; the Japanese tyrant Hideyoshi had attacked China's vassal state, Korea; and Peking was no place for foreigners. However, in May 1600 Ricci tried again, and this time he was more successful. After six months' detention in Tientsin at the hands of the terrible eunuch Ma T'ang, he finally received an imperial summons to the capital. So he entered the city with his presents – it took eight packhorses and over sixty porters to carry them – and expected great things: reception by the Emperor, the conversion of the Emperor, the conversion of China.

In fact, Ricci was never received by the Emperor. For the

Emperor – the Wan-li Emperor, the longest-reigning Emperor for 1,700 years – had by now become a total recluse. Too obese to stand without help, he gave no audiences, neglected business, left offices unfilled, and spent his time building vast palaces and devising his own splendid tomb. No one could communicate with him except through the eunuchs who swarmed around him, shut him off from the world, and oppressed the country in his name. However, Ricci did receive a verbal message from the court, and it was enough. He was told that he could stay in Peking. No longer was he at the mercy of bureaucratic shifts, the changing whims of governors and eunuchs. So he set up in Peking his fourth mission-house, and the last stage of his campaign for the spiritual conquest of China began.

It was indeed an extraordinary achievement, and he could be pardoned for uttering a cry of triumph. The 'enterprise of China', he wrote, was 'the most important expedition undertaken for the promulgation of Christianity since the Apostles went out to evangelize the whole world'. Certainly, by now, it was the most promising Jesuit enterprise in the Far East. The attempt to convert Akbar had failed in India, and now the reaction had set in in Japan: the frightful Hideyoshi had turned against the Christians and was crucifying them in public. But in China Ricci found himself in high favour. The invisible Emperor needed him: to answer questions about Europe – the palaces of its kings, the tomb of Philip II – and to explain and service the presents he had brought: to teach the palace eunuchs to play the clavichord and to regulate the clocks. That ensured his continued residence. It also ensured his social status: in his first year in Peking, he records, he had more dinner invitations than in all his previous seventeen years in China.

Thus established, Ricci no longer had to conceal the real aim of his visit to China. Hitherto the Jesuits had been cautious, afraid of arousing suspicion which would 'impede their immediate purpose of establishing a residence'. But now that that purpose was achieved, 'there was no further cause for delay'. It was full speed ahead. Confident of imperial support, and in alliance with the Confucian literati, Ricci made open war on 'the weird hallucinations of the idol-worshippers' – that is, the Buddhists – and their supporters at court. He made converts among the mandarins; and with their aid he published useful works in Chinese: works on philosophy, ethics, science, songs for the palace eunuchs to sing to the clavichord, a translation of Euclid, new versions of his catechism and his world-map; and he introduced into China, along with Renaissance mathematics, astronomy, clockwork, etc., which, in these days of the Ming, were a step forward, the obsolescent Aristotelian cosmology which, in these days of Copernicus and Galileo, was a step back.[2]

To Ricci, the introduction of the new European science into China was only a means to an end. Always the end was the same: the conversion of China. In fact, the means proved more important, and more lasting, then the end. A century later the Jesuits were still favoured guests in China. They had survived the Manchu conquest and the change of dynasty. They had made distinguished converts. They were high in favour with the Emperor. But they were still at the beginning of their religious task. They had not converted the Emperor. They had not overthrown 'the age-old religion' of China. All they had done was to compromise themselves in Europe by the concessions which they had made to Confucianism. By such methods, in 1600, Ricci had established his mission in Peking. By the same methods, in 1700, his successors found themselves condemned in Rome for surrendering the essential truths of Christianity and reviving heresies which the Church had disowned.[3] It was the first stage in the process which would culminate, sixty years later, in the total dissolution of their Order by the very authority which it had been created to defend.

Their real achievement was not the conversion of China but the introduction into China, for that purpose, of Western science: what Joseph Needham has called the fusion of Chinese science with the universal world science created in Europe. That fusion was the work of a whole century after Ricci's death. He died in Peking in 1610, and was buried in what was to remain the Catholic cemetery, on land granted by the Emperor from the confiscated estate of a disgraced eunuch. His papers were brought back to Rome by his fellow Jesuit, the Belgian Nicolas Trigault. Among them was the manuscript of his *History of the Introduction of Christianity into China*, written in Italian. Trigault translated it into Latin and published it (with omissions and additions) in 1615.[4] It was the first of that series of Jesuit 'Relations' which provided the material for the utopian picture of the government of China as set out in Burton's *Anatomy of Melancholy* and by the *philosophes* of the Enlightenment. Three centuries after its publication, the original Italian text was rediscovered. It was published, together with Ricci's letters from China and other documents, by the Jesuit historian Tacchi-Venturi, at Ricci's birthplace, Macerata.[5] A generation later, in the middle of the Second World War, as a token of the reconciliation of the Vatican and the Italian State by Mussolini's concordat, the first of the three volumes of the 'national edition' appeared: the original sources, edited, with a full and valuable commentary, by a Jesuit who was also a sinologist, Pasquale d'Elia.[6] From these majestic works, which establish the greatness of Matteo Ricci, and from a wide knowledge of the European background, Jonathan Spence, a distinguished historian and sinologist, has written the book which has occasioned this essay.*

One of Ricci's many intellectual gifts was his remarkable memory, of which he gave frequent demonstrations in China. Indeed it became a parlour trick which he was often called upon to perform: he could even repeat a whole sequence of ideographs backward. The Chinese were dazzled by these displays. 'Nothing', he wrote, 'seemed to please them more than an exhibition of his extraordinary memory, which he had developed by a certain technique and practice'. They were particularly interested because a prosperous career in the Empire depended on success in the regular examinations for the bureaucracy, and that success depended largely on knowing the Chinese classics by heart. The mandarins naturally wanted their sons to pass their examinations, and so they pressed Ricci to teach them his method. The method was of course the *memoria technica* which the men of the Renaissance had adopted from the ancient orators, and which has been described for us by Frances Yates and Paolo Rossi.[7] This consisted of building an imaginary palace, memorizing all its features and contents, and relating all the details of one's own relevant knowledge to 'images' corresponding with these features. One of those who were excited by Ricci's parlour-tricks was the Viceroy of the province of Kiangsi, whose three sons were preparing for their examinations. For them, at their father's request, Ricci wrote in Chinese a description of his method. The sons did well in their examinations but not, it seems, thanks to Ricci's rules: as one of them sensibly observed, those rules were no doubt correct, but 'one has to have a remarkably fine memory already to make any use of them'.

---

*Jonathan D. Spence, *The Memory Palace of Matteo Ricci* (New York, Viking, 1984).

Mr Spence makes use of them for a different purpose. He takes four ideographs used as images in Ricci's book (of which only one copy survives) and four religious pictures which Ricci supplied to a Chinese publisher for inclusion in another book, and turns them into artificial memory devices. That is, he seeks, through them, to re-create and bring up the supposed content of Ricci's own memory, as it can be imaginatively documented from external historical sources. In other words, Mr Spence seeks, by a highly artificial method, to re-create selected aspects of the life and times of Ricci: his Jesuit training, his experiences in Europe and Asia, the physical and mental world of Counter-Reformation Rome and Ming China. It is an ingenious project which only a remarkably gifted scholar could have attempted. How far has he succeeded?

Certainly he has succeeded in presenting a series of vivid glimpses into Ricci's world. A picture of two Chinese warriors brings up recollections of war in Europe, the land and sea battles of Alcazar-quivir and Lepanto, social feuds in Macerata, inter-Christian feuds in Macao, Japan's attack on Korea, European schemes of conquest; and each 'memory' draws in its train other details of sixteenth-century life: the low repute of military men in China, the brutal punishment of the bastinado, the purely festive use of Chinese gunpowder, etc. etc. A picture of St Peter floundering in the Sea of Galilee similarly conjures up images of water: the long journey from Lisbon to Goa, the slowness of postal communications between Europe and the East, the frequency of shipwreck, Shakespeare and Cervantes on navigation, religious observance at sea, Portuguese bases in Africa, the trade in negro slaves, Chinese canals, the Yellow River, floods, the travels of the Plantin Bible. So we go on, through Central Asia and Japan, Muslims and Jews, the Spiritual Exercises of St Ignatius, sodomy in Rome, eunuchs in Peking, the Holy House of Loreto, etc. etc. By the time all the recollections evoked by the four images and the four pictures have been drawn up and set out, the reader may feel that he too is floundering in a sea of interesting but disorderly information. Great riches are there, but it is only when he has struggled to the shore, and rested to recover his breath, that he can open his net and sort out the remarkable diversity of the catch.

The trouble about this book is that it is a series of digressions from a central theme which itself is never stated. That theme is the career of Ricci in China. Unless the reader is aware of at least as much of that history as I have set out in this essay, he is likely to give up; for the coherence of the subject is lost.

I feel ungrateful in saying this, for I have profited from reading this book; but I must admit that I prefer to have my information presented differently, and find myself in agreement, on the subject of the Renaissance memory system, with Francis Bacon, who made no more account of it than of 'the tricks of tumblers, funambulos, baladines', and with Rabelais, whose Gargantua (like Ricci) could, by it, repeat whole books backward, but when one wanted intelligent commentary from him, 'it was no more possible to draw a word from him then a fart from a dead donkey'. I wish that Mr Spence, who quotes these two opinions, had shown a little more respect for them and arranged his incomparable scholarship in a less artificial form.

2

Sustaining an Empire:
Two Spanish Imperial Statesmen

The empire of Spain in Europe, unlike that in America which lasted so much longer, was not a rational construction, the effect of gradual expansion or conscious policy. Even more than most empires, it was built up by accident. It had no natural or institutional cohesion; but then Spain itself, throughout its 'golden age', had very little of such cohesion. Its various 'kingdoms' or provinces – Castile, Aragon, Catalonia, Granada, and in the end also Portugal – had distinct histories and brought with them, into the common pool, their particular colonies. Aragon brought in Italy. Granada was a Castilian conquest. The Netherlands and Franche-Comté, the Burgundian inheritance, came by dynastic accident. So did Portugal, which brought Africa and Asia in its wake.

All these countries had their own traditions, sometimes stronger and more ancient than those of Castile. The sixteenth century saw attempts by the Crown of Spain to provide some cohesion to this vast dominion: to centralize its government, to ensure its defence, to protect its communications, to remodel its institutions. The attempt was heroic but costly: without the bullion of America it could hardly have been made. In the end it foundered. The effort to centralize, to rationalize, provoked the usual nemesis of imperialism: revolution fortified by nationalism and religion, and exploited by the *Realpolitik* of rival imperialist powers.

The disintegration occurred in three stages. In 1572 the Netherlands revolted and, after a long struggle, nine of the seventeen provinces were permanently lost. In 1640 the refusal to admit that loss led, indirectly, to the revolt of Catalonia, which would be recovered, and the loss of Portugal and Franche-Comté, which would be permanent. In this last protracted struggle – a struggle which began in 1621 and did not end until 1659 – the communications of the empire were fatally broken, and thereafter the empire itself escaped brutal partition only to see its remaining limbs quietly detached, as they had originally been acquired, by dynastic marriage treaties: Flanders and Milan went to Austria, Naples and Sicily to an independent Bourbon line.

The failure of an empire at particular moments may be organically inevitable, but history commonly assigns the responsibility to individuals. If any one man is blamed for the first stage of the Spanish débâcle, the loss of the Netherlands in the sixteenth century, it is Fernando Alvarez de Toledo, Duke of Alba, who governed the provinces in the name of Philip II for the fateful years 1567–1573. He turned the opposition of an aristocratic *Fronde* into a national revolt: indeed he may be said to have created the Dutch nation. The second stage is even more decisively ascribed to one man: to the statesman who dominated Spain and its King from 1622 to 1643 and whose failure caused hegemony in Europe to pass from Spain to France – '*ce rival pas toujours malheureux de Richelieu*', as Fernand Braudel had called him, '*ce presque grand homme*', Gaspar de Guzman, Count-Duke of Olivares.' Two new books of historical scholarship invite us to take a new look at these unfortunate upholders of the Spanish empire against its disintegration. Let us begin with the first, the Duke of Alba.

When Alba took up his post in the Netherlands – and he took it up very reluctantly, for he was an old man and had already experienced the dangers of serving Philip II at a distance from the court – the provinces were already in commotion. The great nobles were mutinous; the common people, through economic crisis, had taken to violence which Calvinist preachers were prompt to organize. But as yet there was no repudiation of allegiance, no organization of revolt, no leader who could weld together these disparate forces. When he left, six years later, the situation was very different. The 'Sea-Beggars', marauding Dutch partisans, had landed in the north; the Prince of Orange, defeated hitherto, had come to take command of an open rebellion; and Calvinism had become a religion of political defiance, fortifying rebellion against princes in the Netherlands as in Scotland and France. Alba, said his enemies, had found the country submissive and had reduced it, single-handed, to civil war, spending twelve million ducats in the process. Alba, said a Catholic bishop, in six years had done more harm to the Church than Luther, Calvin, and all their followers together.

How had he done it? The Black Legend of the Protestant north has no doubt of the answer. Alba has gone down in history as the man who sought to reduce the Netherlands to obedience by indiscriminate terror and who thereby drove all classes together in resistance to him. He caused the great Flemish noblemen, who had dared to assert the rights of their countrymen, to be publicly executed in the square of Brussels. He set up the Council of Blood to circumvent the lawyers 'who only condemn for crimes which are proved'. He showed 'excessive contentment' at the news of the Massacre of St Bartholomew. He ordered wholesale slaughter in captured towns – 'I am resolved,' he once wrote, 'not to leave a creature alive, but to put them all to the knife'. He openly claimed that his policy was one of reconquest by 'terror'. In the market place of Antwerp he set up a huge statue of himself, in full armour, trampling on heresy and sedition, with an arrogant inscription describing him as the most faithful servant of the King. The statue offended Belgians and Spaniards alike, and was removed by his more tactful successor. In Flemish art he is immortalized as the Herod whose lean, grim features, 'with long, forked beard, piercing eyes and vulturine posture' appear in the younger Breughel's *Massacre of the Innocents*. Such is the picture that has become traditional in Protestant historiography.

In Spain – at least in conservative Spain – the legend has never been accepted, and the late Duke of Alba, in particular, sought to restore his ancestor's good name by publishing his extensive *epistolario*. With this and the other documents that have become available a more balanced judgment is possible, and now Mr Maltby has set out to redraw the picture.[2] He has done his work thoroughly, in the immense and scattered archives of Philip II's empire. He knows all the secondary material – Spanish, Italian, German, Belgian, Dutch. He is sympathetic and judicious and seeks to place his hero in his context. How far has he changed the conventional portrait?

The answer is, not very much. He modifies the detail, of course, and explains the forces to which Alba responded and by which he was controlled: the forces of his Castilian noble tradition, the

pressures of his immediate and unfamiliar task, the intrigues of the
court in Madrid which constantly impeded his work in the Netherlands as it had previously in Italy. But essentially Alba remains
unchanged: a stiff, proud Castilian, limited by his background,
bigoted in his religion, ruthless in his methods. No doubt he had his
virtues, both public and private. He was an efficient administrator,
an able general and quartermaster, a loyal and conscientious
servant of an unresponsive royal master. But he was arrogant and
querulous, of violent temper and language, insensitive to the rights
and feelings of others, contemptuous of foreigners, intolerant of
dissent, confident that all problems, in the end, would yield to
superior force. On his deathbed he declared to his new confessor, the
famous preacher Fray Luis de Grenada, that 'his conscience was not
burdened with having in all his life shed a single drop of blood
against it'. The remark illustrates only the limits of his conscience.
All the blood that he had shed was, he believed, justly shed: was it
not the blood of heretics and traitors? He diabolized his adversaries,
and so he could hardly complain if they in turn diabolized him.

All this makes it surprising that he was ever sent to the
Netherlands, to handle a difficult and delicate situation. After all, he
was sixty years old at the time; he had served Charles V for thirty
years before the accession of Philip II; and in that time he had had
plenty of opportunity to show both the arrogance and the savagery
of his character. His arrogance toward fellow nobles in Spain
seemed, at times, insufferable. At the royal marriage in 1543 he
forced them all to stand: as majordomo he gave a seat to himself
alone. His savagery shocked his contemporaries: in his campaign in
Piedmont in 1555 he insisted on the massacre of every French
garrison that resisted him. And he had shown a particular dislike for
the Netherlands, both country and people. In 1544, when Charles V
had to decide – or thought that he had to decide – whether to part
with Milan or the Netherlands, other counsellors had urged him to
cling to the Netherlands as the 'ancient patrimony' of his house.
Alba had urged – more realistically, perhaps – that they be
discarded as a liability, remote, vulnerable, and disloyal. Milan, he
believed, was the linchpin of the empire: the Netherlands were
expendable. Four years later, when he visited the country with the
future Philip II, master and servant were alike disgusted by that
undisciplined, exuberant people with their vulgar familiarity and
endless drunken feasts.

Why then did Philip II, as King, at a critical moment, send this contemptuous and ruthless old soldier to govern the most difficult part of his empire? The answer is twofold. First – as so often in that reign – the appointment was the result of a court intrigue. Alba was head of a party, and the rival party, the powerful party of Ruy Gomez, Prince of Eboli, wished to get him out of the way. Alba knew this – it had happened to him before, when he was sent to Italy in 1555 – but he was trapped by his own arguments and had to go. Secondly, he was sent, and went, on a false assumption. The assumption was that he would restore order to the Netherlands by military rule and that the King would then come himself (as his best servant, the Burgundian Cardinal Granvelle, always urged him to do) without an army, to settle the country. Alba was to be the hatchetman to do the dirty job and then be relieved. In fact it did not work out thus. The King never came, and Alba was left to carry the can. For this, as he showed, he was not fitted.

Why did Philip not come? It was not merely his habitual indecision, or his personal hatred of the Netherlands. In 1568, the year after Alba's arrival, the heir to the throne, Don Carlos, died, followed, three months later, by the Queen. Then the Moriscos of Granada rose in revolt: a revolt that lasted two years. It was the greatest crisis of the reign: a social and racial rebellion in the heart of Castile itself. For the King 'to leave his country in turmoil and to undertake a perilous journey when there was no one to succeed him was unthinkable'. So Alba had to soldier on in the Netherlands, fighting, by the only methods he knew, the enemies whom he multiplied with every act of brutal repression.

Not that his rule was total failure. He defeated every military challenge. In order to ensure his communications by land he created what was to be the lifeline of the empire: the famous 'Spanish Road' from Milan to Luxembourg. He dealt firmly with the Catholic bigots – the fanatical friar Pope Pius V, with his crusading fantasies, and the Spanish ambassador in London, Don Guerau de Spes, with his troop of English papists plotting against Queen Elizabeth in the interest of the dethroned Mary Stuart. Alba would have none of this. Though he protested that he hated the heretical Queen of England as much as anyone, he put first things first and preserved that peace with England which was essential to his sea communications. He also carried through to completion the great and necessary reorganization of the Netherlands Church, which had been the original cause of all the trouble. This has been described, by a Catholic historian, as one of Alba's greatest contributions as an administrative reformer. It formed 'the basis of ecclesiastical organization in the Netherlands for centuries to come'. Even the famous tax of the tenth-penny, which raised such an outcry, was a defensible device: 'the most equal', as he himself said, 'to all sorts of people'. But no administrative virtue could compensate for the calculated brutality by which he believed that he could end the revolt, and which in fact only intensified it.

Could it have been ended by other methods? Such large hypothetical questions are unanswerable. But a few years later, while Alba, at the age of seventy-four, was carrying out the more successful, and less difficult, conquest of Portugal, another general, no less able than he, but of a very different temper – Alexander Farnese, Duke of Parma – 'reconciled', and reconciled permanently, the greater part of the Netherlands. Farnese combined military genius with diplomacy and tact. So did his Genoese successor Ambrogio Spinola, who completed his work. If Italian diplomacy and tact, instead of Castilian brutality and pride, had been used in 1568, the result might have been different.

By 1609 the Netherlands were firmly divided. 'Flanders' – modern Belgium – was 'reconciled'; 'the United Provinces' – modern Holland – were lost; and an exhausted Spanish government accepted a truce of twelve years. In 1621 that truce ran out and, after a long debate, the Spanish government decided to renew the struggle. There was now a new ruler in Spain, and a new spirit of active imperialism: the young Philip IV was surrounded by men who looked back to the more heroic years of Philip II and Alba. In particular there was Baltasar de Zúñiga, whose long service in central Europe had convinced him that the war newly broken out in Germany could be exploited by Spain. The following year Zúñiga died, and the task of waging the war fell to his nephew, the new King's *privado*, or favourite, the Count – soon to be the Count-Duke – of Olivares.

For the next twenty years Olivares exerted himself to re-create and strengthen the empire of Philip II in Europe: to recover its lost provinces, secure its essential communications, restore its patronage of the universal Catholic Church. The effort that this entailed was enormous – greater than under Philip II, for the Dutch had now become a formidable sea power and France was no longer paralysed by civil war. In order to liberate the energies needed for such an effort, Olivares sought to reorganize Spain itself: to remodel its institutions, reform its finances, change its inveterate social habits. In order to exploit energies thus liberated, he proposed, at last, to create a new unity of government: make his King no longer King of Castile, Portugal, Aragon, Valencia, and Count of Barcelona, but 'King of Spain'.

At first the effort seemed to be rewarded. The year 1626 was an *annus mirabilis* of Spanish victory. But then the tide turned. The turning point was the succession crisis in the Duchy of Mantua, and Olivares's action in ordering the governor of Milan to intervene with force and seize the city of Casale, which was under Mantuan rule. The intervention could be justified – the Spanish position in Italy and Europe would be seriously threatened by the succession of a French duke of Mantua. But it could be justified only by immediate success. In fact it failed, and the consequences were disastrous. The adventure antagonized public opinion, the papacy, the empire, and wrecked Olivares's plans of settlement in the north. Worst of all, it brought France into Italy and, ultimately – in 1635 – into the general war. It was the France of Richelieu, the most ruthless and successful *Realpolitiker* of the age. In the contest with France, the Spanish empire in Europe would be broken, Portugal lost, Alba's 'Spanish Road' disintegrated. Thereafter Flanders would be held at the mercy of France and Holland. For all this, history has held Olivares responsible.

Like Alba, Olivares has had no modern historian – for the late Dr Marañón's work is psychological speculation, not history.[3] For this we can blame the fire which, in 1795, destroyed his personal archive. However, the documents of State survive and no historian has made better use of them than Professor Elliott. He began his career as a historian with a classic study of the Catalan revolt of 1640 and he has since, with his collaborators, published the available documents of Olivares's rule in Spain and a full account of one of his positive achievements: the great palace of Buen Retiro which he built, at immense cost, in the years of war, to illustrate and magnify the authority of his King.[4] His new book is in form a comparative study of Richelieu and Olivares, and is the best kind of comparative history; for by pointing to similarities and differences in the antagonists who dominated the long struggle, it illustrates not only the causes of failure and success but also the common setting within which they operated and the common problems which they faced.[5]

There are some obvious similarities. Both Richelieu and Olivares were younger sons of noble families. Both, after a period of provincial life – one at his home in Seville, the other as Bishop of Luçon – found their way, almost simultaneously, into the court: Richelieu as the protégé of the Queen Mother, whom he would betray, Olivares as chamberlain to the heir to the throne, the future Philip IV, whose chamber pot he would once ceremoniously kiss. Such acts, of treachery and obsequiousness, were necessary if one was to rise in an absolute monarchy. Both men rose. They also survived in power – both of them for twenty years – and amassed great wealth. They indulged their tastes for building – Olivares for his King, Richelieu for himself – for a magnificent style of life, and for intellectual culture: both were well-read men and great biblio-philes who created splendid libraries. Both were reformers who sacrificed reform to war. They fought wars first against their own 'rebels' – here the Dutch, there the Huguenots – finally against each other.

To retain power so long required great skill. Both used the necessary methods. They took the measure of their kings, noted their weaknesses (both Philip IV and Louis XIII were dependent personalities), exalted the royal authority, professed themselves its humble servants, built up clienteles of 'creatures' (here Andalusian, there Poitevin), made themselves indispensable, and then, in moments of crisis, obtained consent to their policies by threatening to resign. The most dangerous moments were when their kings were seriously ill. The death of his monarch would have been fatal to either of them, and in fact both kings were gravely ill at the greatest crisis of the Mantuan affair. Luckily for their ministers, both recovered. There was also the danger that displeasure might be fomented by royal confessors or disgruntled aristocrats. Richelieu had to crush aristocratic opposition again and again. Olivares suffered less from it: the Spanish nobility seldom went beyond talk, or boycotting court functions. It was provincial, not noble, oppo-sition – combined with external defeat – that brought him down.

Richelieu and Olivares are remembered as directors of grand strategy in a struggle for European supremacy. But both began as domestic reformers. They came to power at a time of economic recession and political uncertainty. They followed weak men who had allowed their countries to be weakened, here by neglect and corruption, there by internal dissension; and they wished, in each, to restore the strength and prosperity and reputation of the Crown. 'The present state of the kingdom,' Olivares wrote in 1624, 'is probably, for our sins, the worst that has ever been seen'; and Richelieu, looking back to the same date, wrote that in France 'the Huguenots shared the State with Your Majesty, the nobles behaved as if they were not your subjects, and the governors of the provinces as if they were sovereign powers.' So both set out to unite the resources of the Crown, Olivares by bringing the several kingdoms of the Peninsula under 'the form and laws of Castile, without any difference', Richelieu by breaking the independence of Huguenots and grandees. In order to carry out this programme, both sought to bypass the inherited structures of popular consent – the French States General, the Spanish *cortes*; to abolish the old forms of taxation – the French *taille* and the Spanish *millones*; to reform the economy, to mobilize new resources, to cut out waste. They did not hesitate to challenge the established rulers of religion and finance – to reform monasteries, defy the Inquisition and the Pope, turn to Jewish and Huguenot bankers.

Most of these projects of reform were sacrificed, or adapted, to the needs of war and all-justifying reason of State. As the war dragged on, it became personal: each of the two statesmen saw himself as seeking only peace and security, the other as aiming at universal domination. In fact they were prisoners, rather than makers, of the struggle. Olivares came to power when the war against the Dutch had already been resumed, and he often thought, or dreamed, of making peace with them; for like Alba he judged Italy more important. Hence his fatal error over Mantua, the beginning of French intervention: once the Mantuan succession was open, he could not (he thought) afford to stand aside. But neither, then, could Richelieu. He too saw intervention as a defensive necessity and lamented the predictable consequences: it meant, as he told the King, that he must now 'abandon all thought of tranquillity, of economies and reorganization within the realm'. Olivares had said the same; if the French crossed the Alps, he declared (with remarkable accuracy), it would be the beginning of a war of thirty years, the end of all projects of reform.

Olivares saw himself as fighting a defensive war to preserve the empire. France was threatening its lifeline, that 'Spanish Road' from

Milan to Luxembourg which Alba had created. But one man's lifeline is another man's halter. Richelieu saw France encircled by the same road; and if Spain was going back to the days of Philip II, how could he forget how Philip II had treated France, exploiting its divisions, subsidizing its rebels, fomenting civil war? Was not Olivares seeking to do the same now, supporting noble conspirators, rebels – even Huguenot rebels – against the Crown? In self-defence, as he thought, Richelieu sought to breach the Spanish Road, to secure 'gateways' into neighbouring states, and so 'to shelter them from Spanish aggression when the occasion arises'. Once secured, they would be the gateways through which the armies of Louis XIV would pass not to shelter but to lay waste and dominate the neighbouring states.

For in the end Richelieu won and Olivares lost. Why? The judgment of history, which always backs the winner, is clear enough: Richelieu was a statesman of genius, Olivares was not. Perhaps this is true; but it was not clear at the time. In 1635, when they first went directly to war, both sides expected a quick victory, and at times it looked as if Spain would still win. The year 1636 was 'a terrible year' for France. The army of the Cardinal-Infante, Philip IV's brother, victorious over the Swedes at Nördlingen (it was that victory that had forced France to enter the war), had won the battle of Corbie and was advancing on Paris. Only the reproaches of his Capuchin confessor and counsellor, Father Joseph, then prevented Richelieu from yielding to despair and taking flight. However, he rallied and persevered, and by 1639 it was the turn of Olivares to despair. From then on the disasters multiplied, and the revolts of Catalonia and Portugal began the break-up not merely of the empire but of the Peninsula itself. In December 1642 Richelieu died. Six weeks later Philip IV dismissed Olivares. Two years later he died. The war went on, for another fourteen years; but it was in the long duel between Richelieu and Olivares that the issues had been defined, and the end determined.

What was the secret of Richelieu's success and Olivares's failure? At times all seemed to depend on chance; but, as Professor Elliott observes, there is a difference between those who wait upon chance and those who seize it. Richelieu undoubtedly had good fortune. The Huguenot redoubt of La Rochelle surrendered in 1628 just in time for him to lead the royal army into Italy. Gustavus Adolphus perished at Lützen just at the time when the incompatibility of his alliances with Sweden and Bavaria threatened his foreign policy with ruin. But Richelieu seized these chances. 'Experience shows,' he had written, 'that if one foresees from far ahead the designs to be undertaken, one can act with speed when the moment comes to execute them.' Clear and rational in prevision, ruthless and swift in action, Richelieu could snatch victory out of apparent defeat. Consequently, he created the evidence for the belief that Providence was on his side. Olivares was no less energetic, no less dedicated. But he had less stability, and his confidence dwindled with disaster as Richelieu's grew with victory. His extravagant rhetorical style, so different from the 'imperious brevity' of Richelieu, was combined with a certain stoic fatalism that impeded forethought. The crisis of the Mantuan succession, so momentous for both parties, could indeed be seen from far ahead; but when it came, Richelieu was ready for it, Olivares was not.

When the tide had definitely turned against him, Olivares indulged himself in self-pity and self-justification. He could not see what had gone wrong, or why the Cardinal, who was so much more wicked than he, had been so much more successful. He became obsessed with his own responsibility for the disasters, and saw himself as 'a latter-day Jonah'. 'All the misfortunes of the year', he wrote in 1637, 'are my fault, and once I am thrown into the sea the storm will cease and success and good fortune follow'. Before being thrown overboard he made his will. In it he ordered his executors to establish a Jeronymite convent, to provide for the relief of the poor and the repopulation of deserted villages, to found a college in Salamanca, pilgrim hostels in Santiago, Loreto, and Jerusalem, a hospice and two hospitals for retired soldiers, to rebuild and repopulate Algeciras, and to maintain a squadron of galleons for the defence of the Strait of Gibraltar. After calculating the cost of such fantasies, his confessor dryly remarked 'the gentleman who made this will governed the monarchy for nineteen years in the same style as he bequeathed his inheritance'.

Perhaps, in the end, his mind was unhinged, as it might well be after such disasters. But his moods had always been erratic and extreme; and anyway, what of Richelieu? He, too, could show signs of lunacy, of which there was a streak in his family: sometimes he believed that he was a horse, and his sister dared not sit down, thinking that her bottom was made of glass. Placed, as here, in parallel with his great enemy, Olivares does not seem quite so extravagant, or quite so anachronistic, as some historians have held him, or Richelieu quite so rational and forward-looking. Both grappled with the same general problems. Both attempted to cure the disorders of the State during those critical decades in which so many traditional forms were fractured and remade. Both were in one sense political realists, remarkably free from ideological prejudice. Both also aimed high – impossibly high. As Professor Elliott says, 'the sheer arrogance of their ambition is what most impresses. Both were ultimately attempting to mould a world to their image.' When they clashed, the victory of the one, the defeat of the other, was 'by a hair's breadth'. Whether the Spain oof Olivares, if he had won, could have continued to sustain the burden of empire in Europe is, of course, another matter. All that we can say is that, even in defeat, it preserved its vast American empire for another hundred and fifty years.

Professor Elliott has sought to portray 'an Olivares who is more subtle and complex than he is generally depicted', and he has succeeded in doing so. This is a book that makes all previous writing on Olivares seem very thin. It is brief, but profound, full of insight, and a delight to read. Olivares himself – and Richelieu too – was conscious of his historic role. He looked forward to the verdict of history. It has generally been unfavourable. He would, perhaps, be satisfied with Professor Elliott's more sympathetic reassessment.

3
Medicine at the Early Stuart Court

William Harvey, whose birth we celebrate this year, is the greatest physician in our history: one of the greatest of all physicians. He was also physician-in-ordinary to Charles I, who was, to say the least, one of the more interesting of our kings. Throughout the reign, he was closely associated with the person of the King, both in prosperity and in adversity. In the years of peace, he accompanied him personally on his journeys, travelling three times into Scotland: for the coronation at Edinburgh in 1633; on the military expedition which ended so disastrously in 1639; and in the summer of 1641 when the King sought to raise a royalist party in Scotland to resist the Parliament of England. He was also present at the first battle of the Civil War, the battle of Edgehill on 23 October 1642. He did not of course take part in the battle – he was then sixty-four years old – but spent the time reading a book behind a hedge while the bullets whizzed past his ear. For the next four years he was with the court at Oxford. There we catch a glimpse of him experimenting in the hatching of eggs in Trinity College; then, in 1645, he was appointed, by royal nomination, Warden of Merton College, and continued his experiments there. Finally, in 1646, when the King had fled from that falling capital to the protection, as he supposed, of the Scots at Newcastle, Harvey joined him there. It was only when the King was transferred from Scottish to English custody that he was parted from his chosen doctors, as from his chosen chaplains. Meanwhile, in all his works, Harvey showed devotion to the King. In 1628, as royal physician extraordinary, he dedicated to him his greatest work, on the movement of the heart; in 1642 as a committed royalist, he suffered the sack of his official lodgings at Whitehall and thereby lost all his papers – the most crucifying grief of his life, he afterwards said; and it was to raise his spirits in the total collapse of the royal cause in 1648 that he was persuaded to publish his last work, on the generation of animals.

This being so, the subject 'medicine at the court of Charles I' seems natural enough for the opening lecture at a Harveian conference, and at first I thought that I knew well enough how to handle the topic. However, on closer consideration, I am not so sure. For what in fact is the distinctive character of Charles I's medical patronage? Who, apart from Harvey, were his court doctors, those physicians whom he drew together round his person and his family? Once we ask this question we encounter difficulty. The court of Charles I was certainly distinctive. It was an elaborate, correct, aesthetically oriented society, very different from that of James I or Elizabeth. But his physicians – or at least the most distinguished of them – were not discovered by him. They were all inherited from his father. In fact, we find that it was James I, not Charles I, who was the great innovator. Harvey himself came to court under James I, and it was in that reign that the foundations of his great work were all laid.

This being so, I think it is best to speak of medicine and the court in the time not of Charles I but of Harvey. In this way we can see how James I, by his personal patronage, temporarily altered the pattern of English medicine, giving a new impulse to heretical ideas, and passing those ideas on to the next generation. We can then see how, beneath an apparent continuity, Charles I, by the subtle shift of his patronage, quietly put the clock back; and we can see where, in this process, Harvey fits in.

Of course the court did not operate in a vacuum. There were other, less personal, more continuous, and therefore in the long run stronger institutions beside which the patronage of the court had an accidental, almost whimsical character. In particular there was the Royal College of Physicians, founded by Henry VIII in 1518 and now well established, well organized, sure of itself. The college set out to maintain the standards of medicine, and protect the public, by licensing those physicians whom it approved, banning those whom it did not approve, and keeping the subordinate technicians of the profession – apothecaries and surgeons – in their subordinate place. Its discipline may not have been very effective. Unlicensed practitioners throve in London, protected by powerful patrons, and the apothecaries remained the indispensable physicians of the poor. However, by 1600 the college had established itself as the central organ and the club of the profession, the arbiter of medical standards and medical fashion. Its Fellows knew each other, had similar ideas, and a common base of proper academic training.

Theoretically, all Fellows had to have degrees from English universities; however, in fact many of them had studied abroad. The English universities did not have organized medical schools, and although Henry VIII had founded regius chairs of medicine, and Dr Caius, in the mid-sixteenth century, had introduced the study of anatomy at Cambridge, the best training was still to be found in Continental universities; after which English degrees could always be obtained by incorporation. The most admired foreign university at the time was the University of Padua, with its famous anatomy theatre. Thomas Linacre and John Chambre, the founders of the Royal College in London, were both doctors of Padua; so was its reformer, John Caius. Padua was also the model for the new University of Leiden, founded in 1575 during the Dutch revolt against Spain. Padua and Leiden were the centres of experimental anatomy within a conservative, Aristotelian tradition. There were also other traditions, as we shall see.

Compared with the dignified Fellows of the Royal College of Physicians, the English court physicians of the sixteenth century, it must be admitted, were a miscellaneous lot, picked out by personal accident or personal whim. Some of them were reputable enough, but some would never have qualified for membership of the college. Many were only part-time physicians; for medicine was still a branch of universal natural philosophy. Some were foreigners. Henry VIII had had two Italian doctors – a Genoese, Giovanni Battista Boerio, whom he had inherited from Henry VII and who would employ Erasmus as travelling tutor to accompany his sons to Rome, and a Venetian, Agostino de Augustinis, whom he took over from Cardinal Wolsey. Queen Elizabeth had at least two foreign doctors. The first was an Italian, Cesare Adelmare from Treviso, a doctor of Padua, whom she inherited from her sister Mary. He prospered in England, and his son Giulio Cesare Adelmare would make a great career in the law, ending as Sir Julius Caesar, Master of the Rolls. The second was a Portuguese Jew, Rodrigo Lopez, who had worked for ten years at St Bartholomew's Hospital, the training-ground of so many doctors, including Harvey. Dr Lopez too made his mark, in a way: in 1594 he was hanged, drawn and quartered – no doubt unjustly* – on a charge of seeking to poison the Queen in the interest of the King of Spain. Such conspiracies were a constant source of worry in Renaissance courts, and court doctors were expected to keep up to date, especially, in the subject of poisons and their antidotes.

Other court doctors were eccentric in other ways. Some of them were regarded by respectable physicians as quacks. Certainly they included medical heretics. In the sixteenth century there was one great medical heresy, and the history of medicine, at that time, is largely conditioned by its impact. That heresy was Paracelsianism, alchemical medicine, 'iatrochemistry'.

The new chemical medicine was in some ways a direct protest against, and challenge to, the Galenic orthodoxy of the established physicians. As such it was popular among their rivals, the depressed classes of the medical profession, the surgeons and apothecaries; but it was condemned by almost all the institutes of higher learning. However, by the end of the century certain universities had begun to make tentative compromises with it. At the same time certain princely courts began – not always for disinterested scientific reasons – to welcome chemical doctors. The English court, under Elizabeth, remained conservative, but several European rulers – the Emperor Rudolf II, the King of Denmark, the Landgrave of Hesse and many other German princes – patronized the new medicine and founded laboratories and academies to promote it. This royal patronage sometimes placed the court doctors in frontal opposition to the established medical corporations.

The most spectacular of such confrontations occurred in 1603, the year of the accession of James I. It occurred in Paris and I shall return to it shortly, for it had a direct influence on the medical history of the English court. Meanwhile I shall prepare my ground by stating that at that time there were two main lines of progress in experimental medicine. On the one hand there was the anatomical

*Sir George Clark, *A History of the Royal College of Physicians* I (Oxford 1964), p. 128, says that Lopez 'was almost certainly guilty'. I do not know on what evidence Clark, who in general was notoriously reluctant to venture a judgment, felt so certain in this matter. The fullest account of the affair, which is well documented, is Martin Hume, *Españoles y Ingleses en el siglo XVI* (Madrid 1903), pp. 205–33.

school of Padua and Leiden, conservative, Aristotelian, Galenist. On the other hand there was the chemical school of Paracelsus which had been made reputable by Peter Severinus in Denmark and had penetrated the universities of Basel, Montpellier and Nantes. Both movements had their extremists. In Paris, where passions had been sharpened by ideological civil war, the Medical Faculty was as extreme in its Galenism as the Theological Faculty, the Sorbonne, in its Catholicism. In Germany the Paracelsians ran riot in alchemical fantasies. But we are in England, and in Elizabethan England, in medicine as in religion, there was compromise. The doctors from Padua and Leiden, and the new medical reformers from Basel and Nantes, met amicably in the College of Physicians, and the royal doctors, a race apart, did not influence either medical science or, except in the *cause célèbre* of Dr Lopez, public events.

On one occasion indeed, it seemed that the Royal College itself might quietly yield to the chemical reformers. In the 1580s a committee of the Royal College was set up to plan an official English pharmacopoeia. At the same time a Physic Garden was established under the direction of the famous surgeon and herbalist John Gerard, then superintendent of Lord Burghley's gardens. This project caused great alarm to the apothecaries, who protested in vain against it as an invasion of their preserves. It looked as if the Royal College was about to extend its activities, liberalize its philosophy, and admit chemical remedies. This movement coincided with the admission into the College of an active Paracelsian reformer, who enjoyed aristocratic patronage, Thomas Muffet. Muffet was a doctor of Basel, who had been to Denmark and had known the scientific innovators patronized by the Danish court: the astronomer Tycho Brahé and the reformer of Paracelsian medicine Peter Severinus. He was himself an experimental doctor who had made a special study of insects. He also wrote a didactic poem on silkworms and enjoys perpetual fame because of his little daughter's encounter with a spider.

However, the first reforming period, in the end, came to nothing. After 1594 the project of a pharmacopoeia ran out of steam. The old Queen, conservative in everything, gave no encouragement, and when she died in 1603, nothing had been done. Her court physicians followed her quickly to the grave: Dr Gilbert, famous as the philosopher of magnetism, in 1603; Dr Lancelot Browne, the distinguished Arabist, her first physician and the father-in-law of

Harvey, in 1605. The way was now open for the new King to exercise his patronage, if he wished, in a new way.

King James had already given some hint of his ideas. As King of Scotland he had chosen as his court doctor John Craig, the son of the great Scottish feudal lawyer, Sir Thomas Craig of Riccarton. James had discovered Craig in Denmark when he went there, in 1589, to collect his wife. Craig was an interesting man. Like Muffet, he had taken his doctorate at Basel, and again like Muffet, he had become friendly with the Danish scientists, Peter Severinus and Tycho Brahé. When King James moved to London, he brought Craig with him and kept him as his first court doctor there. The appointment can be seen as a sign that Muffet's enterprise was to be resumed. Next year, another sign pointed in the same direction. The King sent a personal doctor to Scotland to attend to his second son, Prince Charles, now four years old and ill in Dunfermline, and to bring him to London. The doctor he chose was Henry Atkins. Atkins was a doctor of Nantes, another 'Paracelsian' university. In the 1580s he had been on the committee of the Royal College to devise the new pharmacopoeia. In 1593 he had volunteered to sail as a ship's doctor on the Earl of Essex's expedition to Cadiz. This too showed an interest in practical experiment. Most of the Paracelsian doctors, like Paracelsus himself, had sought experience as army doctors, and Muffet himself had accompanied Essex's earlier expedition to France in 1591. When Atkins returned from Scotland with the Prince, King James made him his first English physician in ordinary. Later, another doctor of Basel, Matthew Lister, was appointed physician to the new Queen. He had succeeded Muffet both as physician and as man of affairs to 'Mary, the incomparable Countess of Pembroke' at Wilton, whose estate he managed 'to her best advantage', and whom he is said to have married when she was a widow. He too, like Muffet, was a very successful – i.e. a moderate – Paracelsian.

Thus the new reign was signalized, in medicine and at court, by something of a Paracelsian invasion. The invaders were not always welcome. James I, it is well known, was an extravagant King. The court, its cost, offices, honours – all were inflated in his reign. So was the roll of court doctors. At the end of the reign, a cry was raised against them. Queen Elizabeth, it was observed, had been content with three physicians, one surgeon and one apothecary, at a total cost of £416 per annum, while King James, at his death, was retaining seven physicians, six or seven surgeons, and two or three apothecaries.¹ One of King James's physicians alone cost more than the whole Elizabethan establishment. Most of these doctors are mere names to us, but those whose personality and tastes can be discovered have something in common. Like Craig and Atkins they are unorthodox, experimental, chemical doctors. Sometimes their unorthodoxy seems to verge on charlatanism. But that was in keeping with the character of the court.

For the court of James I was very different from that of Elizabeth. From the beginning, conventional observers were shocked by its undignified, even disorderly character, so different from the hieratic regularity of the old Queen's court. But this unconventionality had another side to it too. Intellectually the new court was remarkably open to new ideas. It became the resort, and the refuge, of adventurers, fortune-seekers, charlatans, but also of philosophers, scholars, scientists of unorthodox genius. In the world of medicine it welcomed both types. James I was very sceptical about medicine in general – his doctors complained that he was a very bad patient – and he positively disliked respectable physicians. He liked eccentrics.

For instance, there was Leonard Poe. The Royal College knew Dr Poe only too well. It condemned him, again and again, as an ignorant charlatan. But he was protected by noble patrons, supported by Privy Councillors, consulted as a scientist by Francis Bacon, who also disliked the established physicians and believed in open-ended experiment. In 1609 James I appointed Poe to be physician in ordinary to the royal household, and the Fellows of the Royal College found themselves obliged to admit him as a colleague. They did so with reluctance, and then changed their rules in order to be able to resist next time.² Then there were the Scotchmen who found it convenient to follow the court to London. One of these wrote his name, in Latin, as Macollo. I suspect it was really McCulloch.* He had taken a degree at the new University of Franeker in Holland and had been chief physician to the Grand Duke of Tuscany. Afterwards he was also described as 'physician in

---

*A John and a James McCulloch (probably the same person) are mentioned as ordinary Physicians to the King of Scotland in 1622 and as having died in office early in 1623. (*Registrum Magni Sigilli regum Scotorum* (Edinburgh 1814–1914) VIII, pp. 315, 455; Register of Retours XXVI fo. 116. I owe these references to Dr A. L. Murray of the Scottish Record Office.

ordinary' to the Emperor Rudolf II.* That alone marks him as an
eccentric. He was a baroque character and wrote books of Paracelsian chemical medicine in a flamboyant Latin style.† James I made
him his physician in ordinary in 1620, together with another
Scotchman, Dr Chambers, who was denizened for the purpose and
succeeded Dr Craig, who had just died. We know little about Dr
Chambers, except that he was once so enraged by anti-Scottish
remarks in a pub in Kenilworth that he pulled down the pub-sign
and threatened to burn it.[3] The English physicians evidently
thought little of him. He was not made a member of the College.

Those were the less distinguished of King James's physicians in
ordinary. Better known was another foreigner who arrived in 1611
from the still smouldering medical battlefields of Paris. This was
Theodore Turquet, who preferred to be known as Theodore de
Mayerne.

Mayerne was the youngest of a triumvirate of chemical doctors,
all Huguenots from Geneva, who held court appointments under
Henri IV of France, and had aroused the furious opposition of the
orthodox Galenist Faculty of Medicine, dominated by two powerful
figures, both called Jean Riolan, father and son. The son would
afterwards draw attention to himself again by attacking Harvey's
theory of the circulation of the blood. Indeed, he was the only critic
whom Harvey would deign to answer. For five years, from 1603 to
1608, the Paris Faculty, led by the Riolans, had attacked the
heretical court doctors, anathematizing them as ignorant charlatans, forbidding them to practise, patients to resort to them, or
apothecaries to make up their medicines. But the battle did not
damage them in the least. The heretical doctors continued to
practise without fear, and Mayerne, who in 1609 was the sole
survivor of the trio, enjoyed a splendid practice in Paris. All the *beau
monde* went to him, Protestant and Catholic alike: the King's
mistress, the Comtesse de Moret; his flamboyant financier Sébas-

---

*The claim is made by the editor of Macollo's posthumously published *XCIX
Canons or Rules . . . for Practitioners in Physick* (1659). It is not mentioned in Macollo's
funeral inscription in St Margaret's, Westminster, quoted by Munk, which
describes him as 'Magni Hetruriae ducis Archiater quondam'. But he may have
treated the Emperor, who was the Grand Duke's brother-in-law. In Arthur
Johnston's *Delitiae Poetarum Scotorum* (1637) there are some Latin poems by Macollo
(there called James Macallo), addressed to various members of the Medici family.

†He published two books on the chemical treatment of venereal disease: *Theoria
Chymica* (Florence 1616) and *Iatria Chymica* (London 1622).

tien Zamet; the now ageing *mignons* of Henri III; the young Bishop of Luçon, afterwards Cardinal Richelieu, whom he cured of *lues venerea*; the dukes of Bouillon and Rohan, rival leaders of Huguenot revolt; the entire *haute société protestante*. He cured them by Paracelsian, alchemical methods, by patient observation, by strange hermetic formulae, and by an irresistible bedside manner; and in his spare time he was diligent in his chemical laboratory, distilling essences, making projections, seeking to transmute metals, to discover the philosopher's stone.

However, although he was not afraid of Riolan and the Paris faculty, Mayerne was frightened of one thing: the loss of royal protection. In 1606, at the height of the Paris battle, he had reinsured himself by visiting England and had scored a great success at the court of James I. He had also taken the precaution of being admitted as a doctor of Oxford University. Two years later, Henri IV had offered him the highest medical post at his court, that of *premier médecin du roi* – but on condition that he became a Catholic; for by now the Catholic reaction was in full swing and the Jesuits were strong enough at court to impose this condition. After some agony, Mayerne refused the post. Two years later, Henri IV was assassinated, and Mayerne decided to act. Through the English ambassador in Paris, he made excellent terms for himself. He was to be first physician to the King of Great Britain with a salary of £600 a year, board and lodgings at court, allowances for apothecaries and servants, and exemption from all taxes. At the same time, he was allowed to keep his titular position at the French court, and a retaining fee. The French ministers, on their side, were ready to pay this price: in the heart of a rival court, Mayerne, they thought, might be useful, as their spy.

So began the phenomenal career of Mayerne in England. His coming was well timed. James I was naturally well disposed; so was his most intellectual minister, Francis Bacon. To Bacon the old Galenic physicians with their traditional, academic theories were as distasteful in medicine as the Schoolmen in philosophy, and he called for a revival of 'the ancient and serious diligence of Hippocrates' – that is, observation and therapy.[4] He was also interested in chemistry and therefore, as he would write, 'partial to poticaries'.[5] To both King and minister Mayerne was thus a welcome visitor. Moreover, in the Royal College of Physicians, the ground had been prepared for him by the influence of men like Muffet and Atkins. In 1616, as royal physician, he was admitted as Fellow of the Royal College. His reception there astonished him. The grandees of the College accepted him not, as he had expected – for it was, after all, the equivalent of the Paris Faculty – 'with hostile faces and oblique glances', but with open, welcoming arms. He was particularly delighted by the friendship of Sir William Paddy, a cultivated high Anglican, who had been one of the projectors of the English pharmacopoeia under Queen Elizabeth and was now one of the royal doctors. He also learned all about Muffet and his work. Afterwards, from Muffet's apothecary, Mayerne obtained Muffet's manuscripts and published Muffet's beautifully illustrated work on insects, with a dedication to Paddy. Thus, thanks to Mayerne, Muffet was more fortunate than Harvey, whose work on insects, the fruit of many years' research, would perish in the sack of his lodgings in 1642.

One of the public effects of this new Jacobean spirit, and of the rise to prominence of a new group of royal doctors, was the success of the apothecaries in emancipating themselves from the control of the grocers, with whom they were inconveniently incorporated, and the resumption, and realization, of the Elizabethan project of a British Pharmacopoeia. Both these results were achieved in 1618, and the moving spirits in the Royal College were the royal physicians, particularly Atkins, Mayerne, Craig and Paddy. The physicians did not, of course, intend to set the apothecaries free – only to free them from the hampering control of the grocers, in order that they might be more closely linked with, and subordinate to, themselves. But it was a welcome change nevertheless, and as the new pharmacopoeia included a whole section on chemical medicine, the victory for the experimental doctors was obvious. That victory was largely due, as the King himself stated, to the initiative of 'our well beloved physicians Theodore de Mayerne and Henry Atkins'.

Once established in the court of James I Mayerne soon built up a large and fashionable practice in England. He also retained his foreign patients. With his courtly manners he was acceptable everywhere and James I used him as an agent in numerous delicate affairs, literary and diplomatic as well as medical. Mayerne thoroughly enjoyed dabbling in international politics. From his position in the English court, he planted a sister in the court of James's daughter the Electress Palatine, Queen of Bohemia; his first wife was the sister of the Dutch ambassador in Paris, his second the daughter of the Dutch ambassador in London. Nearly all English ambassadors abroad, and nearly all foreign ambassadors in England, even including the Spanish conde de Gondomar, were his patients; and he was adept in combining medicine with politics. He was the unofficial emissary of French Huguenot grandees and of the city of Geneva. In 1620 he bought a feudal castle in Switzerland, and set up as Baron d'Aubonne in the Pays de Vaud. As such he became the trusted agent of the canton of Berne, leader of the Swiss Confederation; for the French-speaking Calvinist Pays de Vaud was subject, not altogether willingly, to the German-speaking Lutheran canton of Berne. Mayerne had princely patients in Germany too. He made regular visits to the Continent to see his patients, and took with him secret political instructions. On one occasion he was arrested in Paris and ordered out of the country. That caused a great rumpus, but no explanation was ever offered. There can be no doubt that he was regarded as a Huguenot spy. When the Thirty Years War broke out, he was at the centre of the international Protestant alliance. He advised on treaties, received ambassadors, recommended generals, handled secret intelligence and instructions. His castle of Aubonne was well placed as a listening post and his friend, the old Huguenot hero Agrippa d'Aubigné, now exiled at Geneva, invented a special 'telephone' for long-distance secret communication with him.

In the autumn of 1624 Mayerne set out to revisit his château of Aubonne. Before leaving London he wrote out, for the other royal doctors, a full psychosomatic case-history of the King: to us an invaluable document. Unfortunately the King became mortally ill while he was away, and the royal deathbed was attended, in the absence of the *premier médecin*, by the physicians in ordinary and by some other doctors, including William Harvey, who was now physician extraordinary. Arriving too late to be of service, all that Mayerne could do was to convey the congratulations of the city of Geneva to Charles I on his accession.

By his ill-timed absence abroad Mayerne had missed an unedifying episode which perhaps he could have prevented; for the amateur and infelicitous medication of the Duchess of Buckingham enabled a Scotch adventurer, one George Eglisham, who called himself a royal doctor but had not been present at the deathbed, to declare that the

Duke of Buckingham had poisoned the King. Eglisham,* a Roman
Catholic, was an extravagant, bombastic character who had already
accused the Duke of poisoning his own early friend and patron, the
Marquess of Hamilton. Now he appealed to Charles I and to the
Parliament, demanding that the Duke be tried for the murder of the
King. His demand was ignored, and he judged it prudent to flee to
Brussels; but his accusation, though treated with contempt at the
time, proved very useful afterwards. It was cited in justification by
the assassin who murdered the Duke in 1628; extended to embrace
Charles I, it would be solemnly repeated in the propaganda of his
enemies in the civil wars – in the Grand Remonstrance of 1641
which precipitated the Civil War and in the Remonstrance of the
Army of 1648 which precipitated the King's execution; and it would
be faithfully repeated by the revolutionary propagandist, John
Milton.

I have described the court of James I as open to ideas, tolerant of
heresy, encouraging experiment. Behind its apparent disorder and
occasional absurdity, it was a Baconian court. In medical matters,
the reign was unique in the opposition of the court to the monopoly,
the privileges, and therefore the dogmatism of the established
physicians. Of course, the established physicians themselves were
not caste-bound, as in Paris. It is noteworthy that not one of them
had studied in Paris, although the medical faculty there was
renowned for anatomy and Mayerne himself would send his son to
study there. But royal patronage encouraged the success of the more
liberal, experimental physicians within the college. The liberal
atmosphere and the medical achievements of the reign – the
incorporation of the apothecaries and the publication of the London
pharmacopoeia – were undoubtedly facilitated by the character and
patronage of the court.

What then of the new reign? Outwardly on the accession of
Charles I, there was a great difference. As Lucy Hutchinson, the
widow of the regicide Colonel Hutchinson – no friendly critic –
would put it, 'the face of the court was changed' and 'the bawds and
catamites' of the previous reign disappeared, or at least practised

---

*The name is variously spelt. I suspect it was Englesham, and that he derived
from the village of that name, near Hamilton, his patron's seat – the same village at
which Rudolf Hess parachuted to earth on 10 May 1941, in search of *his* intended
patron, the Duke of Hamilton.

their vices in corners, out of royal sight. The new court was chaste, correct, orderly. It was also much more conservative. It was conservative in politics and in the Church. Everywhere it favoured the reimposition of hierarchy, discipline, tradition. It was conservative in medical affairs too. It saw the reinforcement of the power of the physicians over the apothecaries and the surgeons, the eclipse of chemical innovations, the return to orthodoxy: fortunately, in the person of Harvey, to the orthodoxy not of Paris but of Padua.

Outwardly, indeed, there was apparent continuity. The medical establishment at court remained intact: most positions, after all, had been granted for life. But gradually the inflated court of James I was reduced by death or retirement and new doctors appeared. The first of them was a Scotchman, David Bethune, doctor of Padua, who became the King's physician in ordinary. He had been to Spain – perhaps accompanying the Prince on his famous visit in 1623 – and had picked up some ideas there. He was joined by Matthew Lister, whom we have met as physician to the late Queen Anne. The new Queen, Henrietta Maria, added a new physician, the Roman Catholic Thomas Cadyman. He too was a doctor of Padua, though not a very good one: he was evidently more concerned to exhibit his stylish horsemanship than to advance his science. We have a fine account of him, with whip and groom, putting his horse through its paces.[6] As for Mayerne, his exceptional position as medical supremo was explicitly confirmed, but he soon became aware of a gentle wind of change.

The first blow was the Duke of Buckingham's war with France on behalf of the French Huguenots. This naturally embarrassed Mayerne, who was officially retained by both crowns and had important contacts on both sides. He was now suspect on both sides. In England some saw him, most unjustly, as another Dr Lopez. In France, he suffered an even greater blow. The French government took advantage of the war to cancel his office and retaining fee. Long and loud Mayerne protested. He wrote to Richelieu, he mobilized royalty, ambassadors, apothecaries, but it was no good. From now on, he was physician to the English court only.

Nor was that all. Charles I took the opportunity to forbid him ever to leave England again. Mayerne was very mortified. He was a cosmopolitan, interested and, he thought, influential in international affairs. He had sunk a great sum of money in his baronial estate and fine castle in Switzerland. But Charles I was firm.

Mayerne's medical services, he said, were indispensable to him: he did not wish to be stranded without them, like the dying James I. It is probable that this was not the King's real, or at least his only, reason. After all, he would allow Harvey to go on a long journey to Vienna and Italy in the train of his ambassador, the Earl of Arundel, in 1636. But Mayerne had too many political interests, and his politics were not those of the new court. After 1628 Charles I had had enough of the Protestant International, and he may well have wished to keep this incorrigible busybody under control. To compensate him for the blow, he promised Mayerne anything that he might ask. A few years later, Mayerne cashed this blank cheque. He requested and obtained, with his colleague the equestrian Dr Cadyman and a courtier, Sir William Brouncker, a monopoly of distilling. We may thus honour him as a founder of the Distillers' Company. But he never saw Aubonne again.

Instead, he concentrated on his experiments: medical experiments, chemical experiments, botanical experiments. Around him, in London as in Paris, buzzed a swarm of empirics, apothecaries, technicians, many of them émigrés like himself. He devised new instruments for the distillation of essences and elixirs, extracted and mixed opiates and unguents, experimented with plants, exchanging rare seeds with foreign enthusiasts, produced cosmetics and perfumes for royal and noble ladies and fumigations for costly funerals. He extended his patronage to immigrant goldsmiths and native gardeners: it was on his recommendation that John Parkinson, the famous herbalist, was made botanist royal to Charles I. He also studied the technology of art, patronizing enamellists from Geneva, discovering new colours, inventing new inks for miniaturists, rescuing Protestant goldsmiths from the Inquisition in Milan, questioning great artists – Rubens, who painted his portrait, Van Dyck, Mytens, van Somer – on the secrets of their technique. He wrote, but never published, or even finished, treatises on all branches of medicine. He enjoyed food and wine: he was, it was remarked, 'of somewhat more than liberal diet' – and of somewhat more than normal girth too: in his later years he was immobilized by corpulency. He is even credited with a cookery book: one of the many desperate attempts by foreigners to improve our English cuisine; and at one time he tried, unsuccessfully, to corner the English oyster beds. But this may have been out of chemical and financial rather than gastronomic interests, as he was interested in the 'magistery', and the manufacture, of pearls.

At one time – in 1638, when he was sixty-five years old – the court of France tried to lure Mayerne back to Paris. He expressed great appreciation of this gesture, but declined to come. He hoped one day to revisit France, 'my dear country', he replied; but he was now too old to transplant, and 'all my designs and hopes, in this winter of my age, are confined within the bounds of this most happy island', an oasis of peace in warring Europe, where the King and Queen were so kind to him and insisted on his presence. No doubt they were, and did. Nevertheless, in a sense, this very Jacobean figure was always an outsider in the court of Charles I. He remained always a Huguenot, always a cosmopolitan, always interested in that 'Rosicrucian Enlightenment', as it has been called, which was now the intellectual world of the Calvinist International. He had no sympathy with the policies of Charles I, or with the style of the court, and although he conformed with the Church of England, he positively disliked the clericalism of Archbishop Laud, which severed that Church from the cause of European Protestantism.*

So, when the great crisis came in 1642, and the court left London, Mayerne did not follow it. Physical immobility, professional convenience, love of metropolitan life conspired to keep him in the capital. It is difficult to imagine him, like Harvey, continuing his experiments in the ultra-royalist atmosphere of embattled Oxford, or as the head of an Oxford college. He stayed in his handsome house in Chelsea, which had formerly belonged to Sir Thomas More. His chief concern, in those years, was to preserve his income, and that came, substantially, not from a straitened court but from private practice in London. At one time, the Parliament stopped his royal salary. At another it threatened him with war-taxation. On each occasion Mayerne reacted forcefully. He rehearsed the terms of his contract with James I. He threatened to emigrate. He ostentatiously packed his bags and made preparations to leave for Holland. He forced full-scale debates in both Houses of Parliament. His patients in the Lords and Commons extolled his services to the country, lamented the possible drainage of such a brain, and hinted

*Neither Strafford nor Laud used Mayerne as his physician, although Strafford's doctor, Sir Maurice Williams, took professional advice from Mayerne when Strafford was ill at York in September 1640. Laud's physician was Sir Simon Baskerville.

that he might prove politically useful, since he had influence in the canton of Berne – although what good that might do in the English civil wars was not clear. In the end, he won his point: he stayed in London, exempt from all taxes, appointed by Parliament to care for the health of the royal children. On one famous occasion he was obliged to displace himself. Queen Henrietta Maria was ill in childbirth at Exeter, and a peremptory message was sent from the King in Oxford through the diplomatic bag of Mayerne's father-in-law the Dutch ambassador: '*Mayerne, pour l'amour de moy, allé trouver ma femme*'. The Parliament gave the necessary leave, and the seventy-one-year-old Mayerne, for all his corpulence, and his eighty-year-old colleague Dr Lister, set out, by coach, with a parliamentary safe conduct, to ease the birth of Princess Henrietta, afterwards Duchess of Orléans.

Mayerne never, I think, saw the King during the civil wars and revolution.* At court, he was replaced by his colleague William Harvey, who in the 1630s had gradually acquired the personal favour of the King and in 1639 had succeeded Bethune as physician-in-ordinary. In manner at least, Harvey was much more in tune than Mayerne with the chastened character of the Caroline court. It was not that Harvey himself subscribed to the aggressive new royalism or its neo-stoic philosophy. Certainly he was conservative in his personal habits. He would ride out to see his patients with brocaded foot-cloths on his horse – a 'very decent' fashion, as Aubrey admitted, but 'now quite discontinued'. But intellectually, in many ways, he was a 'libertine', a sceptic. His closest friends, in the intellectual world, were the sceptical lawyer John Selden and the materialist philosopher Thomas Hobbes. Neither of these could be described as traditional royalists: one was a parliamentarian, the other a radical thinker, outside all parties. Harvey's mind was open to all ideas, but he was careful in those that he expressed. His own religious views, and his greatest work, were, as he realized, implicitly heretical. However, anatomy, unlike Paracelsian chemistry, was a conservative discipline; Aristotelianism covered a multitude of sins; and Harvey's staid manner, his refusal to involve himself in politics, and his quiet devotion to research made him

---

*On 6 April 1643 Mayerne received a parliamentary pass 'to go to Oxford to the King and return back again quietly'; but from a further entry in the *Lords Journals* on 11 April I deduce that he did not go himself but sent his assistant, Dr Colladon, instead (*Lords Journals* V, pp. 696, 712).

more attractive personally to Charles I than the flamboyant medical heretic and political *intrigant* Mayerne.

So, in the 1630s, we seem to witness the growing personal ascendancy of Harvey at the King's court, while Mayerne, increasingly, is concerned with the French Queen and the royal children. It was not a change of personnel, but a shift within personnel, since Jacobean times. In 1617 it was Mayerne who had accompanied James I to Edinburgh, and had received, together with many others, the freedom of that then more generous city.* In 1633, when Charles I made the same journey, it was Bethune and Harvey who accompanied him and received the same honour. It was on that journey that Harvey made the visit, which he afterwards described in such vivid detail, to the Bass Rock, that sheer, conical, volcanic islet rising out of the Firth of Forth, in order to observe the breeding habits of the gannets and guillemots 'which make their conflux to the aforesaid island for procreation sake'. Luckily he was nimble and sure-footed. The mind boggles at the thought of the portly well-fed Mayerne in such a situation, perched 'upon a rugged and dangerous clift', looking 'down into the sea beneath you (as from a steep tower or precipice)', treading on paths glazed by the droppings of seabirds. In the same happy decade, Harvey also accompanied the King to his hunting-lodges at Windsor and Hampton Court. There too he continued his researches, regularly dissecting the red and fallow deer which the King had killed and illustrating their anatomy and generation to 'my royal master, whose physician I was and who was himself much delighted in this kind of curiosity, being many times pleased to be an eye-witness and to assert my new inventions'. Once again, it is less easy to envisage Charles I attending the arcane, alchemical conjurings of Mayerne in his private laboratory in London.

Indeed, there is a sharp distinction between Harvey and Mayerne, a distinction that was emphasized by their physical appearance: Harvey small and quick – 'that little perpetual movement called Dr Harvey' as the Earl of Arundel described him; Mayerne – as we see him in Rubens's splendid portrait – of unwieldy, not to say mountainous stability. In medicine Mayerne's great strength was in chemistry and therapy. He was half Hermetist,

*In 1978, when this lecture was delivered, the City of Edinburgh ungraciously refused its freedom to Prince Charles, Prince of Wales.

half Baconian, and in both capacities distrustful of orthodoxy. Harvey was Baconian in his respect for experiment – Sir Geoffrey Keynes would make him more Baconian than Bacon himself – but in every other way he differed from his Huguenot colleague. 'All his profession', says Aubrey, who was his patient, 'would allow him to be an excellent anatomist, but I never heard of any that admired his therapeutique way . . . He did not care for Chymistry and was wont to speak against them with an undervalue'. As for Bacon himself who was also one of his patients, Harvey does not seem to have admired him. His remarks on him are disparaging. He esteemed him much, says Aubrey, for his wit and style, but would not allow him to be a great philosopher. ' "He writes philosophy like a Lord Chancellor", said he to me, speaking in derision'; and Bacon's 'lively hazel eye' he described, unflatteringly, as 'like the eye of a viper'.

Behind these differences of personality and interest lay a profound difference in philosophy. Both men were philosophers, medical philosophers: that, after all, was expected of a Renaissance physician. But the traditions which they represented were different, even opposite. Intellectually Harvey looked back to Aristotle: Aristotle himself, 'the Master', Aristotle as mediated in the Middle Ages by Thomas Aquinas, Albertus Magnus, Peter of Abano, and, in more recent times, by the great doctors of the medical school of Padua. Mayerne looked back to Plato and the neo-platonists, mediated for him by the medieval alchemists Ripley and Dastin and by the Hermetists of the Renaissance: in medicine his modern masters were not Cesalpinus and Columbus but Severinus and Quercetanus, Fioravanti and Sala, Sendivogius and Croll. No doubt, as Walter Pagel has shown, each knew the other's tradition; but they went their separate ways.*

Being so different, how did Mayerne and Harvey agree together at court? It seems that they agreed to differ, and since both were men of great tact they differed amicably enough. We know only one direct communication between them: a letter from Mayerne in London to Harvey, who was attending the court at Newmarket, on the health of the King's nephew, the Elector Palatine. It is an urbane

---

*In his *New Light on William Harvey* (Basel 1976), while demonstrating Harvey's philosophical commitment to Aristotle, Pagel notes that Harvey accepted certain Paracelsian ideas and was a friend of Mayerne; but too much cannot be built on this: the concrete evidence of intellectual contact which he offers is, at best, very limited.

but somewhat magisterial *consilium*: there is a tone of condescension in it. In a private note, Mayerne observed of one of his patients that he had been *'guasté par D. Harvey,*[7] 'ruined by Dr. Harvey'; and in a letter to a Huguenot Paracelsian doctor in Venice he refers somewhat slightingly to the doctors of Padua – *'vos piliers de pratique Padouans'* – who, he suggests (and Aubrey's remark seems to justify him), are rather too casual in their therapy.[8] Of Harvey's anatomical discoveries he seems to have taken no notice.* Of Harvey's views on Mayerne, apart from his general 'undervalue' of chemistry, we know nothing. Here too, as in everything, he was discreet.

Harvey was a man of genius and it is impossible to generalize from him. He does not fit into the pattern of the court, either of James I or of Charles I. The other physicians whom he joined at the court of King James were often interesting men, with advanced ideas, but except for Mayerne they were not profound researchers and some of them were pure adventurers. All of them were on the make. We find them perpetually begging and scrounging for lands and leases, patents and perquisites, confiscations, wardships, fines. They speculated in forfeitures, cornered coal, garbled spices and tobacco. When Charles I succeeded to the throne, the character of the court physicians changed. The new arrivals are perhaps more respectable that their predecessors but they are less interesting and they made no contribution to science at all. Their learning was conservative, decorative and thin. Arthur Johnston, the Scot who succeeded Harvey as physician extraordinary, was a connoisseur, writer and editor of Latin poetry. An episcopalian from Aberdeen, with a doctorate from Padua, he held very sound views on the Kirk and defied its strictures by going fishing on Sundays: as he remarked, if one waited till Monday, the fish might well have moved too far upstream.† Archbishop Laud approved of him (Archbishop Sheldon, that great fisherman, would have approved even more). He was made Rector of King's College, Aberdeen, and died in still Laudian Oxford in 1641. John Wedderburn, another Scot, began as

---

*Copies of Harvey's *De Motu Cordis* (but a late edition, Leiden 1639) and *De Generatione Animalium* (1651) were in the library of Sir John Colladon, which included many books formerly owned by Mayerne; so Mayerne may have possessed them. But his notes show no sign that he read or was interested in them. His observations on the heart, 'De Corde contra Ar[istote]lem' (MS Sloane 2120, fo. 77v), present a purely Galenic account.

†See his poem 'Apologia Piscatoris' in Sir W.D. Geddes (ed.), *Musa Latina Aberdonensis* I (Aberdeen, New Spalding Club, 1892), p. 147.

professor of philosophy at St Andrews. Walter Charleton was an eclectic man of letters who toyed with fashionable medical ideas. Appropriately, it was in the Bodleian Library, not the new Jacobean Physic Garden or Anatomy School, that the King chose to knight the Roman Catholic court physician, Simon Baskerville. Harvey is quite different, from these as from those. His speculations were purely intellectual. He was a researcher, content with his lot. He was never knighted. As he said, he did not need such 'wooden legs'. Perhaps his conservatism made him more at home in the chaste, correct, archaizing court of Charles I than in the swinging court of James I; but it was conservatism with a difference: superficial conservatism only, the conservatism once recommended by one of the greatest teachers at his own university, the university of Padua, *extra ut moris est, intus ut libet*: outward conformity, inner freedom.

4

Hugo Grotius and England

Hugo Grotius's love-affair with England – a platonic love for an idealized England – is a romance in two chapters, with an epilogue. The first chapter coincided with the nine years of European peace which began with the truce between Spain and the Netherlands in 1609 and ended with the European crisis of 1618, the prelude to the Thirty Years War; the second with the time when England was an island of peace in that war, the eleven years of Charles I's 'personal government', between 1629 and 1640. The epilogue can await its turn. But first there is a necessary prologue.

Seen through this end of the historical telescope, Grotius is famous as a lawyer, one of the greatest, most philosophical of lawyers, universally respected as the founder of international law. If you wish to study him in Oxford, you are diverted from the Bodleian to the Law Library. The Grotius Society, which commemorates him, is a society of scholarly lawyers. But Grotius himself would not have accepted that label. He was a lawyer of course, just as Jacques-Auguste de Thou, Francis Bacon and the first Earl of Clarendon were lawyers: it was a necessary preparation for public service. But the study and practice of the law was not what gave purpose to his life. In all his vast surviving correspondence, he seldom refers to what he calls *studia ista arida et inamoena*, those dry and disagreeable studies. He was a humanist scholar, who began his career by editing a minor classical text: the approved first step for an intellectual, the equivalent of the modern Ph.D. Then he went on to write Latin poetry, tragedy, history. Finally, while never abandoning any of these pursuits, he settled for religion: specifically, he sought to restore, while it was still possible, the shattered unity and ruined peace of the Church.

From the very beginning, this problem had haunted him. How could it not, at that time, in that place: in the brief interval between two great holy wars, in the divided Netherlands? In 1601, at the age of eighteen, he published his first poem, *Adamus Exul*, a foretaste of *Paradise Lost*. Its message, as he pointed out at the time, was ecumenical, and in sending a copy of it to Justus Lipsius, he assured that great arbiter of Christian stoicism, that he intended never to write anything that was not 'catholic and ecumenical, as the early Fathers would say'.[1] Thirty years later, writing to the German Socinian Johann Crell, he would summarize his own intellectual biography: 'from my earliest years, while I was thrust from one discipline to another, nothing delighted me more than religious meditation. This was my relaxation in prosperity, my solace in adversity. Then as now I sought means of peace among Christians' – but look now, he exclaimed (for he was writing in 1632, in the midst of the Thirty Years War), and see what Christians are doing to each other . . . ! It was to mitigate the savagery of that ever-spreading war, 'unworthy not merely of Christians but of men', he explained in another letter, that he had written the book by which he is now remembered, and which, like all great works, has transcended the circumstances which provoked it, *De Jure Belli ac Pacis*.[2]

In all this Grotius saw himself as a disciple – an avowed disciple – of his fellow Dutchman, Erasmus. Erasmus to him was 'the universal teacher of humanity', the constant model by which he measured other men and himself. His earliest prose work is lyrical in praise of Erasmus.[3] The books that he wrote throughout his life, the very language that he used in them, recall his master. Like Erasmus, he deplored the schism of the Church and thought that it could be healed if exact scholarship were used to extract the true meaning, and thus show the essential rationality, of Christian doctrine – what Erasmus had called *philosophia Christi*. Then the abuses which had grown up in unenlightened times could be identified and rejected and the inessential but harmless variations, the products of time and custom, tolerated as *adiaphora*, things indifferent. To ensure this, the theologians, with their pedantry and love of controversy, must be kept in order by lay power, by 'the magistrate'; and it would be a good thing if the magistrate were to keep international peace too, for war is not only evil in itself but also inflames the ideological hatreds which the theologians have inspired. In pursuit of this ideal, Grotius, like Erasmus, came to think that a crucial role could be played by England. However, he did not at first ascribe this role to England. Like Erasmus, he came to England by way of France.

For it was in France – the France of Henri IV, after the peace with Spain in 1598 – that the resumption of the Erasmian programme first seemed possible. There, in the circle of Jacques-Auguste de Thou, the architect of the Edict of Nantes, the greatest historian of his age, and one of the central figures in the European Republic of Letters, Huguenots and Catholics conceived the idea of a reunion, within their country, of the two religions, so recently at war, and dared to cite the officially forbidden name of Erasmus. De Thou, writing his great *History of His Own Time*, called on scholars throughout Europe to provide him with material, and he had talent-spotted Grotius while he was still a student – a very precocious student, the star pupil of the great Scaliger – at Leiden University. The young Grotius came to Paris in 1598 with a Dutch delegation to the peace conference – he was then fifteen, and came in attendance on the Dutch representative Johan van Oldenbarnevelt, who would be his constant patron – and there he met members of de Thou's circle and was accepted into it. He missed de Thou himself, but wrote to him afterwards, and they became regular correspondents. Grotius's earliest publications were dedicated to French statesmen and scholars whom he had met in Paris and knew as friends of de Thou.

However, in the end France let them all down. Gradually it became clear that the movement for the reunion of the Churches in France, though initiated in good faith by the Huguenots and the Catholic friends of de Thou, was being used by the hard-line Catholics, the *dévots*, as a trap: a device to soften up the Huguenot élite and then pick them off one by one. The orchestrator of this campaign was the famous and fashionable *convertisseur*, himself a convert, Cardinal du Perron. Its operation is vividly illustrated in the diary and correspondence of the greatest Huguenot scholar after Scaliger, Isaac Casaubon. Casaubon had been lured to France from Holland to be librarian to Henri IV, but then found himself remorselessly pestered by the Cardinal and his acolytes. The climax came in November 1609, when de Thou's *History*, after long resistance by de Thou and his friends, was placed on the Roman

Index of Prohibited Books as too conciliatory to heretics. One of the charges made against it was that de Thou had praised Erasmus as *grande huius saeculi decus*, the great glory of this age. Next year Henri IV was assassinated, and under the regency of his widow, Marie de Médicis, the *dévots* took over in France. Casaubon now decided that he had had enough: he accepted the invitation of the Archbishop of Canterbury, Dr Bancroft, and emigrated secretly to England. England, Jacobean England, had now replaced the France of Henri IV as the possible centre of a reunited, reformed, universal Church.

The omens, in general, seemed good. The truce of 1609 between Spain and the Netherlands had completed the general pacification of Europe begun in 1598. The long religious war had now, it seemed, come to an end and the ferocity of sectarian passions could be abated. In the Netherlands, the architect of the truce, Johan van Oldenbarnevelt, was in power and Grotius with him. That entailed the supremacy of the States of Holland in the Dutch legislature and of the 'Arminian' party, the 'Remonstrants', in the Dutch Church. Grotius, now Pensionary of Rotterdam and so a powerful figure in the States of Holland, had made his own religious position clear by publishing a funeral poem in praise of their intellectual leader, Arminius, who had just died. Meanwhile there had been the revolt of Venice against the Papacy, which would lead to an alliance between Venice and the Netherlands. North and South might now meet on the *via media*.

So too, perhaps, might East and West. Grotius had learned, from Dutch friends who had travelled in the East, of promising developments within the captive Greek Church. For there too Roman aggression, and in particular the creation of the Uniate Church in the Ukraine in 1596, had provoked a counter-movement. This had been articulated by the Patriarch of Alexandria, Meletius Pegas. Like Grotius, Meletius had wished to end the damaging schism in the Church – in his case the Eastern schism – not by surrender to Rome, but by rediscovery of fundamentals and toleration of differences. Grotius therefore saw him as an ally, and between 1609 and 1611 he wrote a treatise advocating religious toleration and entitled it, in memory of the patriarch, *Meletius*. However, Calvinist critics were shocked by Grotius's treatise: they smelt, as they often would in his works, the dreadful heresy of Socinianism – nationalism, corrupt human reason applied to sacred texts. Socinianism was particularly malodorous at that time; the King of England, whom it would be imprudent to offend, was using very strong language about it; and Grotius did not publish his work. It was not published – indeed, it was thought lost – till 1988.[4]

Thus the historical conjuncture now seemed favourable for a return to the Erasmian model. But politically how could it be achieved? Grotius had considered this carefully. Sometimes he saw Poland as his model. Poland, at that time, was the most tolerant country in Europe: complete religious toleration had been guaranteed by its constitution since 1573, and the three main Protestant Churches had a working political consensus: the consensus of Sandomierz of 1570. But Poland also smelt of Socinianism, which had its headquarters there, at Racow, complete with a learned seminary and a printing-press, churning out heretical books.

Politically, Grotius decided, all the indicators pointed to England. The most persuasive of these indicators was Casaubon. Casaubon's letters from England – not only to Grotius in the Netherlands but also to de Thou in France – were lyrical in their praise of England, of its King, James I, and of the Anglican Church: a comprehensive, tolerant Church which had rejected Roman superstition and arrogant Roman claims but had preserved continuity with the past; a Church with learned bishops, decent ceremonies, pure doctrine; a Church which was even now discarding Calvinist rigour and stabilizing itself on the basis of the Greek Fathers – Chrysostom, Basil, Gregory of Nazianzus – so much more civilized than the Roman Augustine, whose grim doctrine of Predestination had set so fatal an example . . . For Casaubon had had some very disagreeable experiences in his native Geneva and hated Calvinist intolerance quite as much as that of Rome.

All this was music to Grotius's ears, and he responded in kind, setting out his programme. It was not an idle fancy, he insisted, but the fruit of careful thought and discussion. The plan was to go back behind the Council of Trent, the source of all the trouble, and begin again where Erasmus left off. On that basis there should be a new General Council. In the first instance it must be a Protestant Council, to draw up the rules: moderate rules, like those of the consensus of Sandomierz in Poland,[5] which liberal Catholics might afterwards be able to accept. If that meant isolating and extruding the extreme Calvinists along with the Pope and the Jesuits, why not? And then, perhaps, the Greek and Asiatic Churches, under leaders

like the late Patriarch Meletius, would come in. As for the meeting-
place of this Council, Grotius had no doubts: 'I have chosen', he
wrote to Casaubon, 'your Britain, and for its president and
moderator the wisest of Kings', King James. Now was the time, for
so favourable a conjuncture might never recur: 'every age does not
produce learned Christian Kings, nor will England always have a
Casaubon' – *Casaubonum Erasmi simillimum*, Casaubon the modern
Erasmus.[6]

'*I* have chosen *your* Britain': so the Dutchman to the Frenchman.
How often has it happened in history? We think of the Polish, Swiss
and Italian immigrants of the mid-sixteenth century, the Scots,
Germans and Czechs of the mid-seventeenth century, and no doubt
many other Europeans who have planned to establish rational
models of society among these bumbling islanders. But let us not
forestall the story. Casaubon duly responded. He saw some difficulties. It was not easy to catch King James: when he was not out
hunting, he was pressing Casaubon to get on with his refutation of
Baronius, and when caught, he was somewhat evasive. Yes, he liked
the idea of a Council; but no, he did not think that he should
summon it: he was a member, not the head of the universal
Church . . . Poof, replied Grotius, that was no problem: we can get
the German Princes to invite him as the obvious person: the
essential thing is to keep the theologians in their place, for no good
comes from their disputes: princes, lay magistrates, are the only
effective reformers. The Dutch Arminians rely on the States of
Holland to control or side-track the Calvinist clergy; the King of
England is the supreme governor of the most perfect of Churches.

Grotius was consumed with zeal for his project. The peace, the
unity, the repair of the Church, are his constant refrain. Then, in
1613, he had his chance. He was sent to England by his friend
Oldenbarnevelt on an official mission – ostensibly a trade mission –
with secret instructions to broach his project: the project of a
General Council of the Protestant Churches, to be held in England.

So, like Erasmus, Grotius came to England, and, like Erasmus, he
was enchanted by what he found there. James I was so friendly, so
erudite – just like the young Henry VIII. The clergy whom he met –
Casaubon saw to it that he met the right ones: Lancelot Andrewes,
Bishop of Ely, and John Overall, Dean of St Paul's – were so
cultured and scholarly, just like John Colet and Thomas More, and
had all the right ideas. He also met Sir Henry Savile, the learned and

magnificent Warden of Merton College, Oxford, who had just published his great edition of Chrysostom. He discovered that there was an independent English 'Arminian' movement, though it was not yet called by that name. The Church of England, in fact, was not at all as it was represented by Calvinists abroad. He even found several theologians who were 'not hard, rough, stiff-necked, but smooth, fair-minded, amiable, both learned and charitable'. Only Archbishop Abbot was rather cool, but Grotius had already been warned about him and was prepared for that. To protect himself he decided to get in first and undermine Abbot with the King. This was not a very good idea. The King listened to him and smiled, but was evidently not very pleased. However, on parting, he invited Grotius to keep him informed about developments in the Netherlands, which was encouraging.[8]

Grotius was now more than ever convinced that religion was too important a matter to be left to the theologians, and when he returned to the Netherlands he made his views very clear, in politics and in a treatise which he published in justification of his politics.[9] The treatise reached King James, who, for various reasons, was not too well pleased: he thought that he ought at least to have been informed more directly. The King was also still uneasy about Socinianism, of which the Dutch Arminians were being accused by their Calvinist rivals. Grotius was eager to clear himself of any such suspicion and wrote a treatise to do so;[10] which however did not improve matters: in fact, rather the contrary; for Grotius then found himself in direct correspondence with real Socinians and discovered a large area of agreement with them, which he was too honest to deny.

Grotius clearly believed that his visit to England had been a great success. He would remember it nostalgically long afterwards. Englishmen were less sure. He had heard what he wished to hear, which was often his own voice. Archbishop Abbot complained that, at a dinner given by Andrewes at Ely House, Grotius had 'overwhelmed them with talk' the whole time. Of course Abbot was an enemy, so he would, wouldn't he? But Andrewes also had some reservations, which he was too polite to show. Neither Andrewes nor Overall, nor other high Anglicans after them,[11] could support Grotius's Erastian views, his insistence on lay control of the Church. Though they were happy to use the royal supremacy when it favoured their cause, as it generally did in their time, they were not prepared to endorse it absolutely. Kings, after all, can change. Grotius sent letters of explanation to both Andrewes and Overall and asked them to put things right with the King, but his explanations did not make matters better. Andrewes respected Grotius as 'a very learned and able man',[12] but he was himself a very cautious courtier-bishop and was not to be hustled in domestic matters by a foreign visitor. Even Casaubon had been shocked by Grotius's language about Abbot, who was, after all, the King's personal nominee. Casaubon did his best to make peace; but in 1614 he died, and so Grotius lost his essential intermediary. This was a great blow to him, as to King James and the world of scholarship.

Undeterred, Grotius pursued his ideal of a reformed, reunited, ecumenical Church which would marginalize the extremists on both sides. Naturally he was soon embroiled with the Calvinists in the Netherlands. His old mentor, de Thou, wrote to him urging him to keep out of such controversies and concentrate on scholarship and public service. He reminded him that Erasmus, Cassander, and others who had tried to reunite the Church had not only failed but also ended hated by all parties.[14] George Cassander was another Netherlander, a Belgian, who in 1564 had drawn up a plan of conciliation between Catholics and Protestants for the Emperor Ferdinand I and then for his successor Maximilian II. Casaubon had recently drawn Grotius's attention to his work, and he had now become second only to Erasmus in Grotius's lengthening list of precursors in that cause.[15] However, Grotius did not accept de Thou's advice. Though he wished to put an end to the divisive controversies of religion, he wanted to win his own controversies first. So he took up his pen to rebut the charge of Socinianism and explored the earlier history of the encouraging 'Arminian' movement which he had discovered in England: the controversies of Peter Baro, the promising developments in Cambridge, the great work of Richard Hooker. To strengthen his cause and correct Calvinist misinterpretations, he also encouraged his learned friend Gerard Vossius, professor at Leiden, to explore the true history of the ancient Pelagian movement, so castigated by St Augustine and his rigid followers.

Besides, there were such encouraging signs abroad, all pointing to England. In France Pierre du Moulin, 'the Pope of the Huguenots', who had supported the French movement for reunion under Henri IV, was now the trusted agent of James I, a successor, as it seemed, to Casaubon: he even hoped to be rewarded with an English bishopric. Philippe du Plessis-Mornay, the founder of the liberal Calvinist college of Saumur, whom Grotius venerated, was at the centre of an international network. In Italy, there was the famous Servite friar, Paolo Sarpi, in touch with England through the English ambassador and with Holland through his Huguenot adviser on foreign affairs, the physician Pierre Asselineau, and Oldenbarnevelt's son-in-law Cornelius van der Mijle. Sarpi was now preparing for publication his devastating exposure of the true history of the Council of Trent: timely propaganda for the cause. Then, in 1615, at a dinner-table in Rotterdam, Grotius met an exciting new convert: Marcantonio de Dominis, the Catholic Archbishop of Spalato, on his way to England to become Anglican Dean of Windsor and Master of the Savoy. In his baggage the Archbishop was carrying the manuscript of Sarpi's work, to be printed. Finally, in the East, there was Cyril Lucaris, Patriarch of Alexandria, a pupil of Grotius's hero Meletius. He was already in touch with the Dutch Arminians, especially Grotius's friend and mentor Johannes Wtenbogaer, and was seeking contact with the Church of England.* After his arrival in England, de Dominis published his own great work, *De Republica Ecclesiastica*, a manifesto for the party, judged by them unanswerable. The author sent a copy to the States General in the Netherlands, and another to the Patriarch in Egypt, urging him to follow his example and unite the Greek Church with 'this most flourishing Church of England'.

What a noble prospect! Venice and the Greek Church – and if Venice, then (it was confidently said) all Italy; and if the Greek Church, then the scattered Christian Churches in the Ottoman Empire, even Muscovy. So the two great schisms of Christendom – the Eastern schism of 1054 and the Western schism of the Refor-mation – would be reversed; the fragmented Christian world would be reassembled, purged of its abuses, in a great ecclesiastical republic, accepting as its model and titular head the episcopal Church of Jacobean England.

Seen in retrospect, this visionary alliance was very fragile. It was not at all clear that the kind of union imagined by all these men was the same. Venetians and Greeks, French Huguenots and Dutch Arminians would soon discover their differences, for all were

---

*See below, p. 92.

conditioned by the special circumstances of their recent history. Even the 'Arminians' of England – who were not yet called by that name and would always disown it – were shy of too close an association with their controversial Dutch allies, and King James, who had responsibilities of government, and had other reasons for distrusting Grotius, was certainly not willing to commit himself to such an alliance. But the time for retrospection has not yet arrived and for the moment we are looking through the eyes of Grotius, who clung to the hope that, in a peaceful Europe, the Arminians of the Netherlands, sustained by the lay authority of the States of Holland, in alliance with the high Anglicans in England, sustained by King James, could lead the way to the reunification of Christendom. Unfortunately, every premiss in this argument would be proved wrong. In the later months of 1617, as the internal struggle in the Netherlands grew more intense, religious differences became political. On one side the Arminians came to be seen as the party of 'appeasement', prepared to sacrifice national unity in order to prolong the truce with Spain; on the other, the Stadholder, Maurice, Prince of Orange, put himself at the head of the Calvinist party, as the party of resistance, and prepared to end, if necessary by force, the rule of Oldenbarnevelt and Grotius; and in this he was supported by King James.

King James's ambassador at The Hague was Sir Dudley Carleton, a diplomatist formed in the Elizabethan tradition. As ambassador, he was a man under orders, but he executed his orders with a will – and also with authority, for he had a seat in the Assembly of the States General: a relic of the Elizabethan protectorate. When he told Grotius, as the spokesman of the Arminian party, that he was instructed to press for the calling of a national synod of the Dutch clergy, in which the Arminians would inevitably be outvoted, Grotius demurred. He suggested that an outside umpire would do better to try to reconcile the parties rather than put his weight behind one of them.[16] This advice, which was no doubt unrealistic, was not liked; the struggle became fiercer; the ambassador emerged as a strong partisan on one side, and Grotius, now deputy to Oldenbarnevelt, as the animator and articulator of the other. Relations between them were soon very strained. The ambassador, in his despatches, denounced Grotius as 'this pedantical fellow', 'one of the chief *brouillons*', a '*boutefeu*', 'a busy brain and an instrument for the rest', marked by 'temerity', 'indiscretion', and 'shameless impudence'. Pamphlets flew, and 'placards' were published against them. Grotius sought to have the ambassador's speech in the Assembly of the States General suppressed. In his own speeches and pamphlets, in order to enlist English support, he likened the Dutch Calvinists to the English Puritans and he assured his countrymen that the established Church of England was on the Arminian side, citing the name of Andrewes. Busy friends promptly reported this to Andrewes, who at once took fright. He had met Grotius only twice, he said: once at that dinner-party, when Grotius had hogged the conversation, and once at supper, and had had no discussion with him except 'what then passed at table'. He was alarmed to learn that Grotius now 'fathered many things upon him which were neither so nor so'. An officious friend advised Andrewes to 'be more wary hereafter', although he added, when informing the ambassador of his *démarche*, that 'for aught I know, he hath used caution enough that way'. Andrewes was a very discreet courtier who took great care not to expose himself.

Grotius, of course, knew nothing of these private reactions. The ambassador's hostility was clear enough to him, but he still naïvely trusted in Andrewes and King James. He hoped to be sent to England again as a deputy: then perhaps he could have undercut the ambassador as he had tried to undercut Archbishop Abbot; but the ambassador knew how to prevent that: he reminded the King that Grotius was 'a young petulant brain, not unknown to Your Majesty'. So, in December 1617, Grotius took a bold step. On behalf of the Remonstrant party he sent an 'express agent' to London with letters to his chief allies there, Andrewes, Overall and Marcantonio de Dominis, asking them to introduce the agent to the King so that he could present their case and correct the reports of the ambassador. Andrewes and Overall prudently did nothing, but de Dominis – innocent foreigner – handed the letter to the King. The King's answer was such that de Dominis, much mortified, did not dare to report it to Grotius. But Grotius would learn it soon enough: the letter, or a copy of it, was sent to the ambassador and would form part of the charge now building up against Grotius in the Netherlands. As the ambassador somewhat smugly reported, 'I have reserved it for so fit an opportunity'.[17]

The 'opportunity' was the ruin of Grotius and his party. For meanwhile the crunch had come. In August 1618 the States General, remodelled by the Prince of Orange, ordered the arrest of

Oldenbarnevelt and Grotius. Three months later the national synod, which they had fought to prevent, met at Dordt. It was a general council of the Protestant Churches all right, but how different from the council envisaged by Grotius five years ago! Not in England under the presidency of a pacific King and a cultivated Anglican episcopate, but in Holland, dominated by the intransigent Calvinist clergy, against a background of revolution and the rumble of approaching war. The Arminian ministers would be driven out, unheard. By the time the Synod of Dordt was closed, having reaffirmed all those harsh dogmas against which the Arminians had protested, a novel court, presided over by a political judge, had sent Oldenbarnevelt to the scaffold, Grotius to perpetual imprisonment. The Princess of Orange, more humane than her husband, called on Carleton and asked him to intercede for Grotius, that his sentence might be commuted to exile; but the ambassador refused: he had no commission from His Majesty, he said. Besides, such an appeal would be useless, 'because they here apprehend the sharpness both of his tongue and pen, being abroad, but whilst he is in their hands, he will be kept in obedience, for fear of the sword'.[18]

The dramatic events of 1618–19 not only ruined the Arminian party in the Netherlands. They also shattered the ecumenical party on which Grotius had built his hopes. Some members of it moved over to the right. Marcantonio de Dominis returned ignominiously to Rome. It did him no good: he would die there in the prison of the Inquisition. Others moved left. Paolo Sarpi supported the stiff Calvinists at Dordt; du Moulin became one of them. So, in effect, did the Patriarch Cyril, and thereby fragmented instead of uniting his Church. Thus ended the chimera of Erasmian reunion and, with it, the political career of Grotius in his own country and the first chapter of his romance with the Church of England.

Imprisoned in the fortress of Loevestein, alone, 'behind iron bars', with the prospect of a lifetime of captivity before him, Grotius had time for reflexion and study. He also had plenty of books, delivered to him regularly in large crates by his devoted wife. But what is study to a prisoner? 'The best solace of all unhappiness, how crude and insipid it becomes without conversation with other scholars!'

In this state of depression, after six months of confinement, he contrived to send a letter to Lancelot Andrewes, whom he still, perhaps naïvely, considered a friend. It is an eloquent, dignified and very moving letter, an apologia for his life and its steady purpose – the restoration of the unity and peace of the Church 'without violence to the truth', and with toleration on the Polish model. As for his political life, he denies any breach of the law: he had acted always under the legitimate authority of the States of Holland. He sets out the injustice of his trial and his present fate. 'I hear that the best of Kings gave some orders on my behalf' – what they were, he knows not – 'I wish that *dominus* Carleton had been a little fairer to me. My friends sought to soften him, but the zeal of party blinds men strangely.' Then comes the positive plea, the purpose of the letter. He longs for liberty: liberty which is almost as dear as life, which some men prefer even to life itself. 'Oh that the most learned of Kings would deign to summon me to some literary work, so that I might be with you until our storms have blown over, or would find some way of succouring this his suppliant! I have not dared to write to him, fearing lest I do it amiss, which is my misfortune.'

Grotius apparently believed that King James had wished to help him but had been frustrated by his ambassador. He apparently recognized, too, that he was not his own best advocate. His *cri de coeur* evidently reached Andrewes (for the letter is in an English archive), but that cool and courtly high churchman was not moved to act, or to reply.[19]

So Grotius resigned himself to solitude and captivity. He read, thought and wrote. In particular he wrote, in Dutch and in verse, what was to become his most popular work, his little book on The Truth of the Christian Religion: the equivalent, for his century, of Erasmus's *Enchiridion Militis Christiani*. In that book Erasmus had expressed his rational, simple 'philosophy of Christ' for ordinary men, and thereby he had captivated Europe. Grotius addressed his similar message, in the first instance, to Dutchmen – merchants and sailors – travelling to the Far East. It was to solace their long journeys and to enable them to convert the Muslims, Hindus and pagans of their new colonial empire. In its later, Latin version, which would be translated into many modern languages, it too, like the *Enchiridion*, would become a best-seller, although of course, since it sought to sustain Christianity by human reason, not miracles, revelation or authority, it too smelt of 'Socinianism', and critics were quick to notice that it nowhere mentioned the important doctrine of the Trinity. In prison, Grotius also, as he wrote, 'resumed the study of the law which had been suspended through my other avocations',[20] and so laid the base for his other famous work, *De Jure Belli ac Pacis*. Then, in 1621, he made his dramatic escape from prison, carried out under the noses of his wardens in one of those great crates which had brought him his reading matter. Once outside the castle, the French ambassador, his old Huguenot friend Benjamin Aubéry du Maurier, had him spirited across the frontier to Antwerp, and thence to Paris. It was there that the new phase of his life began.

At first all promised well. '*Profuit mihi carcer*', he wrote, '*proderit, spero, et exilium*': 'I profited from prison; I shall profit, I hope, from exile.'[21] He had friends in Paris. The French government had supported the Arminian party in the Netherlands, and now the King of France, ignoring the clamour of his Dutch enemies, assured him a pension of 3,000 livres *per annum*. De Thou was dead, but the circle of his friends remained: the *cabinet Dupuy*, ranged around de Thou's librarian and executor Pierre Dupuy and his brother Jean. It was the club of the *libertins érudits* of Paris. They included the great organizer of the Republic of Letters, Nicolas Fabri de Peiresc, who encouraged Grotius to write his *De Jure Belli ac Pacis*, published in Paris in 1625 and dedicated to Louis XIII. Grotius also wrote and published his *Apologeticus*, a clear, impressive and wonderfully magnanimous defence of the defeated party in the Netherlands. Altogether, the first few years after his liberation were productive and happy. He was in an Erasmian milieu in a civilized and friendly capital.

However, as the years passed, life in Paris became less agreeable. Outside the charmed circle, there were the *dévots*, and Grotius, like Casaubon before him, found himself first pressed, then persecuted by the *convertisseurs*. The process had begun on his first arrival in a Catholic city, in Antwerp, when he was still in a promising state of physical and mental disequilibrium after his dramatic escape. There he had been met and cherished by officious Catholic clergy who afterwards followed up their good offices with letters of friendly advice. The Arminian cause, they assured him, was now dead. In Paris he would no doubt have run into his old friend and fellow exile, Peter Bertius. Driven from his professorial chair in Leiden, Bertius was now a Catholic convert. Why then, asked the Jesuit André Schott, did not Grotius accept the same logic? And then there was his other old friend Marcantonio de Dominis. He was now back in Rome, living very comfortably, with eight servants and a generous pension from the Holy Father (he had not yet disappeared into the dungeon of the Holy Office) . . . To all these letters Grotius's replies were friendly but firm. Yes, he had always wished for religious unity, but not on their terms: papal infallibility, mandatory doctrines unsupported by Scripture or reason . . . As for Marcantonio de Dominis, he had lost his personal reputation by repudiating his own profession of faith, but his book, which Grotius had studied in prison, was convincing. 'Truth, supported by valid reasons, must not be rejected, whoever may have uttered it.'[22]

So Grotius stood, unshakeable, on the narrow Erasmian bridge, protesting its solidity even as it was shot to pieces under him and his companions leapt off it, one by one, to right or to left. In spite of his firm answers, his persecutors did not give up. They boasted that he was on the brink of surrender: even his closest friend among the Dutch Arminians, Gerard Vossius, feared the worst.[23] And if this was the pressure from Antwerp, how much heavier in Paris itself! Nor was this all: there was also the Catholic censorship. For many years Grotius had been working on a history of the Dutch revolt against Spain, commissioned at first by the States General when he was collecting material from de Thou. He had also written, in 1614, a work on the authority of the civil power in religious matters, and he was now busy on his *Annotations* of the four Gospels. All these, he discovered, were unacceptable to the Catholic censors and could not be published 'so long as I live in France'.[24] Under these various pressures he began to think of leaving France. He would look for 'some corner' in Lutheran Germany – perhaps Speyer – where he could live in freedom and bring up his family, for France was now in a state of turmoil, with civil war against the Huguenots, 'and I am weary of the pressure to go to mass'.[25]

In spite of these frustrations, Grotius remained in Paris till 1631. By then Richelieu had arbitrarily stopped his pension and emigration was a financial necessity.[26] The situation in the Netherlands had changed too. Prince Maurice had died in 1625 and his successor, his brother Frederick Henry, was well disposed to Grotius. So, in 1631 – not without difficulty, for his enemies were still powerful – he obtained leave to return to the Netherlands. His first stay was in Rotterdam, and his first visit there a pilgrimage to the house of Erasmus. Then he moved to Amsterdam. But he found the atmosphere hostile; his enemies were determined to drive him out; the Stadholder yielded to their pressure; and in April 1632 he was forced to leave. He chose to settle in Hamburg, which he found very dull – no company, no books, he might as well be in prison again – but at least he was not pestered by *convertisseurs*. His stay in his own country had lasted only nine months, but, if I am right, it had an interesting consequence to which I shall refer in my epilogue.

In all this time Grotius had never lost sight of England. It is true, his former friends – or supposed friends – there were dying off: Overall in 1619, Savile in 1622, King James in 1625, Andrewes in 1626. But on his arrival in Paris he became friendly with the British ambassador, the famous deist Lord Herbert of Chirbury (who unfortunately was withdrawn next year);[27] Casaubon's son Meric was now established in England as a canon of Canterbury cathedral; and he had a well-placed Dutch friend in Francis Junius, the learned librarian of that great patron of the arts, the Earl of Arundel. Grotius invited Junius to translate into Latin his book on The Truth of the Christian Religion, and this led to a correspondence through which he discovered some new English admirers. These included Christopher Wren, Dean of Windsor, whose brother, the formidable Matthew Wren, was the leader of the high-Church party in Cambridge, and, more important still, 'Dr Laud, now bishop of St David's, who is in high favour with the Prince of Wales' – i.e. the future King Charles I.

Grotius lost no time: he wrote direct to Wren and sent, through him, a message to Laud.[28] Meanwhile his constant ally, Gerard Vossius, who was the brother-in-law of Junius, was establishing links with England. Soon he would be writing regularly to Laud and thus providing Grotius with another channel to him. So, by 1628, Grotius could feel that he had restored his position in England. When it was reported to him that he was said to have enemies there, he was indignant: 'my writings', he retorted, 'show how much I admired King James. Francis Junius knows that I have friends there. My opinions . . . are supported by the best and most learned of the bishops and the flower of Cambridge University'.[29] By this time his old enemy Archbishop Abbot was in eclipse and Laud, now Bishop of London, was effective master of the English Church.

It is clear from his correspondence that as he became disillusioned with France, Grotius hoped for some formal offer from England. After all, Casaubon, du Moulin, Vossius, Junius, all had been given posts or sinecures in England, so why not he? He had failed with Andrewes, but Laud was now more powerful and more determined, than Andrewes had ever been. In 1631, while still in Paris, and uncertain whether he would be allowed back to the Netherlands, he wrote to Laud, apparently feeling his way. Laud did not reply directly to him: he was just too busy, he told Vossius; but he was in a generous mood and added that he would do anything that he could for Grotius, as for Vossius or Junius.[30] Then came the permission to return to the Netherlands. At first, Grotius hoped that he would be allowed to live there permanently. He could then make a living by practising the law. When that hope failed, he began to look for asylum and employment abroad. News of his difficulties soon reached foreign courts, and several Protestant princes began to show interest.

In February 1632, while he was still in the Netherlands, hints were conveyed to him of a possible offer from Sweden. Gustavus Adolphus was now sweeping triumphant through Germany, and it was known that he had a great respect for Grotius. However, Grotius was unenthusiastic. 'My spirit shrinks from the life of camps', he wrote,[31] and at once he mobilized the faithful Vossius in Amsterdam. Remembering Laud's generous offer, Vossius wrote to him setting out Grotius's predicament in detail and expressing his fear that this great scholar was about to leave his ungrateful country in disgust; 'and this I fear all the more', he added, 'because I know that many kings and princes are trying to lure him to their countries with large offers of honours and benefits. But if he must live outside his own country, I would grudge him to any other country except Great Britain, where I know how useful he could be to His Majesty, our Lord King Charles, and the whole kingdom'.[32] While he waited for an answer to this second and indirect approach, Grotius received renewed hints from Sweden, but again he stalled, 'for a warm breeze has also been wafted to me from England. I must take my time and deliberate before taking the plunge'.[33]

Laud also took his time. When he finally replied to Vossius, his answer was firm and clear, but disappointing. If Grotius should indeed choose to leave his country again, he wrote, how fortunate for him that so many kings and princes are competing to receive him! It is gratifying to learn that he would prefer Britain above all other countries and no one appreciates his virtues more than I, 'but as things now stand with us, such a thing is quite out of the question'.[34] The warm breeze had now become a somewhat chill wind, and Vossius shrank from passing the message on to Grotius, who by now had left the Netherlands and was in Hamburg. In a warm and tactful letter, he advised Grotius to close with the Swedish offer. What other prince, he asked, could compare with his virtuous, victorious admirer, now in Germany, Gustavus Adolphus?[35]

Lonely and bored in Hamburg, Grotius still hesitated. Having apparently drawn a blank through Vossius, he turned to his other chief contact with Laud, Meric Casaubon. To him he sent a letter full of complimentary remarks about Laud and asked Casaubon to show it to Laud. Casaubon did so, and reported that it had been a great success: Laud had expressed his admiration for Grotius, had snatched the letter from Casaubon's hand, read it, and then, 'though otherwise impervious to flattery and singularly indifferent to other men's opinions of him', kept it.[36] This was very encouraging, and Grotius still made no response to the Swedish suggestions. Then, in November 1632, at the battle of Lützen, Gustavus Adolphus was killed, and any argument based on his virtues, victories and personal admiration for Grotius dissolved. That chance, it seemed, had gone.

So Grotius stayed on in Hamburg, becalmed. But then, a few months later, the Swedish offer was renewed. It came in a personal letter from Axel Oxenstjerna, Grand Chancellor and now, after the King's death, Regent of Sweden. Could Grotius, he asked, spare time from his Muses to come from Hamburg to Berlin, to visit him? Again Grotius stalled. A year later, the Grand Chancellor returned to the matter. He sent Grotius a flattering letter, repeating his invitation and enclosing money for travelling expenses. Grotius returned the flattery, but also the money. He could not leave Hamburg at present, he said. To his brother Willem, his regular confidant, he wrote that he did not trust the Swedes, their offers were too vague. 'I know their tricks', why cannot they speak clearly?[37] Besides, other possible patrons were now in the field. The King of Denmark had offered 'a large stipend', and the King of Poland and the Duke of Holstein were interested too[38] – or least so it was said, but still there was nothing concrete. 'If your King wishes to use my services', Grotius wrote to a Socinian friend in Poland, 'once I know in what capacity, I shall not take long to decide'; but he immediately added that in England the new Archbishop – for Laud was now Archbishop of Canterbury – shared all his views: a prudent man, a pattern of primitive Christianity, sound in all his opinions, and as powerful in the State as in the Church; and he sang the praises of the Anglican Church as now constituted: its respect for tradition, its repudiation of Roman abuses, its rejection of the brutal doctrine of double predestination.[39] Evidently Grotius was still looking to England. But still only compliments came back from Lambeth. Vossius and Casaubon together lamented the disgrace of the age, that a man for whom all the kings of Europe ought to compete should suffer the miseries of a wandering exile.

Finally, after two years of procrastination, Grotius surrendered to the only offer which seemed serious. He accepted Oxenstjerna's invitation to visit him in Frankfurt,[40] and in 1635 he returned to Paris as Swedish ambassador to the court of France. One of the first letters which he wrote in his new capacity was to Laud, congratulating him (rather belatedly) on his elevation to Canterbury, praising him for his work in restoring the purity of primitive Christianity, and expressing the hope that he might now have personal access to his good will.[41]

So began the last phase of Grotius's career: his ten years in the service not of his own country, from which he had been excluded, nor of the pacific King of England, which he would have preferred, but of the belligerent, conquering, imperialist monarchy of Sweden. As an ambassador, it is generally agreed, he was not a great success, but at least it was a delicious revenge. Cries of horror rose from his implacable enemies in the Netherlands. Richelieu, who had so meanly squeezed him out of France, was mortified to see him return in grandeur and pressed repeatedly for his recall. But he pressed in vain. The all-conquering Swedes were the arbiters of Europe and liked to show it; so the Cardinal had to swallow the bitter pill. His relations with the new ambassador, predictably, were very bad, and after the first year all contact between them ceased.[42] Grotius's relations with his Dutch colleague were no better: he was the son of Reinier Pauw, the president of the kangaroo court which had condemned Grotius in 1619, and was a mortal enemy. Since France and the Netherlands were the allies of Sweden in the war, this must have been somewhat inconvenient.

Did Grotius care? Perhaps not much, for he was not really interested in politics or war – certainly not in Swedish imperialism. He had different priorities. To him his embassy was a post of honour from which he could continue his more important task of reuniting Christendom. So he satisfied his official conscience by sending to

Oxenstjerna long letters containing (it was said) only the gossip of the Pont Neuf translated into elegant Latin, and meanwhile pursued his own special interests. He edited and translated classical texts, corresponded with European savants – with Galileo on the reckoning of longitude, with Louis Cappel on Hebrew punctuation, with Peiresc on the lost Greek works of Porphyry, with his Socinian friends on Pythagoras – planned the publication or republication of his own writings, and prepared his last great work, his massive *Annotations* on the Bible. These were to serve the same purpose as Erasmus's *Paraphrases*: that is, by correct scholarly methods to extract the true meaning of the sacred texts and provide a universally acceptable, rationally defensible basis of general reconciliation. He also engaged in a series of controversies which did not always further this irenic design: controversies with the dreadful Calvinists Samuel Desmarets and André Rivet – two French Huguenots preaching virulent orthodoxy in the Netherlands – controversy over Cyril Lucaris and the historic doctrine of the Greek Church, controversy over the identity and chronology of Antichrist, over the charges of Socinianism levelled against him, and – a very unnecessary controversy – over the origin of the American Indians. Oxenstjerna thought all of these controversies unnecessary, and said so.[44] He soon became dissatisfied with his ambassador in Paris, and sent other agents, nominally to support but actually to undermine him, and starved him of funds. This did not improve their relations.

However, in Paris Grotius now had one valued friend and ally. In 1635, the same year in which he re-entered the city as ambassador, there arrived also a new British ambassador, Viscount Scudamore of Sligo. Scudamore was not a very successful ambassador. A Herefordshire squire, without diplomatic experience or gifts, he soon became unpopular with the government to which he was accredited,[45] and his own government found it convenient to impose upon him an unwelcome colleague to supply his defects. In all these respects his position was similar to that of Grotius, and made them natural allies. But there was also a stronger bond between them. Like Grotius, Scudamore was an enthusiastic admirer of Laud. He and Laud had risen together in the clientèle of the Duke of Buckingham, to whom the one owed his successive bishoprics and the other his (Irish) peerage. It was to Laud that Scudamore now owed his embassy in Paris. Thanks to this common enthusiasm, he and Grotius soon became friends and had frequent conversations together.[46] Through Scudamore, Grotius now hoped, once again, as in 1613, to offer his programme of Christian reunion to the rulers of England.

Of course the political situation had changed much since 1613; but in England at least it had changed for the better. There the high-Church party was now stronger than ever, England itself was at peace – an island of peace in a warring world – and if the Netherlands had been lost, why should not a new beginning be made with Sweden? Lutheranism – episcopal Lutheranism, the Lutheranism of Melanchthon, whom Grotius venerated only a little less than Erasmus – was quite acceptable and could no doubt be adjusted to the perfect Anglican model; and then perhaps, England and Sweden having set the pace, the Danes too might come in, and even, in certain particular circumstances – who knows? – the French; for there were many sound French bishops who had a great respect for the Church of England. 'Truly, my Lord', Scudamore reported to the Archbishop, when reporting this scheme, 'I am persuaded that he doth unfeignedly and highly love and reverence your person and proceedings. Body and soul he professeth himself to be for the Church of England, and gives his judgment of it that it is the likeliest to last of any Church this day in being.'[47]

Laud, in his reply, poured some rather tepid water on these warm fantasies, at which Grotius, according to Scudamore, 'seemed to be surprised and quailed much in his hopes', but he did not abandon them. Perhaps the Danes and the French should be dropped, at least for the time being, but Anglo-Swedish ecclesiastical union, he insisted, was possible. Admittedly the Swedish bishops being 'stiff Lutherans', were not likely to be very accommodating, but the business should be entrusted to the lay rulers, 'the magistrate', not to them, and of course the Calvinists, being beyond the pale, should be kept firmly out. And why should not this Anglo-Swedish Church union form part of a political alliance, cemented by a royal marriage – the young Prince of Wales with the young Queen Christina? Thus (Grotius suggested to Scudamore) the formidable Swedish army could be engaged to win back the Palatinate for the dispossessed electoral family and the spectacle of such a sound Protestant alliance might even – perhaps – cool the ferocious temper of the rebellious Scots.[48] To Oxenstjerna Grotius sang the praises of Laud and the English Church, urging him to pay no attention to the slanders of his opponents and dwelling with satisfaction on the fulsome compliments which he himself received from the Archbishop and the excellent relations between them.[49]

Oxenstjerna must have been somewhat surprised by his ambassador's *engouement* for the Archbishop of Canterbury. Surely, he must have thought, there was some confusion of interest here: confusion between Grotius's personal programme of religious reunion, to which England was central, and his official function as the representative of Sweden, to which it was marginal, even irrelevant. Moreover, the confusion was compounded by the activities of a rival evangelist preaching a different form of reunion in the same field at the same time: the indefatigable Protestant missionary, John Dury.

Dury, like Grotius, was an idealist, but their ideals were not quite the same. He wished to achieve not reunion for the peace of the Church but union of all Protestants for the holy war: in particular, union of Lutherans and Calvinists. This suited Swedish policy in Germany, and both Gustavus and after him, Oxenstjerna, listened to him. As Swedish ambassador, Grotius might therefore be expected to support Dury's mission, or at least to give objective advice on its prospects. But Grotius already had his own views on the matter. He had no use for the Calvinists, whom he regarded as quite irreconcilable and wished to exclude from any scheme, and he felt confident that Laud, to whom he could represent all Calvinists as Puritans, would agree. He therefore urged Dury, who had consulted him in 1633–4, before he entered the Swedish service, to be ruled by the Archbishop of Canterbury, 'on whose encouragement the welfare of this business will wholly depend'.[50]

Very little encouragement would come from the Archbishop. To him Dury was, at best, a nuisance. He had, indeed, many supporters in England, but they were the interventionists, advocates of English involvement in continental affairs, even in the war, whether for ideological reasons or in order to recover the Palatinate for its dispossessed Elector. Laud was totally opposed to such a policy. He remembered, only too well, what had happened when England was last involved in war, in the 1620s: a turbulent Parliament calling for his impeachment. He was unfamiliar with the complexities of European politics and indifferent to the misfortunes of the Palatine family whose rash adventure in 1618 had started all the trouble. He had no more use for the Swedish Lutherans, whom Grotius would sponsor, than for the German Calvinists whom they both rejected.

He had quite enough trouble enforcing the authority of his Church at home without seeking to extend it abroad. Of course the decencies had to be preserved – the Queen of Bohemia was the King's sister, and Dury's influential English backers had to be humoured – but he preserved them in a somewhat devious way. He gave Dury letters of recommendation to the British ambassador in Germany but wrote privately to the ambassador to pay no attention to them.[51] He can hardly have relished the intervention of Grotius seeking to divert Dury's efforts into his own project of Anglo-Swedish Church union; and perhaps Oxenstjerna did not relish his ambassador's reports of the anyway lukewarm and ambiguous comments of the Archbishop on Dury.[52] Dury was not deceived by all these ambiguities. In the end he regarded both Laud and Grotius as enemies.

If Laud lacked enthusiasm for Grotius's European diplomacy, he had even less desire to be involved in his religious controversies. Laud disliked controversy and – once he had won the competition for power – did his best to silence it in England. He did not want the theological hornets' nest to be stirred while he was at work in the garden, and he would have been glad if his own too vocal supporters – those Cambridge men, for instance: Dr Brooke, Mr Pocklington, and the noisy Peterhouse mafia – would shut up.[53] Grotius was a very distinguished man, respected throughout Europe, and praise from him was gratifying; but why must he rush into controversy so often? On this at least, Laud found himself in agreement with Oxenstjerna.

For instance, there was the question of Erastianism. Grotius was a convinced Erastian. He relied on 'the magistrate' – the Christian Prince or the States of Holland – to keep the theologians in order and thus secure 'the peace of the Church'. In 1614, during the religious struggle in the Netherlands, he had written a treatise on the subject, which he wished to publish. He had sent a copy of it to Overall soliciting his opinion and that of Andrewes;[54] but it had not been relished, and when Grotius escaped from prison, Overall's librarian, Dr Cosin (for Overall had now died), sent it back without comment.[55] Grotius then tried to publish his treatise in Paris, but the Catholic censors stopped that. Undeterred, he now sent it to Laud. The result was predictable. No man profited more from the royal supremacy in England than Laud. He used it again and again to enforce his ecclesiastical policy, and Charles I was happy to put it at his disposal. But to argue for it theoretically was most unsafe. Who could tell what kind of a lay ruler would succeed Charles I? It was better to insist – but not too aggressively – that episcopacy was *jure divino*. Laud did not return Grotius's manuscript. Nor did he comment on it. He sent a message to Grotius through his agent abroad, Stephen Goffe, advising him not to publish it at present, as inopportune. Grotius accepted the advice, and his treatise, *De Imperio Summarum Potestatum circa sacra* was not published till after his death.[56] An English translation would be published after the execution of Charles I, under a government whose Erastian policy fully vindicated the apprehensions of Andrewes and Laud.

Another sign of danger appeared in 1635, when the government of Charles I decided to assert itself at sea, claiming exclusive sovereignty over undefined home waters. In support of this policy John Selden was persuaded to update a legal opinion which he had written in the reign of James I to counter Dutch claims to complete freedom of the seas. The Dutch claim had been set out by Grotius and published in 1609 as *Mare Liberum*. Selden's counter-claim, which had remained unpublished as that particular crisis subsided, was now published as *Mare Clausum*. The Dutch government was thoroughly alarmed, and Laud who had persuaded Selden to revise his work for the occasion, feared that Grotius would re-enter the fray. He therefore wrote to Scudamore expressing the hope that Grotius would be wiser than to waste his time answering Selden. In this case the hint was unnecessary. Grotius was no longer retained by the Dutch government. On reading Selden's treatise he observed that it was very respectful towards him. And he saw clearly enough that his Swedish masters would not appreciate the idea of *Mare Liberum*: they were aiming at *dominium maris Baltici*.[57] So on this issue he remained silent.

Far more dangerous, to Laud, was Grotius's reputation for 'Socinianism': a heresy more damaging even than Erastianism. Not that Grotius was himself, strictly speaking, a Socinian – he had explicitly written against the heresy – but, like Erasmus, he believed that the Christian message, rightly understood, like the ideal system of law, was in harmony with human reason and could be defended by it; and that, in itself, was enough to provoke the charge. After all, was not Erasmus himself the true father of Socinianism? Like other 'rational theologians', Grotius soon discovered that the mere process of defining his position in relation to Socinianism in its narrowest sense strengthened the suspicion that he favoured it in a wider sense, and this suspicion was increased by his friendly discussions with the Socinians in Poland, where it was officially tolerated. The same process occurred in relation to popery: the more Grotius defined his aversion from its particular abuses, the nearer he was said to approach its idealized form. So, having begun by seeking a middle position *inter Socinianam licentiam et papisticam tyrannidem*, he would end by being accused of favouring both. Laud's fate was similar – but the order was reversed. Whereas Grotius was accused at first of Socinianism and later of popery, Laud was already, by 1635, widely slandered as a papist, and had no desire to be still further smeared as a 'Socinian'. And yet this was a charge that too close an association with Grotius could bring.

It was brought dangerously close to him by the case of his own former chaplain Samson Johnson. As chaplain to the British ambassador in Germany, Sir Robert Anstruther, Johnson had met Grotius in Hamburg in 1632 and had become an ardent disciple. In 1635 he had returned to England armed with a strong letter of support from Grotius to Laud. Laud then recommended him as chaplain to the exiled Queen of Bohemia at The Hague. There the sensitive noses of the Calvinist clergy soon picked up a familiar scent: Socinianism of course, and popery. Johnson firmly repudiated both charges. He had a cast-iron defence, he said: he was a disciple of the great Hugo Grotius, whose tract against Socinianism ('for Socinianism!' cried his accusers) he had republished at Oxford. That put the fat in the fire, not only for Grotius but also for Laud. The drum ecclesiastic was beaten and English-speaking spies were sent to listen to Johnson's sermons. They discovered sinister goings-on, and complained to the Queen of Bohemia, who (they said) was much put out: why, she asked, had the King and the Archbishop sent her such a man? Had she not trouble enough already? Letters of violent denunciation also came to Laud. To protect himself, Laud obliged Johnson to clear himself in public, but it did no good. Nor did Laud's official denunciation of both popery and Socinianism in the famous canons of 1640: indeed, they rather rebounded on him, for while they enabled him to get rid of the Bishop of Gloucester, as a secret papist (which he was), the Bishop turned on him and accused him of Socinianism. In 1642 Johnson, who remained on good terms with both Grotius and Laud (and with the Queen of Bohemia), would be accused in the Long Parliament of Socinianism, and finally kicked out of his chaplaincy thanks to the efforts of his former friend, now colleague at The Hague, the evangelist Dury; and next year the rabid Calvinist Francis Cheynell would denounce the whole Laudian Church as a Socinian mafia organized and directed by the Archbishop.[58]

Altogether, it is difficult to escape the conclusion that Laud, like Andrewes before him, found the enthusiastic support of Grotius rather a liability than an assest. He returned his compliments, expressed his respect and admiration, but was careful to give him no encouragement and avoided direct correspondence. He sent his messages through intermediaries, excusing himself for not writing direct: one of Grotius's letters 'was most welcome, but I have no time to reply'; to another, he 'would have had an answer if important business had not intervened'.[59] However, when Grotius was in real need, Laud, unlike Andrewes, came to his aid. In 1639 seemed likely that his appointment in Paris would come to an end. He was *persona non grata* to Richelieu. Oxenstjerna had turned against him, Scudamore had been recalled to England in January of that year, and his successor, his former colleague the Earl of Leicester, had different views. Grotius appealed to Scudamore in England, Scudamore to Laud; and Laud responded. In the name of Charles I, he offered asylum in England for Grotius and his family, if they should need it. Grotius was deeply moved: 'all my life', he wrote, 'I shall labour to show my gratitude by very humble service'.[60]

In fact Grotius did not need to take up the offer. Richelieu was not prepared to expel him, and Oxenstjerna, who would gladly have recalled him, kept him in Paris (we are told[61]) for the sole purpose of annoying Richelieu. Anyway, by the end of 1640, asylum in England was no longer attractive: if anyone then needed asylum abroad, it was the Archbishop, who was in the Tower of London. The overthrow of his Church, the centrepiece of Grotius's plan of reunion, had begun.

After the recall of Scudamore, Grotius had virtually no contact with England. His policy of an Anglo-Swedish alliance, which he was still pressing in the autumn of 1640,[62] was bankrupt. Perhaps it had always been a chimera: since 1638 Charles I had been relying on Spanish support, quite incompatible with it. After the meeting of the Long Parliament, and the fall of the Archbishop, Grotius could only record the increasingly depressing news from England and lament the personal misfortunes of the Archbishop. In 1641 the new

British ambassador, Sir Richard Browne, brought some account of him: he had visited him in the Tower and found him 'strong in body and mind'.[63] Grotius was able to send a message of moral support back to him through another visitor. This was Edward Pococke, the first occupant of the chair of Arabic which Laud had founded at Oxford. Pococke planned to translate Grotius's book on The Truth of the Christian Religion into Arabic, and as he was passing through Paris on his way back from the East, he took the opportunity to call on its author. According to Pococke's biographer, Grotius sent practical as well as moral exhortation to Laud, recommending that the Archbishop escape from the Tower as he himself had once done from the castle of Loevestein; but the advice, though duly delivered, was rejected.[64] As the crisis in England worsened, Grotius must have been painfully reminded of the revolution in the Netherlands over twenty years ago: a great statesman judicially murdered; 'Arminianism' overthrown; its champions scattered, driven into exile, sometimes converted; 'Calvinism' triumphant. And still there was no end to the European war.

As his hopes of support from England faded, Grotius became ever more anxious to declare his message openly to the world. 'I am uncertain how much of life is left to me', he wrote in the spring of 1640, 'and I wish, above all, to leave a testimony of my opinions on the events which are so gravely shaking Christendom'. Therefore it was essential that his writings – all of them, old and new – be published and distributed without delay. If they remained in manuscript, how could he trust his heirs not to let them perish? That had been the fate of so many useful works. So orders, sometimes imperative and testy, flew from Paris to Holland, the only country where they could evade the censors, to his patient and devoted brother Willem, his confidant and literary agent, and to his few reliable – that is, Remonstrant – friends. Meanwhile his pen was busier than ever. He republished, with his own notes, Cassander's plan of reconciliation of 1564, his *Annotations* on the Bible swelled to a huge bulk, polemical treaties were dashed off, the Calvinist hornets swatted as they swooped, buzzing furiously, from their nests in The Hague and Amsterdam. Of course it was an unending battle, but the aim was constant, and it had to be fought. To those, like Vossius, who thought that, in such troubled times, a period of silence would be prudent, he was severe. Such timidity, he wrote, was unworthy of a man of Vossius's age: the temporary success of sedition – he was referring to the trouble in England – should not divert us. It had not diverted Erasmus, Cassander, Casaubon, Melanchthon . . . 'Our lives are not in our own hands. We shall serve either our own age or another . . . If Erasmus and Cassander had waited till there were no popular seditions, they would have condemned themselves to eternal silence.' Of course it was hard work swimming against the current, 'but we are not alone. Erasmus, Cassander, Casaubon went before us; and now there is Milleterius'.[65]

The name of Milleterius comes as a shock, for Milleterius – Théophile Brachet, sieur de la Milletière, a Huguenot layman – was quite unfit for such distinguished company. A noisy controversial-ist, he had begun by advocating rebellion, but had now emerged as a preacher of reunion. Grotius had been suspicious of him at first: what, he asked, could be the motives of this volte-face? Vanity? Exhibitionism? Or was he perhaps a paid hack of Richelieu?[66] For by now Richelieu was seeking – cautiously, obliquely, secretively – to revive the old programme of reunion within France: Catholics and Huguenots to be joined in a Gallican 'patriarchate', largely independent of Rome. It was a return to the early years of Henri IV. The Cardinal's chief agents in this operation were the brothers Dupuy, Grotius's closest friends in Paris, and Grotius was well aware of the machinery behind it. Its patron, he told his brother, was the Cardinal himself, 'a man so fortunate that he had never failed in any of his undertakings'. The movement, he thought, might well succeed – the Cardinal himself was hopeful – so why not back it? Even if it should fail, 'ought we not to plant trees for future generations?' 'Even if we succeed only in reducing mutual hatred and making Christians gentler and more civil to each other, is not that worth our labour and trouble?'[67]

It was in 1640, as he was losing hope of England, that Grotius emerged as a supporter of la Milletière – that is, in effect, of Richelieu's proposed patriarchate. Richelieu seems to have wel-comed his support: perhaps that is why he no longer sought Grotius's recall. The whole operation was conducted behind a veil of secrecy, but by 1642, the sharp-eyed Calvinist vigilantes noted that the Cardinal was transferring his interest from la Milletière to Grotius as a more reputable publicist, and in the same year Grotius managed to insert a few little compliments to Richelieu in his *Prayer for Ecclesiastical Peace*.[68] However, in the end, it all came to nothing.

As before, as afterwards, Rome knew how to deal with such deviations: personal submission first, discussion (if any) afterwards, was its message to those who would treat with it; and on Richelieu's death, in December 1642, the whole project evaporated.*

With the Netherlands lost to militant Calvinism, the mirage of a French 'patriarchate' dissolving, and England, by now, engulfed in civil war, where was Grotius to turn? He was bored with his Swedish embassy and longed to be freed from it. He was bored with France too: his door in Paris was locked against visitors, even old friends. As for the Netherlands, 'I ceased long ago to be a Hollander'. But he remained a citizen of the world: 'my thoughts are not directed to any one country, but to all countries, and I thank God that there are great men in England, Germany, Denmark, Poland, who think seriously of these things'; and he had a message for posterity which must be delivered: 'I cannot tell you', he wrote to his brother, 'how eager I am to see all my works published'.[69] But what was his message to the élite of Christendom, to posterity? Contemporaries were not at all sure. They were sure only that he was not one of them. To the Calvinists he was either a papist or a Socinian or both: *purus putus Socinianus* cried the Dutch Calvinist Johannes de Laet;[70] 'Tridentine Popery!' screamed the Scotch Calvinist Robert Baillie.[71] This was the standard Calvinist view: the view of Richard Baxter and John Owen in England. His fellow-irenist Dury concluded that he was an agent of the Pope, but the Roman Church put his books on the Index. To Gui Patin, conservative, anti-papal Catholic, *libertin érudit*, who knew him in Paris and was devoted to him – they had much in common: love of Erasmus, dislike of monks and Jesuits, hatred of Richelieu, that cold-hearted machiavellian warmonger who had murdered their friend, the son of the great de Thou

---

*For Grotius's involvement in Richelieu's plans, see Pierre Blet, 'Le Plan de Richelieu pur la réunion des Protestants', *Gregorianum* XLVIII (1967); Hans Bots and Pierre Leroy, 'La Mort de Richelieu vue par les Protestants', *Lias* iv.i (Amsterdam 1977). Grotius's support for the plan incidentally raises a teasing question mentioned in my *Catholics, Anglicans and Puritans* (p. 100). The most substantial manifesto of the project was the huge two-volume compilation by the Dupuy brothers on the liberties of the Gallican Church, of which two sets were sent to Laud in 1639 and deposited by him in Oxford libraries as useful to the Church of England. But how did they come to Laud? Were they perhaps sent to him by Grotius – and conveyed (since the work was denounced by the Catholic hierarchy in France) in the diplomatic bags of the returning Lord Scudamore? But this is pure speculation.

– he was a mystery, '*feu M. Grotius, dont l'on ignore la religion*': it had been a complete enigma, he said, for the last twenty years.[72]

Grotius himself knew, or thought that he knew. Again and again, in his correspondence and controversies, he defined his position. He was for the reunion of Christendom on the the basis of the doctrines agreed by the Church in its 'three best centuries', when Greek and Latin Churches were still united, episcopacy was established, and the Roman primacy was no more than a presidency over equal bishops gathered in national Churches and legislating through General Councils: a great ecclesiastical republic as defined by his one-time friend Marcantonio de Dominis. Those doctrines were to be discovered by humanist scholarship and human reason applied to the sacred texts as they had been applied by the great scholars – his master Scaliger, his friend Casaubon – to the classical texts. Then the abuses which had grown up in time could be identified and purged away and the harmless variations from place to place tolerated. This had been the message of Erasmus, who had cleaned the sacred texts and extracted the philosophy of Christ, and that process could be continued. Not only Roman abuses and errors had to be purged: there were also the new Protestant inventions: the identification of Antichrist with the Pope, now mandatory among good Calvinists, and the fable of the female Pope Joan, happily exposed by the Huguenot scholar Blondel. Thus continuing scholarship would establish an agreed basis, ideological confrontations would cease, and the horrible wars of the time, which were born and nourished from such confrontations,[73] would lose their justification, or at least their ferocity and could themselves be regulated by reason, by international law, as set out in *De Jure Belli ac Pacis*.

It sounds so simple, so rational; but how could such a result be achieved when religion had been so deeply entangled in politics and its differences hardened by history? At first Grotius believed that Protestantism, which had already corrected many of the abuses of the Church, should be the starting-point, and he had seen in his own country, the Netherlands, in that golden age 'after the governorship of the Earl of Leicester',[74] until the Synod of Dordt – i.e. from 1589 until 1618, the era of Oldenbarnevelt and the Arminian ascendancy – and in Jacobean England, the England of Hooker and Andrewes, the nucleus around which the other Churches could gradually be reunited. But then the traumatic events of 1618 – the revolution in the Netherlands, his own imprisonment and then exile, and the beginning of the Thirty Years War – had destroyed that hope. From then on, Calvinism, the radical Calvinism of the Dutch preachers and the militant Huguenots of France, was rejected altogether. No reunion, Grotius now believed, could accommodate them. Their horrible doctrine of 'double predestination', their intolerance, their intellectual despotism, ruled them out.

So, in the 1630s, Grotius turned from Calvinism to Lutheranism, from the Netherlands to Sweden. Perhaps the moderate Lutheranism of Melanchthon, of the Augsburg confession, could be fused with the Anglicanism of the Church of England to form the essential nucleus of the new unity. After all, the English 'Arminians' had at first been known as 'Lutherans'. But then, in 1640, it was the turn of the English 'Arminians' to founder in revolution, a revolution very similar to that of the Netherlands in 1618. To Grotius that was a shattering blow, and in his last years, he shifted the basis of his ideal reunion yet again: this time from Protestant (but not too Protestant) England to Catholic (but not too Catholic) France. A union of the Protestant Churches alone, he now decided, was impossible: acknowledging no central authority, they would continue to split into different Churches, congregations, sects, as was happening in England with the rise of the Independents.[75] Therefore the Roman Church must be included in the mixture as a necessary coagulating element. But in order to qualify for such inclusion, it must first pass certain tests. It must accept the Erasmian conditions: abolition of the post-Tridentine papal monarchy, rule by General Councils, repudiation of papal infallibility and claims to depose rulers, abolition or reform of monasticism. Such reforms he hoped to see carried out by Richelieu. It was the kind of reformation carried out in England by Henry VIII – who, however, had been driven into schism, which was perhaps unnecessary: after all, the King of Spain, as King of Sicily, had already secured independence without such an open breach. Perhaps Richelieu would achieve the same.[76]

Of course his enemies seized on this hypothetical acceptance of Catholicism. Did it not justify all their accusations? Even modern scholars have described it as a 'stupefying' volte-face by a lifelong Protestant.[77] But in fact Grotius had always understood reunion to include both the Catholic and the Greek Orthodox Church: it was merely the order of the successive stages of such reunion that he had now been obliged to change. Originally, he had envisaged a Protestant union, on the Erasmian model, to which Romans and

Greeks would be invited to adhere. Now, since the Protestants were unable to form the necessary nucleus, the order was altered: the Romans would be in at the beginning – provided that they made the necessary concessions. When his Calvinist assailants declared that he had been bought by promises, he was indignant. His views were still the same, he maintained: they were those of his Protestant precursors, Melanchthon and Casaubon. If he had been willing to surrender to Rome, he could have enjoyed the ample honours and rewards which had been offered to him in France: he would not have felt obliged, when he had already been imprisoned, despoiled and driven out by his own country, then to leave France for Germany and serve an unknown Protestant kingdom.[78] In other words, he echoed the reply of his friend, Archbishop Laud, when he was offered a cardinal's hat if he would be converted: that Rome would have to be 'other than it is' before he could consider such a step. He would not deny his own deep convictions like Marcantonio de Dominis.[79]

Since that did not happen, he remained a Protestant and, *in foro interno*, an Anglican to the end. The Anglican Church might be in convulsion, but he was loyal to its idea. In December 1644 he even offered an Anglican solution for the religious problems of the Netherlands. Ideally, he then wrote, the Remonstrants should establish episcopacy on the Anglican model: they should choose eminent men who should seek consecration by laying-on of hands from Archbishop Ussher, then at Oxford with the King; then these bishops should consecrate others, and so start the process of return to the good old system whose rejection had led to all the trouble.[80] Four months later, in April 1645, he wrote to his brother that 'the Anglican liturgy has always been held by all learned men to be the best'.[81] Then he left for Sweden, to wait on Queen Christina and discharged from his embassy. On his return journey he was shipwrecked on the Pomeranian coast and died from exposure near Rostock. Had he returned to Paris, being now liberated from his embassy, which had previously inhibited him, he would no doubt have communicated, as he had advised his wife and children to do (and as they did), in the Anglican Church:[82] that is, attended the services in the house of the royalist British ambassador – the only place in the world, it was said, where the now proscribed service of his proposed universal Church was still publicly celebrated.

*

When we look at Grotius's life in its own terms, as defined by him, it has a tragic character. A boy-prodigy, initiated into public life at fifteen, holding high office at twenty-six, an international statesman at thirty, described, by no mean judge, as the greatest universal scholar since Aristotle,[83] at thirty-five his fortune changed, and for the next twenty-seven years he was first a prisoner, then (apart from a few disappointing months in 1631–2) an exile. From beginning to end, his life was dominated by a single purpose, to which all his activities, political, diplomatic, intellectual, were directed. At his death, he had not only failed: he was completely isolated. His former friends and allies, who for a time had shared, or seemed to share, his ideals, had disappeared. Oldenbarnevelt and Laud had perished on the block, Marcantonio de Dominis had died in the prison of the Inquisition, Cyril Lucaris had been strangled in that of the Sultan. It was, once again, a repetition of the story of his hero Erasmus: how prophetic had been that warning of Jacques-Auguste de Thou! Looking back on his career, we may say, with the wisdom of hindsight, that his cause had been hopeless from the start. The division of Christendom was a fact; the several forms of Christianity had been hardened by mutual opposition and welded into the social and political diversity of Europe. The mould had set even in the time of Erasmus, and was far harder a century later in that of Grotius.

However, his ideas had a future which, in his last years, he can hardly have foreseen: a future not in the restoration of religious unity, which remained a chimera, but in the emergence, behind the permanent religious fragmentation, of a new intellectual unity: the unity of that natural law and that human reason which he had seen as providing the essential means to religious unity. Francis Bacon wrote, of the alchemists, that their operations, in their own terms, were futile, but that they were not to be condemned since, incidentally and accidentally, they led to the new science of chemistry. Similarly Grotius, seeking to establish the universal truth of Christianity and the universal validity of law by placing under both a universal human reason, laid a foundation for the philosophy of the next century. Dutch Arminianism, separated from the politics which had at first discredited it, and Polish Socinianism, passing through it into Anglicanism and even into Calvinism itself, by dissolving the bristling theological outworks of the established Churches, cleared the way from the ideological jungle of the Thirty Years War into the open landscape of the Enlightenment. Thereby,

as he had hoped, the ideological heat being taken out of international relations, the savagery of war was, for a time, reduced. As he
himself put it, even if his efforts for reunion should achieve no more
than making Christians gentler and more civil to each other, they
would not have been in vain: *profuturi sumus aut huic aetati aut aliis.*

The subject of this essay is Grotius's relations with England. For
accidental historical reasons – because the English Church, more
than any other, had preserved some continuity with Erasmian
reform and because England had not been sucked into the whirlpool
of the Wars of Religion – Grotius saw England as central to his
programme. I have called it an idealized England, for he knew little
of its reality. On his brief official visit in 1613, he moved in a
charmed, or at least a closed circle. Thirty years later, when
England was engulfed in civil war, he would dwell nostalgically on
his memories of that delightful visit.[84] But what did he know of the
real England? In all his vast surviving correspondence, he shows no
sign of having conversed or corresponded with any Englishman
outside that circle. His scholarly interests did not bring him into
contact with Camden or Ussher or Selden or Cotton or Bacon, his
political interests with Sir Henry Wotton or Sir William Boswell or
Sir Thomas Roe. Self-centred, wedded to his own ideas, inflexible,
somewhat insensitive, and ignorant of the language, he had no
understanding of the tradition which these men had inherited from
Elizabethan times. Perhaps, like Charles I and Laud, he regarded
them all as Puritans: a great mistake. After 1613 his contact with
England was either through foreigners – the two Casaubons, Isaac
and Meric, Vossius and Junius – or through committed members of
the party to which he had attached himself: first Andrewes and
Overall, then the Laudians: Laud himself, Christopher Wren,
Samson Johnson, Scudamore, and Laud's agent in the Netherlands,
Stephen Goffe. The picture of England conveyed by these men was
partisan, black and white. Of the political conditions which limited
the freedom of English statesmen, bishops, ambassadors, he showed
no awareness. No wonder the cautious Andrewes, and even the
incautious Laud, were chary of his support. No wonder Oxenstjerna
found him an imperfect diplomatist. No wonder he was surprised by
the 'sedition' which broke out in England in 1640.

However, there is the epilogue. A few years after his death, when
the political circumstances which had made and marred his career
had changed – when the house of Orange was in eclipse in the

Netherlands, Laudianism and episcopacy itself extinct in England, peace made and the Swedish army no longer formidable in Europe – the underlying philosophy of Grotius began to penetrate European thought, and nowhere more than in England, where the new Anglicanism of Hammond and Sheldon and the new royalism of Clarendon found it a more acceptable intellectual support than the abrasive clericalism of the old Laudians or the radical new absolutism of Thomas Hobbes.[85] Grotius had not realized his hope of seeing all his works published in his lifetime, but his heirs were less casual than he had feared, and his sons Cornelius and Pieter de Groot fulfilled his wishes. They published his still unpublished works – his Tacitean *Histories* and *Annals* of the Netherlands, whose magnanimity towards his persecutor, Prince Maurice, would so impress Pierre Bayle;[86] his defence of Erastianism, which had shocked the clergy of all denominations; his *Annotations on the New Testament*, which would inspire Henry Hammond and convert the great editor of Erasmus and publicist of the eighteenth-century Republic of Letters, Jean Leclerc.[87] They also resolved to publish his complete theological works. This enterprise was delayed by war in the Netherlands and a disastrous fire in the printing house: but when the four folio volumes were at last ready for the press, their editor, Pieter de Groot, could think of no more proper dedicatee than the King of Great Britain: was he not the grandson of King James 'of immortal memory', whom Grotius so venerated, and the supreme governor of the restored Church which he had chosen as the model for Christendom?[88]

In a published essay,[89] I have suggested that the medium through which the ideas of Grotius were separated from present politics and thereby regained their value as an objective intellectual force was the group of independent spirits who gathered in the circle of Lord Falkland at Great Tew. The last question that I shall ask here is, how were those ideas carried into that circle? For nowhere in the surviving correspondence of Grotius do I find any sign that he knew any of them, and on the other side no private papers of Falkland, Chillingworth and their friends at that time survive. However, it is clear that Grotius was well informed about matters which interested him in England; he had many visitors in Paris who are not recorded by him[90] and we need not be deterred from speculation.

Although the chronology of the Great Tew circle is not at all clear, it seems, from a poem by Falkland in praise of Grotius, which was printed with George Sandys's English translation of Grotius's early poem *Christus Patiens*,[91] that Falkland had met Grotius personally. If so this must have been in 1631, when Falkland visited the Netherlands to which Grotius, in that year, had returned.[92] It was also in 1631 that Francis Coventry, a young man at Oxford and a pupil of Gilbert Sheldon, who was one of Falkland's close friends, undertook to translate Grotius's *De Veritate* into English. The translation was anonymous, but Grotius knew the identity of the translator.[93] We also know that Chillingworth, the intellectual leader of the Tew cirlcle, who had just returned, disillusioned, from Douai, was 'not far from Oxford' – which could mean at Tew – in March 1632, when he refused to commit himself to the Anglican Church, to which he was being pressed, at the request of his godfather, Laud, by Juxon and Sheldon, without first going to Holland to consult Grotius. We do not know whether he actually went – probably not, for Grotius was already preparing to leave the Netherlands for Hamburg – but he would hardly have proposed the journey without some encouragement or introduction, perhaps from Falkland. It therefore seems possible that the intellectual starting-point for the reception of Grotius's ideas in England was a meeting of Grotius and Falkland in Holland in 1631. If so, that meeting of one of the greatest of Europeans with a young Englishman of no note or public position had profounder and more lasting consequences than Grotius's long wooing of Andrewes and Laud, and can be seen as a moment in Anglo-Dutch intellectual history.

5

The Church of England and the Greek Church in the Time of Charles I

It is well known that the Church of England, in the time of Charles I, showed a special interest in the Eastern Church. Archbishop Laud patronized Greek and oriental scholarship. As its Chancellor, he enriched Oxford University with Greek and oriental manuscripts and made plans to print them. He projected a Greek press at Oxford and achieved one in London. He obliged the King's printers to print three Greek texts. He also provided the learned press at Oxford with Arabic type. He then sent qualified scholars to the Ottoman empire in search of more manuscripts. Meanwhile he endowed the study of the Hebrew and Arabic tongues.

The impetus behind this patronage was not humanist or scientific: it was theological. The manuscripts which Laud sought, and the texts which he published, were religious. He wished to encourage the study of the Hebrew and Greek scriptures and the Greek Fathers. Even his Arabic interests had the same purpose. The tradition of the Greek Church, in the East, had often passed through Arabic channels. It seemed reasonable to suppose that the Greek saints, like the Greek philosophers, might reach the West in an Arab dress.

This new interest in the Greek Church was well timed, for Laud's rule over the English Church happened to coincide, not only with the revival of Greek studies in Oxford,* but also with the rule over

*The main centre of Greek studies since the Renaissance had been Paris. Although Henry VIII founded regius chairs at Oxford and Cambridge, the subject can hardly be said to have flourished at Oxford until the time of Sir Henry Savile, who, as Warden of Merton College and Provost of Eton, filled both places with

the Eastern Church of an equally energetic Greek archbishop who was eager to respond to it. Cyril Lucaris, Patriarch of Alexandria from 1601 to 1620 and of Constantinople – with dramatic interruptions – from 1620 to 1638, had good reasons to cultivate the Protestant Churches of the West, and he exchanged letters, gifts and emissaries with both Charles I and Laud. His gifts remain: the *Codex Alexandrinus* of the Greek bible in the British Museum; the Arabic Pentateuch and many other manuscripts in the Bodleian Library. Thanks to these splendid testimonies of it, and the tragic fate which engulfed both the giver and the receivers, a special relationship seemed to unite the Greek Church, defending itself against Roman aggression, with the high-Church party in the Church of England, which was also (in spite of Puritan accusations) firmly anti-Roman. This relationship was emphasized a generation later when the documents were collected, and some of them published, by the Jacobite non-juring scholar, Thomas Smith of Magdalen College, Oxford.* The martyred patriarch then joined the martyred primate in the hagiography of high Anglicanism.

On the face of it, this is odd, for Cyril Lucaris was certainly no Laudian. Difficult though it is to pin down and label that elusive clerical politician,† we can at least say that, in the end, in doctrine and in discipline, his ideas were opposed to those of Laud. Those who ultimately destroyed Laud accused him of deviating from the true faith of Calvin and selling the English Church to Rome. Those who ultimately destroyed Cyril were the Romanizing party in the

---

Greek scholars. His famous edition of Chrysostom, in eight folio volumes, was printed at Eton 1610–12, and the Greek type, which he had obtained from Holland, was afterwards presented by him to Oxford University and used for Laud's publications. Till then, the University had not been equipped to print Greek texts, although it had the use of a small type, suitable for footnotes. See Harry Carter, *A History of the Oxford University Press* (Oxford 1975), pp. 25, 30.

*Thomas Smith spent the years 1668–71 in Constantinople as chaplain to the ambassador Sir Daniel Harvey. He wrote, in 1672 and 1676, in Latin, two works which he afterwards translated into English as *Remarks on the Manners, Religion and Government of the Turks, together with a Survey of the Seven Churchs of Asia* . . . and *An Account of the Greek Church under Cyril Lucaris with a Relation of his Sufferings and Death*. In 1707 he also published *Collectanea de Cyrillo Lucario*. These works brought him into controversy with the formidable Oratorian biblical scholar Richard Simon. See especially Simon's *Histoire Critique de la Créance . . . des nations du Levant* (Frankfurt a/M 1684); *La Créance de l'Eglise Orientale sur la Transsubstantiation* (Paris 1687).

†The latest attempt to pin him down is Gunnar Hering, *Ökumenisches Patriarchat and Europäische Politik 1620–1638* (Wiesbaden 1968); a work of vast cosmopolitan erudition and fine scholarship. But he remains unpinned, or at least flutters still.

Greek Church, and they accused him of selling that Church to the Calvinists. Both in fact were accused of sectarianism – but in the opposite directions. In order to resolve this difficulty, and to join the two archbishops in a common cause, the high-Church defenders of Cyril have had to restort to elaborate interpretations and imputations of forgery.* In fact I believe that such efforts are unnecessary.

*Almost all the crucial documents for the religious beliefs of Cyril Lucaris have been either denounced as forgeries or deliberately ignored by historians whose interpretations they might undermine. Three such documents are (1) Cyril's letter to Pope Paul V, of 1608, offering to submit to his authority; (2) Cyril's 'Calvinist' confession of March 1629; (3) Cyril's letter to Bethlen Gabor, Prince of Transylvania, of August 1629, repudiating as 'sin' Bethlen's proposal to impose Calvinism on the Orthodox 'Vlakhs' of Transylvania. The Greek Orthodox historian, Archbishop Chrysostomos Papadopoulos, roundly declares (1) and (2) to be forgeries. See his article on Cyril in Μεγάλη ʻΕλληνικὴ ʼΕγκυκλοπαιδεία (1939) and his article ʼΑπολογία Κυρίλλου τοῦ Λουκάρεως in Νέα Σιών (Jerusalem 1905). The Greek Protestant, G. A. Hadjiantoniou, ignores (1) and (3); see his Κύριλλος Λούκαρις (Athens 1954), translated as *Protestant Patriarch* (1961). The Jesuit G. Hoffmann regards only (1) as binding; see his *Griechische Patriarchen und römische Päpste, II.i. Patriarch Kyrillus Lukaris und die römische Kirche (Orientalia Christiana Periodica* 17 (Rome 1929)). Even Hering, who sees Cyril as a determined Calvinist, seems to me to ease his case by paraphrasing (1) and (3) into insignificance. The actual text, in each case, seems to me much stronger than his paraphrase.

In addition to these three fundamental documents, Papadopoulos has produced two further documents which, if genuine, must be allowed to support his case. They are (4) Cyril's 'orthodox' confession of 1629, Κυρίλλου Λουκάρεως πίναξ ὁμιλιῶν (Alexandria 1913), and (5) Cyril's encyclical letter of 1634 repudiating the charge of Calvinism and urging the Greek Christians of Ruthenia to stand fast in their faith. I have not seen the authenticity of these documents challenged, and Papadopoulos explicitly states that (5) has never been challenged. I therefore do not understand why Hering (op. cit. p. 196) says that (3) is 'the one and only document' on which the defenders of Cyril's orthodoxy rely.

Not only do historians differ among themselves: they also differ within themselves. Emile Legrand changed his mind so completely about Cyril after reading 130 privately owned letters which he was not allowed to publish, that he tore up the biographical notice which he had prepared for his *Bibliographie Hellénique 17ᵉ siècle* IV (1896) and printed his documents without commentary: an act of despair. Mr C. Th. Dimaras tells me that he too changed his mind completely about Cyril between the first and second editions of his ʻΙστορία τῆς νεοελληνικῆς λογοτεχνίας; and he adds that the Greek scholar Manuel Gedeon, on discovering new documents, also destroyed what he had written about Cyril.

New documents continue to appear – and old to disappear. The 130 letters seen by Legrand have never been identified. Seven collections of sermons which Hoffmann, in 1940, wrote that he had seen in the Metochion of the Holy Sepulchre at Constantinople have since become invisible. A large volume of Cyril's draft sermons and correspondence – 278 letters, mostly early – emerged in 1970 from the vast treasure-house of the Phillipps collection (MS Phillipps 7844). It is now in the Rijksuniversiteitsbibliothek, Leiden (MS BPG 122), and has been used by Dr Keetje Rozemond for her publication, *Cyrille Lucar, Sermons 1598–1602* (Leiden 1974). The compiler of the MS (who evidently wrote in the early eighteenth

In this essay I propose to show that they are unneccessary by putting the relations of Laud and Lucaris into their historical context. This entails prior consideration of three determining factors: the Anglican need of historical justification; the ecumenical movement of the time; and the pressures of the Thirty Years War.

The value of the Greek Church as a historical justification of Anglicanism does not need to be emphasized. Roman Catholic controversialists regularly denounced the Church of England as an upstart Church, born of schism. They made the same accusation against the Greek Church which had taken the same path a few centuries earlier. To Anglicans, therefore, the Greek Church was a natural ally. Moreover, because of its continuous tradition, it was an important ally. The propagandists of the English Church claimed for it a continuous history going back to the apostles and bypassing, as a merely marginal episode, the Roman mission of St Augustine of Canterbury; but the earlier part of that history – the stories of Joseph of Arimathea, King Lucius, etc. – were admittedly somewhat fragile. No such weakness could be found in the Greek Church whose well-documented early history eclipsed that of Rome by the glory of its Fathers, and preceded the Roman claims to primacy.

If the Greek Church suffered any weakness in its historical credentials, that was not in its early independence but in its later surrender of that independence. In 1439 the Byzantine Emperor, in the agony of his empire, had vainly sought to purchase Western aid against the Turks by accepting papal terms and submitting, at the council of Florence, to reunion with Rome. However, on his return to Constantinople, the lower clergy and people had repudiated that union, and it was never effective. The Roman Church always insisted on its legal validity, but the Protestants naturally, like the conquered Greeks, dismissed it as an abortive event of no significance. Nor was it of any significance – at least for the first century after the fall of the Byzantine empire. Even in those parts of that empire which were under Catholic rule – the Venetian colonies of Crete, the Ionian islands, Cyprus – the union was not enforced.

century) states that Cyril's correspondence with the Cretan scholar Maximos Margounios, his teacher, who died in 1602, was then preserved in the rich library, in Constantinople, of Nicolas Mavrocordato, Prince of Wallachia. The Mavrocordato library was dispersed in the mid-eighteenth century and many of its documents have also disappeared from view; but the correspondence of Cyril and Maximos was in the Metochion of the Holy Sepulchre (MS 463) at the end of the nineteenth century, when it was printed, from a copy, by Legrand, op. cit. IV, p. ix.

To the Church of England, as to other Protestant Churches accused of schism, the Greek Church was thus an encouraging example, and they naturally wished to see its independence preserved. At first their interest could only be platonic: the parties were separated by distance, had no direct communication, no common language. 'What the Grecians this day think of us', Bishop Jewel wrote in his defence of the Anglican Church, 'I cannot tell.'[1] In the 1570s tentative discussions took place between the patriarch of Constantinople Jeremias II and German Lutheran scholars of Tübingen; but these academic interchanges had no lasting effect. Their most important result was the publication in 1583 of Martin Kraus's, or Crusius's, *Turcograecia*: a work of propaganda which called attention to the plight of Greece under Ottoman rule.

Meanwhile Greece was being threatened from another quarter. In the 1570s the Roman Church, having recovered its strength after the shock of the Reformation, was striking out to the East as well as to the West. It was now determined to end the Eastern schism by reviving and enforcing the union of Florence. The foundation of the congregation for the dissemination of the faith in 1573 and of the college of St Athanasius in Rome for the education or re-education of Greeks in 1577 were stages in the long campaign, in which the Jesuits were the front-soldiers. Their first victory was in Poland. Under the patronage of the Catholic King Sigismund III they established themselves there in strength and wrought havoc among the unprepared heretics of Eastern Europe. In 1581–2 they were in Moscow, seeking to detach the Russian Church from the Eastern allegiance and unite it to Rome. They failed, and would resort, later, to more forcible methods. But meanwhile, in Lithuania, they had achieved a break-through. In 1596, at the second synod of Brest-Litovsk, they set up the new Uniate Churh, Greek in ritual but under Roman supremacy. By this device they hoped to split the Greek Church and bring it, gradually and piecemeal, under the control of Rome.

From the second synod of Brest onwards, the Counter-Reformation Catholic Church made the pace in the East, and this was the continuing background to the agitated history of the Greek Church in the next half-century. In 1606 began the campaign of Pope Paul V against the ecclesiastical independence of Venice: a campaign which roused Paolo Sarpi to defend the autonomy not only of the Catholic Church in Venice but also of the Greek Church in its islands. In the following years, the Jesuits resorted to economic warfare: they sought to buy the votes of Greek bishops and so secure the election of 'unionist' patriarchs. After the outbreak of the Thirty Years War, spiritual and economic aggression would be reinforced by secular arms. Protestantism, already crushed in Poland, was now rooted out of Bohemia. Throughout the 1620s the Habsburg armies drove to victory. Even the entry of France into the war, on the other side, would not weaken the drive against heresy in the East. Richelieu might be the ally and patron of Protestants in the West, but in the East he would compete with Austria to serve (and exploit) the imperialism of the Roman Church. The French protectorate over the holy places would be at the expense of the independence of the Greek Church.

The Protestant Churches were naturally reluctant spectators of this advance. Fortunately, by now, they too had a presence in the Ottoman empire. By the 1580s the English and Dutch had broken into the Mediterranean and had diplomatic representation in Constantinople. By the 1620s their ambassadors would be prepared to counter Catholic intrigues. But before we come to that last stage of the battle, which is well documented and well known, we must turn to a less familiar subject. This is what I have called the ecumenical movement: the movement, which coincided in time with the relatively peaceful years between 1590 and 1620, to repair and restore the universal Church not by total Catholic or Protestant conquest but by agreement on a rational, Erasmian base. Such agreement looked forward to voluntary reunion of all those distinct national Churches, or those parties within such Churches, which were opposed to the extreme sectarian policies of Counter-Reformation Rome and Calvinist Geneva: in other words, the Church of England, the 'Gallican' Church of France, the moderate Huguenots, the 'syncretists' of Germany, the 'Arminians' of Holland – and those earlier 'schismatics', the members of the Orthodox Greek Church.

The ecumenical movement of the early seventeenth century is one of those 'lost moments of history' which have been recaptured by Dame Frances Yates. It seems very remote now: an interlude between the frontal struggles of Catholic and Protestant, a last, ineffective dream before the final, painfully won realization that Christendom was now irremediably plural and must settle, in despair of unity, for a diplomatic balance of power. But at the time its aims seemed not only desirable but attainable. Perhaps, but for the Thirty Years War, they would have been attained. The movement engaged the best spirits of the time: Richard Hooker, Justus Lipsius, J.-A. de Thou, Isaac Casaubon, Hugo Grotius, Lancelot Andrewes – and, in their earlier years, Paolo Sarpi and Cyril Lucaris. Who can say that these men might not have succeeded but for the re-polarization, the return to fixed postures of extremity, caused by the renewal, in 1618, of ideological war: a war that was not, essentially, a war of ideas (though it drove men into opposite ideological positions), but a struggle for power?

The ecumenical programme was essentially an Erasmian programme, a programme of the centre, of moderate men, of men who were prepared to allow that many of the controversies of religion were over *adiaphora*, things indifferent. It was hated by both Tridentine Catholics and stern Calvinists. The basic programme – without explicit ecumenical implications – was set out in England by Hooker. Those implications were drawn out by Hooker's most intimate disciples, George Cranmer and Edwin Sandys.

Cranmer and Sandys, the two friends who, between them, encouraged, financed and guided Hooker's *Laws of Ecclesiastical Polity*, set out together on their foreign travels in 1594. After their return, Cranmer was killed in Ireland; but Sandys wrote down his conclusions in a little book, *A Relation of the State of Religion*, which he presented to Archbishop Whitgift in 1599 and which was briefly published in 1605.[2] This book was his considered plan for a reunion of the moderate Catholics, moderate Huguenots, and Anglicans, at the expense of the extreme Calvinists and the 'papists' of Spain and Italy, and under the presidency of the one national Church which, he believed, they would all accept as a model: the historic, continuous Church of England as defined by Hooker. In the course of his travels Sandys had not – as he had originally intended – visited the East, and his only direct knowledge of Greek Churches was in Venice, where the most ambitious Greeks from Crete and the Ionian islands came for education and employment. But he felt, and expressed, a natural sympathy for men who had preserved the language and literature of the early Church, rejected the corruptions of Rome, and withstood the monarchy of the Pope. Whether enslaved by the Turk, as in the former Byzantine empire, or free, as in Muscovy, the Greek Churches were obvious candidates for inclusion in the new universal Anglican Church.

The trouble was, the Greek Churches, at that time, were so weak. Harassed or seduced in Lithuania and Ruthenia, oppressed and fleeced by their Turkish overlords, torn by the internal dissension of their own bishops, seduced by the new emissaries of Rome, they could not even help themselves, far less give useful help to distant allies. Their only educated clergy, apart from those now processed by the college of St Athanasius in Rome, came from the Venetian colonies. If the Greek Church were ever to be raised up again from its fallen state, two things were essential: first education, then political alliances. These two needs were interdependent. Only if the general level of education were raised could the Greek Church recover something of its old stature and qualify for alliance, against Roman aggression, with the Churches of the West.

Fortunately, at precisely this time, the Greek Church produced its reformer. Cyril Lucaris was a Cretan who had studied in Venice at a time when the Church of Venice was defining its position in relation to the aggressive Tridentine policy of Rome. In Venice he had listened to Paolo Sarpi, already collecting material for his great work on the Council of Trent, which he regarded as the fatal turning-point in the history of the Reformation: the point at which the Church of Rome had become sectarian and blocked the possibility of general reform. Then he had returned to Crete. In 1595 he had been sent to Lithuania, where he had vainly resisted the Catholic triumph at Brest. By 1601 he was Patriarch of Alexandria. There he came, perhaps for the first time, into contact with the Protestant West.

One of those who discovered Cyril in Egypt was George Sandys, the younger brother of Edwin Sandys. In 1611 George Sandys fulfilled his brother's frustrated wish and travelled through the Levant. He too studied the state of religion. He particularly noted that although the patriarchs of Constantinople were in general a disreputable lot, the present Patriarch of Alexandria, 'the worthy Cyril', was quite different, being 'a man of approved virtue and learning', a restorer of public works for the benefit of the Greeks in Egypt, and 'a friend to the Reformed Religion and opposing the contrary'. 'The differences between us', said this worthy Patriarch, 'be but shells, but those are kernels between them and the others.'[3]

George Sandys, like his brother, was an ecumenist: he too believed in a reunited Anglo-Catholic Church, whose centre would be the Church of England. His hero was the great Dutch scholar Hugo Grotius. Sandys would afterwards translate a tragedy of

Grotius, and in the 1630s he would join that group of ecumenical admirers of Grotius who gathered to exchange their views at the young Lord Falkland's house at Great Tew.

For Grotius, though chiefly commemorated as a jurist, in fact devoted his whole life to a single, all-consuming ideal: the restoration of the universal Church. In order to achieve his aim, he put his faith in the new 'Arminian' party in Holland and in their allies the 'Arminian' clergy in England. As he explained to his friend, the Huguenot scholar Isaac Casaubon, now an émigré at the court of James I, the first necessity was to call a general council of all those Churches which rejected the Council of Trent. This Council should draw up a public confession, leaving doubtful or indifferent matters in suspense. Then the moderate Catholics should be drawn in. This should be possible when they saw that good works, decent ceremonies, tradition, etc. were respected. The Council should meet in Britain under the presidency of King James. If Casaubon would prepare the King, Grotius would work on the States General of the Netherlands, then dominated by the Arminian party led by the Grand Pensionary Johan van Oldenbarnevelt. Invitations to attend the Council should be sent to Catholics and Protestants alike. 'Whether the Churches of Greece and Asia should also be invited, I leave you to consider'.[4]

King James proved difficult to win over, but Grotius did not despair. In 1613 he came to England and, with the approval of Oldenbarnevelt, he worked hard for his cause. His English supporters were Lancelot Andrewes, Bishop of Winchester, and John Overall, Dean of St Paul's. Unfortunately he was not very tactful. His enthusiasm alarmed the cautious and courtly Andrewes, and he made no headway, and had no social success, with the new Archbishop, George Abbot. Abbot was a 'high Calvinist', a patron of Puritans, and took a strong dislike to Grotius.

In spite of setbacks, Grotius's plans for reunion went forward. In 1614 he was at work on the French. Two years later, he welcomed an unexpected ally who visited him in Rotterdam. This was Marcantonio de Dominis, Archbishop of Spalato, who in that year ostentatiously abandoned the Roman Church, declared himself an Anglican, and set out to make a new career in Jacobean England.

De Dominis also was an ecumenist. His ideas, like those of Cyril Lucaris, had been formed in the Venice of Paolo Sarpi. Coming from Dalmatia, he knew the Greek world well. The motives of his apostasy, and of his later behaviour, were mixed; but of his fundamental ideas there can be no doubt. He expressed them next year in the first part of his book *De Republica Ecclesiastica*. He sent a copy of this book to Cyril in Alexandria. It evidently had some effect there, for ten years later the Jesuits in Constantinople complained that the heresies contained in it were being circulated in the East.[5] In his covering letter to Cyril, de Dominis commiserated with him on the plight of the Greek Christians, oppressed under a new pharaoh; but at least this Turkish pharaoh, he added, left them their religion, unlike the Roman tyrant, who has brought the Western Church to the most miserable bondage. That is why de Dominis has escaped to the land of Goshen – that is England – from which he now sends this book defending the rights of patriarchs and reducing the Bishop of Rome to his right size; and he ends by urging Cyril to unite the Eastern Church 'with this most noble and flourishing Church of England'.[6]

Cyril was already in touch both with England and with Holland. His Dutch correspondents were, first, Cornelis Haga, who had visited him while travelling in the East in 1602, and who would afterwards play an important part in his life as Dutch ambassador at Constantinople, and, secondly, through him, Johannes Wtenbogaert, the Dutch theologian with whom the young Grotius had lived, and who was now, like him, an Arminian. Wtenbogaert sent the works of Arminius himself to Cyril, and Cyril declared himself impressed by them.[7] Cyril's English correspondent was Archbishop Abbot. It seems that it was Cyril who had initiated this correspondence, probably in 1612.[8] Perhaps he was encouraged to do so by his Dutch allies, who at the time, still had hopes of the new primate; or possibly the idea had come from George Sandys. At any rate, Abbot replied suggesting, in the name of King James, that Cyril send a Greek student to study in England.

Cyril grasped the opportunity. When he received the Archbishop's letter – which must have been through the English ambassador, Sir Paul Pindar – he was in Constantinople, on the way to Wallachia, Moldavia and Poland, to relieve the Greek Christians there 'who are being harassed by the tyranny of Antichrist' (i.e., to Greeks, the Turkish government) 'and the subtlety and wickedness of the Jesuits'. On his return to the city, in 1615, he wrote effusively to Abbot thanking him for his letter. Above all, he said, he was delighted to hear of the friendly disposition of King James, the platonic philosopher-king whose lively image, carried by the voice of Fame, was firmly painted in the hearts of the Eastern Christians. To Cyril, as to Grotius, as to Marcantonio de Dominis, King James was the potential saviour in Christendom, destined to reunite the true Church and defend it against those enemies who were trying to pervert it from the Pauline model. In the East, the immediate need was a learned clergy: 'our clergy', Cyril went on, 'through ignorance, are forcibly silent, and in the words of the Prophet, "I, even I only, am left"'. But what could he do alone? He could not be everywhere at once; even now, he was hurrying back to his duties in Egypt; thence he would send those whom he thought most fit to be educated in England and serve the Church.

In the same year, 1615, another Greek prelate wrote to Archbishop Abbot. This was Gabriel Severos, a well-known literary champion of Greek orthodoxy. He too had a Venetian education – he was a graduate of the University of Padua. Forty years ago he had been consecrated as Archbishop of Philadelphia in Asia Minor; but in spite of the pleas of the clergy and people of that diocese, he preferred – as who would not? – to live in Venice; and there he stayed, for the rest of his life, as 'exarch' of the Greek Church in Venice and Dalmatia, collecting Greek manuscripts, corresponding with Western scholars, and assisting Sir Henry Savile with his great edition of Chrysostom.[9] In his letter to Abbot, this epicurean and sedentary old scholar showed at least a certain imaginary mobility. He sighed for the wings of a dove to fly to his fellow archbishop and discuss not vain philosophy but the pure doctrine of Christ. However, since intervening seas and mountains made that impossible,* he was writing (he said) to send a pledge of his devotion and to urge upon his distant colleague 'the union of the Holy Church of Christ, its true children and its uncorrupted members'. We do not know what response he elicited.

Meanwhile Cyril pursued his journey back to Alexandria. Thence

---

*'μεγάλοις γὰρ πελάγεσιν, ὡς εἰπεῖν, καὶ οὔρεσι μακροῖς εἰργούμεθα'. The learned Archbishop knew his Homer. The letter is in MS Smith 36. fo. 33 and is dated January 1615. Thirty-one of Gabriel's Greek MSS were brought for the Ambrosiana by Cardinal Borromeo; others are now in the Biblioteca Nazionale in Turin. Some of his works were published in Greek in Venice and would be cited by Richard Simon as evidence that the Greek Church was doctrinally Roman Catholic – see his *Fides Ecclesiae Orientalis* (Paris 1674). On Gabriel see M. Jugie's article in *Dictionnaire de Théologie Catholique* 6, and the same writer's essay in *Echos d'Orient* 16 (1913).

he sent his first and most famous student to England. This was Metrophanes Critopoulos, a young monk whom he had picked up, in the course of his journey, from a monastery on Mount Athos, and who would end as Patriarch of Alexandria. When Critopoulos arrived in England, Abbot sent him to Oxford, to his own old college, Balliol.* He was the first of several young Greeks whom Cyril would send to England. The last would be the Cretan, Nathaniel Conopius, who would come to Oxford in 1638, after witnessing the murder of his master, and whom Laud would similarly send to Balliol. He would be remembered as the first man to drink coffee – presumably Turkish coffee – in Oxford.

It was in 1617 that Critopoulos came to England and in the same year that de Dominis published the first part of his book. At this date it is convenient to pause and consider the whole world of the ecumenists. For this was the intellectual world of William Laud. It was also a world which was shattered before he rose to power in the English Church.

The essential fact is that none of these men, with the exception of Archbishop Abbot, whom Cyril Lucaris had most probably approached in view of his office rather than of his personality, could be described as puritan in any sense. All were conservative Protestants seeking accommodation with moderate Catholics on an Erasmian base. They were as hostile to extreme Calvinists as to 'papists'. In Holland, they were the 'Arminians', Wtenbogaert and Grotius; in England, after the Anglican Hooker and his disciples, they were the 'Arminian' clergy, Andrewes and Overall; in France, if not Gallican Catholics, they were 'Arminian' Huguenots like Casaubon or Pierre Daillé or Jean Hotman and Daniel Tilenus of Sedan, the friends of Grotius. Paolo Sarpi in Venice was a Catholic friar; Marcantonio de Dominis was a Catholic archbishop. Gabriel Severos was very critical of Lutheranism and accepted some kind of belief in transsubstantiation.[10] Cyril Lucaris himself came from the same school: though bitterly opposed to papal agression in Poland, he would waver towards the Catholic Church and had even, in 1608

---

*On Critopoulos see especially his 'Confession', published in E.J. Kimmel, *Monumenta Fidei Ecclesiae Orientalis* (Jena 1850), and the biography by M. Renieres, Μητροφάνης Κριτόπουλος καὶ οἱ ἐν 'Αγγλίᾳ καὶ Γερμανίᾳ φίλοι αὐτοῦ *1617–28* (Athens 1893). Further documents are in Legrand op. cit. V, pp. 192–218. I am grateful to the Rev. Colin Davey for allowing me to see his unpublished essay on Critopoulos.

– under what precise stress we do not know – offered his submission to Rome. Critopoulos, the disciple whom he sent to England, was, and would remain, a reunionist: he would quarrel with the 'high Calvinist' Archbishop Abbot on that count and leave England under something of a cloud at Lambeth.* Later events might alter men's lives and thoughts, but in 1617 the advocates of alliance between Eastern and Western were not necessarily anti-Catholic or Puritan. Those in the West were Anglo-Catholic, 'Arminian', Gallican, Erasmian, anti-Calvinist. Those in the East were as yet uncommitted: for it must be emphasized that the doctrines of the Greek Church had not yet been adjusted to the fierce but quisquiliary controversies of the Western Reformation and Counter-Reformation.

However, the ideas which united these men depended on one necessary condition: the continuation of peace in Europe. In this too they were the heirs of Erasmus. Just as, in the previous century, the outbreak of ideological war, by driving men into opposite postures, had destroyed the original Erasmian *via media*, so this new ecumenism, which had only been revived in the years of peace in the early seventeenth century, could not survive the renewal of such war. So, when the war-clouds gathered in 1618, Grotius and his 'Arminian' friends were accused of 'appeasement'; and indeed there was some truth in the charge. Irenism in the Church could take root only if there was peace in the world. War would turn Erasmus into Calvin.

In fact there was to be no peace. In 1618–19, as the great crisis approached, the representatives of international Protestantism met

---

*Abbot's complaint against Critopoulos was outwardly over his return journey: the Archbishop wanted him to return direct by sea but Critopoulos insisted on going by land – and on trying to scrounge money for the purpose. Abbot's letters to Roe on this subject are published in *The Negotiations of Sir Thomas Roe in his Embassy to the Ottoman Porte 1621–8* (1740), pp. 102, 251. There may have been a deeper reason for Abbot's resentment. Critopoulos, by the friends whom he had made in England and by the visits which he was to make in Europe, sufficiently showed his 'Arminian', irenist views. In England, apart from Patrick Young, the King's librarian (who was known as 'the Patriarch of the Greeks', being their general patron in London), his chief friend was Meric Casaubon, the son of Isaac Casaubon, who was at Christ Church, Oxford, while Critopoulos was at Balliol. Critopoulos's correspondence with him is in BL MS Burney 369 fos. 48–64. His correspondence with Young is in Bodl MS Smith 38 and is printed in J. Kemke, *Patricius Junius* (Leipzig 1898), pp. 124 ff. On his return journey, Critopoulos was entertained in Hamburg by the family of Lucas Holstenius, the Vatican librarian; stayed in Helmstedt with the reunionist George Calixtus and in Strasbourg with Grotius's friend Matthias Bernegger; and preached general reunion at Berne and Geneva (Legrand, op. cit. V, pp. 202–8).

in general council. It was the Synod of Dordt. The ecumenists had long advocated a general council which would prepare the basis of reunion and undo the schism forced upon Christendom by the perverted and sectarian Council of Trent. But this was not such a council. At Dordt, favoured by events, the extreme Calvinists, the allies of the war-party, seized the initiative. The Arminians were routed. There was revolution in the Netherlands. Oldenbarnevelt was executed, Grotius thrown into prison. Wtenbogaert had already fled abroad. Their whole international party, such as it was, crumbled. Some of its members, like Peter Bertius and the son of Wtenbogaert, surrendered to the Catholic Church. Marcantonio de Dominis returned to Rome, to recant and die in a papal prison. Others, to avoid that fate, moved over to radicalism. Paolo Sarpi, Sir Henry Wotton, Sir Edwin Sandys became supporters of the hard line of Protestantism. Sarpi and his friends had already moved in that direction under the pressure of events in Venice. Even King James now suspended his pacifism; for his daughter's inheritance was at stake. In such circumstances, the idea of an international *via media* leading peacefully to a restored universal Church was clearly a chimera. And in the East, Cyril Lucaris saw that, once war had broken out, there was only one possible ally against the pressure of Counter-Reformation Rome. It was international Calvinism.

Cyril had already discovered the works of Calvin and had been feeling his way towards a Protestant definition of the still undefined area of Greek doctrine. Now he moved further. It was in 1617–18 that he made the acquaintance of the Dutch councillor of State David de Wilhelm le Leu and, through the Calvinist books supplied by him, was brought over to a firmly Calvinist position. He would become, in the words of the English ambassador, 'a pure Calvinist', 'in religion a direct Calvinist; yet he dare not show it'.[11]

No doubt it was Calvinism with a difference: Greco-Calvinism. Cyril was no more willing to subject the Greek Church to foreign Calvinist than to foreign Catholic control. However low it had now sunk, however drastically it needed to be reformed, it must still preserve its historic identity. It was the Church of St Basil and St John Chrysostom and all the great early fathers. When the Calvinist prince of Transylvania suggested that the Vlakh peasants under his rule should be absorbed into his Calvinist Church, and gave sound political reasons for such a change – it would raise the level of education, it would strengthen his Protestant State, their overlord the Sultan had no objection, it could be done secretly, the patriarch need only stop his ears and shut his eyes as the prophet recommends (Isaiah 30:15) – Cyril would repudiate the proposal indignantly. Calvinism, he agreed, was a Christian, not a pagan, religion; but it differs materially from the faith professed by the historic Eastern Church, and to support such a change, openly or secretly, would be a sin which all earthly torments would not wipe away . . . However, within this historic Church, and in order to restore its power and renew its vitality, a new spirit was needed, and that spirit, he believed, must come from Calvinism. A limited injection of Calvinist doctrine was necessary if the Greek Church was to preserve its identity, and secure effective foreign allies, against the otherwise irresistible onslaught of the Tridentine Catholic Church.*

For the next twenty years, the Greek Church, under the lead of Cyril Lucaris and the impulse of events, was dragged into European politics – the desperate, unscrupulous politics of the Thirty Years War. On one side, the 'Uniate' Greek bishops, headed by Cyril Contaris, Metropolitan of Beroea (Aleppo), were manipulated by the French and Austrian ambassadors, on instructions from the congregation *De Propaganda Fide* in Rome. On the other side were the English ambassador, Sir Thomas Roe, an old interventionist, devoted to the cause of the dispossessed Princess Palatine, Queen of Bohemia, and the Dutch ambassador, Cyril's old friend Cornelis Haga. In 1620 Cyril was elected Patriarch of Constantinople. The election, significantly, took place in the Dutch embassy. His reign would be stormy. In the next eighteen years he would be four times deposed and four times restored. He would be exiled to Rhodes or Tenedos after each Austro-French coup and brought back after each Anglo-Dutch counter-coup. Theoretically, deposition and election were the work of the Greek bishops; but all knew who pulled the strings. Already the rotten Ottoman empire was dominated by foreign ambassadors. As Roe would write, after one of Cyril's depositions, there was no cause for alarm: the deposition would not last: it had been the work of the grand vizier – that is, of the French

---

*Cyril's letter to Bethlen Gabor, in Latin, is printed in *Török-Magyarkori Történelmi Emlékek* 4 (Pest 1869), pp. 137–40. Hering (pp. 190–9) seems to me unreasonably to attenuate its force – and indeed to distort its meaning. He suggests that Cyril's objections were purely political. Cyril himself is quite explicit that they are not: '*non licet enim nobis ob terrena bona, etiam si illa maxima forent, fidem nostram politicis rationibus immolare; salus enim animae praecellit salutem terrenam*'.

embassy working through the grand vizier – but grand viziers, by a little judicious bribery, could always be removed, and so, wrote Roe, 'I am confident to restore him' – as he soon did.[12]

For seven years Roe and Haga sustained Cyril against his enemies. Then, in 1628, Roe was replaced, and Cyril became increasingly dependent on the Dutch. That was a crucial year. Roe's departure was a great loss – the loss of a stabilizing influence. In the same year Laud obtained effective domination over the English Church. Meanwhile, the Thirty Years War was coming to a climax: the triumphant imperial general Wallenstein was on the Baltic shore and against him, a new Protestant power was looming in the East. Like so many others, Cyril would soon be looking with fascination towards the power of Sweden.* Meanwhile, the Dutch ambassador would apply to Geneva for a sound Calvinist minister to serve the Patriarch as assistant and amanuensis. So from a remote valley in Piedmont there would come to Constantinople the man who was to be the *âme damnée* of the Patriarch: the Calvinist enthusiast whose hand must be seen in Cyril's most dramatic gesture – his Calvinist confession of 1629, published in Latin and Greek, for East and West – Antoine Léger.[13]

It was a radical change from the old, pre-1618 days, and nobody felt it more strongly than the man who, in the general débâcle, remained most consistently true to his old ideas, Hugo Grotius. In 1620, in prison in the castle of Loevestein, Grotius wrote, in Dutch, a little work of devotion which was afterwards, in its Latin form, to be a best-seller. This was his *De Veritate Religionis Christianae*, which would be for the seventeenth century what Erasmus's *Enchiridion Militis Christiani* had been for the sixteenth: an expression of rational religious philosophy for all believers, Catholic and Protestant alike. To Grotius, looking around him at the wreck of his hopes,

*For Cyril's courting of Sweden see the letters to Gustavus Adolphus printed in *Monumenta Pietatis et Literaria Virorum illustrium selecta* (Frankfurt a/M 1702); also Pericles Zerlentes, Κυρίλλου τοῦ Λουκάρεως πρὸς Ἀλέξιον Ὀξενστίερναν ἐπιστολαί, in Δελτίον τῆς ἱστορικῆς καὶ ἐθνολογικῆς ἑταιρίας τῆς Ἑλλάδος 6 (Athens 1901), pp. 88–93. These letters are of 1632, but the contact began earlier: the imperial ambassador stated, in 1643, that, on his arrival in Constantinople in 1629, he had found that Cyril not only favoured Calvinism and the Dutch '*sondern selber auch Correspondenz und intelligenza hielte mit dem schwedischen König Gustavo, diesen für der Orientalisch Griechische Kirchen defensor und protector erkannte und aussruffte*'. Eudoxius Hurmuzaki, *Documente privitore la Historia Romanilor IV 1600–46* (Bucharest 1882), pp. 682–91. Compare also *Rikskanseleren Axel Oxenstjernas Skrifter och Brefvexeling*, I (Stockholm 1918), pp. 200–1.

Marcantonio de Dominis would be a disappointment: by his inconstancy and weakness, he had let the cause down. But Cyril was far worse: a deserter, a traitor, who had gone actively over to the opposite enemy. To him Grotius would be merciless: even after his martyrdom, he would hate him.

It is against this background, this radical change of circumstances, that we must see the attitude of Laud towards the Eastern Church. Moulded in the 'Arminian' tradition of Hooker and Andrewes, Laud had imbibed ecumenical views and oriental interests. He was not a *dévot* of ecumenism like Grotius, or himself an oriental scholar like Andrewes, and his intellectual views were narrowed by his somewhat insular mentality and experience, and his practical realism. But he was prepared to envisage union even with Rome, if Rome should be 'other than she is now' – that is, if she would go back beyond the Council of Trent; he spoke fairly of true intellectual reunionists and evidently admired Marcantonio de Dominis's book,* and he defended the Greek Church as a true Church against Bellarmine and other Roman Catholics. In 1622, in his conference with the Jesuit Thomas Fisher, Laud explicitly dealt with the position of the Greek Church. It might err in particulars like the Procession of the Holy Ghost, he said, but its foundations were sound. 'It was wrong to condemn so ample and large a Church as the Greek, especially so as to make them no Church. Heaven's gates were not so easily shut against multitudes when St Peter wore the keys at his own girdle'.[14] Several years later, a Laudian clergyman who admired the Greek Church and wrote copiously in its support, Ephraim Pagitt, would send to Cyril Lucaris and all the Eastern patriarchs 'a learned treatise written in defence of your Church by the most reverend William Lord Archbishop of Canterbury'.†

---

*Laud himself was reticent about de Dominis, but his chaplain Peter Heylyn, who expressed his views, is remarkably sympathetic to de Dominis's intellectual position and describes his *De Republica Ecclesiastica* as a book 'never yet answered by the papists, and perhaps unanswerable' (*Cyprianus Anglicus*, 1668, p. 108).

†BM MS Harl 825 contains Pagitt's letters to Cyril and other Greek and Russian patriarchs, as well as to Polish and Transylvanian Protestant magnates. Together with Laud's treatise, he sent them copies of his own book, *Christianographie or the Description of the Multitude and sundry sorts of Christians in the World not subject to the Pope, with their Unitie and how they agree with us in the principall points of difference between us and the Church of Rome* (1635), most of which is devoted to the Greek Church, and also of the Anglican prayer book in Greek – presumably the translation by Elias Petley (λειτουργία βρεττανική . . . 1638: STC 16432), which, according to Heylyn (op.

These and such ideas brought Laud to the attention of Grotius. In August 1622, three months after the conference with Fisher, hearing that Laud was the rising star among the English Arminians, Grotius sent messages to him and was told that Laud was very anxious to know him.[15] They corresponded periodically thereafter, and communicated also through third parties. However, by 1628, when he came effectively to power, Laud knew well enough that all these ecumenical ideals were chimerical. In the midst of the Thirty Years War, with the Counter-Reformation victorious throughout Europe, and international Calvinism the only common voice of resistance, the ecumenical dream had vanished, and Laud had no time for a lost world. It was in vain that Grotius, now Swedish ambassador in Paris, called upon him to repair the torn and dispersed body of Christ. Laud's hands were full and he had other problems on his mind, far nearer home. He had already severed the Church of England from the Calvinist International. Now he severed it from the ecumenical alliance too. Since the old programme of a universal Erasmian Church had become impossible, he would fall back on a more limited programme: Arminianism in one country.

That meant that there was no longer any need for an ideological alliance with the Greek Church. However, it did not entail brusque severance of links already forged. Laud had inherited several such links. From his intellectual predecessors in the Arminian party he had inherited the idea of full co-operation with an ancient Church, equally continuous. From his immediate predecessor in the see of Canterbury he had inherited a correspondence with the Patriarch based on their common Protestantism. Sir Thomas Roe was an old personal friend.* He had close personal relations with the great merchants of the Levant Company – Sir Paul Pindar, who advanced money to the Crown, and Daniel Harvey, who advised him in

---

cit., p. 398), had been inspired by Laud, and which was dedicated to him. The treatise was presumably Laud's conference with Fisher as published (pseudonymously) in 1624, and explicitly praised by Pagitt in *Christianographie* (p. 119). In his book, which is dedicated to the Arminian Bishop of Ely, Francis White, Pagitt refers to Laud as 'my honourable patron' and cites Sir Edwin Sandys's *Relation*. This places him in the 'Arminian', ecumenical camp, although later, at the age of seventy, he would take the covenant and support the Presbyterian Church as a bulwark against the sects which he catalogued in his *Heresiographie* (1645).

*Lady Roe was the daughter of Laud's first patron, Sir Thomas Cave of Stanford, Northants. On her return from the East, she brought him a cat from Smyrna.

matters of finance.* Decency required that these old links be not brutally snapped. Cyril Lucaris, in his search for allies, continued to cultivate an English alliance. He had planned to send the Codex Alexandrinus to James I; on hearing of the King's death, he re-addressed it to his successor. He sent the Arabic Pentateuch to Laud, with a personal inscription.† He even sent his notorious 'Calvinist' confession of faith to Charles I.‡ But these courtesies implied no political or religious solidarity. That had evaporated with the ecumenical idea.

However, after the evaporation, there remained one small solid deposit. If the present Greek Church was too weak to sustain the burden imposed upon it by the Arminian ecumenists in the years of peace, and was seduced by Calvinist politicians and Calvinist preachers in the years of war, at least the primitive Greek Church remained as the model of an independent, continuous episcopal Church, and the Anglican Church of Laud, which looked back to that model, could become the repository, and the publisher, of its sacred texts. In the confusion of the Thirty Years War, cities were being sacked and monasteries pillaged, and there was a busy traffic in the spoils. The great collectors had their agents in Italy and the East. Laud was determined that the University of Oxford, the intellectual capital of his Church, should profit from these opportunities, and he entered the competition. What he wanted was manuscripts, the documents of the Church. He had his agents in Germany. He secured a monastic library from Würzburg, sacked by the Swedes. But the great opportunities, he believed, were in the Greek monasteries. There the documents of an independent Church might be found; and since all things among the Greeks, including

---

*For Laud and Daniel Harvey see Clarendon, *Life* (1760) I, p. 17. Daniel Harvey also acquired MSS – presumably oriental MSS – for Laud in 1638. See Dr R. W. Hunt's introduction to H. O. Coxe, *Bodleian Library Quarto Catalogues II Laudian Manuscripts*, reprint of 1973, p. xxxiii. He was the brother of the great Dr Harvey. His son, Sir Daniel, would be ambassador in Constantinople in 1668.

†The volume is now Bodleian Library MS Laud Or 258. The inscription, in Cyril's hand, is in both Greek and Latin: in Latin, '*Cyrillus oecumenicus Patriarcha beatissimo et sapientissimo Archiepiscopo Cantuariensi Gulielmo Laud dono mittit praesentem librum in signum charitatis fraternae*'. The sense of the Greek is identical.

‡An apparently autograph MS of Cyril's confession, in Greek and Latin, is in the Bodleian Library (MS Bodley 12). It is a presentation copy, stamped with the royal arms of Great Britain. It had belonged to Thomas Smith, who had acquired it from a London bookseller after the Restoration. Presumably it had left the royal library during the interregnum.

the patriarchates, were for sale, it could be no sin to buy them up. If the Greek Church were to go down, swallowed up by Rome or seduced by Geneva, at least its ancient manuscripts could be saved by its true heir, the Church of England.

For such a policy the ground had already been well prepared. In the early seventeenth century, with the establishment of factories and embassies in the Ottoman empire, the collectors of the West had moved in, and by 1624 great hauls had been made, which imagination and greed had amplified. In that year, when William Petty, the agent of the greatest of Jacobean virtuosi, the Earl of Arundel, arrived – to be followed, hot-foot, by that of his upstart competitor, the Duke of Buckingham – the English ambassador doubted whether much of value was left. 'I doubt he shall find little worthy of his pains in those rude parts', he wrote (for Petty was scouring Smyrna and Milo), 'where barbarism hath spitefully trodden out all worthy reliques of Antiquity. Some few medals or coins he may find rarely; but books have been so often visited that I think Duck-lane is better furnished than the Greek Church'. The only means of making bargains now, he added, was through the Patriarch: he alone had the key to the real treasures of the Church; and he suggested, not obscurely, that his own excellent relations with the Patriarch could usefully be exploited. Would Archbishop Abbot (for he was writing to him) send a personal letter to Cyril to acknowledge 'his many favours and courtesies to me'? This would help 'my purpose of collecting Greek authors that are lost to us and not in print; of which the Patriarch is able richly to store England, and hath thereunto a good inclination'. 'This rich merchandise', he added, could easily be got with a little encouragement.

The encouragement which the Patriarch most needed was printed books for the edification of his clergy, and the capacity to print suitable books for distribution in the East. This had always been a problem in the Greek Church, which had never known the art of printing: for the Turks would not allow that infernal machinery in their empire. Cyril's predecessors had sought to obtain printed texts in Greek from Venice and elsewhere,* and Cyril himself was continually begging for books from the West. Already

---

*J. J. Scaliger, who died in 1609, referred to these attempts: '*Graeci non habent typographiam in Graecia . . . vetitum est quidquam excudi sub Turca . . . tant s'en faut qu'il y ait aujourd'huy des livres en Grèce que le Patriarche de Constantinople en envoye querir. Il n'y a pas long temps qu'il demandoit un Joseph.*' *Scaligerana* (Cologne 1667), p. 98, s.v. *Graeci.*

Abbot had sent him, by the hand of Critopoulos, 'many of the best Greek authors, and among them Chrysostom's eight tomes' – that is, Sir Henry Savile's great edition of the most famous of the Greek fathers.[16] Now Roe was suggesting a formal system of exchange: the Patriarch was to receive a regular supply of printed books in return for a regular contribution of Greek manuscripts. While waiting for the Archbishop to respond, the ambassador thoughtfully lubricated the system on his own account. He presented to the Patriarch Paolo Sarpi's *History of the Council of Trent*: a work, he explained, which illustrated to the life the arts, frauds and tricks of the papists; and he added that the Patriarch would further the same good cause if he would ease the discovery of the books and manuscripts '*quae plura latent in librariis vestris*'.[17]

Archbishop Abbot took the ambassador's hint. He undertook to write personally to the Patriarch. 'I do marvellous well like of your trafficking with him for his Greek copies, which there do no good, and may serve for singular use here', he wrote; and he promised to send 'a good library of books'. So the traffic began. It was no longer a mere interchange of compliments: it was a systematic trade. Before long Roe boasted that he had acquired through the Patriarch 'the jewel of his library', an Arabic manuscript of the first councils, and had been able to introduce Arundel's agent 'into the best library known of Greece, where are loads of old manuscripts', of which, 'with the help of my servants' he abstracted twenty-two. Then came the Codex Alexandrinus: 'what estimation it may be of', reported Roe, 'is above my skill; but he values it as the greatest antiquity of the Greek Church'. The Patriarch was by this time deeply involved in his programme of Calvinist reform and was prepared to part with anything. He promised Roe that before leaving Constantinople 'I shall see what he hath, and take my choice freely'. Then the ambassador added darkly, 'There is another business intimated to me from the Patriarch, which I dare not mention, for his sake, without a cypher; which may bring a treasure of books into the protection of His Majesty, and which some other states have sought; whereof I will find means to advertise Your Grace by some safe way.'[18] This other business was the Patriarch's plan to solve his problem by setting up a Greek press in Constantinople itself.

The central figure in the story of the Greek press was Nicodemos Metaxas, a Greek monk from Kephallenia in the Ionian islands, then under Venetian rule.[19] The Metaxas family was prosperous and well known in the islands: Nicodemos's uncle was Bishop of Kephallenia, Zacynthos and Ithaca, and his brother, who was engaged in the currant trade, had settled in London. Nicodemos had studied in Athens under the neo-Aristotelian philosopher Theophilos Corydalleus, a friend of Cyril Lucaris; then, in 1622–3, he had come to England and continued his studies there, perhaps at Oxford, perhaps under the patronage of John Williams, Bishop of Lincoln. He had stayed altogether four years in England, and in those four years he had caused to be printed a series of Greek works, beginning with one by his teacher Corydalleus, the manuscript of which had been provided, through Metrophanes Critopoulos, by the Patriarch. The printed texts had then been sent to Venice for distribution among the Greek clergy. However, this system was uncertain, and after Critopoulos's return to the East the Patriarch evidently decided to reduce the difficulties, but also increase the risks, by bringing the press under his own direct control.

In the spring of 1627 Metaxas sailed to Constantinople bringing with him a printing press, Greek type, a Dutch printer, and 'many cases of Greek books' already printed and ready for distribution. On arrival, he reported to the Patriarch and, by permission of the deputy vizier, the press was set up, under the protection of the English and Dutch ambassadors. Its first production in Constantinople was a work by the Patriarch himself, against Judaism. Unfortunately it was also its last. The Jesuits were indignant at this apparent Protestant take-over of the Church which they were trying to capture for Catholicism. Declaring that Metaxas was disseminating 'the heresies of the Archbishop of Spalato', i.e. their great enemy Marcantonio de Dominis, they prodded the French ambassador. The French ambassador put pressure on the deputy vizier; the deputy vizier changed his mind; and so, while Metaxas took refuge in the protective English embassy, 150 janissaries broke into the printing-house and seized its contents. Roe, of course, protested, and contrived to win the next round. The Jesuits, it was agreed, had gone too far. They were expelled and the press was returned to its owner. However, in Constantinople no victory lasted long. Soon the Jesuits were back: the press it was that went. So did Metaxas. Within a few months he would be back in his native island, of which he was elected Archbishop, and we next hear of him printing anti-Catholic tracts on a printing-press 'brought from England' and now installed in a local convent.

So far, therefore, the Jesuits had won – at least in Constantinople. However, even there, their victory was soon marred. Shortly afterwards, Roe's embassy came to an end, and when he left the city they looked with horror on his great haul of manuscripts, carried away under their noses 'with the knowledge and consent of the schismatical anti-Roman Patriarch'. Their report (which greatly exaggerated the haul) caused horror in Rome too. The Pope's nephew, Cardinal Barberini, a great collector himself, was most upset. So was the librarian of the Vatican. Heretics from the ends of the earth, they complained, were carrying off the treasures of Greece which ought, of course, to have gone to Rome. First the Arundel marbles, now these Greek manuscripts, not to speak of the great Barocci collection of 240 Greek manuscripts, mainly patristic, recently sold in Venice and bought in London by the Earl of Pembroke, and the incomparable art-gallery of the Duke of Mantua, secretly swiped by Charles I . . .[20]

Abbot had handled the correspondence, but it was Laud who received the spoils. By the end of 1627 the Archbishop was a back number. Stripped of his jurisdiction, confined to his private house in Kent, he was powerless to delay any longer the omnipotence of Laud. It was to Laud, as the instigator of the purchase, that the Earl of Pembroke handed over the Barocci collection. Almost at the same time, Roe's manuscripts were brought in and were also given to Laud. It was Laud who sent the two collections down to Oxford in May 1629. They had been catalogued by two of his scholarly assistants, the Grecian Augustine Lindsell and the orientalist Peter Turner – names which recur in the history of Laud's patronage of learning. Augustine Lindsell, afterwards Bishop of Hereford, was the most learned of the Laudian bishops. He collected Greek manuscripts and was editor-in-chief of the Greek texts to be published by Laud's Greek press at Oxford. Peter Turner, fellow of Merton College, was a versatile and worldly don – 'a thorough-paced mathematician . . . a most curious critic, a politician, statesman and what not' – who dazzled mere college codgers by his grand acquaintance and political influence. He was (says one such codger, from his own college) 'of a proud, haughty mind, because of his great parts and intimate acquaintance with archbishop Laud and the great heroes of that time'. Indeed, he was so 'much beloved of archbishop Laud, and so highly valued by him', that he could have been secretary of State or clerk of the Privy Council; but he preferred to stay in his college, 'entertaining hopes of being Warden thereof'.[21]

Thus already, in Abbot's time, Laud was thoroughly familiar with the means of acquiring Greek (and other) manuscripts. When he became Archbishop he continued, in this at least, the policy of his predecessor. But he also carried it further. Abbot had been prepared to receive manuscripts as payment for books, but Laud, by setting up a Greek printing-press under his control, proposed to convert the manuscripts which he thus obtained into the printed texts which, in turn, would pay for them.* This could be an ideological service to the Anglican Church. It was also (provided that they agreed on the texts) precisely what Cyril wanted for the Greek Church. By sending his manuscripts to England to be printed, he was using Laud's Greek press as the unofficial printing-house for his own Church. Or rather, as one of such printing-houses: for he was using others too. In 1632 he would send a manuscript commentary on the Book of Job to the King of Sweden. It was a complimentary present, but the ulterior purpose was explicitly stated. Cyril suggested that the King submit the work to his theologians and, if they agree, have it printed for distribution in the East, where it would be very welcome.†

When Laud became Archbishop in 1633, Roe had left Constantinople, but his successor, Sir Peter Wych, entered into the game. Meanwhile Laud had discovered two new agents. These were Edward Pococke and John Greaves.[22] Laud had already used the services of Pococke as a collector of Greek and oriental manuscripts and coins when he was chaplain to the English factory at Aleppo from 1631 to 1636. Greaves was a fellow of Merton College, who had been brought to his notice by the Merton activist Peter Turner, and had spent two years in Italy, probably on Laud's account. Like Turner, he was an orientalist, a mathematician, and an out-and-out royalist and Laudian.

In 1636 both Greaves and Pococke were back in Oxford, where

---

*In planning his Greek press Laud explicitly stated that it was 'for the printing of the library manuscripts' – that is, the manuscripts which he had given, or would give, to the Bodleian Library.

†Cyril to Axel Oxenstjerna 1/11 July 1632, quoted by Zerlentes. The Codex Alexandrinus sent to Charles I also included a series of commentaries on Job, and these were specially printed, on Laud's orders, for the Patriarch (see my *Archbishop Laud* p. 275). It looks as if Cyril was particularly anxious to provide the Greek Church with commentaries on Job – no doubt a valuable text for a suffering Church.

Laud appointed Pococke as his first professor of Arabic. Then both set out to Constantinople, Pococke to perfect his knowledge of Arabic, Greaves to make astronomical and geographical observations. They had letters from the Archbishop and a full power to buy manuscripts at whatever price they thought fit. Naturally they found their way to the Patriarch. The Patriarch, as ever, was obliging. Laud had particularly instructed them – on the advice of Archbishop Ussher – 'Greece having been so often gleaned', to 'see what Mount Athos will afford you';* and the Patriarch, learning of 'His Grace's honourable designs in the edition of Greek authors', was eager to help. He granted Greaves, as the more adventurous traveller, free access to all the monasteries of Mount Athos; authorized him to examine and catalogue their manuscripts; and having genially dispensed the monks from 'the anathemas which former Patriarchs have laid upon all Greek libraries, thereby to preserve the books from the Latins', bade him godspeed as he prepared to take ship for the Holy Mountain.

Unfortunately, this liberal gesture came too late. Before Greaves could set sail, the enemies of the Patriarch achieved their master-stroke. They persuaded the Sultan that the capture, two years ago, by the Don Cossacks, of the fort of Asad on the Sea of Azov – a painful stab in the back during the Persian war – had been organized by the Patriarch in alliance with the Czar of Muscovy. The Sultan did not wait for evidence. This time Cyril was not exiled to Rhodes or Tenedos. He was arrested, strangled, and his body thrown into the Sea of Marmara. His old enemy, the romanizing Cyril of Beroea, returned in triumph to the throne from which he had twice been deposed. He would only last a year, but it would be time enough in which to be revenged on his enemies and to repay his friends: he submitted to the Church of Rome.

---

*As Greaves put it, '*Forsan quod in Byzantio desideramus, Athos suppeditabit*' (Thomas Smith, *Vita . . . Johannis Gravii*, 1699, p. 8). The valuable MSS in the monasteries of Mount Athos, and the illiteracy and indifference of their monkish custodians, had been remarked by George Sandys, *Relation of a Journey begun A.D. 1610* (1615), p. 64. On the other hand Pierre Belon, who had visited the monasteries half a century earlier, had found that there was nothing of value there (*Les observations de plusieurs singularités et choses memorables trouvées en Grèce*, etc. Paris 1553). They had, in fact, been cleaned out by Janus Lascaris for Lorenzo de' Medici in 1491–2. But the myth died hard, as is shown by that splendid work, Robert Curzon's *Visit to the Monasteries in the Levant* (1849).

This dramatic revolution in the Greek Church was naturally felt as a great blow in the Protestant West. It wrecked the attempted Calvinist take-over of the Greek Church. It was also a blow to Greaves and Laud. But for it, the remaining manuscripts of Mount Athos would now be in Oxford, more effectively protected by the stricter anathemas of the Bodleian Library. As it was, Greaves not only had to abandon his proposed expedition: he also had to surrender some of his previous gains. 'For fear of worse inconvenience', as he put it, he found it prudent to return, without compensation, 'fourteen good manuscripts of the Fathers' just acquired from 'a blind and ignorant monastery which depends upon the Patriarch'. The only consolation was that the Dutch ambassador had to disgorge even more.*

Laud received the news calmly. No doubt, he accurately prophesied, the new Patriarch would soon come to an equally bad end. Meanwhile, he was just in time to recall a present which he was about to send to Cyril. It was a special edition of two texts from the Codex Alexandrinus, printed by the learned press at Oxford, and personally inscribed, in Greek, to the Patriarch. The inscription indicated that more was to come. No more would come. The frustrated gifts were re-directed to the Bodleian Library.

When Greaves and Pococke returned separately to England, they did not, after all, come empty-handed; but they found a revolution there too, and their own Archbishop also overthrown. Greaves took his manuscripts, which included a fine text of Ptolemy's *Almagest*, 'stolen by a Spahy (as I am informed) from the king's library in the Seraglio', to Oxford, and there settled down to sustain the royal cause in college politics. His triumph would come in 1645, when, as Sub-warden of Merton College, he secured the deposition of the anti-Laudian Warden, Sir Nathaniel Brent, the translator of Paolo Sarpi's *History of the Council of Trent*, and the election, in his stead, of a sound royalist, the great Dr Harvey. Unfortunately that triumph did not last long: next year Oxford would surrender, and when the parliamentary visitors arrived to purge the University, their presi-

---

*Greaves's own account of his adventures and misadventures is given in two letters printed, from the drafts in the Bodleian Library (MS Savile 47 fo. 45), in his *Miscellaneous Works* II, pp. 434–8 and again in Kemke, op. cit. pp. 83–6. The letters were probably addressed to Peter Turner.

dent was found to be Brent. He would naturally purge Greaves, who would thus be obliged to return to oriental scholarship. It is fair to say that he returned with zest: he would publish ten considerable works in his remaining six years.

Meanwhile, Pococke too had returned. On his way back, he had stopped in Paris and there called on Grotius, whose ecumenical manifesto, *De Veritate Religionis Christianae*, he proposed to translate into Arabic. By him, Grotius was able to send to Laud, now a prisoner in the Tower of London, a last message of comfort. Thus, in his last years, Laud was reminded, by one and the same visitor, of his old ecumenical aspirations and their new practical application, now all alike in ruin.

If we look at Laud's relations with the Greek Church as a whole, we can see that they fall into three phases. First, there is the ecumenical stage, dating from the years of peace and bound up with the Erasmian ideals of the Arminians, which Laud inherited from them: ideals which embraced Catholics, Protestants and Greeks, excluding extremists of all kinds. Secondly, there is the period of war, in which those ecumenical ideas could not survive, but were replaced by a polarization of ideologies, the revival of a militant international Protestantism. In these years, it can be said, ecumenism shifted its base and became a purely Protestant alliance, with no enemies to the left. This was a development congenial to Abbot. It was welcomed by Cyril, who thus split the Greek Church; and it was repudiated by Laud, who thus split the Church of England. Finally, having accepted the fact that the old ecumenism was dead and that the modern Greek Church had been captured by the Calvinist party, Laud set out to make the best of a bad job and at least secure what he could out of the spoil. For that limited purpose, he preserved relations with Cyril Lucaris; but his final judgment of him, as an ecclesiastic, would probably have been similar to that of Grotius. Grotius accused Cyril of adding to the misery of the Greeks by introducing a new schism. For purely external political reasons, he said, the Patriarch had changed the rites and the faith of his Church to a Calvinist form, 'without a Synod, without the consent of the Patriarchs or of his own metropolitans'. He had adulterated the Greek faith and usurped the rights of others. What an outcry there would have been if the Pope had behaved thus! Cyril, said Grotius, was rightly condemned by the synod of Constantinople which met after his death.* Laud, of course, would incur exactly the same accusations and the same fate – for an opposite deviation.

However, these stages in the story of the two archbishops are not entirely distinct: each is blurred by the residue of its predecessor. The old ecumenical ideal, which dissolved after 1618, nevertheless still shed a lingering glow over the harsh reality of divergence, and the complimentary exchange of politically calculated gifts concealed the incompatibility of immediate aims. So the Anglo-Catholic supporters of Laud were able to romanticize, and sought to re-forge, the links which, in truth, he had inherited only to attenuate.† For between Laud, the austere, undiplomatic English champion of ancient authority, and Lucaris, the supple Greek enthusiast for Calvinist reform, there could be no real understanding. Their aims were not only different but opposite.

*H. Grotius, *Animadversiones in Animadversiones A. Riveti* (Paris 1642), p. 25; *Votum pro Pace Ecclesiastica* (np 1642), p. 57: *Riveti Apologetici . . . discussio* (Irenopoli 1645), pp. 86–7. The condemnation of Cyril by the synods of Constantinople (1638) and Jassy (1642), repeated at Jerusalem (1672), effectively excluded Calvinist influences from the Greek Church, and in 1701 a Scotch Presbyterian could explain the reticence of the Book of Revelation on the subject of the Greek Church by the assumption that it was 'but a limb and a branch of that great apostasy and backsliding from the truth foretold in Revelation', indistinguishable from popery, and so, 'it may very well be comprehended under the Whoor, Beast and False Prophet', *Early Letters of Robert Wodrow 1698–1709*, Scot. Hist. Soc. (1937), pp. 152–3.

†The continuity of high-Church reunionist ideas, retrospectively associated with the name of Cyril Lucaris, can be illustrated by the activities of three men.

(1) Isaac Basire was a high-Churchman who, in the 1630s, corresponded with Vossius and valued the Greek Fathers only less than the Bible. After the civil wars, he refused to comply with the new regime, deposited his family in London with the famous Dr Busby, and set off to convert the surprised peasantry of Greece to high Anglicanism. Among the spiritual weapons which he used, or hoped to use, were the prayer book in demotic Greek and the confession of Cyril. He returned to England, from Transylvania, in 1660 and spent the rest of his life as archdeacon of Northumberland under the congenial rule of Bishop Cosin. See N. W. Darnell, *Life and Correspondence of Isaac Basire* (1831).

(2) After the Restoration, Thomas Smith's studies of the Eastern Church in general, and of Cyril Lucaris in particular (see above p. 84n), were envisaged by him as part of a programme of general reunion. See his *Pacifick Discourse of the Causes and Remedies of the Differences about Religion which distract the Peace of Christendom* (1688).

(3) Paul Rycaut, who was secretary to the ambassador, Lord Winchelsea, and to the Levant Company in Constantinople from 1660 to 1667 and consul in Smyrna from 1667 to 1677, was also a general reunionist and thought that the process could begin with a union of the Church of England with the Greek and Armenian Churches. As precursors, he named Cassander, Melanchthon, Bucer, James I and – Cyril Lucaris. See his *Present State of the Greek and Armenian Churches* (1679), written at the suggestion of Charles II.

Nevertheless, beyond all differences of aim, there remains a certain similarity between these two dynamic but ill-fated contemporary primates. Both were men of resolute energy, determined to reverse the apparently irreversible slide of their Churches into what they saw as disaster: into Puritanism here, into Romanism there. Both relied on their personal zeal and courage, for neither of them had a solid party – only the party which they created and which depended on them. Both felt themselves isolated, struggling alone, in a corrupt age, to restore the threatened independence and the historic culture of their Churches. Laud, said Sir Simonds D'Ewes, was 'the little active wheel that set the rest on work'; Cyril could say of himself that, like the prophet Elijah, he alone was left. In order to achieve their ecclesiastical aims, both involved themselves deeply in secular politics. Both, being overpowered by their enemies, were instantly abandoned by their creatures: Laud's officers deserted him and even Critopoulos, under pressure, signed the condemnation of Cyril. Both at last perished, in their old age, amid the ruin of their life's work, at the hands, one of a public, the other of a secret executioner.

6

The Plunder of the Arts in the Seventeenth Century

Art has many functions, social as well as individual. It has one function for the artist, another for the patron. To the artist and the aesthete it expresses a Platonic conception of beauty or a personal conviction; to the patron it may represent this, but it also represents other things: propaganda, pride, prestige. To the city state of ancient Greece or medieval Italy it illustrated the independence of the republic, the *virtù* of its citizens; to the Renaissance monarchy it illustrated the continuity and strength of the dynasty, the personal magnificence of the prince; and age after age, the Church, the greatest of all patrons, made it yet another instrument to capture, elevate, even hypnotize the devout mind. These are truisms which there is no need to emphasize. Without these 'second causes' of art, art itself would be very different – and there would be much less of it.

Every weapon of propaganda inevitably provokes opposition. If art, at times, is an instrument to enslave men's minds, heretics who wish to set them free will find themselves also enemies of art – or at least of that art. Like the Iconoclasts of eighth-century Byzantium, or the Puritans of Reformation Europe, they will seek to destroy this aesthetic arm of the enemy; or at least, like modern Communists in Russia or China, they will try to neutralize, to sterilize it, by separating it from its living context. Equally, if art gives an aura of prestige to a city or a dynasty, rival cities or dynasties, which set out to conquer and humble them, will seek also to destroy their 'myth' by depriving them of this aura and appropriating it to themselves, like cannibals who, by devouring parts of their enemies, think thereby to acquire their *mana*, the intangible source of their strength.

At least they will do this in certain periods of history: in times, particularly, of ideological struggle, when wars are fought not for limited objectives, between temporary enemies respectful of each other's basic rights and independent authority, but totally, to destroy altogether hated systems of government, to break and subject independent powers, to create a New Order.

Such periods are vivid in our minds. The memoirs of Albert Speer describe Hitler's resolve to convert Berlin into the capital of conquered Europe and to deck that capital with the artistic loot of Europe. A century and a half before, Napoleon had sought to do the same for the benefit of Paris. The process has been described in fascinating detail by Mr Cecil Gould.[1] But these attempts both failed: the victors of 1815, as of 1945, insisted on the restoration of the artistic, as of the political, *status quo ante*. To find an effective dislocation of art on a comparable scale, we must look farther back in history. The subject with which I am concerned is the last unredressed violent artistic upheaval in Europe: the upheaval which coincided with the great ideological convulsion of the Thirty Years War.

It is a particularly dramatic upheaval, for several reasons. First, all the conditions of aesthetic cannibalism, which I have mentioned, were present. The struggles of Protestants and Catholics were holy wars, wars of annihilation. The Habsburgs sought not merely to restore their political empire in northern Europe and in Germany but also to stamp out Protestantism and to eliminate Protestant principalities; and their great adversary, Gustavus Adolphus, King of Sweden, when he swooped down from the Baltic to the Danube, as the lion of the north, the avenging angel foreshadowed in the books of Daniel and the Apocalypse, was no less ambitious to

> cast the kingdom old
> Into another mould.

In England, in those same years, a political struggle led rapidly to a social, ideological revolution. The monarchy was overthrown, the King publicly executed, and a new experiment, both social and political, was defended by an unexampled military dictatorship. Secondly, the European princes, at that time, were princes of a special kind. They were not just secular kings. They were princes by divine right, priest-kings who combined religious with secular power; and they illustrated this double power by an ostentatious courtly culture which combined the pagan magnificence of the Renaissance with the learned or artistic propaganda of their Church.

What a subject they provide, the collector-princes of Renaissance Europe.[2] We can trace their history from the fifteenth-century Valois dukes of Burgundy, those incomparable patron, who drew the artists of Europe to Dijon and Flanders, or from the usurping princes of Italy who stole the aesthetic *mana* of the old Italian communes and secularized it for their own dynastic glory. In the next century, the Burgundian tradition was carried by heredity into the house of Habsburg and transferred to Spain, while in France the rival house of Valois, cut off from Burgundy, refreshed itself from conquered Italy. Intermarriage, family competition, mere fashion soon did the rest. To be philistine, not to patronize or collect, merely (like some German princes) to gorge and hunt, was an undignified rusticity, unworthy of royalty. By 1600, 'the taste of angels'[3] had become general throughout Europe.

Of course the taste was not entirely new. Its rudiments were there, even in the dullest northern courts. Every prince had always had his treasure, his *Kunstkammer*, his jewels and dynastic portraits; these were part of the ordinary apparatus of royalty, like the crown and sceptre, the unction and the thaumaturgical power. But now this was not enough. Around this elementary nucleus had been built a rich, elaborate crust of secular magnificence. Now, if he were to be in the fashion, a prince must be a Maecenas: he must be a patron of art and learning. He must have great galleries and great libraries. And from the mid-sixteenth century, with the Reformation and Counter-Reformation, when princes, Protestant and Catholic alike, became the defenders, almost the proprietors of the Church in their dominions, their galleries and libraries acquired a spiritual character too. There was Caesaro-papism in the arts no less than in politics, as the princely patrons of the Church set out to dazzle their subjects and eclipse their rivals by their theological learning and iconographical magnificence.

What began as a royal monopoly soon became an aristocratic fashion. By the end of the sixteenth century, when the hierarchical form of society had been positively accentuated throughout Europe, the aristocracy everywhere had sought to follow the royal example. Spanish grandees and Bohemian magnates imitated, in their petty courts, the cultural fashions set by Philip II and Rudolf II. Great ministers like Cardinal Granvelle, great financiers like Ulrich von Fugger, would eclipse even princes by their collections of pictures and tapestries, books and bindings, manuscripts and miniatures. And in the next century, at the courts of that greatest of royal aesthetes, Charles I of England, and that greatest of royal culture-vultures, Queen Christina of Sweden, illiterate parvenus like the first Duke of Buckingham and Count Magnus de la Gardie, having begun by following the fashion, would end as discriminating collectors and patrons of art.

Much of it, of course, was mere fashion: a social or a political necessity. But among these royal and aristocratic collectors there were some who, like Charles I of England, had a genuine love of art and a fine or original taste in it. Philip II of Spain, for instance, that cold bigot of the Escorial, whose inflexible Catholicism nevertheless rested on twisted pillars (his most intimate intellectual advisers – his librarian, his geographer, and his printer – were all secret heretics), was a passionate aesthete, with a particular taste for the tortured fantasies of Hieronymus Bosch.[4] Philip's cousin, the Archduke Ferdinand, the first systematic collector among the Austrian Habsburgs, turned his Tyrolean palace of Ambras into a museum of all the arts. And then there was Ferdinand's nephew, that melancholy neurotic hermit, the greatest of all collectors, the Emperor Rudolf II. Isolated in his palace at Prague, inaccessible to his ministers of state, and only rarely to be spotted by strangers as he wandered, disguised as a groom, through his stables or menageries, that most eccentric of all the Habsburgs built up around himself, as a bizarre protective shell, the richest and most fascinating collection in Europe. To enjoy his patronage there came from all Europe painters and sculptors, tapestry-makers, clockmakers and astrologers; the Emperor himself painted and carved, wove tapestries and made clocks among them; and the Leonardos and Titians, Raphaels and Dürers which he bought were joined in the Hradčany Palace by the new works which were specially painted for his own ambiguous tastes: the zoological fantasies of Breughel and Roelant de Savery, the mannerist *bravura* of Giambologna, the animated and mechanized vegetables of Arcimboldo.[5]

Such lavish purchases and cut-throat competition among princes naturally bred opposition among those who ultimately paid for their extravagance, their subjects; and as the zeal of the collectors was merged in ideological orthodoxy, so the economic indignation of the taxpayers was gradually fortified by religious heresy. Armed by this double rage, Protestant iconoclasts, in the sixteenth century, had smashed the seductive treasures of the established Church. At the end of that century the princes, as heirs to the Church, began to incur the same hostility. The Bavarian estates, in particular, grumbled at the heedless expenditure of their Wittelsbach dukes. The Bavarian nobility had but recently been weaned from Protestantism and they did not relish the sight of the flamboyant new Jesuit churches, the cost of whose splendid decoration and elaborate music fell ultimately upon them. They demanded the reduction of Albert V's proliferating choirboys and William V's 'corrupt collection of strange and useless things' – that is, pictures, organs, *objets d'art*.[6] But in general this opposition was held firmly down; and after 1598, when peace gradually restored prosperity to all Europe, the competition quickened as never before. Those were the years when the European art-market was first organized to supply a whole continent; and it was a continent at peace – the peace of Philip III and James I and Rudolf II and 'the Archdukes': an ever-expanding peace of opulence, extravagance and display.

This new international art-market was organized, above all, in Flanders – i.e. the Spanish Netherlands, now Belgium – and, particularly, in the old economic capital of the Netherlands, Antwerp. Italy was still a storehouse to be ransacked by Spanish governors, French and English ambassadors, but already by the 1560s the centre of new production had moved north, to the Netherlands. As Cardinal Granvelle wrote from Rome in 1568, *'nous n'avons icy les painctres à la main comme au Pays d'Embas'*: Michelangelo was dead and Titian *'fort caducque'*; and he recommended the Netherlands, from which he himself had just been driven by the mutinous Burgundian nobility, as the best hunting-ground for new talent. And the Netherlands rose to the economic as well as to the artistic opportunities of the time. There the manufacture of works of art was a highly organized industry, their sale a closely guarded monopoly. It was in Flanders that the great foreign buyers placed their commissions, in Flanders that old masters were sold (and faked) on a large scale, from Flanders that the new artists set out to make their fortunes at the courts of London, Paris, Prague, Madrid. The ruler of Flanders, the Archduke Albert, brother of the Emperor Rudolf, was himself a great patron and consumer of the national

industry; and the greatest of all the painters of his time was a
Fleming: Peter Paul Rubens, whose busy workshop filled the
devastated churches of Flanders, repaired the damage wrought by
iconoclasm, Calvinism and war, and supplied the great propagandist paintings of the courts of Europe: the triumphs of Henri IV and
Marie de Médicis for the Palais du Luxembourg at Paris, the
apotheosis of King James for the Banqueting Hall of Whitehall in
London.[7]

So far, so good: in those years of swelling peace the mechanism of
the market functioned. Supply then kept up with demand, communications were easy, princes had (or thought that they had)
money to spend, and ideological passions were still or stifled. But
soon that happy state was to end. In retrospect we can see that the
twenty years from 1598 to 1618, those years of general peace, the
extravagant, magnificent years of Philip III and Lerma, of Henri IV
and Marie de Médicis, of James I and the Archdukes, of Rudolf II
and Maximilian I of Bavaria, were an Indian summer, the last years
of the Christian princes of the Renaissance, and their bizarre, exotic,
competitive courts. In the next thirty years that elaborate, Ptole-
maic system would go down in revolution and civil war, and the
smooth working of the international art-market would be quickened
and distorted by a new force: the pressure of Puritan iconoclasm and
the piracy of the great art-gangsters.

The Thirty Years War, that last, most convulsive phase of the
ideological wars of the Reformation, began (as we now reckon) in
Prague when the princely figurehead of international Calvinism,
Frederick V, Elector Palatine, was suddenly declared,by a revolutionary Protestant assembly, King of Bohemia. Prague had been
the capital of Rudolf II, who had assembled there the common
treasury of the house of Austria. Since Rudolf's death in 1612, some
of his collections had been taken to Vienna; but the great bulk
remained in what seemed, in those days of Turkish wars, the safer
capital of Prague. Now they were threatened not by foreign war but
by revolution at home. In August 1619 the rebellious Bohemian
nobility, having deposed the Habsburgs (at least on paper), proposed to convert their treasure into cash in order to finance their
revolution. There was a silver fountain, they pointed out, worth a
fortune, with which the Prince of Liechtenstein had bought his
princely title: the Jamnitzer fountain, now in Vienna. There were all
those silver writing-tables, clocks, etc., in which the late Emperor

had delighted. There were also 'statues and paintings, many of them shameless representations of naked bodies, apter to corrupt than to enlighten men's minds'. All these, the rebels suggested, should be appraised by artists and then pawned to the merchants of Nuremberg . . . So, already we see that mixture of ideological Puritanism with the economic needs of revolution which would achieve its great triumph in England in 1649. We should not forget that Prague, in that brief period 1618–20, was the holy city, the centre of the messianic Puritanism of Europe. But this time the act was not completed. The inventory of Rudolf's collection was compiled; but the battle of the White Mountain forestalled the sale; and if any of the treasure was lost, it was paid to its Bavarian rescuers, not sacrificed to ideological zeal.[8] The first cultural victim of the Thirty Years War was not the Habsburg treasure of Prague but that of its infelicitous usurper, the Elector Palatine.

For the battle of the White Mountain near Prague, which ended the independence and the Protestantism of Bohemia, was soon followed by an even more spectacular disaster to European Protestantism: the invasion of the Palatinate by Spinola in 1620, the storming of Heidelberg by Tilly in 1622, the dispossession and flight of the rash prince who had dared to disturb the balance of power in Germany. This second disaster exposed to pillage a treasure as great, in the eyes of Protestants, as Rudolf's *Kunstkammer* could be to the house of Habsburg: the great library of the princes Palatine in Heidelberg. For if Catholic princes gloried in their picture-galleries, good Calvinist princes, who distrusted such pagan or popish imagery, gloried above all in their libraries; and all such libraries, in the early seventeenth century, were eclipsed by the glory of Protestant learning, the *Palatina*.

The Palatine Library had been founded in the fifteenth century. In the next century it had been fostered by a succession of humanist princes, and enriched by the spoils of German monasteries. But its greatest period began in 1602 with the appointment, as librarian, of the famous Dutch scholar Jan Gruytere, known to the learned as Janus Gruter.[9] Unfortunately, in those very years of peace in which Gruter was nursing this great Protestant library, another famous scholar, Cardinal Baronius, was giving similar attention to the papal library in Rome. It was on the advice of Baronius that the Vatican Library was at last stabilized, and its manuscripts catalogued; and this process was completed in 1620, the very year of the

battle of the White Mountain.[10] When that great victory for the
Church had been followed by the capture of the usurper's own
capital, what more natural than that the Pope should signalize his
triumph by cannibalizing his most dangerous enemy: by absorbing
his intellectual sustenance, his *mana*; by swallowing up the *Palatina*
in the *Vaticana?*

The Duke of Bavaria, the victorious generalissimo of the Habsburgs and the Counter-Reformation, duly made the offer, and Pope
Gregory XV eagerly grasped it. In 1622 he sent to Heidelberg Leo
Allatius, a learned Greek, a *dévot* of the Uniate Church, who was
already employed as an archivist in the Vatican Library.[11] The
unfortunate Gruter, who had fled for safety to Tübingen, learned of
the ruin of his work as the busy Greek seized the entire collection of
manuscripts and the best of the printed books. Gruter's own
personal library, together with that of the University and the
collegium sapientiae, was thrown into the general stock. In order to
reduce the weight, the bindings and wrappers were removed, and
with them the evidence of former ownership. In vain the people of
Heidelberg obstructed the act of spoliation: Tilly ordered his troops
to support Allatius; borrowed books were traced and forcibly
recovered; and in February 1623 a long train of mules, each wearing
round its neck a silver label with the inscription '*fero bibliothecam
Principis Palatini*', set out from Heidelberg to carry up the Rhine and
over the Alpine passes into Italy the 196 cases in which were packed
the stripped relics of the greatest of German libraries. It was not till
1624 that the slow mule-train arrived in Rome, to deliver its burden
to the new Pope, Urban VIII. Except for a few manuscripts of
purely German interest reluctantly disgorged by Pius VI to the
King of Prussia in 1815, they are still there.

The deliberate plunder of the Palatine Library was an act of
robbery unexampled in the previous wars of the European nations –
although not of the Italian princes. But the example, once given,
was soon followed. The Thirty Years War was to see a progressive
deterioration in the laws and conventions of war; and the process
was quickened by the competitive greed of the princes and their
ministers, by the collectors' gluttony which characterized the age of
Richelieu and Mazarin, Philip IV and Charles I. A few years after
the seizure of the Palatine Library, that quickened process was
illustrated by the greatest national sale until the tragedy of Charles
I. In form, it was a peaceful sale; but the shock which it sent through

Europe, and its intimate connection with that tragedy, causes it to fit into the pattern of plunder. I refer to the dispersal, in 1627–30, of the Mantuan collection.[12]

The collection of the Gonzaga, dukes of Mantua, had been famous for over a century. It had been built up by patronage and plunder: the patronage which successive dukes had extended to the great Italian masters – to Mantegna, Leonardo, Perugino and Correggio – and the plunder of Urbino by Cesare Borgia in 1502. All through the sixteenth century the dukes of Mantua prospered and their palaces were enlarged and decorated to advertise their prosperity. At Mantua Giulio Romano worked in the 1520s and 1530s; there Rubens studied in the 1590s. By 1600 the citizens of Mantua gloried in what seemed to them not a private collection of the Duke but a national gallery, the possession of their city. They were soon to be reminded, forcibly, that this was not so.

The trouble was that Mantua, like all the industrial cities of North Italy, was in economic difficulties. From 1612, the silk industry, the basis of its prosperity, was in crisis and the dukes could no longer keep up their lavish court out of a dwindling income. They were reduced to pawning their jewellery. In due course they had to choose whether to lose their jewels or to redeem them by selling something else.

Of course, if the dukes of Mantua had been like the dukes of Bavaria – or indeed any other princes of Europe – they would not have sold their treasures. Such treasures, to any self-respecting Renaissance prince, were the symbol of his strength. They would have sold something else – offices, titles of honour, anything – or imposed new taxes, or just let the debts mount. Unfortunately, the two dukes of Mantua who reigned from 1612 to 1627 were not self-respecting princes: they were disreputable ex-cardinals whose ruling passion was not for works of art but for mistresses, relics, food and drink, and, above all, dwarfs and parrots. This being so, their subjects, in those years of financial stringency, reasonably began to tremble for those pictures – *their* pictures – which had made their city one of the artistic wonders of the world.

Already in 1623, the year when the Palatine Library was being transported to Rome, the Duke of Mantua dropped the first hint. He dropped it to the Countess of Arundel – the wife of that greatest of English noble *virtuosi* – and to the painter Antony van Dyck, both of whom happened to be staying at his court. The hint soon bore fruit. Three years later, a strange, cosmopolitan figure, of uncertain nationality, arrived in Mantua from Venice for secret conversations with the ducal Grand Chancellor. The name of this visitor was Daniel Nys, and he called himself a merchant: he supplied the court of Mantua with mirrors, perfumes, vases, furs and other bric-à-brac; but he also had another, more significant function: he was the secret artistic agent of Charles I, and also of the Earl of Arundel and the Duke of Buckingham. Soon afterwards, Nys was joined by Nicolas Lanier, the Master of the King's Music, who stayed in his house and acted under his direction. Together, these two negotiated, in close secrecy, for the sale of the collection to Charles I.

Of course the facts leaked out and at once there were protests. The ex-treasurer of the court, Niccolò Avellani, solemnly warned the Duke that 'if it is true that these pictures are to be sold, being such that the whole world had not the like, all friends of the house of Mantua will grieve'. But the only response to this protest was still greater secrecy at court. Then, in August 1627, the deal was clinched. Nys bought the bulk of the pictures, including Titian's *Twelve Caesars*, Raphael's *Holy Family* ('for which the duke of Mantua gave a marquisate worth 50,000 scudi and the late grand duke of Florence would have given the duke of Mantua, 25,000 *ducatoni* in ready money'), a work of Andrea del Sarto, two of Correggio, one of Caravaggio, and many others. For all these he undertook to pay £15,000.

When the news of this sale broke, there was a terrible outcry in Mantua. The Duke was so alarmed by it that he even, for a moment, talked of raising a loan and buying back his pictures. But just at that moment he learned that a particularly desirable she-dwarf had come on to the market in Hungary, and that decided him. Subsiding in his villa at Maderno, he solaced himself with perfumes obligingly sold to him by that universal purveyor Daniel Nys. 'What is done is done,' exclaimed the ex-treasurer Avellani, 'but God pardon whoever proposed such a sale.' Nys, of course, was jubilant. Of all his deals, he said, this had been the most difficult: 'I myself am astounded at my success.' He added that the city of Mantua and all the princes of Christendom were astonished that the Duke should have parted with his pictures, 'and the people of Mantua set up such a cry that if the duke had been able to get them back, he would gladly have paid twice the sum, and his people would have found it for him'. It was particularly gratifying to Nys that Charles had pipped the Emperor and the Grand Duke of Tuscany to the post. The collection was 'so wonderful and glorious that the like will never again be met with; they are truly worthy of so great a king as His Majesty . . . In this business I have been aided by divine assistance . . . To God then be the glory!'

Nor was this the limit of Nys's success. Within a year he was telling the King that there were still more treasures in Mantua. The Duke had reserved from the sale 'nine great pictures', the pick of the whole collection, Mantegna's *Triumphs of Julius Caesar*, *'cosa rara e unica al mondo'*: 'he who does not have them has nothing' – and, moreover, Cardinal Richelieu was after them. And then there were statues, including sleeping Cupids said to be by Praxiteles and Michelangelo, 'and believe me, all the statues in England are bagatelles compared with these'. There was danger of losing all these, since they were much coveted by the Queen Mother of France and the Grand Duke of Tuscany. However, in the end all was well. Once again the King of England got in first: he bought the lot for just over £10,000.

The purchase of the Mantua collection was regarded by Charles I as the greatest triumph of his generally unsuccessful reign. Contemporaries regarded the sale as a European scandal. Rubens protested that the Duke of Mantua should have died rather than allow it. But in fact the world probably gained rather than lost by it. For barely had the ducal treasures arrived in England when the Thirty Years War came to Mantua. In 1630 imperial troops captured and sacked the city and all the remaining contents of the ducal palaces simply disappeared. In vain the Empress, herself a Gonzaga princess, implored her husband to secure the return at least of the most precious treasures. Nothing was ever recovered. Eight years before, in 1622, at her marriage to the Emperor, which had been celebrated in Mantua, all the treasures of the house of Gonzaga had been displayed there to honour 'the greatest princess in the world' and to dazzle the royal and princely wedding-guests. Now all had gone; the palaces were stripped bare. The best of the treasures were safer – for the time being – in England.

It is worth remarking, as an illustration of the intermixture of art and politics, and as a sidelight on the priorities of King Charles I, how he paid for his great triumph. At the very time of the sale, he was sending an expedition, under the Duke of Buckingham, to the Isle of Ré, to relieve the Huguenot citadel of La Rochelle, hard pressed by the army of Cardinal Richelieu. The financing of this expedition, as of all Charles I's operations, was handled by his regular international financier, Sir Philip Burlamachi. But just as the expedition was about to sail, Burlamachi received the bill for the Mantuan pictures. He was aghast. 'I pray you', he wrote to the King's secretary, 'let me know His Majesty's pleasure, but above all where money shall be found to pay this great sum. If it were for two or three thousand pounds, it could be borne, but for £15,000, besides the other engagements for His Majesty's service, it will utterly put me out of any possibility to do anything in those provisions which are so necessary for my lord duke's relief. I pray you let me know what I must trust.' The Duke's expedition, thus starved of money, was a disaster; La Rochelle was reduced; and Cardinal Richelieu, imitating Pope Gregory XV, cannibalized its library.[13] But Charles I had got what he wanted. Having secured the pictures, he was glad to get out of the war. The agent who got him out was none other than that great preacher of peace, Peter Paul Rubens, who came to England as ambassador of Spain and was quickly booked to decorate the Banqueting Hall of Whitehall.

But if peace came to England, in Europe the war went on, gathering momentum, and the plunder of the arts gathered momentum with it. In 1632 it was the turn of Munich. For by now the tide of war had turned: the Protestant powers, beaten to the wall in the 1620s, had been reinforced by a new and terrible ally from the north; and the same duke of Bavaria who had so light-heartedly presented to the Pope the looted Palatine Library, was now to suffer an appropriate nemesis in his own capital.

For thirty-three years the duke – now Elector – Maximilian I had been building up his collection, regardless of trouble and cost. He was the first of his house to break the spell of Italian taste, seeking out German and Flemish masters. Particularly he looked for Dürers. No trouble, no price was too great for him if a Dürer was in the market. He outbid even the Emperor Rudolf for Dürer's *Assumption of the Virgin*, and he would repay the city of Nuremberg for having at last yielded up to him the *Four Apostles*, which Dürer had specially painted for it, by ordering his army to spare the lands of that obsequious city. By 1632 the Wittelsbach collection was the greatest collection in Germany after that of the Emperor. But in May of that year, the work of a whole generation was undone. The Swedish army of Gustavus Adolphus captured Munich, and when it left, and the Elector returned to his capital, what a sight greeted him! His collection, his *Kunstkammer*, his picture-gallery, all were ruined. In vain he wrote letter after letter seeking to recover his lost Dürers, Holbeins, Cranachs. In the end he gave up. Though he would reign for another twenty years, he had not the heart to re-create his picture-gallery, whose treasures were now dispersed or destroyed, or decorating the upstart palaces of Sweden.[14]

For now a new robber court had entered the market: a court which was collecting with the indiscriminate greed of a parvenu and the unashamed methods of a bandit. Gustavus Adolphus had entered Germany in 1630 as the champion of Protestantism, the avenger of Heidelberg. He bequeathed to his successors a brief robber-empire in the Baltic and an even briefer cultural centre in Stockholm. Wherever the Swedish armies went, they seized and sent back to Stockholm the artistic spoils of Europe: Russian icons from Riga and Pskov, altarpieces from Stargard and Braunsberg, pictures by Matthias Kräger from Würzburg, altarpieces by Grünewald from Mainz (which were lost at sea on the way to Sweden), libraries from Würzburg, Bremen, and the looted Jesuit and Capuchin churches of Olmütz. Gustavus's own great haul was at Munich. Six months later he was dead, and his throne was occupied by his daughter, the child who would become the most famous and most predatory of royal blue-stockings, 'the Hyperborean Minerva', Queen Christina.[15]

Queen Christina was a glutton for culture. She would summon to her court the greatest intellectual figures of Europe; and on the boat they would find themselves jostling with printers and bookbinders, 'pipers, fiddlers and *chefs de cuisine*', all hastening northwards to the same destination. She would kill Descartes by forcing him to give her tutorials in philosophy at 5 a.m. on Swedish mornings. She bought libraries wholesale as they came on the market.[16] She had agents in London, The Hague, Rome, watching for bargains. German cities were laid under tribute and crate after crate of books, manuscripts, pictures and jewels was sent constantly northwards to the insatiable Queen. And of course the fashion, once set, was quickly followed. Just as English aristocrats copied their King, so Swedish noblemen copied their Queen: de la Gardies, Wrangels, Brahe, Skytte, Oxenstjerna, Königsmarck filled their grotesque new palaces with their share of the loot.

The greatest treasure of all, of course, was still the Emperor

Rudolf's collection at Prague. In 1639 the Swedes occupied Prague; but on that occasion they missed their prey. The imperial Chamberlain, Dionisio Miseroni, had removed it in time to a safe hiding-place. But nine years later the Swedish troops were again at the gates of Prague, and by now the Queen was of age and determined not to miss the spoil. She was also determined to act quickly, for already the plenipotentiaries had assembled in Münster to conclude a general peace and if she did not strike now, she might be too late. So she ordered her generals – her cousin, Prince Charles Gustavus of Zweibrücken, afterwards her successor as Charles X, and Count Königsmarck – to lose no time. Prague must be taken; and this time the imperial treasures must not escape.[17]

The generals did their part. Just in time – just before the signing of the peace of Westphalia – Prague was captured and sacked. This time there was no opportunity for concealment, and the Queen's commands were explicit. 'Take good care', she wrote, in a private postscript to her cousin, 'to send me the library and the works of art that are there: for you know that they are the only things for which I care.' So all – or almost all – that remained of Rudolf II's picture-gallery, all the statues and *objets d'art*, the whole imperial library, and even a live lion from the imperial menagerie, were seized and loaded on to five barges which then set off, sailing slowly down the Elbe towards the north. Many of them, of course, disappeared *en route*; but 570 of Rudolf's pictures arrived ultimately in Stockholm. So did a huge collection of books and manuscripts – which soon also began to leak out through the dishonest librarians of the voracious but incurious Queen. When Christina came to the throne, there had been only one picture – and that Swedish – in the royal palace. Twenty years later, Stockholm was one of the artistic capitals of Europe. It was a capital stocked entirely with loot.[18]

A few years later, a further episode dispersed them still further. In 1654 the Queen, who had sought so forcibly to drag the culture of Europe northwards to Stockholm, suddenly changed her mind. At the age of twenty-eight she decided to give up the effort and, instead, to follow culture to its natural centre in the south. She entered the Roman Church, abdicated her crown, shook from her feet the dull, Lutheran dust of her dreary country, and migrated to the more congenial climate of Rome. There, for the next thirty-five years, this tyrannical spinster would both eat her royal cake and have it, gossiping with worldly cardinals, enjoying royal precedence without any of the tedious responsibilities of a crown. With her she took most of her spoils; and if she was obliged to leave some of them in Sweden, she soon refilled the gaps. Her way south lay through Flanders. There she stopped for a year, to see the great gallery of the Archduke Leopold William in Brussels and haunt the sale-rooms of Antwerp. To pay her huge travelling expenses, she sold many of her treasures, but ended by buying others. Even in Rome she reverted to her old methods: she pillaged the Farnese palace, which its owner had kindly but imprudently put at her disposal. (Cardinal Mazarin was wiser: when she visited Paris, he excluded her firmly from his gallery.) When she died, in 1689, she left all her property to 'that divine man', as she called him, Cardinal Azzolino; after which her collections had a varied history of bequest and sale until the royal library of Stockholm, like the electoral library of Heidelberg, sank into the Vatican Library, and the royal picture gallery was dispersed and now lies, to a large extent, embalmed in a series of aristocratic English collections.[19]

So, through the wilfulness of one woman, the imperial treasures of Rudolf II were scattered over the world. Well might Alfons Lhotsky, the historian of the Habsburg collection, describe the capture of Prague as 'an infamous robbery'. Only the catastrophe of the Mantua collection, he writes, can be compared with it: those two disasters, of 1630 and 1649, 'are unquestionably among the most grievous losses in European cultural history'.

For meanwhile the collection of Mantua had also gone the same way as the collection of Prague. Within a year of the ruin of Rudolf II's *Kunstkammer* occurred the catastrophe of the Stuart gallery; that marvellous personal gallery built up with such undeviating zeal and exquisite taste by the most unfortunate of English kings; that gallery to whose formation politics had been sacrificed and which was now, in turn, sacrificed to political and ideological revolution. For Charles I's collection was not merely a victim of war or plunder. It was not merely, like the Mantuan collection (now included in it), liquidated to pay economic debts. It was the victim also of an iconoclastic movement: a movement that was moral and social as well as political and which went back to the Reformation and beyond.

To the iconoclast of the sixteenth century – to those zealots of reform who hewed down the organs, smashed the stained-glass windows and decapitated the statues of northern Europe – these works of art were the visible symbols of a hated social system. They were fetters whereby the old Church had enslaved the minds of simple men, 'dead images' to whose costly maintenance 'the lively images of Christ' were being daily sacrificed. In the seventeenth century the lavish princely courts, having taken over so many of the functions of the established Church, had also inherited its enemies. Princes, it now seemed, had separated themselves from their subjects, elevated themselves beyond their reach, withdrawn into a narrow circle of connoisseurs. So, at the crisis of the English Revolution, the gallery of Whitehall would pay the price. The English Puritans had already hewn down the great cross of Cheapside in London. They had already desecrated the exquisite chapel of Henry VII at Westminster and decapitated the effigies in the English parish churches. They had destroyed the Queen's chapel and thrown a painting by Rubens into the Thames. They had voted to sell the English cathedrals for scrap. Finally, when Charles I had been decapitated too, they turned to his incomparable collection of pictures and, since their needs were pressing, did not destroy them, but put them up for sale.

Some indeed were given away privately, in settlement of old debts or claims, and some very explicitly reserved, as Oliver Cromwell appropriately reserved Mantegna's *Triumphs of Julius Caesar* to decorate his apartments at Hampton Court. But in general, the best of them were sold. And what a sale it was! The kings of Europe, whom Charles I had so often undercut or outbid, now saw their opportunity. While still uttering scandalized protests at the act of regicide, they sent their agents furtively to London. In the shocked words of Clarendon, instead of making common cause against the enemies of royalty, the barbarous assassins of an anointed colleague and kinsman, 'they made haste and sent over, that they might get shares in the spoils of a murdered monarch'.

So there we find them again, all the old predators, each hidden behind his secret agent, as Charles I himself had hidden behind Daniel Nys. The Spanish ambassador, through a cut-out, recovered for Philip IV the Titians which Charles had collected in Spain. The ambassador pretended to be acting for the royal favourite, Don Luis de Haro; and Don Luis, in his turn, kept up the pretence: on receiving the pictures, he declared them too fine for a subject and obsequiously laid them at his master's feet. Cardinal Mazarin,

though himself in trouble from the revolutionary *Frondes*, nevertheless contrived, through the French ambassador, to secure his share.
Queen Christina, unsated by the spoils of Prague, sent her agent
Michiel le Blon to bid for the jewels. The Habsburg Governor of
Flanders, the Archduke Leopold William, who so loved to be
painted by Teniers, surveying his own splendid collection, seized his
chance. From his vantage-post in Brussels, he had already fished in
the remains of two great English collections, wrecked on the rocks of
revolution: those of the Duke of Buckingham and the Earl of
Arundel. Now he secured an even richer prize. The fifth of the great
purchasers, somewhat incongruous among these kings and statesmen, was a Cologne banker, now resident in Paris, Everhard
Jabach, who bought both for Mazarin and for himself. Jabach, we
are told, returned to Paris at the head of a convoy of wagons, 'loaded
with artistic conquests, like a Roman victor at the head of a
triumphal procession'. The kings of whose purchases Clarendon
wrote with such withering scorn were at least a little more delicate
than that. Indeed, Clarendon himself, who was at that time
ambassador of the exiled Charles II to the court of Spain, was
discreetly ordered away from Madrid lest he should see, coming into
the city, the dusty train of eighteen mules which had carried from
Coruña the spoils of the murdered monarch.[20]

But if the sale of Charles I's pictures was the most spectacular, it was
also the last of those great acts of artistic plunder which
accompanied the Thirty Years War. The mid-seventeenth century,
here as in so much else, was a watershed in history: a period of
separation, of disintegration. If politics thereafter were separated
from religion, art also was detached from the ideological pattern in
which, hitherto, it had been set; and because it was so detached –
because it no longer seemed part of the *mana*, the prestige, of a
particular system of government or belief – iconoclasm too, which is
the moral or social hatred of art, lost its purpose. Ideological wars
now went out of fashion, and with them went some at least of the
ferocity of war. In the limited wars of the next century, rules and
conventions were observed. Princes and generals no longer looted
each other's palaces or deliberately stole each other's property.

Besides, were these treasures really their personal property? In
1649 the people of England had undoubtedly been shocked by the
execution of Charles I and the destruction of monarchy, but they do

not seem to have felt a national loss when his pictures were sold. Only the people of Mantua seem to have regarded the loss of the ducal pictures as an insult to themselves, a national insult. But in the following century the views of the people of Mantua gradually became general. The great royal collections might remain legally private but in fact they became national collections. The collections of Richelieu, Mazarin, Jabach – all concentrated in the hands of Louis XIV – became the nucleus of the Louvre; that of Philip IV was transformed into the Prado; that of the Archduke Leopold William, who returned to Austria in 1656, fed the Kunsthistorisches Museum in Vienna. So it is in these three national museums that we will find, today, the Titians which once belonged to Charles I. Appropriately, Queen Christina, that eccentric anachronism, was the last monarch to carry off, as her personal property, a national collection . . . and even here the Swedish government made some faint, unavailing remonstrances, seeking to distinguish between private and public possessions.

In the last three centuries the artistic treasures of the world have indeed changed hands, on a huge scale – how else would the museums of America be stocked? – but it has been by private sale. Though the princes may have gone, the great European princely collections have remained – with few exceptions – intact. They have been, *de facto* or *de jure*, nationalized. The plunderers, it is true, have not ceased. Napoleon and Hitler did their best. But, in the long run, they did not succeed. Unlike Pope Gregory XV and Queen Christina, they did not get away with their spoils.

7

Archbishop Laud in Retrospect

William Laud was the last Archbishop of Canterbury to hold high political office: indeed to dominate the government of England. He was also the last to suffer a violent death. Controversy pursued him through his life: the controversies of religion. Controversy still pursues him: the controversy of historians. To some he is a hero and a martyr; to others an obstinate enemy of progress and enlightenment. This is not surprising, since his whole career was bound up with the revolution in which he perished, and that revolution – the English Puritan Revolution – is itself a subject of unresolved controversy still.

Consider the changing history of his reputation. In his lifetime, in his years of power – that is, from 1629 to 1640, the eleven years of the personal rule of Charles I – he united the articulate classes against him. Few men in our history have been so loudly, and apparently so universally, vituperated. It was not a fanatical Puritan preacher but an educated baronet and member of Parliament who described him, in 1640, as 'the stye of all the pestilential filth' that had infected Church and State. When he fell from power, no voice was raised in his defence. His former colleagues and supporters saw him only as a liability to be discarded as quickly as possible. Once in the Tower, he was forgotten; for civil war was at hand and Parliament had other things to do. But the passions aroused by his name were not abated. Nearly five years later he was dragged out, condemned and executed, not because he was feared but because it was expedient to harness those passions: he was an expendable pawn in revolutionary politics, a cheap sacrifice which could be offered to the radical populace, their bloodthirsty Puritan preachers, and the bigoted Scots. Thereafter, for fifteen years, he was hardly mentioned. He was the symbol of a past era which the quick pace of revolution had left, as it seemed, far behind.

However, in 1660, he re-emerged: not very defiantly indeed, for the bitter consequences of his errors were still fresh in memory; but at least his writings were collected and his name was uttered with respect by the new high-Churchmen of the Restoration. Then, with the Glorious Revolution of 1688, he sank, once again, out of sight. This time his eclipse seemed final. Politically, doctrinally, intellectually he had no place in the England of the Whig ascendancy, the latitudinarian Church, and the Enlightenment. Only those 'internal émigrés', the non-jurors, cherished his memory; and the non-jurors as we all know, were not conspicuous for political sense.

To the historians of the eighteenth century Laud was an incomprehensible figure, an archaism embedded in a lost world. Even David Hume, who hated Puritans and liked to exasperate the Whig establishment, could not muster much enthusiasm for him. Hume would 'shed a generous tear for Charles I and the Earl of Strafford', but the most he could say for Laud was that his errors were the most excusable of all those which prevailed during that zealous period, and that the parliamentary leaders should have had the sense to ignore him. The high Tory statesman and historical philosopher Lord Bolingbroke dismissed him no less summarily. Laud, he wrote, echoing the regular charge of the Archbishop's aristocratic opponents, 'had neither temper nor knowledge of the world enough to be entrusted with the government of a private college'. Bolingbroke would not even have left him as president of St John's College.

In the eighteenth century I know of only one man of the world who dared to raise his voice in defence of Laud. In 1773, in a debate on a motion to abolish the test of subscription to the Thirty-Nine Articles in the universities, an ignorant member of Parliament described those articles as an 'accursed farrago' devised by Laud, whom he characterized as 'a despicable ecclesiastic'. He was corrected both as to fact and as to judgment by Charles Jenkinson, afterwards first Earl of Liverpool, father of the Tory Prime Minister. 'Candour must allow', Jenkinson protested, 'that Laud, with all his faults, was a very great man'.

Such candour, in the eighteenth century, is refreshing. It could not last. The nineteenth-century Whigs soon restored the old view.

To Macaulay, Laud was 'a ridiculous old bigot', 'a superstitious old driveller' who never, in word or action, rose above 'the ordinary capacity of an old woman'. To Carlyle, who differed so fundamentally from his Whig contemporaries, he was 'an ill-starred pedant', the archetypal 'college tutor whose whole world is forms, college rules'. Only the Anglo-Catholics of the Oxford Movement ventured to dissent. Laud, wrote Newman, in his Anglican days, was 'a character cast in a mould of proportions that are much above our own, and of a stature akin to the elder days of the Church'. It was the Anglo-Catholic successors of Newman who collected and published Laud's works, resuming, in this, the work of the old non-jurors of whom they were the heirs, in scholarship as also (their enemies would say) in lack of sense.

These writers of the nineteenth century, of course, were fighting their own battles. They saw the seventeenth century, with its royalists and parliamentarians, its prelates and Puritans, through the eyes of modern Whigs and Tories, Anglicans and dissenters. Newman loved Laud because he saw him as a precursor, a proto-Tractarian, and Macaulay and Carlyle condemned him for the same reason. To Macaulay, Newman was the type of 'rabbinical futility' sunk in abject, childish supersition; to Carlyle, he had 'the mind of a half-grown rabbit'; and what went for Newman naturally went for Laud too.

Perhaps the only men who saw Laud objectively in the nineteenth century were those with divided loyalties: the Catholic Liberal Acton, who recognized that Laud was more tolerant than the professed 'liberals' of Victorian England, and the high Anglican Liberal Gladstone, who said to Morley, 'Do you know who I find the most tolerant churchman of that time? Laud!'

Let us forget these later judgments, which have so little relevance either to the seventeenth century or to us. Let us move back to Laud's own time and try to see him in his own context: the context which bred him, in which he lived, to which he responded or reacted, and which he sought, with almost heroic energy, to change. In this lecture I shall try to look at Laud first as a man of ideas, then as a man of action, seeking to realize those ideas; and as even ideas spring not out of the head, or out of other ideas, but out of objective circumstances, I shall begin by looking at the circumstances of Laud's youth, the period when his ideas took shape.

*

It is a dark period, for he was of humble birth – his father a clothier in Reading; he came late on to the public stage – he was forty-eight before he was a bishop; and he was never, except by necessity, a writer. For over thirty years the centre of his life was St John's College, Oxford, and we hear of him only in an academic context through the occasional controversies, indiscretions or disputed elections in which he was involved. However, the mere date of his birth tells a tale; for he was born in 1573, and he came to Oxford, as an undergraduate, destined for the Church, in 1589. That was a very critical time in the history of the English Church. For that year – the year after the Spanish Armada which had mobilized so much Protestant hysteria – witnessed the most formidable Puritan attack on the episcopal Church until 1640. It was the attack associated with the Marprelate Tracts: a concerted attack, launched simultaneously, and with great ferocity, in the country, in Parliament and in the press. St John's College, Laud's college, had a conservative, not to say Catholic tradition. He had a conservative tutor there, John Buckeridge; and it is probable that already in his undergraduate days he trembled for the survival of the historic, traditional Church of England, still poised upon the precarious base of the Elizabethan compromise. Then, in 1593, when he was twenty, he would have read the great work which, more than any other, turned the tide of ideological radicalism: the first four books of Richard Hooker's *Laws of Ecclesiastical Polity*. Those years, Laud's student years, can thus be seen as the period when the Church of England was in its greatest danger since the reign of Edward VI. But they were also the years when it evoked its strongest intellectual defence. The great question was, could this purely intellectual defence be turned into a practical restoration, or was it already too late?

For already, in the fifty years after the Reformation, the orginal, limited aims of the English reformers had been far outrun. Those reformers had not intended to weaken the Church. Rather, they had meant to purge, reanimate and strengthen it. Henry VIII and Thomas Cromwell had dissolved monasteries, but they had intended to use their endowments to create new bishoprics. Unfortunately it had not happened thus. The Crown needed money and the laity saw opportunities. So, gradually, those endowments had fallen into lay hands, carrying with them tithes and Church-patronage; and the appetites thus whetted had soon turned to feed on the episcopal Church itself. Long leases, forced alienations, artificial vacancies, unequal bargains, had reduced the wealth of the Church. The new lay-patrons used their power to promote radical ideas and their own interests. Foreign wars were costly, foreign examples contagious. Episcopal revenues were raided and in the Marprelate Tracts the hierarchy itself was directly attacked. By the 1590s the Anglican Church seemed weak indeed. Unless practical steps were taken, its intellectual justification might prove to have come too late. Hooker himself wrote as if he thought it too late.

In fact, in those same 1590s, the reaction began. Its architect was Richard Bancroft, Bishop of London, a vigorous administrator who was prepared to uncover the underground operations of the Puritans, to challenge them at all levels, and to use all the machinery of the law for the defence and repair of the Church. In 1604, when King James had come in and Archbishop Whitgift died, Bancroft succeeded to Canterbury, and continued his work on a wider scale. There was a great deal to do, and a great deal to undo; but the new Archbishop did not flinch from the task. He only lived for another six years, but his work in those six years has been described as 'the restoration of the English Church'.

All this time Laud remained basically at St John's College, first as a scholar, then as a fellow. He held some external positions – a chaplaincy, or a vicarage – but the centre of his life was in Oxford, for it was there that much of the strategy of the Church was planned, there that the clerical army was recruited, there that ideological battles had to be fought. And Laud was never afraid of battles. By temperament and by college loyalty he was essentially conservative. He had entered the Church at the moment when the tide was turning, and conservatism had acquired intellectual respectability. Moreover, this respectability was not merely parochial, English. At this moment it was acquiring a new cosmopolitan dimension. It was becoming European, ecumenical: in the language of the time 'Arminian'.

The Christian Church is by definition ecumenical even when it is factually divided by schism. Neither Luther nor Calvin intended to split the Church: they sought to reform it, and to reform it whole. Similarly, the English reformers did not intend to create a distinct Church: they envisaged a reformed universal Church of which their own Church would be a part. During the ideological wars which followed the Reformation, this ideal was difficult to pursue. War polarizes ideas. But in the twenty years of peace which followed the death of Philip II of Spain in 1598 the idea of a reformed ecumenical Church was revived, and it happened that England, and the Church of England, was at the centre of it. All those foreign Calvinists who believed that Calvinism, in the years of struggle, had become narrow and intolerant, some of those Catholics who were dismayed by the new course of Tridentine Rome, looked to the episcopal Church of England as the truest realization of the old Erasmian ideal which had foundered in the destructive wars of religion. And since England, after 1603, was ruled by an intellectual king who pursued universal peace, they saw great practical possibilities. A union of moderate Catholics and moderate Protestants, they thought, would provide the beginning of a new reformed universal Church; and although Rome and Spain would be excluded from membership, the Greek Church, which had forestalled northern Europe in repudiating papal claims, would probably join it. For although the Greek Church was now a poor thing, depressed under Turkish or Muscovite depotism, it was still the heir of the greatest of the early Fathers. The Latin St Augustine had been taken over by the Calvinists. The Latin St Thomas had been taken over by Rome. But the true Church looked back to the great Eastern Fathers, Basil, Gregory of Nazianzus, Chrysostom; who were Greek.

The lifelong champion of these ecumenical ideas was the great Dutch scholar Hugo Grotius. In Jacobean England he had allies among the cultivated clergy whom James I loved to honour: particularly Lancelot Andrewes, the orientalist Bishop of Winchester, and John Overall, Bishop of Lichfield. These ideas found advocates in the two universities, and gave an impetus to Greek and oriental studies: the great edition of the works of Chrysostom which Sir Henry Savile published at Eton in 1610–12, and which began serious Greek printing in England, was one of their products. In 1613, Grotius himself arrived in England in order to sell his programme. Unfortunately, he found that a recent change there had blocked his path, as it blocked the whole programme of Anglican reconstruction. In 1610 Archbishop Bancroft had died, and James I had made a somewhat whimsical appointment. Instead of Lancelot Andrewes, who was generally expected, he had appointed, as Archbishop, George Abbot, who had been of some help to him in restoring episcopacy in Scotland. Abbot, till recently, had been Master of University College and Laud's great enemy in Oxford. Long afterwards, looking back on the history of the Church, the Earl of Clarendon would see its fatal turning-point in 'the never enough to be lamented death of Dr Bancroft'. If only Bancroft had lived, or if he had been succeeded not by Abbot but 'by bishop Andrewes, bishop Overall, or any man who understood and loved the Church', history, he thought would have been very different.

It was not only that Abbot had no sympathy with the new ecumenical ideas: that he snubbed Grotius and blocked the promotion of Laud, who spent the next ten years as head of his college at Oxford. Abbot was a lax, indolent man who allowed all Bancroft's work of reconstruction to slide. And he lasted twenty-three years. In those years Laud watched impotently, getting older, while the Puritans recovered the ground they had lost. When he finally came to Canterbury, he was sixty years old: an old man in a hurry. After those lost years he felt (as a seventeenth-century writer put it) that there was no end of yielding and that it was time to stand firm, even if that led to frontal collisions.

I have mentioned the ecumenical movement because it was of great importance in the background of Laud's thought. Laud was not a profound scholar. He was also somewhat insular. He never went abroad. But ecumenical ideas, Greek patristic studies, an interest in oriental learning, were never far from his mind. In the long years of waiting he came to know Grotius and his friends and used their language. He would speak of reunion as an ideal. These interests would be misinterpreted by Roman Catholics, who saw him as a possible convert, and by Puritans, who would accuse him of seeking to bring England back to Rome. In fact (as he himself recorded) he was twice discreetly offered a cardinal's hat. The Puritans would make much of this when they discovered it. They did not dwell on Laud's answer, that 'something dwelt within me which would not suffer that, till Rome were other than it is'. In other words, the Roman Church too would have to go back to Erasmian times: to the times when its reform still seemed possible, before Catholicism had been hardened and fixed in a new sectarian mould by the Council of Trent.

However, by the time when Laud was important in the Church, the steam had gone out of the ecumenical movement. The first setback came in 1617, and was something of a comedy. It was the case of Marcantonio de Dominis, the Catholic Archbishop of Spalato, who declared himself a convert to the Church of England, and arrived in London to a fanfare of Anglican trumpets. He was

regarded as a great catch, was fêted and cosseted, made Dean of
Windsor and Master of the Savoy. He published a great work on the
ideal ecumenical Church, which was regarded as unanswerable.
Unfortunately he then changed his mind and went back to Rome.
The high Anglicans who had welcomed him in England and cried
up his book were very mortified, and denounced him as an
irresponsible changeling. The Roman Church did not welcome the
returning prodigal. He died in disgrace. In him, the ecumenical idea
had become ridiculous, and was universally condemned.

De Dominis had his explanation, of course. He argued that the
Church of England had let him down. By supporting the rigid
Calvinist party at the Synod of Dordt in 1619, it too had become
sectarian. That Synod had killed moderate Protestantism just as the
Council of Trent had killed moderate Catholicism. It nearly killed
Grotius too. He was thrown into prison in the Netherlands, and
although he escaped, concealed in a crate of books, for most of the
rest of his life he was an exile, preaching vainly to unheeding ears.
For by now European war had driven men back into extreme
positions and 'reunion' had become a dangerous word, like
'appeasement' after 1939.

So the years passed and Laud, who in his youth had seen the
promise of restoration, could only watch impotently while that
promise was betrayed. The villain in his eyes was Abbot; for it was
Abbot who had allowed the work of Bancroft to crumble, Abbot who
had pushed Andrewes and Overall aside, Abbot who had aligned
the Church of England with the Puritans at home and the Calvinists
abroad. However, Laud did not despair. He was ambitious,
determined and active. If he could not dominate the Church, at least
he would dominate a party in it. And if he was regarded as a trouble-
maker, at least that might bring him to the attention of a patron. For
a patron was essential if he was ever to break through the apparently
solid ring of procrastinating courtiers who surrounded the throne of
King James.

His first patron was Richard Neile: a busy clergyman who had
begun as a servant of the Cecils and who now, as Bishop of Durham,
turned his London house into the headquarters of the 'Arminian'
party in the Church. There Laud soon became accepted as the
strongest personality in the party. As such he attracted the attention
of a far more powerful patron. This was the new royal favourite, the
all-powerful Duke of Buckingham. Buckingham at last overcame

the resistance of King James and helped Laud to his first bishopric. It was only a poor bishopric in Wales, but it was a beginning – provided that he did not actually go and live in Wales but stayed near the court, and Buckingham.

For by now Buckingham controlled the entire patronage of the Church, and needed an expert adviser. His natural adviser would have been Archbishop Abbot, his own original patron, who had personally selected him and groomed him to catch the roving royal eye. But here Laud had a piece of luck. In 1621, the Archbishop accidentally shot and killed a keeper while out hunting, and the high-Church party made much of this misfortune. A man of blood, they said, was unfit to exercise a spiritual office. Laud himself refused to be consecrated by those tainted hands. The Archbishop was gradually pushed aside, rusticated to Kent, and other clergy jostled to fill the tempting void. Since the Duke's own religious views were somewhat labile, the appointment did not depend on doctrine. There were Puritans as well as Arminians in the running. However, in the end, Laud won the race. Four years later, King James died, and the last obstacle in Laud's rise was removed. Buckingham recommended him to the new King 'as fittest to be trusted in the conferring of all ecclesiastical preferments . . . and from that time', says Clarendon, he 'prospered at the rate of his own wishes'. Whatever his formal position, whether Bishop of St David's, or Bath and Wells, or London, or Archbishop of Canterbury, 'he entirely governed that province without a rival'.

Consider the position in which Laud found himself in 1625. An active man, who knew what he wanted to do, he had been, as he saw it, artificially kept down 'till the vigour of his age was past'. He had seen a great work of reconstruction suddenly halted and allowed to slide. To resume that work was now more than ever necessary, and yet it was also, thanks to that interruption, more than ever difficult. Bancroft had died in a time of universal peace. How easily his work could then have been continued! Now all Europe was at war and passions were high. Moreover the government on which he depended was new and unpopular. His immediate patron, the Duke of Buckingham, was hated as the cause of every misfortune: corruption at home, defeat abroad. How was it possible for one man, starting from such a position – a man who had no natural source of strength, no formidable following, no ancient alliance, no political experience, and not a great deal of tact – to carry through a whole, long-deferred programme of restoration, a programme which, of necessity, implied a frontal challenge to some of the most powerful interests in the country: landlords who would resent the attack on their lay-patronage, common lawyers whose jurisdiction would be threatened, corporations denied their right of election, vocal Puritan clergy whose whole programme was in jeopardy? On the face of it, by human calculation, it was impossible. However, Laud did not flinch from it, and in fact he nearly achieved it. Even in failure, he left behind him a model which has become permanent in the historic English Church.

I suppose the answer is that Laud came to power with an absolutely clear idea of what he wished to achieve. He saw, in his mind, the Church which he intended to restore: its structure, its organization, its doctrine, its place in society. He also knew the methods by which he could achieve it. And he simplified these methods by the rigidity of his own categories. He saw everything in black and white. Those who were not for him were against him. There were no subtleties in his mind, no half-lights in his vision. On the accession of Charles I, Buckingham asked Laud who should be promoted in the Church. Laud replied by submitting a list in which the clergy were placed in two categories, summarized as O and P. O meant orthodox, P Puritan. It was as simple as that.

And what was Laud's ideal of the Church? First of all, it was to be a strong Church, an estate of the realm, the sole guardian of morality and truth, respected by all, for all were members of it: 'whosoever is a member of the Commonwealth, the same is also a member of the Church'. The Church was to comprehend the Commonwealth, to be co-terminous with it; no one was to be outside it; those who lingered outside must be persuaded, or forced, to come in.

On the other hand, in matters of belief, such a Church was not to be intolerant. Since society was not plural, but unitary, toleration was not external, but internal. Externally, there was no toleration, for no man was allowed to stand outside the Church; but internally, provided men conformed, there was room for difference on the niceties of doctrine. The Laudian Church, however oppressive to non-conformists, could be liberal to those who obeyed the rules. Its theology too was liberal, even sceptical. By the hard-liners on both sides – by the old-fashioned crypto-Catholic Bishop Goodman and the Calvinist bigot Francis Cheynell – Laud was himself accused of rotting the structure of belief by rationalism, 'Socinianism', the most dangerous of heresies. Calvinism, in the seventeenth century, like Counter-Reformation Catholicism, was theologically intolerant. Laudianism was not. Laud harried men for practical non-conformity, but not for intellectual deviation. He was opposed to controversy. Indeed, he tried to silence controversy. Provided men accepted the external limits of the Church, that was enough for him. Internally there was to be latitude. There was even the possibility – shocking to good Calvinists – that Christ had died for all: that all men might be saved.

A Church that was to dominate men's souls must also appeal to their senses and their minds. It must be a visible Church, visible in monuments, ceremonies, decent ritual, imagery, music – all those external forms which create the outer context of inner devotion and which Laud summarized as 'the beauty of holiness'. So he determined that churches should be rebuilt where they had fallen into decay, and beautified when built, that the Church services should be dignified, and that that beauty and that dignity should be so designed as to enhance authority, order, hierarchy. There was to be an end to the jejunity, even slovenliness, of Puritan service. Churches and chapels should be solemnly consecrated for divine worship. The holy table should be an altar, fixed permanently at the east end of the church, not a moveable table shuffled into the aisle for the occasion. There should be candles, candlesticks, copes, surplices, organ music, stained-glass windows: all those appurtenances of worship which the Reformers had regarded as indifferent and the Puritans as superstitious and abominable.

To Laud, as to the early Fathers, these external symbols were the means of encouraging devotion in ordinary men. But his Church must appeal to the élite also. It must be a learned Church, and it must be able to prove its continuity, its legitimate descent from the apostolic Church. That continuity, he believed, was not to be found in the Roman Church, which had first deviated into error, and then been fixed in it by the Council of Trent, but it was inherent in the Church of England which preserved, in spite of occasional lapses, the authentic traditions of the earliest, the Greek, Fathers. To prove and maintain this tradition, Laud would educate the clergy in sound learning. He would reform the universities in which they were trained, encourage the printing of orthodox works, discourage unorthodox, establish a learned press, obtain and print authentic manuscripts of the Greek Fathers.

And when such a Church had been established, how was it to function in society? As it was to be an established Church, the Church of the whole commonwealth, so it was to maintain the bonds of that commonwealth, promote and preserve social harmony, social justice. In the last century, Laud believed, individualism had run riot, encouraged and sanctified by radical doctrines which made every man his own priest, responsible only to his own conscience. Hence arose heresy, which was individualism in religion; hence also economic individualism, the disruption of society and its traditional communities by private greed. The Church must resist that: it must stand on the ancient ways. It must correct the acquisitive, be they never so great, and protect their victims. At court, in council, from the pulpit, the Church must always resist 'what the Prophet hath called, in a very energetical phrase, grinding the faces of the poor'.

All this presupposed a strong base: an economic base and a political base. The economic base, in the last century, had been sadly whittled away. Laud would restore it. He would recover alienated patronage, and the tithes that went with it. He hoped, he once told an astonished landlord, to leave not so much as the name of a lay-fee in England. If he could not persuade, he would use the law. He would hunt out old titles, discover and break those fraudulent or collusive bargains by which the patrimony of the Church had been lost. In this great campaign of economic recovery – the resumption of Bancroft's work – the bishops must play their part. They were to be his general staff. Therefore they must be chosen for their efficiency. They must not be, as under James I, court intellectuals, dilettante ghost-writers for a royal exhibitionist, but strenuous administrators, resident in their dioceses. If they claimed that such residence was difficult, because their palaces had been alienated, they must build new palaces. Elizabethan bishops had often bought their sees by alienating their lands and houses. The new bishops must buy theirs by undertaking restoration.

It was a huge programme. How could one man, coming late to power, hope to carry it out? Well, in one respect, Laud would limit it. His 'Arminian' precursors had seen the Church of England as the model and potential head of Christendom. Laud was a practical man, and he was prepared to narrow his aims. For him, it would be enough to realize the plan in one country only. The European war had anyway dissolved the ecumenical dream. Calvinism might now be international: it was a fighting creed; Arminianism, which was an ideal of peace, could not. So Laud would be content if he could re-establish the Church, according to his plan, in his own country, in England only. If he had kept to England only, he might have succeeded. Unfortunately Charles I was King of Ireland and Scotland too, and Great Britain, as the men of the seventeenth century were continually reminded, was indivisible. It was Laud's alliance with Strafford in Ireland, and his part in the frontal attack on the organized Church of Scotland, that would precipitate his fall.

For the monarchy of Charles I was Laud's political base. On it he depended, absolutely. Under James I, neither he nor his ideas had made progress. At that time, the royal supremacy, court patronage, had been against him: the King had regarded him as a trouble-maker, the Archbishop as an enemy. Even Buckingham had only been able to secure him a poor Welsh bishopric. But once Charles I had succeeded to the throne, all was changed. The royal supremacy, court patronage, now operated for him and he accepted its con-ditions gladly. Whatever his formal position in the Church, he was now in effective command, sole ecclesiastical adviser of the Crown, directing its prerogative as well as his own. And the prerogative of the Crown stretched far beyond the province of Canterbury.

Admittedly, at first, there were difficulties. For the first three years of his reign, Charles I was locked in frontal struggle with a series of angry parliaments; and their anger was directed against failure in war and appeasement of popery. As the Protestant cause was steadily beaten back in Europe, and the 'Arminian' clergy steadily advanced in England, all the rage of Parliament was concentrated on the heads of Buckingham, 'the cause of causes', and his creature Laud. Laud would never forget those traumatic years, in which he too was threatened with impeachment and his patron, in the end, assassinated. He survived, but, like Charles I, he had had his bellyful of parliaments and never wished to see such an assembly again. For eleven years, he never did; and it was in those years that he carried out his long-prepared programme of restoration.

From the start, he laid down its guide-lines. He drew up royal instructions to the bishops. He also laid down private instructions for himself; to repair episcopal palaces, to recover impropriations, to found a learned press at Oxford, to bring into conformity foreign Protestants in England, and English merchant companies abroad, etc., etc . . . And as each stage of his programme was completed, he would tick it off on his list, with the satisfactory word 'Done'.

How was it done? Ruthlessly, quickly, efficiently, by legal means or executive action, leaving many wounds, bruises and resentments; for Laud, by now, was short of time and in no mood to be thwarted. His energy, in those eleven years, is staggering, and as he met with opposition, or found his own allies or agents unsatisfactory, so he continually added to his own burdens. He sat regularly at the Privy Council Board, in the Star Chamber, on the Court of High Commission. He was added to committees for Foreign Affairs, Overseas Plantations, the Treasury. To equip himself for these secular duties he took tutorials in economics from a neighbour, a great Levant merchant. He extended the powers of the Church courts, and the claims of the clergy. He put bishops into secular office and sent his own officers to visit their bishoprics. He showed scant patience with more dilatory, more self-indulgent, or more tactful colleagues. 'Thorough' was his motto, and high-minded aims, in his view, justified high-handed methods. Petitioners against his measures received short shrift. They were 'choked with a pair of lawn-sleeves' and went away steaming with indignation against that 'little low red-faced man', that 'little meddling hocus-pocus' who had treated them so brusquely. As a judge, he was merciless: there is something chilling in the record of those 'preroga-tive courts' in which the Archbishop invariably casts his vote for the severest punishments, – branding, whipping, ear-cropping, 'with the highest in all things'.

Meanwhile, as the power of the Church spread and thrust down new roots, it revealed itself outwardly in a new cultural efflor-escence. Oxford, its seminary, received new buildings – the beauti-ful Canterbury Quadrangle of St John's College, the gothic porch of St Mary's Church. The rich were dunned and fines raised so that St Paul's Cathedral could be rebuilt by Inigo Jones.

Laud's most uncontroversial, and most lasting, work was achieved in Oxford, and it was there that his memory was most honoured. As chancellor of the University, he equipped it with new statutes: statutes which bore the imprint of his mind, for they were authoritarian, conservative, disciplinarian. Aristotle was to be 'paramount' in philosophy; the heads of houses were to rule; hair was to be cut short. Those statutes remained in force for two centuries. Even more permanent was his work for printing at Oxford. He is the true founder of the Oxford press. His aim was to take the publication of learned works out of the hands of 'mechanic craftsmen' who merely looked for profit, 'caring not at all for the beauty of letters or good and seemly workmanship', to give the university its own press, and to make it publish what he wanted: that is, the *pièces justificatives* of the continuous, independent Church of England. So he sent emissaries to fetch manuscripts from the sacked cities of Europe and the monasteries of the Levant; Arabic and Hebrew type was brought from Holland; Henry VIII's chair of Hebrew at Oxford was re-endowed, and the Laudian chair of Arabic was founded. We have it still.

It was in Oxford, in 1636, that Laud celebrated, by a royal visit, the zenith of his power. Laudianism was then as firmly established as the personal monarchy of Charles I on which it depended; and if, as many historians believe, that personal monarchy could have been made permanent, then Laudianism could have been made permanent too. Of course, it had its weaknesses. It had many enemies, who were not only 'Puritans'. It also had few friends. For it was not, as it now seems, in long retrospect, 'traditional'. To contemporaries it seemed aggressively novel: its details were attacked as 'innovations'. Even the old Jacobean 'Arminians' disliked it, for Laud, they thought, had narrowed and hardened their ideas. He had rejected their ecumenism, made the English Church provincial and sectarian, cut it off from foreign allies. He had also retreated from their liberalism. Neither Hooker nor Andrewes had supposed that episcopacy was divinely ordained. They had supported it as the best and most convenient, but not the only valid form of Church government. They, after all, wished to preserve their Continental allies. Laud, who preferred confrontation to compromise, rejected that view. Some of Hooker's works which had been left in manuscript were in his hands, but they were never published in his time. Indeed they were suppressed. So the true heirs of Hooker, Andrewes and Grotius stood aside from the Church of Laud. Nor did the poor, whom Laud sought to protect, thank him for his efforts on their behalf. To them the Church was represented not by a distant archbishop preaching social justice but by a newly confident parson at their doors claiming tithes of corn and greens, poultry and pigs. Nevertheless, we cannot say that Laud's work was doomed to fail. All lasting historic changes have weak beginnings. Given time and peace, the Laudian Church might still have taken root – provided that the personal non-parliamentary rule of Charles I, on which it depended, had also endured.

However, that rule did not endure, and when it could no longer sustain itself – when the King was forced to call the Parliament which he had so long kept at bay – then all Laud's unceasing work, still so recent and so resented, still incomplete, came tumbling down. Then indeed its weakness was revealed. Everything still depended on him. He (as one said in Parliament) was 'the little active wheel which set all the rest on work'; and when that wheel was removed, the whole machine stood still, a lifeless, unresisting structure which could be dismantled piece by piece. The prerogative courts which he had used were abolished. The clergy whom he had favoured deserted him, or were harried from their livings; tithes, so rigorously exacted, were withheld; the hierarchy, which he had exalted, was laid low; churches were denuded, images, stained-glass windows, organs destroyed. The new St Paul's remained unbuilt. Later, as passions were inflamed by civil war, the process would go further. Episcopacy, which he had declared to be by divine right, would be abolished. The lands of the Church, which he had laboured to increase, would be sold. The bishop's palaces, which he had renewed, would be secularized. Lambeth Palace itself would be turned into a prison, then sold to the most radical of the regicides. The manuscripts in Laud's study disappeared and have only returned, 300 years later, through the serendipity of Mr Fairhurst and the enterprise of the present librarian.*

None of these acts of violence had been intended in 1640, but the momentum, and the frustrations, of civil war carried fundamentally moderate men, most of whom were episcopalians, into extreme courses and radical gestures, and Laud himself, in his years of power, had built up against himself a bank of hatred on which it was only too easy to draw. So, in 1644, in a critical period of the struggle, he was taken out of prison and put on trial. The trial was a travesty of justice, his execution a gesture of defiance. Even that act of bloodshed did not silence his enemies. A member of Parliament, one of the greatest of Anglo-Irish landowners, a man who would be ennobled by Charles II, heckled him indecently on the scaffold; and immediately after his death, a Puritan clergyman, soon to be

*The papers were discovered by Mr James Fairhurst at Alderley in Gloucestershire, the home of the descendants of the great judge Sir Matthew Hale. Confiscated by the Long Parliament, they had been entrusted to John Selden and had passed, on his death in 1654, to Hale, who was one of his executors. The bulk of them were acquired for Lambeth Palace by the librarian, Mr E.G.W. Bill, in 1963.

rewarded with a chair of divinity and the headship of an Oxford college, preached a vindictive and gloating sermon comparing him with Mattan, the priest of Baal, justly butchered, and his pagan altars and images destroyed, on the orders of Jehoiada, the priest of God.

It is sometimes said that Laud's work survived him and that its strength is shown by the victory of the 'Laudians' after 1660. Certainly the high Anglicans of the Restoration looked back to him with respect. He was, after all, their martyr. But martyrs are generally ahead of their time – that is why they are martyred – and Laud especially, as it seems to me, was the victim of his own haste. When we look at those who fell with him and at those who restored the Anglican Church twenty years later, we are obliged to notice that the fall of the Laudian Church was final and that its apparent restoration was in a different style and on an altogether different ground.

For who were the Laudians in the 1630s, the days of Laudian triumph, and what did they do to defend his Church, or to protect its inheritance, in the 1640s, when it fell? History knows their names but has no need to recall them, for none of them lifted a finger to save their master or his work. Some went to ground in the country, others fled abroad and turned papist, others conformed with the new Puritan establishment. The young whipper-snappers – Laud's chaplain Peter Heylyn, his amanuensis John Birkenhead – became court-journalists. There is not a single 'Laudian' bishop whose career after 1640 effectively served the Anglican cause. Even the most reputable of them, William Juxon, Laud's chosen successor as President of St John's College and Bishop of London, whom Laud made Lord Treasurer of England, spent those twenty years in rural ease, hunting his excellent pack of hounds in the Cotswolds. If he was made Archbishop of Canterbury in 1660, that was simply to provide a necessary continuity. He was the senior surviving bishop after nearly twenty years of freeze; and at the age of seventy-eight he would not last long.

On the other hand, when we look at the younger men, those who breathed new life into the Restoration Church, we discover that almost all of them had been, in one way or another, distrusted or kept down by Laud. Sheldon, Morley, Hammond, all had aroused his disapproval and had looked to other patrons. For intellectual stimulus they had turned from Laudian Oxford to Sir Henry

Wotton's lodge at Eton or to Lord Falkland's house at Great Tew, where the ecumenical ideals of Hooker and Grotius were preserved; and the atmosphere at Great Tew was certainly not Laudian. In 1641 it was Falkland who rose in Parliament to denounce the Laudian bishops for their secular activity and popish innovations. Even Clarendon, who did so much to restore the episcopal Church in 1660, and who paid, in his *History*, a moving tribute to Laud, was not, in the 1630s, a Laudian. He too was a *habitué* of Great Tew. In 1640–1 he supported the attack on the instruments of Charles I's personal rule on which Laud had relied; he worked for the ruin of Laud's great ally Strafford; and he never, as far as we know, spoke in defence of Laud.

In retrospect, what does the Church of England owe to Laud? Directly, I think, very little. Except in Oxford, he survived everything that he had created, and much that he had inherited, and if the Church was afterwards restored, it was because other men went back to an older tradition and rebuilt it on sounder foundations – and because the Church itself had, by then, been transformed by passage through the catacombs.

The great change was in its relations with the laity. Laud's Church was aggressively clerical. He saw the laity as the authors of the process which he had set out to reverse. It was lay landlords who, in the past century, had detached the lands of the Church, lay patrons who had appropriated its tithes and who appointed unorthodox clergy to their churches, lay lawyers who challenged the Church courts, lay corporations which endowed Puritan lectureships in the towns. Therefore he declared frontal war on the laity. In every parish, the parson was to stand up to the squire and the bishop to support the parson. This was not the way to win lay support for the Church. So, to finance his constructive work – to augment stipends, repair churches, rebuild St Paul's – Laud had to rely not on generosity but on coercion: political pressure, economic squeeze, steep fines. Naturally the laity resented it and saw the Church as their enemy. But in the 1640s and 1650s all this was changed. Dispossessed clergy then found relief in the houses of the gentry; a new sympathy was generated by common misfortune; and the Church was reconstructed at the grass-roots by an alliance that would last for over two centuries.

The laity is the measure of the Church. This truth, which Newman discovered in adversity, under the Catholic clericalism of

Manning, was learned by the Church of England in its adversity, after the fall of the Anglican clericalism of Laud. Seen in retrospect, through those twenty years of misfortune, his harsh and thrusting rule acquired a new image: an image to which Hooker and Andrewes, George Herbert, Izaak Walton and Jeremy Taylor contributed more than he did. His contribution was not, in the end, the victory which he celebrated so complacently in 1636, but the halo which he acquired by his subsequent fall and martyrdom.

8

'Little Pope Regulus': Matthew Wren, Bishop of Norwich and Ely

The bishops who were raised to power by Archbishop Laud have not, in general, had a very good press. For a brief period they seemed to have achieved their aim. They stemmed the tide of Puritanism within the Church, strengthened its hierarchy and discipline, restored its disused ceremonies, exalted the institution of episcopacy, and used the authority which they had acquired by favour of the Crown to support the Crown in its political aims: the creation of a new synthesis of hierarchical Church and authoritarian State. In 1640 that policy was shown to be bankrupt. *Bellum Episcopale*, 'the Bishops' War' against the Scots, precipitated its collapse. Six years later, the Archbishop of Canterbury had been publicly executed, the episcopate abolished, its lands put up for sale. Fourteen years were to pass – fourteen years of revolutionary power and ecclesiastical confusion – before a broken remnant would return to resume a more modest role under the restored monarchy of Charles II.

Of the nine Laudian bishops who thus returned to their sees, none had been more notorious than Matthew Wren, Bishop of Ely. No churchman, after Archbishop Laud himself, had been more hated than he. Against none of them had so many vitriolic pamphlets been published. In the literature of theological hatred, his name was regularly coupled with that of Laud. It was supposed by many, and hoped by some, that he would share the fate of Laud. He did not do so; but he spent seventeen years as a prisoner in the Tower of London. When he finally emerged, an old man of seventy-five, his long imprisonment (as 'honest Tom Fuller' put it) had 'converted many of his adversaries into a more charitable opinion of him'.

Many, but not all. Nothing so shocked the inexorable Scotch Presbyterian Dr Baillie as the news that the restored King had listened, in the Chapel Royal, to a sermon by 'Dr Wren, the worst bishop of our age after Dr Laud'.[1]

It would be pleasant to be able to discover some contemporary voice raised in defence of Bishop Wren. Since he was a fellow and benefactor of this college, and one of my own predecessors as Master of Peterhouse, I have strained my ears to catch such a note. I have not been very successful. Edward Hyde, Earl of Clarendon, was a man who, as a historian, strove to be fair to all. A good Anglican, he admired the person and aims, though he opposed the policy and methods of Laud, and wrote movingly of him. But for Wren he expressed no such sympathy. He described him as 'a man of a severe, sour nature, but very learned and particularly versed in the old liturgies of the Greek and Latin Churches': a bishop who, by his 'exorbitant acts' and 'great pride and insolence' had provoked 'all the gentry, and in truth most of the inhabitants', of his diocese.[2] This indeed is the general verdict of history on Matthew Wren.

However, if Wren had few defenders in his own time, he had loyal and grateful relations. His younger brother Christopher, who followed him, at a discreet distance, up the rising stair of the Church, was the father of the great architect, Sir Christopher Wren, who owed his first commissions to his uncle; and Sir Christopher's son, yet another Christopher, a Tory member of Parliament, collected the materials for a family history, which in due course was published by his own son Stephen. This history – *Parentalia or Memoirs of the Family of the Wrens*, published in 1750 – begins with the Bishop, who was indeed the founder of the family fortunes; and though mainly an assortment of quotations glued together by charitable interpretation, it preserves the text of several private documents of which the originals have since perished. It is, I think, the only work which actually praises my present hero; and in my lecture I shall try to improve his generally unflattering image by dipping occasionally into the documents, and occasionally into the glue.*

Where then shall I begin? Where indeed, but in Pembroke College: the Pembroke College of Lancelot Andrewes, in the last

---

*A modern work on Wren is Peter King, 'Matthew Wren, Bishop of Hereford, Norwich and Ely 1585–1667' (Ph.D. thesis, Bristol University, 1969), to which I am indebted, particularly for Wren's patronage and economic activities in his dioceses.

years of Queen Elizabeth and the first of King James. For Wren was an undergraduate during the mastership of Andrewes, was indeed his favoured pupil, became his chaplain, lodged in his London house, and remained all his life his faithful disciple. In the answers which he wrote to the articles of his impeachment he dared to cite 'that learned and holy prelate' under whom he had been brought up and on whom he had depended for over forty years; and in the brief 'diary', or rather calendar of memorable dates in his own life, which he would write on a blank page of Pond's *Almanac* in the Tower in 1652, he especially notes the date of death of Andrewes twenty-six years before.

To a superficial view this may be surprising. It is difficult to discern the spirit of Andrewes, that suave, Olympian clergyman, so liberal, so humane, so diplomatic – that smooth, non-committal courtier, as some would say – who carried his immense learning so lightly and won such universal praise, in the 'sour, severe', abrasive disciplinarian Wren; but then it is equally difficult to discern it in the sharp-tongued, peremptory, bustling, dynamic Laud. And yet it was there in both of them, if overlaid by the deposit of another generation and hardened by more exacting times. All the Laudians, including Laud himself, though an Oxford man, looked to Andrewes as their mentor, 'our Gamaliel', as they would call him. Like him they wished to recover for the Church of England some of the Catholic content of Christianity which Erasmus had sought to save but Calvin had driven out: a liberalism of doctrine, if not necessarily of discipline; a place in the continuous tradition of the Church, not in the broken tradition of its heretics; and what Laud would call the beauty of holiness: ceremony, decorum, an aesthetic dimension in worship. They also all looked back not to the Roman but to the Greek Fathers: not to St Augustine, the Founding Father of Calvinist Predestination, or to St Gregory, the herald of papal imperialism, but to St Basil and St John Chrysostom and those purer traditions which still survived in the captive Churches of the now Muslim East. Andrewes himself had been an oriental scholar, the greatest patron of Arabic studies in his time;[3] Laud would found a chair of Arabic in Oxford and exchange gifts with the Greek Patriarch; and Wren, as Clarendon observed, was particularly learned in the documents of the Greek Church.

Such was the intellectual inheritance of Laud and Wren. But we are concerned with its application: with its translation into action in the tough, resistant world of early Stuart England. This did not happen till the reign of Charles I. For most of the reign of James I, Wren, like Laud, lived in the cloister. He was essentially a college man, devoted to the interests, the traditions, the good order of that little society; and being a man of great energy and industry, with 'a vast comprehension and memory of particular and minute circumstances'* – not a sparrow could fall to the ground in Pembroke College but he knew it – he soon became, as such men sometimes do, a college activist, who did not shrink from exposing the weaknesses of the Master. The Master, at that time, was Samuel Harsnett: a sound churchman indeed, but a frequent absentee (he was also Bishop of Chichester) whose nominated deputies did not give satisfaction to the other fellows, especially in the management of the college property. Wren, who had no patience with inefficiency or waste, soon became the leader of a caucus of fellows opposed to the Master; and in 1615 a fortunate accident strengthened his hand by bringing him to the notice of the court.

The accident, in itself, was trivial. King James had visited the University, as he liked to do, from his hunting-box at Newmarket. As usual, the University put on an Act – that is, a learned debate, which the scholar-King preferred to the tedious frivolities of the theatre. The question debated was, can dogs make syllogisms? Yes, insisted the proponent, Dr Preston: observe how sagaciously the creatures hunt. No, Dr Wren began to argue; but the King, a passionate devotee of the chase, would not have his own hounds thus devalued and interposed a protest on their behalf. It was a tricky moment; but Dr Wren was equal to the occasion. The royal hounds, he declared, were exceptional: they hunted by royal prerogative and were thus exempt from the laws of Nature governing common dogs. This judicious reply pleased the King, who took to Dr Wren. Next year, the fellows of Pembroke elected Wren as their President – that is, their Vice-Master – and when he led a delegation of them to wait on the King at Thetford, with a petition on the misgovernment of the college, it was well received. A tactful hint then caused Dr Harsnett to resign his mastership; and under the rule of his two successors Dr Wren, first as President, then also

---

*S. Lloyd, quoted by P. King, op. cit. As Mr King remarks, the same point was made by the hostile *Wren's Anatomy* (1641), which describes Wren as 'subtle and fault-finding, aggravating small things'.

as Bursar, effectively controlled the discipline and the finances of the college.

Thus Wren, while still active in his college, had found a foothold at court. He also had a finger near the levers of power. For by now he was chaplain to Bishop Andrewes, with rooms in his London house, and thus enjoyed regular contact with the new anti-Puritan or 'Arminian' pressure-group organized by Dr Neile, the vigorous new Bishop of Durham, from his London residence, Durham House in the Strand. There the party – for it was now a party in the Church – regularly gathered, preparing for action when the time should be ripe. The time would be ripe, they believed, when King James should die and Charles, Prince of Wales, became King.

How would the Prince of Wales turn out as King? At present – we are now in 1622 – it was not clear: he seemed to be dominated by his father's favourite, the Duke of Buckingham; and the Duke's allegiance was not clear either: he seemed to be dominated by the fashionable Puritan preacher Dr Preston – the same who had maintained that dogs could syllogize, and who had now moved up in the world, and become chaplain to the Prince. However, by this time Wren too was moving up: in 1622 he too became chaplain to the Prince. It was therefore a toss-up between the two chaplains. The question was, who would win?

In 1623 English society was astonished, not to say affronted, by an extraordinary episode. Weary of diplomatic negotiations for a Spanish marriage, the Prince and the Duke of Buckingham went off themselves to Spain to force the issue. With him the Prince took two chaplains. Both were Cambridge 'Arminians'. One was Dr Mawe, Master of Peterhouse; the other was Wren. We can be sure that, before setting out, they had their instructions from Andrewes and Neile. We know that, on their return, Wren, who alone had stayed the course (for Mawe had fallen out after an unfortunate contretemps with a Spanish mule), was summoned to a special meeting at the London house of Lancelot Andrewes, now Bishop of Winchester.

On arrival at Winchester House Wren found only three men: Lancelot Andrewes himself, Neile and Laud (now Bishop of St Davids). It was a council of State of the heads of the Arminian party, and they had summoned him to question him about the character of the master whom he had come to know intimately in the past two years. How, they asked, would the Prince stand to the Church of

England? Wren reassured them: the Prince's judgment, he said, was 'very right'; he would uphold 'the doctrine and discipline of the Church of England'; he was more to be relied on than his father who had shown 'much inconstancy in some particular cases'. In the circumstances, and considering the persons present, and the extreme secrecy of the episode, which was long preserved,* we can be sure that the danger which worried the three bishops was not of Spanish popery but of English Calvinism, and that Wren's reassurance was not that the next King would be a sound Protestant (such an assurance needed no secrecy) but that within the Protestant Church of England he would support, as his 'inconstant' father had not done, the 'Arminian' party.

Wren's judgment was sound. From the moment of his accession, Charles I showed where his sympathies lay. Succeeding to an expensive and unsuccessful war, which required parliamentary grants, he could not impose his policy at once, but of his intentions there could be no doubt, and when he felt free to do so, he showed his hand. He plumped for the Arminians in the Church and they plumped for him in the State. As an earnest of his intentions, he at once promoted the two 'Arminian' chaplains who had accompanied him to Spain. Dr Mawe was made Master of Trinity. That was easy, for the Mastership was in the gift of the Crown. The Mastership of Peterhouse, which he vacated, was then bestowed, *invitis sociis*, against the wish of the fellows, by a 'peremptory royal order', on Dr Wren.

From now on, Wren was the chief agent of the new policy in Cambridge, the trouble-shooter for the court and for his Oxford ally, now intimate with the Duke of Buckingham, Dr Laud. Two episodes showed him at work in the University.

The first was in 1626 when the Earl of Suffolk, Chancellor of the University, died, and the King sent word that he wished the University to elect, in his place, the Duke of Buckingham. The Parliament, at that very time, was impeaching the Duke for high crimes and misdemeanours. Naturally it was very angry. Its supporters in the University were angry too. They put up a rival

*This meeting is known only from an account given by Wren himself, shortly before his death, to William Sancroft, afterwards Archbishop of Canterbury. Sancroft recorded it in writing and urged Wren to do the same. The two documents, Wren's own record and Sancroft's version of it, are printed in *Parentalia*, pp. 45–6, 48–9.

candidate – an unheard-of impertinency when the royal wish had been expressed. There was a bitter contest, in which the whole Durham House party took an active part: indeed, they made the pace. Mawe and Wren were the great organizers in Cambridge. They dragooned their own fellows, bullied and cajoled other Heads, sent their friends round to canvass. In the end the Duke was elected, but only by five votes. His sponsors were delighted: not only had they gained credit at court; now at last, they thought, the University would get a new library to rival the Bodleian at Oxford. For the Arminians, we must not forget, were not only a political pressure-group: they were a learned party, with learned ambitions – although their idea of learning was of a special kind, and had its limits, as the second episode was to show.

The second episode was the affair of Dr Dorislaus. In 1625, Fulke Greville, Lord Brooke, the friend of Sir Philip Sidney, had decided to found a chair for the study of civil – that is, secular – history at Cambridge to compete with the similar chair founded by his friend William Camden at Oxford. Wren and his friends were suspicious of these innovations, especially when Camden's chair at Oxford went to a man whom they regarded as a Puritan. 'I hope', wrote one of the party, when he heard of Lord Brooke's benefaction, 'it will be better employed than the donations are at Oxford'.[4] At first it looked as if it would be, for Lord Brooke offered the chair to G. J. Vossius, the great Dutch Arminian scholar, who was a friend of Laud and whose son would soon be admitted by Wren as an undergraduate at Peterhouse. However, after some hesitation Vossius declined the offer, and the professor finally appointed was another Dutchman, Isaac Dorislaus. Dorislaus was a doctor of Leiden University, and he came recommended by the greatest of Dutch Arminians, Hugo Grotius. That sounded all right; but one could not be sure. Dutch Arminianism might be theologically sound, but politically there was a difference. Holland was a republic; and Charles I did not like republics, or Holland.

Dorislaus began his lectures in Cambridge on 7 December 1627.* They were on the *Annals* of Tacitus. Wren himself attended the first two. He was thoroughly alarmed by them. Dorislaus had discussed monarchies and republics, and although he 'spoke with great

---

*For the affair of Dorislaus see Kevin Sharpe, 'The Foundation of the Chairs of History at Oxford and Cambridge', in *History of Universities* II (Avebury 1982), pp. 127–52.

moderation', declaring that monarchy was the best of all forms of government and paying special tribute to the English monarchy, his tribute was somewhat ambiguous, for he praised it as resting not on divine right but on popular consent. Such doctrines were not now fashionable at court, and Wren reacted at once. He raised the matter with senior doctors of the University who had been present at the second lecture. Did they not agree that the lecture had been packed with 'dangerous passages . . . applicable to the expectation of these villainous times?' When they did not agree, he put pressure on the Vice-Chancellor, Dr Bainbrigg, to investigate. Meanwhile he blocked the Congregation which was to incorporate Dorislaus as a doctor next day, and he wrote secretly to Laud – he insisted on secrecy, 'except where my service will be rightly accepted' – to warn him of the snake that had slid into the Cambridge grass. With his letter he included choice passages from the lectures which, he said, he had 'privately gathered'. At the same time he wrote to the Duke of Buckingham, urging him to intervene as Chancellor. The result was satisfactory. While the Vice-Chancellor, whose enquiries had satisfied him that the lectures were unexceptionable, was seeking to compose matters, a peremptory royal message, brought down to the University by Bishop Neile, vetoed any further lectures by Dr Dorislaus. That was the end of Lord Brooke's chair – and indeed of the study of history in seventeenth-century Cambridge. In this way the Master of Peterhouse protected the students in his University from any modern or whiggish taint. A few months later he himself succeeded the unsatisfactory Dr Bainbrigg as Vice-Chancellor.

It was unfortunate for the Arminians in Cambridge that, just at this time, their Chancellor, the Duke of Buckingham, was assassinated. Cries of anguish went up from the whole party. They had invested very heavily in the Duke. As Vice-Chancellor, Wren wrote to the King to express the anguish. 'This fatal blow', he wrote, 'hath so astonished your university as, like a body without a soul, she stirs not till Your Majesty's directions breathe life again in the choice of another'.[5] No nonsense, we note, about election this time: the King was to nominate. His nominee did not in fact prove very satisfactory, but for the moment that did not matter, for Buckingham, by now, had served his purpose.

By the beginning of 1629, with the dissolution of Charles I's third Parliament, the new course in politics and religion was established. The ground had been cleared, and the essential agents of the new synthesis were in place. Laud was now Bishop of London, effective primate, royal councillor, Dean of the Chapel Royal, controller of the press. Soon he would be Chancellor of Oxford University. Wren was trusted by the court, Dean of Windsor, Register of the Order of the Garter, Judge of the Court of High Commission, a powerful figure in Cambridge. Together they would now set out to reform the two universities, and, through them, the whole Church.

The two men were in many ways similar. Both were demons for work, attentive to detail, careful stewards of property, jealous assertors of rights. Both were builders and rebuilders of the fabric of the Church. Both were martinets, accustomed to the uncourtly discipline of university colleges, of which they had risen to be heads. Both were fifty years old, or near it, before they were bishops and councillors. Both were puritan in their cast of mind: haters of extravagance in dress, long hair, 'cavalier' luxury. It would please the poet Milton, so easily inebriated with the exuberance of his own verbosity, to describe the Laudian bishops as 'swan-eating and Canary-sucking prelates', 'revelling like Belshazzar with their full carouses in goblets and vessels of gold snatched from God's temple', 'snoring in luxurious excess', and 'warming their unctuous and epicurean paunches with the alms' of the impotent poor. Nothing could be further from the true image of that austere, indefatigable pair, Laud and Wren.

In 1635 Wren gave up the mastership of Peterhouse for the bishopric of Hereford. He had left his mark on Peterhouse: a mark which is still visible. In particular, he had built the new chapel. This was in tune with Laudian policy. Laud was insistent that colleges should have their own chapels, within their walls. It was not enough to have a parish church next door as Peterhouse had in Little St Mary's: as Wren explained to the Bishop of Ely, when applying for leave to build his chapel, he wished to keep the undergraduates in after dark and it was irksome for the fellows to go even those few yards outside the college walls in winter before sunrise.[6] So he collected money and saw the chapel built. When it was built, he had it consecrated by the Bishop of Ely (now a sound Laudian) as Visitor of the college. The Laudians were great sticklers for the consecration of churches – a practice that had fallen into disuse in the last half-century and was repudiated as popish by the Puritans. Lancelot Andrewes had devised a form of consecration, which they used or varied for such occasions. Wren's chapel was a plain building, somewhat austere, as befitted his character – the frills would come later from his more aesthetic successor – but the Laudian beauty of holiness was introduced into the services: a Latin liturgy; an altar, fixed and railed; and mandatory bowing towards it. Wren had already established all these practices at Windsor. Now they were brought to Cambridge. Soon he would seek to establish them elsewhere.

In Peterhouse Wren also busied himself with the college archives. As his great-nephew put it, 'he rescued their writings and ancient records from dust and worms, and by indefatigable industry digested them into a good method and order'.[7] Wherever he was placed, he did this, his sharp eye incidentally discovering obsolete rights to be enforced, forgotten dues to be paid, and arrears of debts to be exacted. So at Pembroke College he had started a register, reconstructed the history of the college, organized the library, and compiled a splendid illustrated record of its benefactors.[8] Similarly at Windsor, as Register of the Order of the Garter, he had written a history of the Order, and discovered, and exacted, long-forgotten financial obligations of the Knights.[9] As a later college antiquary would write, 'Bishop Wren was a true antiquary, and may be traced by his collections wherever he came: At Pembroke-hall where he was Fellow; at Peterhouse, where Master; at Windsor, where Dean; and Ely where Bishop'.[10] Unfortunately, added an Oxford antiquary, those collections, 'being left in loose scattered papers, are in danger of perishing', as many have since done: 'the Cambridge men are much wanting to themselves in not retrieving the remains of their worthies'.*

Wren left Peterhouse, as he thought, in good order. His great-nephew assures us that he had 'exercised such prudence and moderation in his government that he had reduced all the Fellows to one sacred bond of unity and concord and excited the scholars to constancy and diligence in their studies'. What college head can hope to achieve more than that? The college was so docile that he

---

*Reliquiae Hearnianae, ed. Philip Bliss (1869) III, p. 8. The language of Hearne and of Attwood as cited in *Parentalia* is so similar as to argue a common source. It looks as if Hearne (whose entry is dated 25 June 1728) is citing Baker, the antiquary of St John's College, who may also be Attwood's source. Hearne says that some of Wren's MSS were in the hands of Bishop Tanner, who had no doubt (as so often) filched them. Some are still among the Tanner MSS in the Bodleian Library. Others, now lost, were copied and published by Christopher Wren III for *Parentalia*.

even thought that he could fix the succession: a rash thing for any Master to do. Always mindful of his family, he persuaded the fellows to elect his younger brother Christopher, whom he had already caused to be incorporated at Cambridge, presumably for that purpose. But higher powers would not have that. A word to the Bishop of Ely, Visitor of the College, ensured that the new Master was the most extreme and aggressive of all the Laudians, John Cosin. Poor Christopher, however, did not starve. Soon afterwards Matthew Wren was made Dean of the Chapel Royal, and Christopher, who had already followed him as chaplain to Andrewes and to the King, would then succeed him as Dean of Windsor.

With his appointment to a bishopric, Wren moved, as it were, out of the closet. Hitherto he had operated and prospered within the protective context of his colleges in Cambridge and his deanery in royal Windsor. Now he had to face the realities of provincial England: not academics and courtiers, bowing towards the risen sun, but squires and their parsons, town merchants and their lecturers, few of them sympathetic to the new Laudian synthesis, many of them positively Puritan. Hereford indeed was not a great problem: in that loyal county he could rely on an ally who was a Laudian *dévot*, Sir John Scudamore, for whom he would cause the great church of Abbey Dore to be ceremoniously consecrated. But he only stayed a few months in Hereford. Then he was promoted to Norwich; and it was there that the trouble began.

For Norwich was one of the largest and most difficult dioceses in England. It contained the counties of Norfolk and Suffolk. Its old industries – especially in Suffolk – were in decline. Its new industries had been imported by Dutch and Walloon immigrants who had been allowed to form their own congregations outside the established Church. They were particularly numerous in Norwich. Its gentry were notoriously independent: they lived to themselves and resented metropolitan intrusion; and, like the gentry everywhere, having done well out of Church lands, leases and great tithes in the last century, they looked with suspicion on Laudian clergy determined to recover them. As Laud himself reported to the King in 1635, after his metropolitan visitation, 'I find . . . that the whole diocese is much out of order . . . but I hope my Lord that now is' – that is, his new Bishop, Dr Wren – 'will take care of it, and he shall want no assistance that I can give him.'[11]

Wren certainly found the bishopric in a bad state. The spire of his cathedral had fallen down. Foreign Protestants had taken over his episcopal palace at Ludham. The gentry had not only absorbed Church property: they had invaded the churches themselves, raising the height of their own pews, blocking the chancel with their family tombs, so that the officiating clergyman, if he stood at the east end, could not be seen by the congregation. That was one way of preventing the return of an altar. And then there were the unlicensed Puritan preachers, maintained either as private chaplains by peers – like the new Lord Brooke, whose father had imposed Dorislaus on Cambridge – or as lecturers by towns like Ipswich and Yarmouth: men who, by preaching unsound doctrine in improper afternoon sermons, drew excitable crowds and thus threatened disorder. To Wren, the whole diocese seemed rotted with neglect. It was also far too big, especially for a bishop who lived mainly in London, Dean of the Chapel Royal, Judge of the High Commission, tipped to be secretary of State, Lord Treasurer, what not? It ought, he believed, to be divided in two. Finally, to make everything worse, there was an epidemic of plague.

Whatever might be said against Wren, he could not be accused of lack of courage. He set out at once to put things right. He ordered a visitation of the diocese by his chancellor: a vigorous man, who often outran him in zeal. He insisted on fixed and railed altars and imposed the full Anglican liturgy in places where it had never been heard before. There was not a parish church in the diocese in which his hand was not felt. Everywhere the form of service was altered, and the communicants were ordered to come up to the altar. The Bishop suppressed afternoon sermons. He turned the foreign Protestants out of his palace, and proceeded – as Clarendon complained – 'passionately and furiously' against them. He forbade Lord Brooke's chaplain to preach and when Lord Brooke threatened to appeal to the King, told him that 'no Lord in England should affront him in his diocese'. He deprived Sir Thomas Gawdy of his chaplain and ordered his pew to be cut down to size. He demanded that the family tomb erected by Sir William Withypool in St Margaret's, Ipswich, be levelled so that the altar could be seen, which was regarded as insolence. Relenting, he ordered the chancel floor to be raised instead, which was regarded as popery. He twice ordered Lord Maltravers, the son of the Earl of Arundel, the greatest magnate in Norfolk, to remove the gunpowder which he had conveniently stored in his parish church. And of course he introduced, in his cathedral, the full Laudian ritual as established in the Chapel Royal. This too was regarded as popery.

However he might afterwards defend himself, it is evident that Wren's rule in Norwich was one of disastrous confrontation. When he boldly went to stay in Ipswich, the main centre of Puritanism in Suffolk, there was a riot. Angry citizens, armed with sticks and guns, and summoned by the ringing of church bells, besieged the house in which he was lodging, and 'would have done violence to his Lordship if they could have met him'.[12] At Norwich, the mayor and half the corporation petitioned the King against him. When their petition was rejected, their leader, Alderman Atkins, left for London, where he would become a leader of the City radicals during the Civil War, and would be invited, though he funked it, to try the King. The flight of 'many thousands' of artisans to Holland not only ruined the local cloth industry, but also, it was said, 'which was worse, transported that mystery into foreign parts';[13] so the Bishop was accused not only of suppressing the religion but also of destroying the economy of his diocese.

Wren was particularly unfortunate in that the Puritans of East Anglia were in league with the illicit London press. One of the charges afterwards made against him was that he had silenced 'that ancient famous good and painful man, Dr Ward of Ipswich'. In fact it was impossible to silence Dr Ward of Ipswich, who was an old hand at public controversy and playing the media. He had shown this ten years ago, when he had supplied material for the first great parliamentary attack on Arminianism.* Now a press campaign against Laud was being organized in London by a formidable triumvirate: William Prynne, already in the Tower for previous libels, Henry Burton, a discontented clergyman, and a radical physician from Colchester, John Bastwick. In 1636 this combine turned against Wren. A violent pamphlet, almost certainly concerted by them, was published in London, entitled *News from Ipswich*. It was said to have been written by Burton,[14] and its matter was probably supplied by Ward.

News from Ipswich was a work of hysterical propaganda. It accused Wren – 'little Pope Regulus' as it called him – of launching a persecution of God's ministers unparalleled since the time of Mary

---

*Ward and Yates, his colleagues in Ipswich, had written the pamphlet against Richard Montagu which launched the attack on him in the Parliament of 1625.

Tudor, of shutting up the mouths of painful preachers, of prohibiting sermons, encouraging profanity and debauchery, introducing the worship of the Pope and the Devil, and thereby drawing down the wrath of God in the form of plague and bad weather at Ipswich; and it called upon the King and nobility of England to hang up this lecherous, proud, insolent prelate, raised from the dunghill, and all other such true-bred sons of the Roman Antichrist, and thereby stay the plague and improve the weather.

Grotesque though it was, this scurrilous pamphlet nevertheless had its effect. It created the public image of Wren, presenting him as the stereotype of the tyrannical antichristian prelate, soon to be taken up and repeated throughout Puritan England. Hitherto the assailants of Arminianism had directed their fire mainly against Laud and Cosin – Cosin for his activities as prebendary of Durham, where he had aroused an adversary as formidable as Dr Ward at Ipswich. Wren's operations behind the scenes in Cambridge had hardly been noticed outside the University. But now he replaced Cosin as bogey-man number two after Laud. In the same year, 1636, Sir Simonds D'Ewes was writing his autobiography. A respectable Suffolk squire of scholarly, antiquarian tastes, he had already satisfied himself that he was one of the Elect and that the Pope was Antichrist; but now he found that he could go further: the Pope and his cardinals, he wrote, were 'saints' compared with Laud and Wren.[15] Five years later Sir Simonds, as MP for Sudbury, Suffolk, would be able to spell this out in detail as chairman of the committee to frame the impeachment of Wren.

Wren was Bishop of Norwich for only two years. In 1638 he was removed to Ely. Outwardly it was promotion: Ely was a grander see, a palatinate, like Durham. But it was also a smaller and less challenging diocese, and it may be that Laud recognized that he had been a failure, or a liability, in Norwich. Laud defended him at the time, in his report to the King, as Wren would defend himself afterwards, in his proposed answer to the charges of the Parliament. He claimed that, although there were over 1,500 clergymen in the diocese, he had censured or suspended less than thirty of them, and those only for obstinate and wilful resistance. However, his methods were clearly provocative; nor do they seem less provocative in the eulogy of his Tory great-nephew: 'for the space of two years and upwards, he detected the impostures, restrain'd the restless, seditious endeavours, and broke the spirits of all refractory schismatics'.[16] It is to be observed also that Laud replaced him in Norwich by Richard Montagu, the most notorious of Arminian controversialists. This suggests that he intended to continue the policy but to change the man; and Montagu himself, when he looked on the problems that he had inherited, admitted that his predecessor had gone too fast and too far. That indeed was the general weakness of the Laudians: they set out to reverse, at a late hour, and in a short time, a process that had been continuous for eighty years – and nowhere more effective than in the diocese of Norwich.

In removing Wren from Norwich to Ely, Laud was, in a sense, bringing him back to Cambridge; for at Ely he would dispose of patronage for reliable Cambridge men. Besides, the Bishop of Ely was Visitor, and could determine the headships, of two Cambridge colleges, Peterhouse and Jesus. For this reason Laud liked to see a sound man in that see. Wren too seems to have eased off at Ely. He lived in London, at Ely House, and used the revenues of the see to improve his own income and to provide jobs for his relations. As Count Palatine he had valuable rights in the Isle of Ely: he licensed alehouses, controlled ferries and windmills, owned large herds of cattle which he fatted for the Cambridge colleges, traded in beer, turf and hay, exploited his profitable fishponds. His letters, says Mr Peter King, were now 'more like those of a gentleman farmer than a bishop', discussing mutton, corn, beer, fuel, wine, poultry, and their prices: 'the whole tenor of his correspondence, which at Norwich had been full of references to Holy Communion and preaching, underwent an almost complete change'. The result however was much the same. By securing exclusive rights to exploit the Fenlands he once again exasperated the nobility and gentry. By cornering the turf and sedge he provoked riots of the peasantry at Wisbech. The recovery of Ely House entailed a long battle with Lady Hatton, whose husband's family had obtained it, by dubious methods, in the reign of Elizabeth. In 1640, when Parliament met, one of the many petitions it received was from the county of Cambridge against the exactions of the Bishop as Count Palatine. But at least those exactions could not be represented as popery.

By that time, of course, the tide had turned, and the bishops were on the run. Wren stood his ground to the last. On 19 December 1640 – the day after the impeachment of Laud – there was 'much dispute about Bishop Wren and his wicked doings and fears that he would flee away'. He was accused of idolatry and superstition, of seeking to uproot and destroy 'all religion and piety',[17] and bound over in £20,000 to stand his trial. A committee was appointed to investigate him; petitions against him poured in to it; and in July 1641, on its report, he was impeached. The dreadful pamphlet *News from Ipswich* was reprinted; and was followed by others – *Wren's Anatomy, The Wren's Nest Defil'd, The Goldfinch and the Wren* – all dwelling heavily on his activities as Bishop of Norwich. He was described as a monster engendered by a decaying world, a devouring serpent in the bishopric, a tyrant who had made war on his own people and, of course, a wren in the episcopal aviary: 'the least of all those birds, but one of the most unclean ones'. By the end of the year he was, with other bishops, in the Tower, charged with the additional offence of high treason. Released with them after four months, he was then re-arrested and re-imprisoned indefinitely. He was not brought to trial – on seeing his answers to their charges, his persecutors decided not to take that risk – but the impeachment was not withdrawn: the threat still hung over him. Radical preachers from Norfolk and Suffolk, brought up to London by their patrons, excited Parliament against him. Throughout the Civil War, in all the terms offered to the King, he, like Laud, was excepted from pardon. At any moment he might be sacrificed, like Laud, to please the City radicals or the Scots.

How did he spend those long years in the Tower? For some time he continued to act as Bishop. He kept his register with his own hand till 1644. Then things got worse. Laud was executed in 1645. Wren's wife, who was allowed to be with him in the Tower, died in 1646. After that came the abolition of episcopacy, the revolution, the execution of the King, the Republic, the rule of the Saints. These public events must have been very distressing to him. Even when the more conservative, more stable, more conciliatory Protectorate was set up, no move was made to release the prisoner. In the words of a clergyman who had no love for the Laudians (but time and suffering had softened those old animosities), 'God had punished his enemies with such hardness of heart that he, being never yet brought to answer to the objections of his persecutors, after ejection out of all his estates, and after twelve years of imprisonment in the Tower, continues still in that cruel durance'.[18] That was written in 1654: the durance would continue for another six years.

However, Wren was not too uncomfortable in prison. His life had always been austere – up at five in the morning, long hours of study, frugal meals, never a drop of wine. No doubt it was like being back in Pembroke College. He received visitors and discussed liturgical matters. He walked for exercise, 'on the leads of the Tower (by connivence of his warder)', where, says his great-nephew, 'upon a just computation, he walked round the world'. He also studied and wrote, seeking always to defend his concept of the Church against the twin dangers of Presbyterianism and Socinianism: against the Scotch Covenanters with whom the royalists seemed likely, at times, to compromise for the sake of peace or reconciliation, and against the 'rational' disciples of Grotius and Chillingworth who seemed dangerously inclined to rot the doctrine of the Church from within. It was a difficult path to tread, for the strongest intellectual defenders of Anglicanism in those dark days – Henry Hammond and his disciples – were themselves attacked as Socinians. Indeed, Laudianism itself was now declared, by Presbyterian bigots, to have been a vast Socinian conspiracy agains the true reformed Church.[19] But Wren had never shared the tolerant scepticism of these true 'Arminians', nor did he wish for toleration for his Church at the expense of any concession. So he pored over the 'Racovian catechism' of the Polish Socinians, wrote his vast, and never fully published, refutation of their damnable doctrines, and sent out carefully guarded letters, written in the third person and signed with false names – A. Cleveland, Benjamin Hide – to keep Hammond and his friends on his own narrow and funambulatory track of orthodoxy.* In this he was not entirely successful. If Hammond had consulted Wren more often, wrote a nineteenth-century Tractarian, he would have avoided an unfortunate 'gnostic tendency' in his writings, and not fallen into some 'absurd mistakes' about the early Church.[20]

As time passed, and tempers mellowed, the continued imprisonment, without trial, of this old man began to seem futile; and one day the Lord Protector, dropping in at dinner-time at the house of his son-in-law John Claypole, chanced to meet the Bishop's nephew, the young Christopher Wren, who was being entertained there; for Claypole had mathematical interests and enjoyed learned

---

*Wren's correspondence from the Tower was published from a 'private collection' by N. Pocock in *The Theologian and Ecclesiastic* VI, VII, IX, XV (1849–53). His enormous Latin work against Socinianism is preserved in Peterhouse, Cambridge. Part of it was published by his son Matthew under the title *Increpatio Bar Iesu* (1660).

conversation. In a genial mood, Cromwell told Christopher Wren that his uncle could be free for the asking. Having been assured that the offer was serious, Christopher carried the glad news to Uncle Matthew. But Uncle Matthew would not ask. He would not be beholden for his liberty to 'that miscreant', he said, but would 'tarry the Lord's leisure' and owe his deliverance only to Him.[21]

Soon afterwards, Cromwell died, and it seemed that the hour of the Lord's leisure might now be at hand. At the exiled court of Charles II, Edward Hyde, later Earl of Clarendon, was preparing for the restoration not only of the Crown, but also, what required even more tact, of the episcopal Church. To ensure this he was anxious that the Church should already have some substance in England. But how was this substance to be created in the England of Oliver Cromwell? It was fifteen years since the last bishop had been consecrated; the surviving bishops were few and cautious; and the cathedral chapters which, legally, should elect any new bishops, were dying out too. In these circumstances Wren, as the most learned and most resolute of the survivors, was their natural spokesman, and several attempts had been made to prod him into some decision or action; but always without effect.* Now Hyde tried again, more insistent than ever. He approached Wren through a secret intermediary, Dr Barwick, who visited him periodically in the Tower, and urged him to recommend sound clergymen whom the King could nominate as new bishops and who could then be formally elected by the chapters before it was too late.

Hyde – as we have seen – had no great love for Wren, but now, in letter after letter to Barwick, he courted and flattered him. He 'much preferred the Bishop's judgment and advice before any man's', he wrote. 'I beseech you present my humble service to [the Bishop], upon whom no man looks with more reverence'. 'I pray remember my service with all imaginable reverence to my Lord of Ely'; 'you must never forget my service to my Lord of Ely; and if he please to recommend some of his friends to the King, they will find the fruit of it in all ways'. But curiously the old curmudgeon would not respond. He made implausible excuses. Not a single name would he suggest. Hyde became urgent, then almost desperate: 'the King hath done all

---

*In October 1651, Sheldon and Hammond pressed Wren on the matter (*The Theologian and Ecclesiastic* IX (2), p. 288). Another more concerted attempt was made in 1655 (*Clarendon State Papers* III, nos. 135, 136, 138). Cf. J. W. Packer, *The Transformation of Anglicanism* (1969), p. 41.

that is in his power to do, and if my Lords the Bishops will not do the rest, what will become of the Church?' Already the chapter of Carlisle was reduced to a single aged canon, and 'God knows, it will be almost a miracle if the winter doth not take away half the bishops that are left alive'. But Wren would not be moved. He never suggested a single name: the secret channel of communication, so carefully created and maintained, was useless. Effectively he sabotaged the plan to strengthen the Church in opposition.[22]

How are we to explain this curious indifference? The sclerosis of old age? Genuine lack of information about English churchmen of the next generation? Personal distrust? Perhaps all of these, and possibly particular distrust of Hyde. Hyde was not only an old critic of Wren: he was also a conciliator, determined to restore the monarchy by agreement; and who could tell what concessions he might exact from an episcopate which, as yet, had no power of its own? Wren was never a conciliator. So far as he was concerned, the Church of England might die out in the catacombs so long as it died pure.

Luckily the Restoration came in time. But if Wren thought that the old Laudians were to resume control of the Church, he was mistaken. They had had their day. Nor could he personally, at seventy-five, hope to be a force in it. His great liturgical knowledge was used in the preparation of the new Prayer Book of 1662 – as it had been used in the disastrous Scottish Prayer Book of 1637, the beginning of the Troubles – but otherwise his chief activities, after the recovery of his bishopric, were to provide for his family. As Clarendon would write of the restored bishops (and I fear that he had Wren particularly in mind), they 'had been long kept fasting' and 'had now appetites proportionable'. So the revenues of the diocese and the Palatinate of Ely were raised and sons and sons-in-law, nephews and kinsmen of the Bishop accumulated offices and benefices within it. They became rectors, prebendaries, archdeacons, JPs and deputy lieutenants, bailiffs and constables: a clientele to be firmly rooted in the Isle before the old man should die.

The Bishop also made full use of his power in Cambridge University. He had a special barge built to convey him thither in state, and he did not forget his rights in Jesus College and Peterhouse. He was particularly anxious to provide for his protégé Joseph Beaumont, whom he had brought as an undergraduate to Peterhouse and then married to his stepdaughter, the heiress of a rich merchant of Ipswich. In 1660 he inserted Beaumont – already amply beneficed in the Isle – as Master of Jesus; but then, in 1663, the mastership of Peterhouse falling vacant, 'by a stretch of power' he swept aside the 'two deserving persons' proposed by the fellows and nominated Beaumont, thus incidentally clearing the way for his chaplain Dr Boldero at Jesus. Even his admirer Dr Attwood of Pembroke College found this hard to digest; 'it must be allowed', he wrote, 'that he was arbitrary to the last'.[23] But after all, that was how he himself had become Master of Peterhouse, *invitis sociis*; and anyway, who am I to object, since it is to this arbitrary stretch of power that I owe, indirectly, my fine residence in Trumpington Street?*

Meanwhile, the Bishop had not forgotten Pembroke College. We are told that, while a prisoner in the Tower, he vowed that, if he emerged alive, he would endow some worthy memorial of his delivery; and having already employed his young nephew Christopher to build a little doorway to the cathedral at Ely, he now decided to entrust him with the design of a new chapel at his own original college. It would be presumptuous of me, in this place, to speak about that work: let it suffice to say that Bishop Wren has the distinction of having built, here in Cambridge, two college chapels, almost opposite each other, both, strictly speaking, superfluous: one – at least as finished by his successor – baroque, looking outward to the Counter-Reformation, the other classical, but with an elegance and lightness of touch which looks forward to the famous churches of Restoration London.

Wren consecrated his new chapel on his name-day, St Matthew's day 1665. Two years later he was dead, aged eighty-two, and was buried in the vault of it, without, as far as I know, any monument; but in this place I suppose we can say of him, as in St Paul's of his much greater nephew, '*si monumentum requiris circumspice*'.

Indeed, if we look at his career as a whole, I think we should see Matthew Wren as essentially a college man. The course of his career has a certain aesthetic regularity, a cycle of emergence and return. It began in a college. Thence, by college service, college politics, he rose to authority within a collegiate university. Then, when he was fifty years old, he moved out of college. The middle-aged disciplin-

---

*Joseph Beaumont's son, Charles, whom, as Master, he was able to insert as a fellow of Peterhouse, built the house for himself in 1702 and bequeathed it to the college as Master's Lodge.

arian don, with his blunt manners and summary methods and limited views, turned to deal with a very different world; and dealt with it very unsuccessfully. Those two years as Bishop of Norwich, which made him a national figure and provided nearly all the evidence for his impeachment, were clearly a personal disaster. The move to Ely was a return towards the University; and in the Tower, he was back again in a kind of college, not very comfortable indeed, but comfortable enough for him. There we can envisage him reading and writing, discussing liturgical problems, expressing downright opinions, making endless learned notes, avoiding public responsibility, snubbing the great, or taking his unvarying walk on the leads of the familiar roof. Perhaps it was with a touch of nostalgia that he would afterwards give his famous snub to Charles II, who had urged him, for the sake of peace, to be less exacting in his diocese: 'Sir, I know my way to the Tower.'

Thomas Carlyle once wrote of Laud that he was the archetypal college tutor of the old style, concerned only with forms. I do not think this is quite fair to Laud, who had a far wider conception of society and a more liberal idea of the Church than Carlyle credited him with: who believed in the social function of the Church and who could be accused, by one of his own bishops, of 'Socinianism'. But it seems to me true of Wren, who remained always a somewhat crusty scholar, conservative, crotchety, critical, but devoted to his college: with 'so great a love of that place' (as his great-nephew put it) 'that neither the length of his days nor the injuries of the times could obliterate or diminish his affection'.[24] And therefore, though his name is seldom praised by historians, and it might be rash, even now, to celebrate it in Ipswich, we can safely do so in the college which, to the end, he showed that he loved best.

9

Edward Hyde, Earl of Clarendon

Few men have loved Oxford as Edward Hyde did. He was there as an undergraduate, at Magdalen Hall, where his old Wiltshire friend Thomas Hobbes had been before him. He returned often to it. Oxford friends surrounded him throughout his life. After the battle of Edgehill, when the King set up his court in Oxford, Hyde lived for over three years in Oxford. When the city fell to the Parliament and the Parliament purged the University, he was far away; but he afterwards noted with satisfaction that even 'that wild and barbarous depopulation' failed to 'extirpate all the learning, religion and loyalty which had so eminently flourished there', for 'the goodness and the richness of the soil . . . choked the weeds and would not suffer the poisonous seeds, which were sown with industry enough, to spring up'. Oxford, in fact, as so often, absorbed its reformers. In 1660, on his return to England, Hyde, already Lord Chancellor of England, became Chancellor of the University; and in 1667, when the fallen minister fled hastily abroad, never to return, his first act on arriving in Calais was to send to the Vice-Chancellor a moving letter asking the University to accept his resignation and to elect another Chancellor who could now serve it better than he, although 'I am sure he can never be more·affectionate to it'.

Hyde's long affection for Oxford may not have begun at Magdalen Hall. He admits that his undergraduate years were not fruitful, 'the discipline of that time being not so strict as it hath been since, and as it ought to be', and he was glad that his father (whom he describes as his best tutor) soon took him away. Thomas Hobbes, we may recall, had spent his time in the same college snaring jackdaws. Hyde's real romance with Oxford began, I suspect, a little later: at Great Tew, the Oxfordshire home of the young Lord Falkland who – though himself a Cambridge man – was to be the intimate friend of his life. It was there that Hyde discovered his philosophy, there that he made his permanent friendships, there too, perhaps, that he built up that extraordinary erudition which made him one of the most learned of our great statesmen.

Hyde had always been a lover of literature. After leaving Oxford, he had studied and then practised law and enjoyed the patronage of Lord Keeper Coventry; but in his leisure hours he had haunted the literary world, and written occasional pieces. He was a friend of poets – of Ben Jonson, Edmund Waller, Tom May – and of the greatest, most scholarly, most historically minded of lawyers, the most learned of Oxford benefactors, John Selden. He was also a student of history, an admirer of the greatest of English 'civil historians', William Camden. In August 1628, when the news was brought of the assassination of the Duke of Buckingham, it found the nineteen-year-old Hyde reading Camden's *Annals of Queen Elizabeth* aloud to his father. Hyde was a lifelong admirer of Camden, whose portrait he would afterwards secure to hang in his great picture-gallery at Clarendon House. But then, in the 1630s, he moved on from literature to philosophy. His philosophy was discovered at Great Tew.

Much has been written about Lord Falkland's circle at Great Tew, but nothing so eloquent, so lyrical, as Hyde's own account. Warmth flows from his pen whenever he recalls it. Falkland kept open house for his friends, who were scholars, poets, and men of the world; to them it was 'a college situate in a purer air', 'a university bound in a lesser volume', and they came to it, from Oxford and from London, 'not so much for repose as study'. There they read and talked, forming a perpetual *convivium philosophicum* like the Tusculan retreat of Cicero, or the Cassiciacum of St Augustine, 'nor did the Lord of the house know of their coming and going, nor who were in his house, till he came down to dinner or supper, where all still met'. Throughout the 1630s this intellectual club continued, till the disasters of the 1640s broke it up.

Hyde's account of the death of Falkland at the first battle of Newbury in 1643 is the most moving passage in his work: it was a loss, he wrote, which by itself alone made 'this odious and accursed civil war . . . infamous and execrable to all posterity'. However, even that and other losses could not destroy the close-knit alliance of his surviving friends. At every stage in his life Hyde would turn to them. With him they would protect Falkland's family and estate; with him they would plan the survival of the Church in its eclipse; with him they would restore Church and Crown. They would be the designated overseers of his will, guardians of his family, arbiters of his work; and the last pages which he would write, in the last year of his life, would be in vindication of 'that unparallel'd Lord', Lord Falkland.

The Great Tew group was so constant a force in Hyde's life that we must ask who they were and what philosophy united them. Its composition is well known. There were the Oxford clergy, Gilbert Sheldon, George Morley, John Earle, Henry Hammond, and 'the ever memorable John Hales of Eton'. There were philosophers like Hobbes and Chillingworth, poets like Ben Jonson, Edmund Waller, Abraham Cowley, George Sandys. The sons of Lord Keeper Coventry, pupils of Sheldon, would be there: so, afterwards, would Hyde's old Oxford friend, who became Falkland's chaplain, Hugh Cressy. As for their ideas, confusion has been spread by those who are ready to conclude without reading the evidence of their works. But there is really no mystery. All their writings and discussions show that they were the students and disciples of Erasmus and Hooker, and that their philosophy for their own time was drawn from the great living Dutch scholar and thinker, the conscious heir of Erasmus, Hugo Grotius.

I will not go far, at present, into the philosophy of the men of Great Tew. It would lead us into the spiritual and intellectual crisis of the seventeenth century, what has been called the 'Pyrrhonian crisis', the crisis of scepticism.[1] But I must say something about that crisis, because, without some idea of it, the character of the Great Tew circle cannot be understood, and indeed, in my opinion, has been generally misunderstood.

It began as a religious crisis, but soon became a crisis of knowledge. By the early seventeenth century the mutually destructive criticism of the religious parties had undermined, on each side, the foundations of belief, and intellectuals looked desperately for a solid base on which to rebuild it. Some of them – Sir Thomas Browne, Robert Boyle – were driven almost to suicide by the lack of such a base. Others clutched at desperate expedients. In Oxford and London, Jesuit missionaries urged wavering souls to cease from struggling and settle on the firm rock of St Peter. In Cambridge, Joseph Mede, the famous scholar of Christ's College, took refuge in the millenarian certainties of the Apocalypse. Robert Boyle found an alternative relief in empirical science. Hobbes, like Descartes, discovered certainty in the infallibility of mathematical reason.

It is against this background that the discussions at Great Tew must be seen. Falkland and Chillingworth had been victims of the Pyrrhonian crisis. Falkland had seen all his younger brothers and his sisters seduced to popery by his formidable mother. Chillingworth had himself been caught by a Jesuit at Oxford and had gone abroad to the English College at Douay before finding that he had been deceived. When he returned to England, he was taken into Falkland's household and became the intellectual leader of the group. But his own intellectual master was Grotius. When Archbishop Laud, who was his godfather, sent to him to offer him a benefice in the Anglican Church once he was resettled in Protestantism, he gave a stalling reply. Before deciding, he said, he must 'go over and confer with Grotius'.

The philosophy of Grotius was a constructive scepticism which led, in religion, to ecumenism: that is, to a religion which, having shed sectarian differences, justified itself by natural reason and historical continuity. Grotius himself had dreamt of a tolerant religion which would unite moderate Catholics and moderate Protestants under the control of the lay magistrate. This ideal had been expressed, in 1605, by Edwin Sandys, a favourite pupil of Hooker, whose brother, the poet and traveller George Sandys, was one of the Tew circle. Grotius believed that the leadership of such a Church should be exercised by the Church of England. He went to England in the reign of James I in the hope of forwarding his design. He there placed his trust, especially, in two distinguished 'Arminian' clergymen, Lancelot Andrewes and John Overall. In order to achieve this result, he saw the need for uninterrupted peace and an agreed system of international law. But in 1618–21 all these hopes were shattered. European war broke out; the Dutch Arminian party, the party of peace, was destroyed; and Grotius himself was thrown into prison. After his escape he fled abroad and wrote his *De Jure Belli ac Pacis* in response to the savagery of the Thirty Years War. Such, in general, were the opinions of Grotius. All of them were regarded, by good Calvinists (and indeed by others), as heretical and were denounced as 'Socinian'.

All the men of Great Tew venerated Grotius. Falkland addressed a poem to him, George Sandys translated his poetry, Francis Coventry his prose. Henry Hammond would adopt his religious arguments. Robert Boyle, a later friend of Falkland, would even have them translated into Arabic. Grotius was the oracle of Chillingworth. Consequently they too were all accused of Socinianism. Though some were more 'Socinian' than others, the accusation was not unjust. Falkland's library was full of Socinian books. When his heir sold it, in the 1650s, it was bought by Sheldon and found a home in Oxford, in Sheldon's own college, All Souls.[2]

As one of the men of Great Tew, Hyde undoubtedly shared their basic philosophy. He did not go quite as far in scepticism as Chillingworth, but he agreed with them all in their veneration for Erasmus, Hooker, and Grotius. He shared their insistence on rational religion and on ultimate lay control: he could, at times, be anticlerical. He shared their ecumenical aspirations, their belief that the Church of England was, potentially, the most ecumenical of Churches. He regretted that Archbishop Bancroft had not been succeeded by one of the two friends of Grotius, Andrewes or Overall. He was convinced that the Church of England and the legal constitution of England were validated by history and historic continuity. And he foresaw the gradual victory of Grotian ideas, if only the world were at peace. Fortunately in the 1630s, England, unlike the tormented continent of Europe, was at peace.

It was an idyllic peace, at least to those who enjoyed the life at Great Tew. In the distractions which so soon followed, Hyde would often look back to it with nostalgia. But let us not suppose that these young men were epicurean idealists only. They were reformers, eager for action. Always in that little group, and in Hyde, perhaps, most of all, two spirits were at war. On the one hand, literature, philosophy, Virgilian love of country life; on the other, the call of public virtue, strenuous exertion for the commonwealth. Throughout Hyde's whole life we can see this tension; nor was he alone, at that time, in feeling it. We think of Milton at Horton and Hammersmith, in these very years, studying, meditating, writing those enchanting uncommitted early poems *L'Allegro* and *Il Penseroso*, and yet repudiating the idea of a cloistered and fugitive virtue in favour of active intervention in public affairs; and a few years later Andrew Marvell, in the delightful garden of the Fairfaxes at Nun Appleton, would reveal, through the imagery of the glow-worm and the mower, the tension between pastoral love of letters and the iron necessity of political strife. To Hyde, England in the 1630s was a garden – 'the garden of the world' – and even Scotland was 'but the wilderness of that garden'; but it was a garden which needed some vigorous weeding before it could bloom at its best.

For the ideas of Great Tew were not the ideas of the rulers of England: far from it. Theoretically, Archbishop Laud was an Arminian, like Grotius. Theoretically, Charles I was continuing the system of Queen Elizabeth. But in fact both were distorting the tradition they had inherited. The ministers of Charles I, by their new taxes and misuse of the law, were straining the accepted English constitution, narrowing the definition of liberty. Archbishop Laud, by his insularity and intolerance, was similarly narrowing the definition of the English Church. He had contracted its membership, cut it off from foreign Churches, exalted the clergy above the laity, converted it from a potentially ecumenical Church into an intolerant clerical sect. For these reasons the men of Great Tew, although loyal subjects, were distrusted by the government, and the clergy among them, though 'Arminian' in doctrine, received no promotion from Archbishop Laud.*

It was here that Hyde saw his personal opportunity. He observed Laud closely and came to admire the real virtues – the integrity, the idealism, the courage – which lay behind that 'cholerick disposition' and 'uncourtly quickness, if not sharpness of temper'. The Archbishop's greatest infirmity, Hyde believed, 'was (besides a hasty sharp way of expressing himself) that he believed innocence of heart and integrity of manners was a guard strong enough to secure any man in his voyage through this world, in what company soever he travelled, and through what ways soever he was to pass; and sure never man was better supplied with that provision'.

What Laud needed, thought Hyde, was 'a true friend who would seasonably have told him of his infirmities' and faithfully helped him to remedy them. Hyde himself had, as Sir Charles Firth has written, a genius for friendship, and he offered himself as such a friend. Unfortunately, the result was not fully satisfactory. Laud accepted

---

*The one member of the group whom Laud wished to favour was his godson, Chillingworth; but Chillingworth refused his offers, at least partly because of the 'sectarian' character of the Laudian Church. See Robert R. Orr, *Reason and Authority: The Thought of William Chillingworth* (Oxford 1967), pp. 36–41.

the friendship so warmly offered, but rejected the advice. He went on his way, single-minded, to his doom.

Meanwhile the general battle was being joined. In 1640, when the Long Parliament met, the men of Great Tew were on the side of reform. Hyde, Waller, Falkland worked together to attack the Prerogative Courts, the royal judges, the Laudian bishops. Hyde himself voted for the attainder of Strafford – though he would be reticent about it afterwards. Then, when the abuses had been corrected – at least on paper – they rallied to the support of the Crown. Hyde became the propagandist of a new royalism, a liberalized Anglican Church. More than that, as previously to Laud, so now he offered himself to the King as a 'true friend' to point out his errors and propose remedies. Unfortunately, once again, the result was unsatisfactory. Like Laud, the King accepted the friendship. It became a real personal friendship: the crusted pedant Antony Wood thought that it went too far, that Hyde's familiarity 'savoured too much of impudence'. But, like Laud, Charles I also ignored the advice. He might listen to his friend 'Ned Hyde', but he yielded to the Queen, the courtiers, the 'swordmen'. He too went on his way to his doom.

In May 1646, when Charles I fled from the besieged citadel of Oxford and surrendered to the Scots at Newark, Hyde was no longer there. He had been sent with the Prince of Wales, first to the Isles of Scilly, then to Jersey. When the Prince was ordered to France, Hyde stayed on in Jersey. So long as there was an inch of English soil unconquered, he refused to go abroad. He stayed in Jersey for a year before he too was forced into exile in France.

What was Hyde's state of mind in those long months of confinement after the defeat of himself and his cause? We might assume that it was one of dejection. We are therefore surprised to hear him saying, again and again, that he was wonderfully happy. We must remember, of course, that we are still only in 1646. The Civil War had been lost but the political settlement was still to come. The 'swordmen' having failed, perhaps the King would now listen to the politician. Moreover, the survivors of the Great Tew group were there to help. Their alliance had been cemented when court and University were together at Oxford. Falkland indeed was dead, killed at Newbury, and Chillingworth was dead, dead of 'barbarous usage' in captivity at Chichester, and Waller had deserted in order to save his life after the failure of his plot – a plot to bring peace concerted with Hyde and Falkland. But Hammond and Sheldon were still there, with the King, when allowed by his captors; Earle was with the Prince; Morley was at Oxford, organizing resistance to the Parliamentary Visitors. Besides, Hyde, now the only lay politician among them, had been given a special task. Early in 1646, to counter the parliamentary history of his former friend Tom May, he had been instructed by the King to write a true history of the rebellion.

Hyde had taken up his pen in the Isles of Scilly: under the roar of the Atlantic breakers those sonorous periods had begun to roll. Now, in Jersey, he set systematically to work. He lived in the Governor's castle at St Helier. The Governor showed 'extraordinary kindness and friendship'. He also had a good library. The war was over; there was conversation at need; there was delicious rural solitude for study. Jersey, 'this blessed isle', was like Great Tew again.

Besides, there was a serious public purpose. Whatever the King's original plan, Hyde had no intention of writing mere propaganda, like Tom May, whom he rightly despised. He still saw himself as 'a true friend' of the King, an intimate political adviser, who would seasonably tell him of his infirmities, and how to remedy them. So he was resolved to set down, in the form of a historical narrative, the mistakes of the past, including – in more tactful language – the King's own mistakes, as a warning, and a guide to action in the future. He would spare no man, he said: his book would 'make mad work among friends and foes' if it were published; but it was not to be published: it was 'unfit in this time for communication'.

Nor was the work to be only tactical. Below the narrative of fact, it was to be a work of political philosophy. Hyde was determined to plumb 'that unfathomable abyss of reason of state'. He would reveal the mechanics of history. For the late misfortunes were not due, as the Puritans supposed, to the will of God, or the working of Providence: they had sprung from 'the same natural causes and means' as had operated in other times and places. Hyde's method would be that of Tacitus, or of the modern Tacitus, the Venetian Enrico Davila, whose history of the French wars of religion uncovered the secret springs of rebellion. Davila's work was regarded by royalists as the manual of the rebels – 'Mr Hampden's *vade mecum*' – and at this very time Hyde's brother-in-law was translating it for the King, who read it (we are told) 'with such eagerness that no diligence could write it out fair so fast as he daily called for it'; for he saw there, as in a mirror, the original of his own troubles.*

On a higher, more philosophic level, Hyde's model was Hooker. The very first words, penned in Scilly, make that clear; for they are a conscious imitation of the first words of Hooker's *Laws of Ecclesiastical Polity*. As Hooker's great work had been a philosophic defence of the historic English Church against Puritan attack, so Hyde's *History* would be a philosophic defence of the historic English State against Puritan Revolution.

Finally, it was to be a work of literature in its own right. Of course it was to be accurate as history. Hyde was careful to collect accurate material for his work – State papers, pamphlets, eye-witness accounts – and he was careful to interpret them correctly. But his ordinary reading at St Helier was not contemporary matter. Even as he wrote, he was studying the great classical models: Livy, Tacitus, Cicero. We have his letters which describe his method; we also have the commonplace books which he kept at the time.[3] They are filled with annotations and extracts from Thucydides and Josephus, Livy, Plutarch, Tacitus, as well as from the great modern political writers, Commines and Camden, Machiavelli and Sarpi, Bacon and Grotius. Hyde's letters from Jersey breathe a positive exhilaration as he dwells on his work. He is conscious of his high aims: he will achieve the Olympian tone of great history. Does Sheldon think his epitaph on John Hampden too eulogistic? He is writing, replies Hyde, for posterity, and 'I am careful to do justice to every man who hath fallen in the quarrel, on which side soever'. Is his eulogy of Falkland too long? 'It is not much longer than Livy is in recollecting the virtues of one of the Scipios after his death.' Anyway, if it is too long,

---

*For Davila see *Clarendon State Papers* ii, p. 334; E. Davila, *History of the Civil Wars of France*, translated by William Aylesbury and Sir Charles Cotterel, 1647 (The Printer to the Reader), 2nd edition 1678 (Preface by Cotterel). The phrase 'Mr Hampden's *vade mecum*' is used by Sir Philip Warwick, *Memoires* (1701), p. 240. It has been cited, by those who would have the Puritans to be always the Moderns, as evidence that Hampden and the Puritans were readers of Davila. In fact it only shows that royalists read him. Aylesbury was Hyde's brother-in-law; Cotterel was a confidant of Hyde and afterwards entertained Hyde and Morley in his house at Antwerp. The royalists described Hampden as a pupil of Davila in the same sense in which Robert Dudley, Earl of Leicester, was described by his enemies as a disciple of Machiavelli: they did not mean that he actually carried the work – a stout quarto of over 1,000 pages in Italian – about with him in his pocket.

it can be published separately, and sooner: 'you know Tacitus published the life of Julius Agricola before either his *Annals* or his *History*'.

The letters and notebooks of Hyde in Jersey are evidence of his resiliency, his confidence, his inextinguishable love of literature. He was 'abundantly satisfied with our condition', he wrote, 'in wonderful contentment', 'never better in body or mind in my life'. 'How do you live?', he wrote to another ruined minister. 'Do you study and find your spirits refreshed by being somewhat unbent to business? Have you the pleasure of the *suavissima vita, indies sentire se fieri meliorem*, which Sir Francis Bacon says is the benefit which learned men enjoy in retirement?' How miserable, he reflects, in his notebook, is the 'bold and illiterate' courtier, once out of place: 'he knows not how to do nothing, nor what it is to descend into himself . . . whereas the learned man can ever be idle, ever alone; his own thoughts are always company and supply him with a variety of considerations'. And indeed he wrote down his own 'cursory and occasional considerations', some of which would be very surprising to those who see him as an archaic, backward-looking conservative in a context in which, by definition, the Puritans are the Moderns.

For in his philosophy Hyde is essentially a modern, a Baconian. He constantly quotes Bacon. He has no patience with 'stupid reverence for Antiquity'. Is not science always progressing? Did not Galileo, with his telescope, daily discover new stars?* And is not 'the growth and improvement of arts and sciences' a very proper subject of history? He is as impatient as Bacon of the Schoolmen, as contemptuous as Milton of monkish contemplation, monkish chroniclers, even Church Fathers. Long afterwards he would summarize his philosophy in two essays. In the first, 'Of the Reverence due to Antiquity', he would reject the authority of the past unless it was confirmed by the superior knowledge of the present. The ancient philosophers and the Church Fathers, he would write, were entitled to respect: we have 'a just reverence for them as great lights which appeared in very dark times'. But neither in science nor in religion are they to be accepted as our guides: the philosophers were grossly ignorant in astronomy and 'we have much to answer for' if our knowledge of religion is not better than that of the Fathers. The

---

*Hyde's interest in Galileo and astronomy may remind us that his father-in-law Sir Thomas Aylesbury was the friend, disciple, and executor of the famous mathematician and astronomer Thomas Harriot.

second essay is 'On the Active and Contemplative Life'.[4] Contemplation without action, he there declares, is barren. Even a historian must be a man of action, as all great historians and political writers have been from Demosthenes and Cicero to Davila and Grotius. As for the monkish Schoolmen, 'it had been happy for religion and the Church of God if they had all been bred ship-carpenters or locksmiths or gunsmiths or granado-makers or any other subtle artificers' and never put to school beyond to read and write. They have contributed nothing to true learning or the use of mankind, for 'the dry tree of solitude' bears no notable fruit. Indeed, when vigorous spirits are 'first mortified and moped with the absurd documents of contemplation before they know anything to contemplate on, they can never be revived out of that dull and lazy lethargy, to be applied to any magnanimous activity'.

Hyde could afford to be confident in 1646–7 for he still looked forward to political recovery. It was inconceivable to him that the course of history could be violently broken and changed by a mere political episode. The misfortunes of the Civil War, he believed, were the accidental result of discernible mistakes and weaknesses. If those mistakes could be corrected, those weaknesses exposed, then the naturally healthy English constitution could be repaired and improved. The Civil War, he always insisted, was quite unnecessary. No one had wanted it – not even 'the great contrivers'. Pym, Hampden, Essex, and their friends were all essentially moderate men. He knew them all, and could say so confidently. But moderate aims had been frustrated and moderate men either converted into radicals or swept aside, not because there was a 'revolutionary situation' in the country – there was not – but because, on both sides, there was a lack of coherent philosophy, of moral conviction, of courage.

For, although he was a sophisticated political and social observer – no contemporary is more acute in his social analysis – ultimately, to Hyde, the Great Rebellion was caused by a moral failure. Like Oliver Cromwell, he believed that the rulers of the nation had not performed their trust. And he pointed out their failure in no uncertain terms. How he hated those great lords who thought only, in prosperity, of their own wealth and grandeur, and, in adversity, of their own safety: the Earl of Arundel, for instance, who 'resorted sometimes to the court because there only was a greater man than himself, and went thither the seldomer because there was a greater man than himself'; or the Earl of Holland, who thought 'poverty the most insupportable evil in the world'; or the Earls of Salisbury and Pembroke, who, though royalist at heart, 'had rather the King and his posterity should be destroyed than that Wilton should be taken from the one or Hatfield from the other; the preservation of both which from any danger they both believed to be the highest point of prudence and politic circumspection'.

Among the Commons, too, how he despised those 'half-hearted and half-witted' members who, though a majority in the House, would not stand up and be counted: who, 'having assumed their country's trust, and, it may be, with great earnestness laboured to procure that trust', then, 'by their supine laziness, negligence and absence' from crucial divisions, allowed the radicals, a mere 'handful of men', to prevail, and thus 'to show that three diligent persons are a greater number in arithmetic, as well as a more significant number in logic, than ten unconcerned'. Certainly no one could accuse Hyde of betraying his trust, neglecting his duty, lack of energy, care for wealth or comfort. The next decade was to prove that.

For after 1647 everything went wrong for the royalists and Hyde never had a chance to present his finished *History* to Charles I, whom he would never see again. By the spring of 1648 he had carried his narrative down to 1644; then a royalist revolt in England precipitated a new series of events which destroyed all hope of restoring and continuing the old system. After the Second Civil War, the victorious enemies of Charles I were in a new mood. They would tolerate no more of his evasions. They resolved on a surgical discontinuity. They cut off his head.

When Cromwell abolished the English monarchy and set up a military dictatorship in England, Hyde was on the Continent, and there he remained, with the exiled court of Charles II, for ten years. They were years of poverty, frustration, and, to many, despair. Particularly there was despair of the English Church. That Church, which Grotius had envisaged as the head of Christendom, was now, as it seemed, utterly destroyed. Among the scattered and disconsolate émigrés, the Roman missionaries went to work. There was an epidemic of apostasy. One of the first to surrender was Falkland's chaplain, Hyde's old friend Hugh Cressy. He now justified his desertion by saying that the English Church had been inwardly rotted by Socinianism – the Socinianism of Great Tew.* Equally, in the State, weak spirits yielded to present power. And not only weak spirits. In 1651 Hobbes – an *esprit fort* if ever there was one – shocked Hyde by publishing his *Leviathan*, with its implied argument that the Republic was now the legitimate sovereign of England. Hyde had read Hobbes's earlier works and had sensed the widening gulf between them. This book revealed it, stark and clear. He asked Hobbes why he had written it; Hobbes replied sardonically that he had a mind to go home; and he went.

Others might not despair of a royal restoration but they argued that the English monarchy could only be restored by jettisoning the English Church; for what support, they asked, could be expected from a Church which was now totally powerless: proscribed in England, non-existent abroad? All around him, the young King heard voices urging him to rely on Catholic help: to seek a foothold in Ireland or armed support from France or Spain; or, alternatively, to buy a passage through Calvinist Scotland, with the support of his Calvinist brother-in-law in Holland. Catholicism and Calvinism were at least real forces: the Church of England, on the other hand, had no battalions: it was a liability, a ghost.

For ten years Hyde stood firm against all such proposals. Almost alone, he insisted that the English Church and State must be restored together, and by Englishmen alone. Such an aim might seem impossible now. The power of the usurper in England was irresistible; the English royalists were scattered and dismayed; his own position at the exiled court was constantly undermined by his old enemies, Queen Henrietta Maria and her courtiers. But he never gave up. It is impossible not to admire the firmness with which he stood his ground in that quaking, slippery court, the skill and patience with which, from that precarious position, he still sustained and heartened the defeated and divided royalists and Anglicans at

---

*Cressy's apologia is his *Exomologesis* (Paris 1647). In this work he states that he had been led into error by the arguments of Chillingworth and had reached the same false position as Grotius; from which he was saved by his conversion to Catholicism. Anthony Wood (*Athenae Oxonienses*, ed. P. Bliss (1813–20) III, p.1014) says that 'this *Exomologesis* was the golden calf which the English papists fell down and worshipped. They brag'd that book to be unanswerable and to have given a total overthrow to the Chillingworthians, and books and tenets of Lucius Lord Falkland.'

home. It was firmness which sprang from a deep conviction of the historic continuity and independence of English institutions.

For Hyde – again like Cromwell – was an English patriot, perhaps even an English nationalist. One of the errors, or crimes, for which he would never forgive the parliamentary leaders was their introduction, into a purely English dispute, of the alien Scots. In 1641 John Pym had got rid of the Scotch armies which had been used to force a Parliament on the King, and all England had been relieved. There had been a day of thanksgiving and bells had been rung throughout the country. But in 1643, to avoid defeat in the field, he had summoned them back, and what a price he had paid! The English Church, even English liberties, had been sacrificed and the Parliament's surrender to the Presbyterian Scots explained (although to Hyde nothing could ever justify) the King's no less disastrous surrender to the Catholic Irish.

To Hyde the surrender to the Scots was unforgivable. The Scots, to him, were 'a foreign contemned nation', 'those vermin' who, from their native wilderness, had brought pestilence into the garden of England. How was it conceivable, he asked, that a mature, civilized country should hand itself over, bound and helpless, to a primitive society composed of 'numerous, proud and indigent nobility' and of 'ignorant and insolent clergy', 'whose infectious breath governed and corrupted' a slavish people? Fortunately, even English Puritans soon came to agree with Hyde, and it was with some satisfaction that he afterwards saw Cromwell put both Scots and Irish in their place. Hyde preferred the Independents to the Presbyterians, partly because they were less clerical, partly because they were at least purely English. When Cromwell was dead, and the Scots thought that they could once again interfere in English affairs, they knew their enemy. The condition of the King's return, declared Professor Baillie in Glasgow, was that Lord Chancellor Hyde be first dismissed: only thus could England be secured in its ideal state, as a Presbyterian colony of Scotland.[5]

In his long struggle, Hyde was supported by his old friends from the past. With him in exile were Earle and Morley: for three years Morley shared his house in Antwerp. In England, Sheldon and Hammond organized the Anglican catacombs and, incidentally, in so doing, built up that alliance of gentry and clergy which was to be the backbone of the Tory party for the next two centuries. They also looked after the interests of the Falkland family. The place of Great

Tew, as an intellectual centre, was taken by Westwood in Worcestershire, the home of Lady Pakington, daughter of Lord Keeper Coventry. There Hammond wrote his scholarly works defending what his enemies sourly called 'the Grotian religion', while Earle, abroad, was translating Hooker's *Laws of Ecclesiastical Polity* into Latin for Europe. At the same time Sheldon, when not busy with the Church or fishing in the River Trent, was transmitting the rationalism of Great Tew to a young pupil who would be the great English sceptic of the next generation: George Savile, Marquis of Halifax, the Trimmer.* Thanks to these strong links and this consistent policy, the terms of the Restoration, when it came, were made not by Professor Baillie or the English Presbyterians, but by Hyde, and the Church that was restored was – against all odds – the Anglican Church.

It was not the old Laudian Church. In the catastrophe of the 1640s, the Laudians had collapsed and fled. Those who had stood firm in the dark days were those whom Laud had rejected, the 'Socinians' of Great Tew, who, now at last, were in a position to carry out the policy they had envisaged in the 1630s. They carried it out together. Sheldon, now Bishop of London, Morley, soon to be Bishop of Winchester, and Earle, soon to be Bishop of Salisbury, formed a close committee for the reconstitution of the Church. They also preached their old doctrines. The works of Grotius and Hooker were now reprinted in England.† It was at Sheldon's request, and in Morley's house, that Izaak Walton wrote his life of Hooker. After Earle's death in 1665, Hyde sent his son, Lord Cornbury, to Salisbury to secure his Latin version of Hooker's *Ecclesiastical Polity*.

---

*That Sheldon, in the 1650s, was tutor to Savile has not been noticed by Savile's biographers. It is revealed by the private correspondence between Hammond and Sheldon now in the British Museum (Harleian MS 6942). This volume is an invaluable source for the survival of Anglicanism, and the continuation of the Tew circle, in the 1650s. See also J. W. Packer, *The Transformation of Anglicanism 1643–1660* (Manchester 1969). Savile's mother was the sister of Lady Pakington.

†Many of Grotius's theological works, which had been particularly attacked, during the 1650s, by John Owen, Cromwell's Vice-Chancellor of Oxford, and by Richard Baxter, were reprinted in 1660 at Oxford, Cambridge and London. The great edition of Grotius's *Opera Theologica*, though planned much earlier, was not completed – and dedicated to Charles II – till 1679. Hooker's works were reprinted in 1662 with a life of the author by John Gauden. It was the unsatisfactory nature of this life which caused Sheldon and Morley to commission a new life by Walton (see Izaak Walton, *Lives*, Dedication and Preface; also Preface to Life of Hooker).

Unfortunately, he was told, he had arrived too late: the Bishop's servants had put it on the fire.*

At the height of his new power, in 1663, Hyde, now Earl of Clarendon, emphasized this return to the 1630s by an almost symbolic act. He was then living in London, in Worcester House, which he had rented. Later, he would build his own town house, Clarendon House, whose magnificence would delight Pepys and Evelyn. There he would hang his famous collection of portraits, the first personal portrait-gallery in England. But meanwhile he decided to build a country house, to be the seat of his family. For this we might expect him to look to his native Wiltshire, whence he drew his title. But he did not. Instead, he had settled at Cornbury in Oxfordshire, eight miles from Great Tew; and there, on the pediment of the new classical front which Hugh May built for him,

---

*The fate of Earle's translation of Hooker is somewhat mysterious. There are two distinct accounts which, at first sight, seem incompatible.

The first account is contained in a letter sent by the non-juring antiquary Thomas Smith to his friend Thomas Hearne on 13 September 1705. In this, Smith writes that Lord Cornbury (afterwards 2nd Earl of Clarendon) 'more than once' described to him how he had visited Mrs Earle at her house near Salisbury about a year after Earle's death, only to be told by her that the manuscript, 'being written in loose papers, onely pinned together, and put into a trunke', had been regarded as waste paper and used, after his death, by the Bishop's servants to light their fire or put 'under their bread and their pyes'. Cornbury himself saw several scattered and discontinuous pages which 'had not then undergone the same fate with the rest' (Bodl. MS Smith 62, p. 29; draft in MS Smith 127, p. 87).

This account is authoritative and circumstantial and commands belief. On the other hand David Novarr, in his book *The Making of Walton's 'Lives'* (Ithaca 1948), p. 207n., prints a MS note found in the margin of a presentation copy of the *Lives* (1670) in the Yale Library which tells a different story. This note reads: 'at Bishop Earle's death this work, unperfect and deficient, came to the hands of Bishop Morley of Winton, who commanded Dr. Adam Littleton to finish it. But the Doctor on perusal found the stile so inimitable that he said, if he should proceed upon it, the translation would not look all of a piece, and that it were better for some one person of leisure and ability to begin the work anew, which non, I think, hath undertaken to this time 1697'. Further, Mr W. Speed Hill tells me that the Folger Shakespeare Library at Washington has recently purchased a mid-seventeenth-century manuscript Latin version of the first five books of Hooker's work (Folger MS V.b. 314) which may well be Earle's manuscript, or a copy of it. There is thus good evidence that Earle's version was not irremediably destroyed, as Mrs Earle supposed.

All this evidence can be reconciled if we suppose that the manuscript which was destroyed by Earle's servants, and of which Lord Cornbury saw the remains, was a rough copy; that the fair copy had already been secured by Morley; and that Mrs Earle was either unaware of this fact, or did not recollect it.

In any case, the affair shows the common interest of Earle, Morley and Clarendon in the promotion of Hooker's work.

he caused to be inscribed the Virgilian line '*Deus nobis haec otia fecit*'. No doubt he looked forward to re-creation, in his old age, of the golden years at Great Tew.

But was it possible, in the 1660s, to realize the dreams of the 1630s? Was the omnipotent Earl of Clarendon, intellectually, the same person as the young, hopeful Mr Hyde? Age transforms all men; revolution transforms them even more. It is sometimes supposed that revolutions liberate the spirit; more often they contract and harden it. Simple souls, excited by the beginnings of a revolution – Milton in 1641, Wordsworth in 1790 – suppose that the old world will vanish like a scroll and a brave new world emerge without travail to replace it. Hyde was not a simple soul. He knew that ancient walls do not fall at the sound of trumpets, and he knew that the ideals of his party needed peace, not war, for their realization. Like Chillingworth, who 'did really believe all war to be unlawful', and like Falkland, who had gone to his death 'ingeminating "Peace" ', Hyde believed that 'no reformation is worth the charge of a civil war'. He had constantly sought to abridge the First Civil War. After the end of it, he could still retain his old hopes. But, when the Second Civil War had been followed by revolution and regicide, his temper changed. Even the victors in that revolution were soured by the struggle: how different is the Milton of the 1650s from the Milton of 1641! For the defeated, the disillusion was greater. After 1650, quite apart from the natural processes of age, and the natural divergences of experience, Hyde and his friends were all, inevitably, less genial, less tolerant, less broadminded men.

We see it in the shrinking of their religious ideals. In the 1630s they had looked forward to a rational, ecumenical Anglican Church. Even in 1645 Hyde and his Oxford friends had argued for a guarantee of toleration by the Church.* Even in 1647 he had wished to welcome foreign Protestants into it. He then condemned Laud's imposition of conformity on the foreign Protestants in England and repudiated 'the testy and imprudent carriage' of Lord Scudamore, the Laudian ambassador in Paris, who had refused to attend the Huguenot services at Charenton. He himself attended those services and urged his friends to do so: 'if you and I were in Germany', he

*See the 'Proposals of the Clergy', printed from Clarendon's MSS by S. R. Gardiner in *English Historical Review* (1887), p. 340. The clergy who made the proposals included Sheldon, Hammond, and Christopher Potter, Provost of Queen's College, Oxford, who was closely connected with the Great Tew group.

wrote to a fellow-exile, 'we should communicate with all charity and alacrity' with Lutherans ('and yet our differences in opinion are not insubstantial'). But after the execution of the King he changed his mind. The French Protestants had justified rebellion against the King of England (though not against the King of France), and he would have nothing to do with them. When he returned to England in 1660, his Anglicanism might be internally as liberal, as rational, as ever; but its frontiers were more closely drawn and more heavily defended.

This hardening became apparent in his last years of power, when the euphoria of the Restoration had worn off and a series of disasters – plague, fire, and defeat in war – united all the dissatisfied in the search for a scapegoat. And what scapegoat could it be except the all-powerful minister who, by now, was so accustomed to command that he overrode opposition, and who, by the royal marriage of his daughter, was raised almost above the rank of a subject? The King, by now, resented his dependence on him; the old cavaliers resented the limits set to their appetite, or their revenge; the courtiers complained that Hyde's settlement had deliberately restricted the King's revenue to keep him dependent on Parliament; the King's mistress, Lady Castlemaine, newly converted to popery, detested him; the people were enraged to see his London palace rising in splendour in the midst of national disaster; and Clarendon did not conciliate his adversaries by showing himself, as he admitted, 'too proud of a good conscience'. It was the same fault, he wryly observed, that he had himself once censured in Archbishop Laud.

Unquestionably, Clarendon's personal attitudes helped to concentrate opposition to him. His conviction of his own integrity, his tendency to see moral causes for political events, his favoured role as a candid friend, all became oppressive when combined with the unanswerable authority of long experience and great power. In a good mood, he could be charming: Pepys was charmed by his effortless mastery of business and lucid, elegant exposition of it. But he suffered terribly from gout, and could be testy as well as pompous. So the King, who declared that he had become 'insupportable', awaited his opportunity. In October 1667 he seized it and gratified his indolent, frivolous court by dismissing the over-mighty Chancellor.

At the news of Clarendon's fall the court went wild with delight. The Keeper of the Privy Purse, Bab May, 'fell upon his knees and ketched the King about the legs' and told him that now at last he was really King, 'being freed this great man'; and Lady Castlemaine 'ran out in her smock into her Aviary looking into Whitehall Gardens' to gloat at 'the old man's going away'.[6] Once he was dismissed, the Commons impeached him of high treason; to his appeal for royal protection, the only reply of the King, who was so eager not to go on his own travels again, was 'bid the Chancellor begone'. When he had fled to France, his plea of innocence was burnt by the hangman and he was banished without hope of return.

The last seven years of Clarendon's life make melancholy reading. Gone were his hopes of Virgilian retirement at Cornbury. Long and dangerously ill at Calais, beaten up and robbed by English sailors at Evreux, persecuted by the French government, he moved from town to town till he found a haven at Montpellier. He was without his books and papers; it was declared treason to communicate with him; he was so crippled by gout that he often could not hold a pen. And yet, once again, the old man astonishes us by his extraordinary energy and internal resources. As soon as he had arrived at Montpellier, he recovered, as he tells us, 'a marvellous tranquillity and serenity of mind'. He learnt languages, read the great modern historians of France and Italy, and sat down to write. He wrote a series of works which, together, reveal or re-state the philosophy of his life.

First, he wrote his own apologia, his *Life* up to 1660. Then, when his son was allowed to visit him, bringing the long-buried manuscript, he completed his *History*, using the *Life* as a quarry of material for it. Then he continued his *Life* up to the present. Neither of these works was written by him for immediate publication. The *Life* was for the eyes of his family only. The *History* was to remain in manuscript in the hands of his heirs. Whether and when it, or any of his papers, should be published was to be decided by them on the advice of the two men whom he named as overseers of his will, the Archbishop of Canterbury and the Bishop of Winchester: that is his old friends from Great Tew, Sheldon and Morley.

Meanwhile, the indefatigable old man was writing a number of shorter works, devotional, historical, polemical. He completed the *Meditations on the Psalms* which he had begun during his first exile. He showed his vast historical reading in his examination, over twelve centuries, of the relations between Church and State in Christendom. It was now that he wrote his essay on the active and the contemplative life. And in two polemical works, which he hoped to see published at once, he reasserted the continuity of English institutions against two old friends who had deserted the ideals of Great Tew, Thomas Hobbes and Hugh Cressy.

Hobbes had once been a historian like Hyde. He had translated Thucydides and declared that knowledge of history was essential to a statesman. But then he had solved the Pyrrhonian problem of his time in his own way, by abandoning experience for the abstract certainties of geometry. The result was a political theory which dispensed with history, traditional institutions and all their loyalties, and which validated novel, unhistorical blueprints of total power. Cressy had despaired of the English Church and become a Benedictine monk. At the time, Hyde had deplored his conversion but sympathized with his weakness – 'apostate', he wrote, 'is too hard a word for a friend'. But then Cressy had justified his apostasy by writing an apologia. He had left the Church of England, he said, because that Church was already finished: even before the Parliament had proscribed it, it had been rotted by Socinianism.

Thus both Hobbes and Cressy had justified their desertion – the one to Cromwell, the other to popery – by declaring that English institutions had failed: the King was no longer an effective sovereign, the Church was no longer a sound Church, and both were logically doomed to wither away. Such arguments were frontal challenges to Hyde's central philosophy. In the 1650s he had had no time to controvert them himself: action was then more important than controversy. Now, in his last exile, he turned and dealt swingeing blows at them both. Against Hobbes, whom he portrayed as an academic pedant, a contemplative Schoolman disqualified for political philosophy by his inactive life, he defended the historic constitution of England. Against Cressy, who had recently aggravated his offence by pointing his charge of Socinianism directly against his former patron Lord Falkland, he defended his old ideal – obscured but not forgotten in practice – of a rational, tolerant, ecumenical Church. He even defended those who, in Cromwellian times, had supported an unsectarian Independency; and as for the charge of Socinianism, if to apply reason in religion was Socinianism, then, he declared, he himself was a Socian too.[7]

Why did Hyde, after more than twenty years, launch this fierce attack on Hobbes and Cressy? Was it merely an old man's return to the battles of his youth? I suspect that there was a more positive reason: a reason which was supplied to him by his own recent experience, but which also looks forward to the future and explains, in part, the long inheritance of Clarendon in the English Tory party.

Ever since the outbreak of the Civil War, Hyde had fought to keep the Stuart monarchy on a consistent base. He had deplored Charles I's flirtation, however insincere, with Presbyterian Scots and Catholic Irish. Charles II, from the beginning, had wavered between popery and materialism, between the seductions of his tutor Hobbes and of his mother Henrietta Maria; and that wavering had never really ceased. Nor had Hyde's resistance to it.* Up to the time of his fall, he had kept the monarchy firmly on a restored Anglican base; but, after his fall, that base was once again in danger. Charles II then repudiated the Anglican Church: with Clarendon, his friend Morley was exiled from the court. The rule of the 'Cabal' which followed was an administration of the King's friends, the patrons of popery and Dissent: that was the time of the Secret Treaty of Dover of 1670, and the Declaration of Indulgence to Catholics and Dissenters in 1672. Afterwards, when that policy had foundered in the turmoil of the Popish Plot, it was Clarendon's heirs who would be brought in to help in the restoration of the old system; but the fall of the Hydes in 1686 would be the signal for the resumption of that policy, which would lead to the second fall of the house of Stuart. In his last exile, Clarendon was careful never to criticize Charles II: after all, he hoped to return; but through his attacks on Hobbes and Cressy he reasserted the philosophy from which he believed that the Stuart monarchy, so arduously restored, was deviating at its peril. And, factually, who can say that he was wrong?†

In 1688, when James II followed his father-in-law into a second and final exile, Clarendon's *History* was still unpublished. It was not till the Anglican–Tory alliance was reconstituted, in the reign of Clarendon's grand-daughter Queen Anne, that that great work was

---

*That Clarendon, throughout his administration, was engaged in a continuing struggle to preserve the Anglican establishment from erosion by Catholicism and Dissent patronized by Charles II, has been persuasively argued by Mr Ian Green in his book *The Re-establishment of the Church of England 1660–1663* (Oxford 1978).

†It is ironical that James II, in his last exile, described the dismissal of Clarendon in 1667 as the beginning of the fall of the house of Stuart (J. Macpherson, *Original Papers concerning the Secret History of Great Britain* . . . (1775), I, pp. 39–41). In 1667 James had supported Clarendon; but his own policy after 1686 had been a more headstrong version of Charles II's policy after 1667.

at last printed at Oxford and became the historical bible of the Tory party, of which the Hyde family remained the secular head and Oxford University the spiritual centre. It was appropriate that the fallen Tory minister, Lord Bolingbroke, should address his *Letters on the Study of History* to the active head of the family, Lord Cornbury; appropriate that, throughout the eighteenth century, Oxford University should collect and publish the other works, and finally the State Papers of Clarendon.

But if we are to judge Clarendon in the twentieth century, it will not be by the party loyalties which he created and which represent, perhaps, the narrowing of his philosophy after 1660. Who would judge Sir Walter Ralegh by his Puritan disciples in the seventeenth century or Milton by the Whigs and Non-conformists who looked back at his later political writings? Ultimately, the greatness of Clarendon lies not in his administration or in his political inheritance. It lies in a *History*, which is the profoundest and most magnanimous history of his times – what other royalist historian would have dared to praise the 'great heart' of Cromwell? – and in a historical philosophy which, being nourished by deep intellectual roots, looks forward over the head of all his contemporaries, to the philosophical historians of the future: to Hume, Burke, Acton. And to this we must add his courage: courage which, against apparently overwhelming immediate odds, turned the course of history and made his philosophy become true.

10

Prince Rupert, the Cavalier

Politically calculated marriages rarely work out according to plan. In 1612 a marriage was arranged between Frederick V, Elector Palatine, the senior prince of the house of Wittelsbach, and Elizabeth, daughter of James I of England. The matchmaker was the bridegroom's uncle Henri, duc de Bouillon and Prince of Sedan, the diplomatic leader of the French Huguenots. To the duc de Bouillon, the marriage was designed to strengthen that international Calvinism on which the Huguenots depended for foreign support. King James accepted it in order to strengthen his position as the arbiter of Europe: with his daughter married to the leading Calvinist prince and his son, as he hoped, to a Spanish infanta, he would hold the balance between the religions and so be able (as he thought) to preserve the peace of Europe. The Elector accepted it as a means to raise his status in Germany and, perhaps, increase his power. All these hopes were soon disappointed. Within a few years the peace of Europe was destroyed in the greatest of 'wars of religion', King James's policy was in ruins, the Elector was deprived of his Electorate, the Huguenots were reduced to impotence. All this was the result of that marriage, and of the ambitious coup which it engendered: the Elector's fatal acceptance, or usurpation, of the Bohemian Crown.

The positive and more lasting results of the marriage were equally unexpected. The Wittelsbach-Stuart alliance, instead of bringing English influence into Germany, brought Germany into English politics. Of the thirteen children of that marriage, four would be closely involved in English affairs. In the struggle between Charles I and his Parliament, the Elector's heir, Charles Louis, backed the Parliament, and even, at a critical moment, undeterred by his father's fiasco, imagined a second usurpation: he fancied that he could displace his uncle as King of England. His younger brothers Rupert and Maurice took the other side: they fought throughout for the Stuart cause. The twelfth child, Sophia, was more patient: by survival, and by persistence in the Protestant religion, she would ultimately be designated to replace the Stuarts on the throne of Britain, and her direct descendant sits on it today.

I am concerned, primarily, with Prince Rupert,[1] the third son, famous in English history as the most brilliant and dashing of Charles I's generals, the inventor, almost, of the cavalry charge – with the proviso, however, that his cavalry charges always became disconnected from the main battle and, though completely successful in themselves, did not lead to victory. Of them it could be said, as the French general said of the famous charge of the Light Brigade in the Crimean War, '*C'est magnifique, mais ce n'est pas la guerre*'. In spite of Rupert's brilliant actions, Charles I lost the war; and I am afraid that it was in this sense that Disraeli afterwards described a political colleague as 'the Prince Rupert of parliamentary discussion'.

However, although it was his cavalry charges which made Prince Rupert legendary in English history, they are not his sole claim to fame. He was as active by sea as by land. After four years fighting for Charles I in England, he spent another four years continuing the struggle in the Atlantic and the Mediterranean, in the Caribbean Sea and off the coast of Africa. Later, he was the admiral of Charles II in three great battles against the Dutch. He was active in colonial enterprise, a founder-director of the Africa Company and of the Hudson Bay Company which is the beginning of British Canada. He left his name there in Rupert's Land and the Rupert River. He was a scientist, too, who, as a general devised his own weapons –

At once the Mars and Vulcan of the war.

In peacetime, he would become a Fellow of the Royal Society. And he was a skilful artist who painted, carved and engraved and who has been credited, here too, with technical innovations and improvements.

He was schooled in adversity. Born in the European limelight, in Prague in 1619, in that brief winter when his father reigned as King in Bohemia, and named after the most famous of his Wittelsbach ancestors, the Emperor Rupert III, he was soon bundled into exile – tossed as an afterthought into a fleeing coach – and grew up in the impoverished court which his parents maintained, on English and Dutch charity, at The Hague. When he was thirteen years old, his father died, a penniless émigré. The death, a few months earlier, of Gustavus Adolphus had removed all hope of recovering his inheritance through Swedish patronage; and to the now widowed Queen of Bohemia – for among Protestants she always kept that title – there seemed no hope of providing for her large family except by turning to her brother, Charles I of England. England was then an island of peace in war-torn Europe, and English diplomacy, or English patronage, she thought, might repair their broken fortunes.

So in 1635 the new Elector, Charles Louis, was sent to London, and was joined there, next year, by Rupert, then aged seventeen. The two brothers were very different. In the nursery at The Hague, Charles Louis had been known as *Timon*. He was cynical and calculating, and his whole aim was to recover by prudent diplomacy what had been lost by rash adventure. Rupert was himself an adventurer. In the nursery he had been known as *Robert le Diable*, and in his brief stay at the University of Leiden his thoughts had been 'so wholly taken up with the love of arms that he had no great passion for any other study'. The difference between the two brothers became apparent in London. There the young Elector recognized that there was more sympathy for his cause among Puritans, who supported the Protestant cause in Europe, than at the royal court, and he offended his uncle by openly cultivating 'puritan' opponents of royal policy. Rupert, on the other hand, became a favourite at court. Their different inclinations were nicely respected in the books which were given to them by Archbishop Laud, when they accompanied the King on a ceremonial visit to Oxford in 1636. To Charles Louis Laud gave Hooker's *Laws of Ecclesiastical Polity*, the great defence of the Anglican Church against the Calvinism which had been the ruin of the Palatinate. To Rupert he gave the *Commentaries* of Julius Caesar, in English: for Rupert, though a good modern linguist, was never a Latin scholar.*

However, if the English court offered opportunities, it also

---

*It is fair to add that by 1677 Rupert possessed two sets of Hooker's *Laws of Ecclesiastical Polity*.

contained dangers. One was the danger of popery. The Queen of Bohemia was a strict Protestant. The Queen of England, Henrietta Maria, was an active Catholic. She was surrounded by Catholic courtiers, and in 1636 – the year of Rupert's arrival – they were reinforced by a busy papal envoy. All these made much of the younger Prince. This was very alarming to his mother. Almost as alarming was a project, hatched in the Queen's court, to send him in charge of an expedition to Madagascar and set him up as king of the island: a project which seemed to his mother to come straight out of *Don Quixote*: had not Sancho Panza been promised the government of an island, still to be conquered? She would have none of her sons to be knights-errant, she wrote. Fortunately, the East India Company, whose support was essential to such a project, was equally opposed to it, and it had to be dropped. But perhaps it was not so fantastic after all. Eighteeen years later Rupert would find himself sailing up the Gambia River and fighting with African negroes in adventures hardly less quixotic than the conquest of Madagascar.

Between fear of popery and fear of knight-errantry, Rupert and his brother were recalled from England and set out together, with a little army of their own, under Swedish patronage, to the European war. In October 1638 they fought a battle at Vlotho, on the River Weser, in Germany. It was typical of many battles in which Rupert would afterwards be engaged: he himself fought with conspicuous valour, and the battle was lost. He was taken prisoner, and spent the next three years in imperial captivity, mainly at Linz. There he 'diverted himself with drawing and limning' and invented an instrument for drawing in perspective, which he would later give to the Royal Society. He refused his freedom at the price of conversion to Catholicism, and ultimately obtained it through English diplomacy, against a promise not to bear arms against the Emperor. It was a promise which he could give without difficulty; for it was now late in 1641 and his military gifts would soon be needed in England.

From Linz Rupert returned first to his mother's court at The Hague. Then he visited his uncle Charles I, nominally to thank him for his part in procuring his release. They met at Dover in February 1642. Charles I had then left London, resolved to return to it only on his own terms: if necessary, as a conqueror. He was now preparing for war. What passed between him and Rupert at that meeting, we do not know; but when Queen Henrietta Maria left for Holland to raise money for a civil war, Rupert accompanied her; and six months later, when the King raised his standard at Nottingham, Rupert at once returned to join him and was named General of Horse, with a command independent both of the nominated commander-in-chief and of the King's political advisers. The Prince to whom these exceptional and dangerous powers were given was an impetuous and self-willed young man of twenty-two.

In many ways he deserved his post. He was genuinely devoted to his uncle, with a romantic, unqualified devotion. Equally he inspired loyalty in his troops: a loyalty which was well deserved, for in spite of his cavalier panache – he was very tall, strikingly handsome, and 'sparkish in his dress' – he was a brilliant leader. His energy and courage were combined with scrupulous attention to detail, efficient organization and strict honesty. In the Netherlands and in Germany, at the court of the warrior Prince of Orange and in the battles of the Thirty Years War, he had studied both the art and the technique of war. He was not only a military hero but a military engineer, and he brought his own engineers with him to England. Compared with him the other generals of Charles I were amateurs. He was a professional.[2]

Unfortunately, he was also a foreigner. He had no knowledge of England, apart from its court, or of English politics, or indeed of politics at all. The other generals of Charles I may have been amateurs, but they were also Englishmen who, like all Englishmen, deplored the Civil War and wanted to end it with as little bloodshed as possible. They were noblemen or gentry with a stake in the country, and therefore necessarily politicians. They naturally distrusted this brilliant German adventurer in their midst. The King's civilian advisers, whose whole business was to find means to reconcile the King with his subjects, were even more distrustful of one who seemed positively to enjoy war. The ablest of them was Edward Hyde, afterwards Earl of Clarendon, the statesman who would bring back the Stuart monarchy in 1660 and write the greatest contemporary history of the Rebellion. He complained that Rupert was a stranger 'to the government and manners of the kingdom, and utterly unacquainted with the nobility and public ministers, or with their rights'; that his heart 'was so wholly set upon actions of war that he not only neglected but condemned the peaceable and civil arts' which were necessary even in war; and that his methods and manners made him unpopular, for he 'was rough and passionate and loved not debate'. This charge cannot be dismissed as arising merely from personal opposition. Twenty years later, the ablest of English naval administrators, Samuel Pepys, would repeat, about Rupert as an admiral against the Dutch, what Hyde had said about him as a general in the Civil War.

Nor was it only Englishmen who were alarmed by Rupert's appointment. His own family were equally dismayed. The Queen of Bohemia, as the widow of a Calvinist hero, was popular with the Parliament. She was also kept solvent – or semi-solvent – by a pension from England, which, being based on the customs, was now payable only by the power which controlled London – that is, by Parliament. On every account she wished to see King and Parliament reconciled, and it was for that purpose, she said – 'to settle peace betwixt His Majesty and his two Houses of Parliament' – that she had returned to England in 1641.[3] Her eldest and still favourite son, the Elector, was even less of a royalist. His chief aim was always the recovery of his lost inheritance, the Palatinate. To that end Charles I, even at the height of his power, had done nothing effective, and he was unlikely to do more even if he should win the Civil War. Therefore, the Elector, who had always looked to the Puritans for help, now openly backed the Parliament. In 1641, when it seemed that a Puritan government might replace the unsympathetic rule of Strafford and Laud, he too had returned to England, in flat disobedience to his uncle's orders; and now when civil war had broken out, he secretly absconded from the royal headquarters and returned to the Netherlands *via* parliamentary London. For this act of desertion, and its sinister implication, the King would never forgive him; and there was worse to come.

In these circumstances Rupert's commitment to the cause of royal absolution, royal conquest, was highly embarrassing to his own family, and at the beginning of the war his mother and eldest brother publicly separated themselves from him. In a petition to the Parliament, they openly 'disclaimed and discountenanced all his uncivil actions'. The Parliament published the petition and, throughout the war, exploited the internal division of the Palatine family. The only member of that family who consistently supported Rupert was his younger brother Maurice. Maurice obviously worshipped his elder brother, from whom he was inseparable in all his actions, by land and by sea; and his devotion was returned. Perhaps the greatest personal blow which Rupert suffered was the loss of Maurice, drowned in a storm in the Caribbean in 1652. It does not seem, however, that Maurice had any great personal gifts. Like many *dévots*, he seems to have been rather dull. He 'had never sacrificed to the Graces', says Clarendon, 'nor conversed amongst men of quality, but had most used the company of ordinary and inferior men'; and he goes on to describe him as proud and stupid and understanding 'very little more of the war than to fight very stoutly when there was occasion'.

Disliked by the councillors, courtiers and generals of Charles I – even, in the end, by Queen Henrietta Maria, who had taken him up on his first visit to England; disowned by the leading members of his own family; arrogant, impetuous and tactless; unable to co-operate, impatient of discipline, without political sense . . . Such is the character of Prince Rupert as it emerges from all sources during the English Civil War – and indeed afterwards. And yet, at the same time, he was indispensable. He was the most brilliant, the most successful, the most charismatic of Charles I's generals. The military men at court – 'the swordmen', as the responsible civilians described them – loved him; men clamoured to serve under him; and for the first two years of the war he seemed invincible: if anyone could have won the war, it seemed, it was he.

His first success came at the very beginning of the war, in a preliminary skirmish. A party of royalist soldiers had been surprised at Powick Bridge, near Banbury. Rupert soon reversed the surprise. Leaping on his horse, he roused his men and improvised a cavalry charge which, by its sudden shock, dispersed the enemy. That little episode made his name. A few days later, at Edgehill, the first major battle of the war, his cavalry charge totally routed the parliamentary cavalry, and could have won the battle if they had been able to stop; but – as would often happen – they returned after their triumph to find the victory lost. Even so, the way to London was now open, and Rupert urged his uncle to take it; to advance and enter his capital as a conqueror. The King's civilian advisers resisted and prevailed: they believed that it was not by sacking his own capital that the King would recover the hearts of his subjects.

These early victories made Rupert's fame and determined its character. He was the master of the cavalry charge, to which he gave a new form and a new force. He taught his men not to fire their pistols, as was usual at the beginning of an action, but to charge at once, in close formation, using their swords until the enemy broke and scattered, and only then to use their firearms. This innovation he had learned in Germany, in the school of Gustavus Adolphus, and it was instantly effective in England. Where he regularly failed was in controlling his own men after the rout of the enemy. Here Oliver Cromwell would succeed; and it was Cromwell's success in keeping control over a victorious cavalry that would ultimately end Rupert's career of undisciplined victory.

After Edgehill, Charles I set up his headquarters in Oxford, and throughout the next year Rupert was engaged in numerous local actions intended to enlarge the area under royal control and to open the way for new royal armies to converge on London. In these operations he was almost invariably successful. He drove back the parliamentary armies by lightning raids, took their towns by storm, and captured the great city of Bristol, the second city of England and the gateway to Ireland and the west. This was a great blow to the Parliament, which court-martialled its governor, Nathaniel Fiennes – and indeed nearly executed him, though he was a member of Parliament and the son of one of the great organizers of their party. Two years later this episode would have a dramatic sequel when Rupert himself lost the same city. But we shall come to that.

By January 1644 Rupert's record of success raised him above all other royal commanders, and the King recognized it by appointing him captain-general of four West Midland counties and President of Wales. He established himself at Shrewsbury, on the Welsh border, and at once reorganized the royal forces, raising money, enforcing his orders, and extending his authority in all directions. His most spectacular victory was the relief of Newark: a victory, as even his enemy Clarendon admitted, 'as prodigious as any that happened throughout the war'. The King described it as a 'beyond imaginable success' and hailed his nephew as the saviour of the North.

However, even at the height of his success, Rupert aroused intense hostility, among royalists as well as among parliamentarians. This hostility was not merely due to jealousy on the one side, or defeat on the other. It was caused both by his aims and by his methods. His aim was total victory, victory by conquest. His methods, it was said, were the methods of barbarism.

To aim at complete victory in war seems reasonable enough. To Rupert, the issue was simple: the parliamentarians were rebels and had to be crushed. But to most Englishmen, on both sides, the issue was far less clear. To them the Civil War was a regrettable breakdown in government which ought never to have happened and the sole purpose of the war was to find a basis of agreement for the future. This being so, it was important not to embitter the adversary by unnecessary humiliation: for they would have to co-operate with him afterwards. As one of the parliamentary commanders, the Earl of Manchester put it, 'if we beat the King ninety-and-nine times, yet he is King still': no alternative system was thinkable. On the royal side, many men, and particularly the civilian counsellors, thought similarly about the Parliament. Such men were deeply suspicious of Rupert, who treated the struggle as a purely military contest, to be directed on the advice of soldiers, and particularly of himself, alone.

Even more resentment was aroused by Rupert's methods. Parliamentary writers regularly accused him of unnecessary severities, illegalities, even atrocities: of illegal extortion of money, of pillage in the countryside, of sacking towns and slaughtering prisoners. It was said that it was he who had introduced the new word 'plunder' – a word 'born in Germany' – into the English language.* He was nicknamed 'Prince Robber'. Some of this can be discounted as war-propaganda. Any war needs a bogey-man, and Rupert, being the most famous and most successful commander on his side, and a foreigner too, was an obvious choice. Rupert's modern defenders have shown that some specific accusations are untrue: that his own behaviour in victory was often chivalrous and humane; that most of the excesses attributed to him derived from the indiscipline of his victorious troops, not from his orders; and that the occasional severities ordered by him were according to the laws of war as applied by parliamentary commanders and, particularly, by Oliver Cromwell. However, certain obstinate evidence remains which cannot be dismissed, since it comes from his own side, and from a man as committed as himself to total victory: the King.

Early in the war, when Rupert, using the King's name, demanded money by threats from the city of Lincoln, the mayor protested to the King, who promptly replied that he utterly disavowed and disliked his nephew's demand and absolutely freed and discharged the city from compliance with it. After the battle of Edgehill, the King thanked Rupert for his 'great valour and loyal services' but deplored the excessive bloodshed, since 'all in both armies are our

---

The Oxford English Dictionary gives the first use of the word as in *The Swedish Intelligencer*, 1632 – that is, in reports from the war in Germany. It is first used in an English context in 1642, in connexion with Prince Rupert. Cf. Thomas May, *History of the Parliament* (1647) III, pp. 1, 3.

subjects' for whose loss he was deeply grieved. He urged his nephew 'to mingle mercy with severity and look on our people as capable of reclaiming, though now misled'. Six months later, when Rupert was besieging Lichfield, the King repeated these warnings in urgent terms, begging Rupert to remember that 'we desire nothing so much as the good, happiness and peaceable government of our Kingdom, and not the effusion of the blood of our subjects'. Later, according to Clarendon, the King was offended to learn that Rupert had stormed and sacked the city of Leicester 'without any distinction of persons and places', churches, hospitals and houses being 'made a prey to the enraged and greedy soldier'. In 1644–5, during the negotiations at Uxbridge, Rupert and Maurice, on learning that they headed the list of war criminals who were excepted from pardon, both burst out laughing; whereupon the King, we are told, 'seemed displeased and bid them be quiet'. In the face of such evidence we must allow some credit to the charge that Rupert embittered an English political struggle by importing into it the brutal methods of the European war: the methods of Mansfeld and Tilly, Wallenstein and Gustavus Adolphus.

Methods of terror can be justified only by quick success. In the first year of war Rupert was remarkably successful: so successful that in 1643 the Parliament, despairing of victory, appealed to the Scottish Covenanters for military help. The Scots were willing (at a price), and early in 1644 they sent an army into northern England, where it joined the two parliamentary armies already there, and shut up the royalist army of the Marquis of Newcastle in the city of York. This immobilization of his northern army threatened ruin to the King's plan of campaign. 'If York be lost', he declared, 'I shall esteem my crown little less', and in an urgent but ambiguous letter he ordered Rupert to relieve York and liberate the besieged royalist army. Rupert at once suspended his immediate plans and marched north. Fighting his way through a series of victories he appeared with his army before York, relieved the city, and was saluted by the delighted Newcastle as 'the redeemer of the North and the saviour of the crown'.

However, this victory, the climax of his military career, was soon thrown away by an unnecessary sequel. Believing that he had been ordered by the King not only to relieve York but to destroy the opposing armies, Rupert challenged them at Marston Moor – and there, in 'probably the biggest battle ever fought on English soil', he met his match. Dismissing the reasoned views of his fellow general, Newcastle, with his usual disdain, he insisted on his own plan; and the plan went wrong. This time it was not the infantry, it was Rupert's own cavalry that was defeated. That famous force, 'which formerly had been thought unconquerable', was scattered by the cavalry of Oliver Cromwell; the North had been saved only to be lost again; and the victor of so many charges only escaped (it was said) by cowering in a beanfield. From that moment Cromwell rose to eclipse Rupert as the greatest leader of cavalry in the English Civil War. In another respect too Cromwell would resemble and outdo Rupert; for he too believed not in 'accommodation' but in total victory, and he outdid Rupert in being able to secure it.

At first Rupert's eclipse was not visible. The King still expressed confidence in him. Indeed, in November 1644, after a successful campaign in the west, he appointed him general of all his forces in England. But Rupert would never win another important victory, and after the battle of Naseby, in June 1645, he recognized that the total victory on which he had staked all was now impossible. He therefore changed his mind, and urged the King to make peace. 'His Majesty', he wrote to the King's cousin, the Duke of Richmond, 'hath no other way to preserve his posterity, kingdom and nobility but by treaty. I believe it to be a more prudent way to retain something than to lose all.' Unfortunately this conversion to a policy of 'accommodation' was now too late. It only served to ruin Rupert by giving a new weapon to his enemies at court.

The weapon was ready for use in the autumn of 1645. The parliamentary army, under Sir Thomas Fairfax, was then attacking Bristol, that same city whose capture by Rupert had so disconcerted the Parliament two years before. Rupert was in command of the defence, and confidently promised the King, who intended to join him there in order to introduce new forces from Ireland, that he could hold the city for four months. This was a rash promise. In fact, after the loss of an outlying fort, he found it indefensible and, to avoid capture by assault, he accepted the advice of his Council of War and surrendered it in four days. Had he insisted on holding out until the citadel was stormed, the whole garrison, by the laws of war, would have been put to the sword. The negotiations between Rupert and Fairfax were conducted with great civility, and when the terms of surrender were agreed, Rupert, we are told, rode out 'clad in scarlet, very richly laid in silver lace, mounted upon a very gallant black Barbary horse'. The parliamentary officers who escorted him were delighted by his urbanity, so different from the popular image of 'Prince Robber'. 'I am confident', wrote one of them, 'we are much mistaken in our intelligence concerning him. I find him a man much inclined to a happy peace', one who 'will certainly employ his interest with His Majesty for the accomplishing of it'.

Vain hope! Rupert had now no interest to employ. When the King heard of the sudden surrender of Bristol, he was naturally shocked, and his shock being exploited by Rupert's enemies, he reacted violently. Without waiting for explanations, he summarily dismissed Rupert from all his employments and ordered the arrest of the governor of Oxford, who was Rupert's nominee. In a letter of unparalleled bitterness, he reproached Rupert for 'so mean an action (I give it the easiest term)', and summarily ordered him 'to seek your subsistence (until it shall please God to determine of my condition) somewhere beyond seas, to which end I send you herewith a pass; and I pray God to make you sensible of your present condition and give you means to redeem what you have lost'.

The King clearly believed that Rupert had betrayed him. It is easy to understand his emotions. He knew that his nephew had given up hope of victory, and he also suspected him of acting in concert with his brother, the Elector. For in 1644 Charles Louis had returned to England, as furtively and as ambiguously as he had left it two years before. Unexpected and unannounced, he had turned up in London and had begun a series of intrigues with the parliamentary leaders. He had subscribed the Solemn League and Covenant, and had pledged his support for 'the people of God' against the popish, Jesuitical advisers of the King. The Parliament had rewarded him with a pension of £800 a year and allowed him to reside at Windsor Castle. At this time there was talk of deposing the King, and the Elector clearly thought that the Stuart line might be replaced on the throne – as it ultimately would be – by that of Wittelsbach, and hoped that, if he could not recover his Electorate, he might compensate himself with the crown of England, which he would be happy to wear on parliamentary terms. Seen against this background, Rupert's unexpected surrender of Bristol could be made to seem very sinister, and Charles I evidently suspected that his most trusted general had deserted to the would-be usurper of his throne. Such was exactly the position which would occur forty-four years later when Marlborough, the commander of the royal forces, treacherously deserted James II and supported his usurping nephew William of Orange. But this time it was not true. Whatever his faults or errors, Rupert's loyalty was unconditional. It never wavered for a moment, even in Charles's defeat, or after his death. In this he was the perfect cavalier.

Rupert refused to be condemned unheard. He forced his way through the enemy lines and confronted his uncle at Newark, the scene of his own great victory. He demanded to be tried by court martial – as Nathaniel Fiennes had been when he had lost Bristol for the Parliament. He obtained his wish. The court martial duly cleared him of any lack of courage or fidelity, but not of indiscretion. So his honour was saved. But he would never receive back his commission. After a second stormy interview, he was ultimately reconciled to the King, but it was too late to serve him in arms. The royal cause was now lost, the King a prisoner, his last citadel taken; and in July 1646 Rupert went abroad to take service in the French army till Charles I, or his son, should call for him again.

Although Rupert's services to the Stuart Crown did not cease in 1646 – he would serve it, with undimmed loyalty, for another thirty-six years – he would never again occupy the centre of the stage. His martial activities, from now on, were marginal and, in the main, indecisive. They were also on another element. From the land he turned to the sea.

The Second Civil War, in 1648, began with a naval revolt against the Parliament, and Rupert, now back in The Hague, took command of the royal fleet. He made his base at Kinsale in Ireland, and it was there that he learned of 'the bloody and inhumane murther of my late dread Uncle of ever renowned famous memory'. When the fleet of the English Commonwealth, under Blake, forced him to leave Kinsale, he moved to Lisbon, which the King of Portugal allowed him to use. Thence he preyed on English shipping and increased his fleet by converting his prizes into warships. One of them, the *Marmaduke*, he converted (until she broke away after a mutiny) into his flagship, renaming her *Revenge of Whitehall* – i.e. revenge for the murder of the King. When Blake pursued him into Iberian waters and forced the King of Portugal to close Lisbon to him, he crossed the Atlantic to support the royalists who still controlled the island of Barbados. Finally, he left the Caribbean and continued his operations off the coast of Africa. These activities kept him busy till 1652, when he joined Charles II's court at Cologne. They had no effect on the English Revolution, but they prepared Rupert for his post as admiral in the Dutch Wars of Charles II.

At sea, as on land, Rupert showed all his old qualities: vigorous administration, technical expertise, impetuous courage – and also his old weaknesses: lack of co-ordination, sacrifice of strategy to spectacular partial victory, and ruthlessness. His sea-war against the Parliament was little more than continuous piracy. It was also ineffective: while he preyed on English shipping from Kinsale, Cromwell was able to sail unopposed into Dublin, to begin the total conquest of Ireland. From Lisbon he preyed on Spanish as well as English ships and became a general nuisance: Blake was able to call on the King of Portugal to suppress Rupert and Maurice (for Maurice was inseparable from him on sea as on land) as mere pirates, 'that most nefarious tribe, the enemies of the world'. For the sake of such piracy, he delayed his expedition to the West Indies till it was too late; when he arrived, Barbados had submitted to the Commonwealth, and thenceforth he had to maintain his fleet among desert islands in the Caribbean or on deserted shores of Africa. In the end, when he arrived at the exiled and penniless court of Charles II, he was welcomed with overflowing affection, for it was thought that he had come laden with booty. The affection soon dried up when it became clear that his piracy had paid only for itself.

In his later sea battles against the Dutch it is much the same. In the Admiral of Charles II, we recognize the old cavalry leader of Charles I. He would co-operate as uneasily with Albemarle and Sandwich by sea as formerly with Wilmot and Newcastle by land. In the battle of Sole Bay in June 1664 he fought splendidly – 'Prince Rupert', wrote Clarendon, who had not always admired him, 'did wonders that day'. In the Four Days Fight off the Downs in June 1666, as at Edgehill twenty-four years before, his impetuous but unco-ordinated courage won a spectacular partial victory which was lost in the total result. He believed in 'the *mêlée*' as against 'formal' warfare, in individual initiative as against centrally con-trolled strategy. As he once said to Samuel Pepys, 'I can answer but for one ship, for it is not as in an army, where a man can command everything'. But even in an army, he had answered but for one arm, the horse. 'Individual initiative', 'the *mêlée*', had been his method there too. To the end he was an individualist, a law to himself, alone.

Indeed loneliness is the most obvious quality in his life. Though he felt, and inspired, absolute loyalty, he always seems to have had more enemies than friends. He was temperamentally unable to co-operate on equal terms, for he recognized no equals. When he returned to the English court in 1660 – the easy, affable court of Charles II – he was, says Pepys, 'welcome to nobody'. Always intolerant and quick tempered, misfortune had made him silent and morose. His personal life was lonely too. He never married – though he had at least two mistresses, of a lower social class, in later life, and left two illegitimate children. His relations with his brothers and sisters (always excepting Maurice, his colourless satellite) were not close, and with his elder brother, the Elector, positively hostile. How could he ever forgive that brother who had clung so long to the Parliament, gaping after his uncle's throne, and had earned general contempt by remaining in England even after the execution of the King? Only when the Parliament abolished the monarchy, and therewith his own hopes, had the Elector left England. By then the Treaty of Westphalia had restored to him half of his Electorate, and he could return from republican England to a desolate Palatinate and a ruined castle in Heidelberg.

In 1654, after his return to France from four years of piracy at sea, Rupert attempted to make peace with his elder brother, and to obtain his own rights in the Palatinate, as confirmed by the same treaty. So he paid a formal visit to Heidelberg, with a train of twenty-six persons, including three blackamoors picked up in his African expedition. However, this interested reconciliation did not last long: on his next visit, his brother refused him admittance to the castle, and he left swearing a solemn oath – which he would keep – never to set foot there again. At one time he nearly made war on his brother, offering himself as a general to the Catholic Bavarian branch of the Wittelsbach family – the same branch which had deprived his own father of his lands and his Electorate a generation before.

After the death of his brother Maurice, Rupert's closest friend was another German: William VI, Landgrave of Hesse Cassel, whom he met in 1655. Like Rupert, the Landgrave was interested in chemistry and art, and Rupert corresponded with him on both subjects, describing his inventions and experiments: his pumps and powder-flasks, his varnishes and drops and medical cures. For by now Rupert was involving himself more and more in chemical and artistic experiments. '*Il avait le génie fécond en expériences de mathématiques*', says Grammont, '*et quelque talent pour la chimie*'; and at the close of his life, as royal governor of Windsor Castle – the same post which his brother had held under the Parliament – he set up a laboratory, forge and workshop in the castle. The list of his library, which survives,[4] includes many books on chemistry, as on mathematics, architecture, fortification, history and the arts. As for his artistic interests, several of his own works survive. He had been taught to paint at The Hague by Gerard van Honthorst, who painted the fine portrait of him in the National Portrait Gallery in London, and on his first visit to England he had shown the royal physician, Sir Theodore de Mayerne (who was a great expert both in chemistry and in painting), how to paint in ink.[5] He also engraved in mezzotint. At one time he was credited with the invention of mezzotint, but this is disputed: the inventor, it is now generally agreed, was the Dutchman Ludwig van Siegen, and Prince Rupert learned it from him at the court of his friend the Landgrave of Hesse.[6] But in any case, Rupert improved the art – his print of *The Great Executioner*, after Ribera, is one of the finest of early mezzotints – and it was he who introduced it into England.

Like many fundamentally misanthropic men, Rupert loved animals. In this he took after his mother, who was said to prefer her menagerie to her children. In his early captivity at Linz he had enjoyed the company of 'a rare bitch called Puddle, which my Lord Arundel gave him', and of a tame hare which 'lay upon the Prince's bed' and would open his bedroom door with its mouth. The 'bitch called Puddle' may well have been a poodle whose name has been confused. Perhaps it was the mother of the white poodle, Boy, who accompanied Rupert on all his campaigns and became a royalist army mascot. Good Puritans reported, with pious horror, that the debauched cavalier soldiers drank profane healths to 'sergeant-major Boy', and suggested that the dog was Rupert's familiar, his accomplice in witchcraft. In the end Boy slipped his collar, followed his master into battle, and was killed at Marston Moor. His death inspired a vindictive Puritan elegy:

> Lament poor cavaliers, ay, howl and yelp
> For the great loss of your malignant whelp!
> He's dead, he's dead . . .

etc., etc. Throughout his life Rupert, like Charles II, was surrounded by dogs, but Boy was the most famous, and shared the most exciting part of his life.

A man of intense loyalties but few friends, proud, reserved and morose, uncompromising, unpolitical, undiplomatic, single-minded in his chosen craft of war, which he saw as a personal adventure under his own command – such was Prince Rupert of the Rhine. Though he lived long in England, he seems never to have understood it, or loved it, or its people: only his uncle, Charles I, and – to a lesser extent – his cousin Charles II who, on his restoration, would reward his services with offices and revenues. For the rest, he lived to himself, in a private world, with his blackamoors and his poodles, his books, his laboratory and his instruments of art. Perhaps his mother was not altogether wrong in 1637, when she likened him to a knight-errant. This 'vagabond German', as his English enemies would call him, with his undivided loyalty and his *'visage sec et dur, lors même qu'il le voulait radoucir'* (as Grammont described it), was surely not very different from that famous 'knight of the doleful countenance', Don Quixote; and his brother Maurice, the peasant prince who 'had never sacrificed to the graces' but followed him so faithfully, was his Sancho Panza.

11

The Continuity of the English Revolution

In our history, the twenty years from 1640 to 1660 are, at first sight, years of desperate, even meaningless change. It is difficult to keep pace with those crowded events or to see any continuity in them. At the time, men struggled from day to day and then sank under the tide. Even Oliver Cromwell, the one man who managed, with great agility, but spluttering all the time, to ride the waves, constantly lamented his inability to control them. When all was over, men looked back on the whole experience with disgust. It was a period of 'blood and confusion' from which no one had gained anything except the salutary but costly lesson of disillusion. How different from the Glorious Revolution of 1688: that straightforward aristocratic revolt against a King who had so considerately simplified the issues, and ensured a quick neat result, by seeking to convert the nation, like himself, to a hated religion!

It is the function of historians, happily separated from such distant events, to see past the details which it is also their function to reconstruct, and so to extract their significance. But do we in fact do any better than contemporaries? Are we not ourselves, unless we are the driest of antiquaries, parties in the struggle: royalists and parliamentarians, Presbyterians and Independents, Levellers and Anabaptists, successively hoisting and submerging each other in the same turbid stream? In the nineteenth century most historians were political historians, and they saw the revolution of the 1640s as a series of broken political experiments, convulsive stages in the struggle for parliamentary sovereignty. But then, by a happy coincidence, just about the time when the Labour party was stealing the lead from Whigs and Liberals, that interpretation lost favour. Social equality, not parliamentary power, then became the real purpose of the revolution, and the Levellers replaced the Parliament-men as its heroes in the pantheon of Progress. But not for long; for soon, in the tense 1930s, when the Communists claimed the leadership of 'progressive' forces, 'radical Puritanism' became the intellectual force of the revolution, Fifth Monarchists stirred again, and the voice of the Digger was heard in the land.

How recent those days are, and yet how remote they now seem! For now our history has been revised again. Toryism, a new kind of Toryism, has emerged: not the old patrician Toryism of Clarendon, or the revised consensus Toryism of Namier, but an uncompromising populist, rather aggressive variant of it – the Toryism of Peter Heylyn perhaps (who was a very learned man). Since 1980, we are told – I wonder why that date – all previous interpretations have been superseded: Lilburne, Winstanley and Hannah Trapnel have followed Pym, Hampden and Cromwell into the voracious historical dustbin, and the revolutions of 1641 and 1688 are alike dismissed as 'petulant outbursts', disconcerting, but not diverting, the smooth and stately operations of the English *ancien régime.*[1] To the Whigs, the consistent purpose of the revolution was political. To the socialists it was social. To the neo-Tories it had no purpose at all: in fact it hardly happened.

In the face of these changing fashions, and this convenient but chastening synchrony of historical with political philosophy, some humility is in order. For if we all date, who can claim exemption from a universal law? Indeed, a recent reviewer of some writing of mine has made the point rather sharply. I am 'anachronistic', out of date, he says, and the proof is in my very language: do I not, like the Gladstonian Liberal S. R. Gardiner and the modern Marxist Dr Hill, refer to 'the Puritan Revolution'?

Well, of course, I do. Hang it all, one has to call it something, and I am not sure what the approved term now is. Perhaps we have gone back to Clarendon's 'Rebellion' (I was once declared 'anachronistic' for using that term: one is driven from pillar to post), or to that anodyne lawyerly archaism 'the Interregnum' – which also has its difficulties. However, I am not much concerned with these semantic niceties. Words, says Hobbes, are wise men's counters but the money of fools. If you find me referring, in this lecture, to the Puritan Revolution of the 1640s or the Glorious Revolution of 1688,

I ask you to believe that these conventional tokens claim no purchasing power. I do not regard the one as inherently puritan or the other as particularly glorious, though I confess that I think Puritanism was not entirely absent from the former and that the latter was, on the whole, in its time, a good thing.

With these cautious and protective provisos, recognizing the danger as well as the advantage of afterknowledge, I turn to that most controversial era of our history and ask myself what continuity, if any, there was in those revolutions; and what most impresses me is the tenacity, over two or more generations, of those who, for all their differences and tergiversations (which are the normal incidents of politics, especially revolutionary politics), opposed and finally broke the Stuart monarchy. Men – especially conservative, traditionalist men of property – do not engage in revolution lightly, and persevere in it through changing times, merely through self-interest or inability to extricate themselves from the mess they have made. To suppose this is to trivialize both their aims and the risks that they took. For after all, the men who mounted the first great attack in 1640, and who never thought that they would find themselves challenging royal sovereignty, far less fighting a civil war with all its consequences, nevertheless, when faced with these consequences, refused to change course. In spite of everything, they persevered in a stubborn, costly and dangerous resistance, first to their legitimate King, then to all the alternative forms of government set up by the army which they had created to defeat him, until they, or their sons and successors, acquiesced, on conditions, in a system which seemed to secure their original aims; and when they found that it did not, and that the Crown, in spite of its previous experience, was resuming its former policy, then, in spite of their previous experience, and the reaction to it, and all their no doubt genuine disclaimers and promises, they did it again. This does not suggest mere 'petulance' or private interest or even mere 'high politics'. It argues a consistent purpose, or at least a consistent fear.

What then was this purpose, this fear? Obviously we must begin with the organizers of opposition: 'the great contrivers', as Clarendon called them, the men who, in the last years of the personal government of Charles I, at high risk and by intense machiavellian preparation, forced the King to face a Parliament in which they had ensured their own predominance and were ready to seize the initiative. The skill with which they had secured this advantage, and the energy, determination and speed with which they exploited it to incapacitate the royal ministers is astonishing. How different from the noisy, extemporized, bungled impeachment of the Duke of Buckingham fourteen years earlier! This time nothing seemed extemporized, all had been planned. Thorough met Thorough, head-on, and took it by surprise. The personal rule of Charles I was to be not merely replaced but destroyed; and the measures for its destruction quickly followed: radical, rationally planned and forcefully executed.

On this they would never weaken. Whatever else was negotiable in the long struggle which followed, this was not. Tory historians, beginning with Clarendon, have argued that the initial differences were relatively slight, that the King was merely seeking to repair the old Tudor system, and that it was only by a succession of 'untoward accidents' and misunderstandings that the original rift was widened into the chasm which ultimately engulfed them all. But this is surely to overlook an important factor which Clarendon found it convenient to play down: the absolute, unremitting hatred, or rather fear, of Strafford and Laud. It was a fear born of the conviction that the government which these two men in particular represented and sustained was, if not a 'tyranny', at least the first stage of a process leading to 'tyranny' – that is, not to tyranny in the classical or propagandist sense, but to a legally institutionalized authoritarian monarchy on the Continental model.

It has often been argued, and now it has become fashionable again to argue, that the struggle was over religion. But how are we to disentangle religion from politics in a revolution? Religion may form the outlook of an individual. It may serve as an ideological intoxicant for a crowd. But in high politics it is a variable. In 1640 the attack was on high Anglican episcopacy; in 1688 the high Anglican bishops were on the other side. The constant was 'absolutism' – whether of King or Protector, whether Anglican, Puritan or Catholic. Neither Anglicanism nor Puritanism nor Catholicism was objectionable *per se*: in spite of all the rhetoric, Roman Catholics suffered little persecution except when a scare was deliberately raised – and it was raised always for political purposes. They enjoyed a particularly comfortable time under the Cromwellian Protectorate. We may say that the issues were religious if we like, but what do we then mean by religion? Is it a difference of religion that troubles Ulster today? The charge of popery served to whip up popular hatred against Laud, but when he was brought to trial before his peers the accusation was political, of seeking to support absolutism. The peers who condemned him would be happy to settle for episcopacy; but it must be non-Laudian episcopacy, 'moderate episcopacy', severed from absolutism in the State.

Were their fears justified? Well, perhaps it is not for us to say. They were there; we were not. They had observed the signs, both at home and abroad. Particularly, perhaps, abroad, for there the consequences were spelt out, the comparison was clear. There they had seen how, in precisely those years, Richelieu had crushed the Protestant nobility of France and built up, at its expense, a royal absolutism sustained by a centralized national 'Gallican' Church. Sir Thomas Roe saw Laud as the Richelieu of England,[2] and Laud in 1639, took special steps to recommend to his clergy the example of Richelieu's 'patriarchate'.[3] His enemies could see his drift. 'Better a Pope at Rome than a Patriarch at Lambeth', they retorted: a Patriarch sustaining royal absolutism, as in France.

An authoritarian State on the Continental model, that was what the aristocratic leaders of opposition foresaw and feared. It might not exist yet, but they believed that it was coming, and must be stopped. The particular charges which they made in their campaign of resistance were pretexts: devices to enlist or retain necessary support. The charge of popery was mere propaganda, as many of them knew and admitted. The grievance of ship-money was trivial and tactical. When that stage was past, and its passions cooled, ship-money would be extolled, in a Cromwellian Parliament, as a model of equity.[4] Objections to the liturgy were equally tactical. Most of the parliamentary leaders used the Prayer Book in their chapels; some of them patronized 'Arminian' clergy,* and who cared about the susceptibilities of the noisy preachers supported, for their own purposes, by 'our brethren of Scotland'? All these charges

---

*The Earls of Pembroke, Leicester and Northumberland insisted on pressing for the inclusion of the 'Arminian' Henry Hammond in the Assembly of Divines (*Common Journals* II, p. 595; *Lords Journals* V, pp. 84, 95–7). Northumberland's father had greatly valued Richard Montagu, Augustine Lindsell, and others whom Montagu regarded as 'honest men' (e.g. Francis Burgoyne). See *The Correspondence of John Cosin DD* (Surtees Society 1868) I, pp. 68, 73n.

were pretexts, to be discarded after use. But opposition to a restoration of royal authority as exercised in the 1630s, or of an Anglican Church on the Laudian model, was constant. To prevent such restoration these men would not shrink from extreme measures: mendacious propaganda, judicial murder, mob violence, intimidation, vandalism, civil war. It is difficult to refute the statement of Lord Saye and Sele, 'Old Subtlety', the mastermind (as some thought – and think) behind the Parliament, that 'it was not for a Service Book or for abolishing episcopacy that this war was made' but because the King had set out 'to destroy the Parliament of England, that is the government of England, in the very root and foundation thereof'.[5] Or, as it was put in more general terms by James Harrington, the only reasons why the people of England blew up their King was 'that their Kings did not first blow them up'.[6]

But if this was the compelling fear which united the opponents of Charles I and caused them to mobilize against him those other forces which in the end submerged them, what was their positive policy? The men who went to such lengths to change the form and course of government cannot have been without plans for its future exercise. If we look beyond immediate tactics and immediate responses to changing circumstances, we should be able to discern something of those plans. I believe that we can do this, and that the plans were both political and social, but that the unexpected course of events caused them to diverge, with significant results in both political and social history.

　Publicly, from the start, the men who forced the King to call the Long Parliament demanded a return to the system of government, which they idealized, of Queen Elizabeth. Many of them were themselves old Elizabethans with family traditions of public service and honour in Tudor times, and they looked back with nostalgia to Elizabethan precedents in foreign policy, religion and war. The Stuart Kings, they believed, had betrayed the Elizabethan inheritance, particularly – if a date is to be chosen – since 1612, with the death first of Robert Cecil, Earl of Salisbury, the last political link with Elizabeth, and then of Prince Henry, the white hope of the future. It was then that the cult of Queen Elizabeth took off – the annual celebration of her accession day, the painting of her tomb, etc., all very distressing to King James; from that time that the lament for the good old days, now past, is heard from men like Camden, Sir Robert Cotton, and Fulke Greville. By the 1630s the nostalgia was undisguised and royalists had to take note of it. 'I am neither unmindful of nor ungrateful for the happy times of Queen Elizabeth', protested Clarendon, but still, the 1630s were just as happy, if not happier;[7] and Charles I, under pressure in 1641, would assure his critics that he had no other ambition than to restore all things to the state they were in in the time of Queen Elizabeth.

What did that mean? To the parliamentary leaders it meant government not of course by Parliament but by a Privy Council of which they would be members, managing co-operative Parliaments when necessary and exercising lay control over an established Protestant episcopal Church. However, in order to sustain that happy system, certain reforms would be necessary. Such reforms had been proposed by Salisbury, but they had not been carried out. In particular, there was Salisbury's plan to rationalize the finances of the Crown so as to remove the grievances of the gentry: a plan made possible by his combination of the two great financial offices of State as Lord Treasurer and Master of the Wards. Had he succeeded, the oppressive feudal dues – wardship, purveyance, forest fines – would have been abolished and the royal revenue settled on impositions on expanding trade. In fact he had failed, as Lionel Cranfield after him had failed, and the feudal dues, instead of being abolished, were exacted in the 1630s more efficiently than ever, so helping to finance the personal government of Charles I but at the expense (as Clarendon put it) of leaving 'all the rich families of England, of noblemen and gentlemen exceedingly incensed and even indevoted to the Crown'.[8]

From the surviving papers of the Earl of Bedford, the political leader of the reformers, it seems that he intended, once installed as Lord Treasurer, with his ally Lord Saye and Sele as Master of the Wards and his client John Pym, who was 'wholly devoted' to him, as Chancellor of the Exchequer, to resume the old policy of Salisbury: a policy in which Pym had been active as an official. In his commonplace books Bedford copied out and annotated some of Salisbury's plans; he set out a scheme for new impositions on trade, to be sanctioned by Parliament; there is a 'project upon the Wards', a 'scheme for raising money for the King by freeing lands from wardship'; he discussed ways and means of rationalizing Crown lands and royal forests with the great financier and customs farmer John Harrison; he planned a complete rationalization of the expenses of the Crown; and 'to my knowledge', says Clarendon, 'he had it in mind to endeavour the setting up the excise of England as the only natural means to advance the King's profit'.[9]

In the hopeful days before the execution of Strafford, all seemed set to ensure a quiet transition to a new government which would seek to carry out this programme. It was to be an inside job, fixed perhaps through the Queen. Outsiders were unaware of it. They could not understand why, after Strafford and Laud had been imprisoned and Lord Keeper Finch and Secretary Windebank had fled abroad, two of the most important ministers of the old regime, Juxon and Cottington, Lord Treasurer and Master of the Wards, one a Laudian bishop the other a 'popish Lord', were unmolested. Scotch Baillie hoped to see Cottington at least following Strafford on the route to Tower Hill.[10] Insiders knew better. They understood the mechanics of policy. The rhetoric against Laudian bishops and popish lords was tactical only. Juxon and Cottington had made a private treaty: their security was guaranteed in return for a quiet surrender of the offices essential to the new programme.

A restoration of aristocratic government, a Privy Council working with Parliament, a rationalization of Crown finance, abolition of feudal dues – such was the form of government which would have replaced the personal rule of Charles I – had Charles I been willing to renounce it. No doubt there were contradictions in it which time would have brought out. However Charles I was not willing and time was not granted. Within a few weeks, Strafford's death had made the King irreconcilable; Bedford was dead too; and a new train of events made all such projects, for the time, chimerical. Of Bedford's policy only fragments would be realized, not by royal government but by parliamentary ordinance, and for a very different purpose: the excise, introduced by Pym to finance war against the Crown, the abolition of the feudal dues in 1645.

But if the form of government was indefinitely postponed, what of its content, its policy? Here too the lineaments had been adumbrated in the 1630s. The same men who pressed for a return to Elizabethan forms of government called also for an (equally idealized) Elizabethan policy. It was an aggressive Protestant policy: England was once again to lead Protestant Europe, to intervene in the Thirty Years War, to strike Spain in the West Indies.* But it was also a policy of social reform: a policy which looked back to the 'Commonwealth men' of the mid-sixteenth century and their Elizabethan successors – reform of the Church, reform of the law, reform of education. Though Protestant ideals, these were not necessarily Puritan and they were certainly not revolutionary. Many of them had been advocated by Bacon, whose works were now widely published. It was only the polarization of the 1630s which wedded them to 'puritan', or at least anti-Laudian, ideas and even to millenarianism, which also could be discovered in – or read into – Bacon's works.†

In fact, for convenience, we can call the social programme of the reformers of 1640 Baconian as the political programme can be called Cecilian. How such ideas were sharpened and given detail and amalgamated within an ideological context by Protestant refugees from the Thirty Years War has been set out, with great erudition, by Mr Charles Webster.[11] Here I need only say that the amalgam, which included simplification of law, re-allocation of Church property, extension of popular education, reform of universities, diffusion of useful knowledge, Protestant union, became the property of those who challenged the very different social ideals of the Caroline court and the Laudian Church. Its patrons, in those years, define themselves: old Elizabethan churchmen like Archbishops Abbot and Ussher; opposition magnates like the Earls of Bedford and Warwick; parliamentary activists like Bedford's two clients John Pym and Oliver St John; advocates of intervention in Europe like Sir Thomas Roe and the whole interest of the exiled Palatine family; anti-Laudian bishops like Davenant and Morton; but not a single Laudian. Its grandest clerical patron was Laud's great enemy, the slippery Bishop Williams, now at last (it seemed) caught and lodged in the Tower. He had been Bacon's executor and,

*One of the 'extravagant particulars' referred by the House of Commons to its standing committee for the recess in the autumn of 1641 was the setting up of a West India Company on the Dutch model (*Commons Journals* II, p. 288; Clarendon, *History of the Rebellion* I, pp. 386–7). The Dutch Calvinist scholar Johannes de Laet, who was a governor of the Dutch West India Company, was called in to give advice but found the proposals very amateur. See his letters to Sir William Boswell in the Boswell MSS (British Library, Add. MS 6395 fos. 120, 126, 131), and cf. The Grand Remonstrance.

†Bacon's supposed millenarianism was found in his *Novum Organum* and *New Atlantis*, and was explicitly cited by the millenarian prolocutor of the Westminster Assembly in his opening address.

as Lord Keeper, his successor in office: a founder of libraries, a patron of scholars and scholarship, foreign Protestants, educationalists, 'puritan' ministers and 'all good causes', but, as one of his more cautious clerical protégés added, 'how far to trust him, I know not'.[12] On the whole, most people found it wise not to trust him too far.

When the Long Parliament met, Laud was sent to the Tower and Williams came out of it. Soon he was in command, regular in the House of Lords, constant on its committees,* chairman of two committees to reform the Church, eager to undo the work of his hated metropolitan, advising the King to let Strafford die, soon to be rewarded with the archbishopric of York. Meanwhile an assembly of clergy was nominated to meet and re-define doctrine and foreign advisers were summoned to be the architects of Baconian reform. When the great Czech reformer, philosopher and teacher J.A. Comenius, a professed admirer of Bacon, responded to the call and arrived in London, he was welcomed by the new intellectual establishment and invited to dinner by Bishop Williams. He too believed that a new government was round the corner, which would carry out all these reforms.

Of course it did not last. The Irish rebellion changed everything. By the end of the year, Archbishop Williams was back in the Tower. His committees had ceased to meet. The assembly of clergy had not begun. In Church and society, as in politics and government, projects of reform were suspended. Nothing had been achieved. Irish rebellion had started the slide into civil war.

History is often at the mercy of accident. It is often linked to individual lives. If the smallpox – that terrible new disease of the century – had carried off Strafford instead of Bedford, or had taken Charles I as it would afterwards, at an equally critical moment, take his son-in-law William II of Orange, who can say what would have happened? As it was, the moment was lost. But whereas the programme of political reform had foundered indefinitely, the ideal of social reform which had been envisaged in 1640, and for which the ground had been prepared, was not forgotten. In all the succeeding years of civil war and revolution, we see it regularly re-emerging as

---

*The *Lords Journals* show that Williams was one of the most active of peers in committee – far more than any other bishop.

the consistent aspiration of the parliamentary leaders. Inevitably, in those years of turmoil and frustration, circumstances changed, tempers worsened, resources shrank, and as each attempt at settlement failed, a fresh price had to be paid in order to satisfy creditors, preserve alliances and keep further revolution at bay. The Anglican liturgy would be sacrificed to the Scots, Church lands sold to pay the army, Ireland pawned to war financiers, 'images' abandoned to the mob. But in spite of this the basic aims remained constant: parliaments 'freely' elected; an established Protestant Church without coercive powers, Erastian and, to some extent, tolerant; reform of the law; reform of education. In proposed treaties with the King, in compositions with royalists, in regulations for the sale of Church lands, and in specific ordinances throughout the period of war, these aims are reasserted or implemented; and after 1649, under changing forms of government, the same course is pursued. For forms of government in themselves, it is repeatedly said, are indifferent: the King's head was not cut off because he was King, nor the Lords abolished because Lords, nor the Long Parliament expelled because a Parliament, but because they had 'betrayed their trust'. And that trust was social as well as political.

It was a zigzag course. Take reform of Parliament – freedom of election, equality of representation. Though the electoral patronage of great lords had been used to create the Long Parliament (how else were Pym and St John elected?), such patronage worked both ways, and from the beginning it was attacked. In challenged elections, the committee of privileges decided, almost always, in favour of the candidate supported by the wider franchise. In December 1641 Oliver Cromwell, as yet a mere backbencher, moved that letters of commendation be altogether disallowed. In the 'recruiter' elections of 1645 they were explicitly forbidden: even the Earl of Warwick, the great patron of Puritan gentry and Puritan ministers, was not permitted to recommend his son. At the same time projects of a new general franchise were being canvassed and hitherto unrepresented areas, like the county palatine of Durham, demanded representation. In 1653 these projects were realized. County Durham was represented in the Barebones Parliament, and the new Protectoral constitution provided for a completely new system. The franchise was lowered, the borough seats were slashed, the rotten boroughs disappeared, the independent county seats were multiplied. New industrial towns – Manchester, Leeds, Bradford – were separately represented. It was the first and only systematic reform of the electoral system until 1832.

Or take the reform of the Church. The national assembly elected in 1641 had not then met, but by the end of the war its surviving non-royalist members composed the Westminster Assembly. Bishop Williams's committees had been overtaken by events, but their proposals re-surfaced during the Civil War. In the sequestration of lands, provision was regularly made for the augmentation of livings. The corporation of Feoffees for Impropriations, an institution designed for that purpose in the 1630s, was freed in 1645 from the judgment given against it in Laudian times, and encouraged to resume its work. A series of ordinances provided for the better maintenance of ministers. Commissions for the propagation of the Gospel were set up. When the radical attack on tithes had been beaten off, the Protector put out his ordinance setting up Triers and Ejectors. The radicals screamed that this was worse than the old High Commission; but if we look at the lists, we find that this only means that the few radical agitators had been dropped from the old commissions. It was of this settlement that the 'Presbyterian' Baxter would afterwards write, 'I bless God who gave me, even under a usurper whom I opposed, such liberty and advantage to preach his Gospel with success which I cannot have under a King to whom I have sworn and performed true subjection and obedience',[13] and under it that many Anglican clergy – to the dismay of the Laudian stalwarts – were tempted to join the new non-episcopal establishment.*

Then there was reform of the law, long ago advocated by Bacon.[14] That cause too was damaged by radical advocacy. But the Long Parliament, the Rump, and the Cromwellians did not abandon it. The Rump passed laws in favour of poor debtors and for the Englishing of legal proceedings. Once the radical distractions were over, Cromwell returned to the problem. In his first nine months as Protector he produced the ordinance for the reform of Chancery: a measure which had been advocated by Bacon himself as head of that court. In his second Parliament, he demanded reform of the criminal law. It was a reform that would be made effective only in the nineteenth century by Sir Robert Peel. The legal reforms of the

---

*The correspondence of Henry Hammond and Gilbert Sheldon in British Library, Harleian MS 6942, shows the concern of the orthodox at these developments.

Rump, having been reversed in 1660, would similarly be made effective in the nineteenth century.

Finally there is reform of education. Bacon, who thought that in his time, 'of grammar schools there are too many',[15] had advocated a multiplication of elementary schools, the creation of local universities, and the reception of 'the new philosophy' in the universities. His disciples preached these doctrines in the 1630s and patronized the 'Baconian' educational reformers. Samuel Hartlib, John Dury, and, when he came to England in 1641, Comenius. In 1642, on the outbreak of civil war, Comenius left in despair, but Hartlib and Dury remained as the advocates of educational (and other) reform, pensioned by the Parliament. From 1646 onwards there was a continuous expansion of elementary schools.[16] At the same time Oxford and Cambridge were 'reformed' and the demands for local universities were repeated. Under the Protectorate both processes were continued. Oxford had become the centre of the new Baconian science, the nucleus of the future Royal Society. Cromwell, in his last year, realized the dream of the Long Parliament, the project of the Rump, and founded Durham College – its professors all drawn from the Hartlib circle.[17] His son Henry, as Lord Deputy in Ireland, planned a similar college in Dublin as a rival to Trinity College – as Durham College had been seen as a rival to Oxford and Cambridge. By then it was too late. Durham College died with its creator: the new college at Dublin was never born. Both were ultimately realized, in a different form, in the nineteenth century: Durham University in 1832, University College, Dublin, in 1851.

What for convenience we may call the Baconian reforms of 1641–59 were at best tentative and fragmentary. Always they were at the mercy of more immediate, more pressing problems: problems first of war, then of the defence and stabilization of the Republic. Some of them, perhaps, were unpractical. But we may still ask what would have happened if they had been given a chance: if the Cromwell dynasty had taken root and become, like the equally usurping Tudor dynasty, an established monarchy. This evidently was the hope of 'the Kingship party', the men who, from 1656, sought to demilitarize and legitimize the *de facto* monarchy of Cromwell and place it on the old civilian base, with two houses of Parliament and an established Erastian Church. If they had succeeded, Cromwell would, in many ways, have forestalled William of Orange. Indeed, in some ways he did forestall him: in the conquest of Ireland, union with Scotland, the return of England as a military power to Europe. In that case the decisive breach with the past would have been political; for how could such a new monarchy have resumed the broken thread of traditional politics with a legitimate Pretender waiting in the wings? To a dynasty founded in regicide, Carlism would have been a more serious threat than Jacobitism after 1688. However, the new monarchy would presumably have retained and continued some at least of the social reforms which were the substance and justification of the revolution. The political breach would have been matched by social continuity: a breach with the past, continuity with the future.

In fact, since the Protectorate failed, the formula was reversed. In 1660 the revolution was rejected and political continuity with the monarchical past was restored – restored with lawyerly precision, from the moment of its breakdown in 1641: that is, from and including the reforms of the aristocratic 'great contrivers' which Charles I had accepted on paper but not, perhaps, in his heart. By this strictly legal formula the whole period from 1641 to 1660 was defined as an aberration: the parliamentary bills to which the King had formally assented were accepted as valid; the parliamentary ordinances automatically lapsed. So the prerogative courts remained abolished, ship-money and forest-fines remained condemned, the Triennial Act remained in force. Even those parts of Bedford's programme which had not the benefit of statute were rescued from the ruined heap of ordinances and legitimized: the excise, the abolition of the feudal dues, were re-enacted by statute. So the aristocratic leaders who had lost control in the 1640s, who had stood aloof during the military usurpation, who had refused to countenance Cromwell's House of Lords, now returned to resume political life where they had left off, on their own terms.

However, they returned with a difference. In the 1630s they had patronized a social programme with a long pedigree behind it. Now they did not. That programme, which originally was neither Puritan nor revolutionary, but which had been polarized by the struggle of parties, was now fatally compromised by its association with political revolution: regicide, republic and military rule. A few piecemeal reforms of the 1650s were indeed adopted after 1660. County Durham, in 1663, recovered its parliamentary franchise (the old unreconstructed Laudian Bishop Cosin resisting to the end), though Manchester, Leeds and Bradford did not. Some law-proceedings were Englished. But systematic parliamentary reform (already jettisoned with its constitutional warrant, the Instrument of Government of the First Protectorate), like systematic law reform, redistribution of Church lands, reform of the universities, the foundation of new universities, had to wait till the nineteenth century. How appropriate that the tireless prophet and formulator of such reform, Samuel Hartlib, disappeared from the historical record after his death in 1662 until the mid-nineteenth century and that his massive archive should have lain hidden till our own time!*

History does not stop, and from the new base, established in 1660, politics continued as before. The chastening memory of the recent past, a new generation, a new climate of opinion, brought a change of attitude. But before long the old tensions returned. On one side was the renewed drive of the Crown towards a legally institutionalized 'absolutism', on a Continental model, supported by an established, hierarchical national Church; on the other the determination of the aristocracy, animated by half-feudal, half-Whiggish doctrines, to resist and contain that drive. Often, on this side as on that, the families are the same: the heirs or successors of Bedford, Essex, Leicester, Northumberland,† Argyll against the sons of Charles I with their new courtier nobility. Sometimes a single life, like that of Shaftesbury, links the two movements. The appeal, on both sides, was to the same arguments: Filmer, who had written during the first revolution, provided reasons against the second; Whigs drew on republican, John Locke on Leveller precursors.[18] The methods were the same too: conspiracy abroad (in Holland this time, not Scotland), alleged popish plots, unscrupulously exaggerated and exploited (though this time more plausibly), parliamentary and municipal manipulation.

Once again what must strike us is surely the tenacity of the opposition. They took the same risks and showed the same resolution in resistance, the penalties for which, after all, were not slight:

*Hartlib emerged from his long obscurity, thanks to the dedication to him of Milton's treatise *Of Education*, in D. Masson, *Life of John Milton* (1859–94). His papers, last recorded in 1667, were rediscovered in a solicitor's office in Chester in 1945.

†The Percy earldom of Northumberland was extinct in 1670, but the family tradition was very consciously maintained by the ninth Earl's grandson, the Whig martyr Algernon Sidney; see Jonathan Scott, *Algernon Sidney and the English Republic 1623–1677* (Cambridge 1988).

indeed they were now far greater than before. To forget that is to trivialize a great struggle. And now, as then, they drew strength from the European context within which that struggle was fought. Then it was the early Habsburg triumphs of the Thirty Years War and Richelieu's reduction of the Huguenot (and not only the Huguenot) nobility of France; now it was the conquests of Louis XIV and the mounting pressure leading to the wholesale expulsion of the Huguenots. And once again it was a damned close-run thing. Charles I, in 1640, had all the advantages of law and possession: what a huge effort had been necessary to mobilize resistance to him! Politically, James II's position was better: no Scottish war drained his strength and forced his hand. If only he had not madly tried to shift his ideological base from the national Anglican to the anti-national Roman Church, perhaps he would have succeeded where his father had failed. At least he would not have collapsed so quickly.

Perhaps then we would have had another civil war, in which the political and social radicalism which had been defeated in 1660 would have had a second chance. Certainly its advocates were prepared to take that chance: better prepared than fifty years earlier. For this time men were ideologically more alert: they thought in terms of revolution, even political assassination; then they had waited till events forced them to think. Now the men controlled the events. They were also served by luck: the luck that James II, who had an army, lost his nerve, while Charles I, who had no army, kept his. Hence the 'glory' of their revolution which, by its speedy success, confirmed the political achievements of 1641 and 1660 and stopped social revolt before it could begin. This time, control never left their hands; the coalition of 1688–9 did not split as that of 1640–1 had split – as it would have been split but for the popish folly. Since it held firm, the radical heirs of the Levellers found no point of entry into the fray; if William III was another Cromwell, he was a Cromwell with two great assets: a presumptive title and no radical past.

The classical Whig historians of the last century, looking back from a time of Liberal triumph, saw the revolutions of the seventeenth century as stages in the battle for parliamentary sovereignty and the supremacy in Parliament of the House of Commons. They had some contemporary warrants for such an interpretation, and certainly the process led, or pointed, in that direction. But it is a mistake to deduce intentions from results,* and very few wars end by achieving the purposes for which they were begun. Carlyle, who created the public image of Cromwell as a living historical figure, dramatized his hero's failure as the beginning of nearly two centuries of torpor and stagnation. Perhaps his grotesque personalization contains a glimmer of truth. Looking back from the revolutionary 1840s, he was aware, as few of his contemporaries were, of the social dimension of revolution, whether English or French. Perhaps these two interpretations, both now unfashionable, are not incompatible with each other, or even, if suitably qualified, with historical truth.

---

*As is elegantly shown in J. S. A. Adamson, 'Eminent Victorian, S. R. Gardiner and the Liberal Hero', *Historical Journal* (1990).

12

The Glorious Revolution of 1688

The Glorious Revolution of 1688–9 was made by an alliance of three parties, or at least of three political or ideological groups: Whigs, who provided its necessary motive force; Tories, who provided its necessary parliamentary majority; and radicals who sought to provide its philosophy. Without the Whigs it would never have got up the necessary steam; without the Tories it would never have been carried through; without the radicals it would have lacked a continuing philosophical appeal. These three parties, united against James II, preserved their uneasy unity so long as there was a possibility that he, or his male descendants, being Roman Catholic, might be restored to the throne. They continued to preserve it long afterwards on ritual occasions. And yet on each such occasion their internal differences would break through, adding a nice flavour of controversy – a sign of its continuing significance – to the interpretation of the Revolution.

After 1715, when the Revolution had been secured by the Hanoverian succession, the Whigs, being settled in power, imposed their own interpretation on it. It became their revolution, almost their monopoly. It was they who trumpeted its glory; and although, in their practice, they conveniently modified some of its original aims, in their public utterances they presented their ancestors as its true authors and themselves as its rightful heirs. Meanwhile they took over some old Tory practices and adapted – some would say exenterated – some old radical ideas. Having thus adjusted it to their taste, they placed it at the centre of English history and saw to it that it was properly celebrated. Every year it would be 'thankfully

remembered in the public services of the restored Church', and
societies with appropriate names – the London Revolution Society,
the Constitutional Society, the Society for the Defence of the Bill of
Rights – would meet to commemorate it with sermons and dinners.
The chosen day of commemoration was 4 November, the birthday of
the Great Deliverer, William of Orange, the eve of his landing in
Torbay. That was no doubt a very proper response to the annual
sermons and celebrations on 30 January, when Tories remembered
the royal martyr, Charles I.[1]

However, these ritual exercises could not altogether submerge the
original passions which had concurred in making the Revolution.
All through the years of the Whig Ascendancy the voice of 'real
Whigs' could be heard, often from the provinces – from Scotland,
Ireland, America – protesting that the original 'Revolution Principles' had been betrayed by the political establishment. Then, in
the 1770s, the American Revolution gave a new, disquieting power
to these voices; but there was even worse to come. How unfortunate
that the first centenary of our Glorious Revolution should be
followed so closely by a much less respectable, indeed in the end a
terrifying revolution in France! The consolidating fears which had
held the various parties together had, by now, dissolved. The
Jacobite threat had been extinguished in 1746; the Stuart dynasty,
reduced to one elderly bachelor in Rome, was all but extinct; and
without this necessary cement the old internal divisions could easily
be re-inflamed and exposed.[2]

They were exposed – and how splendidly they were exposed – in
the famous controversy between Edmund Burke and Tom Paine: a
controversy fired initially by the commemorative sermon of the Rev.
Richard Price to the London Revolution Society at Old Jewry on
4 November 1789. It was Price's sermon, ending in a dithyrambic
exaltation of the American and French Revolutions with their
rational new constitutions,[3] which provoked Burke to launch his
famous tirade, defending the ancient, organic, elastic constitution of
England, which the pragmatic Revolution of 1688 had preserved,
against the 'geometrical and arithmetical constitution' of the French
National Assembly; and it was Burke's tirade which, in its turn,
would provoke Paine to write his equally famous rejoinder, the
Rights of Man. In that controversy two revolutions faced each other,
the historical and the philosophical. Burke was able to prophesy the
capture of the French Revolution by a Bonaparte and to supply a

gospel of European resistance to French imperialism. To Paine all this was 'spouting rant', 'a chivalric rhapsody', a 'pantomime'. As for the Glorious Revolution of England, so cried up by Burke, that, he exclaimed, in another century would be altogether forgotten: 'mankind will then scarcely believe that a country calling itself free would send to Holland for a man and clothe him with power, on purpose to put themselves in fear of him, and give him almost a million sterling a year for leave to submit themselves and their posterity, like bondmen and bondwomen, for ever'.[4]

Paine would be proved wrong. A century later the Glorious Revolution was not forgotten. How could it be, when Macaulay had put it back so firmly and so magisterially in the centre of our history – and indeed had given it a new significance as the motor of economic progress? Just as Burke, in his *Reflexions on the French Revolution*, had trounced the 'geometrical' constitutions of the French assembly, so Macaulay, in his essays on Mill and Mackintosh, trounced the 'geometrical' constitutions offered by the English radicals and utilitarians of his day. Politics, he insisted, was an empirical, not a logical science, and the glory of the English Revolution lay not in its ideas but in its lack of ideas, its pragmatism. It was a compromise indeed, but a compromise which, because it rested on organic strength, could be the basis of later progress, whereas any more systematic and coherent revolution, running ahead of its time, would ultimately have foundered, like the French Revolution after it or the English Puritan Revolution before it, in the reaction it would have provoked.

Macaulay's interpretation was classical for the rest of the nineteenth century, and indeed beyond. So in 1888, when the second centenary came round, the Glorious Revolution still held its place in our public history, or mythology. It is true, the commemorations of that year were somewhat muted. Queen Victoria's Jubilee had just taken place and it would have been tactless to cap that royal apotheosis with too public a celebration of an event of which she did not like to hear. Perhaps also it was a bad time at which to boast of the victory of the Boyne. But Whigs were still around, active and powerful. A committee was formed to do justice to the occasion; a statue of the Great Deliverer was set up at Torquay, to commemorate his landing; and in Derbyshire the Duke of Devonshire, as Lord Lieutenant, organized a church service, a gigantic procession, formed or witnessed (we are told) by 40,000 persons, and a great banquet.[5] The Cavendish family had done very well out of the Revolution, and were very conscious of their ancestor's part in it, as the pompous Latin inscription in the new hall of Chatsworth showed.

Today Whig mythology, even the Whig history of Macaulay, is out of fashion: out with the Whig party, whose relics were destroyed by Lloyd George, out with the death of Macaulay's intellectual heir and continuator, G. M. Trevelyan. Into the vacuum thus created moved the heirs of the other parties. First the allies whom the Whigs, in their days of triumph, had eclipsed: the radicals, the Marxists, who now saw the Revolution as the triumph of the capitalist bourgeoisie, and the Tories, disciples of Sir Lewis Namier, who saw it as an episode in 'high politics', with no deep social or economic content. These, of course, were still 'Revolution Tories', the heirs of Halifax and Nottingham, of those Tories who had been parties to the consensus of 1688. Then, in 1980, when English Toryism cut itself free from consensus, there emerged another historical party, the self-styled 'revisionists', the new Jacobites, who rejected the Revolution altogether, dismissing it as a mere 'petulant outburst',[6] insignificant except as a bold bad act of treachery to an anointed King. With them we are back in 1688: Locke, Burke, Paine are outdated; Filmer and Brady live again.

Not regarding myself as an adherent of any of these parties, but aware of their flickering knives, I wish to start from the safety of undisputed ground. Whatever their differences, all the historians of the Revolution agree that, whether treacherous or glorious, superficial or profound, it was a decisive act. Men did not blunder into it unwillingly, as they had blundered into the Civil War of 1642. They took firm decisions, knowing full well the probable consequences. They knew that their action demanded great political skill, careful planning, strong nerves, and that it entailed enormous risks: risks of disaster through disunity, delay, mere ill luck. How could they not know? Their whole lives had been spent in the shadow of the civil wars, the Republic, the usurpation. All those disasters had stemmed from a well-prepared programme of reform which had gone wrong. And then there were their own fierce internal divisions, only a few years ago, during the struggle over the Exclusion Bill. Nevertheless, laying aside these divisions, they were now drawn together in a perilous adventure by a conviction of overwhelming imminent danger. In their secret invitation to William of Orange they urged him to come without delay, to save the liberties of England 'before it be too late'.

William did indeed come speedily. But he came for his own reasons, not theirs, to save the liberty not of England but of his own country, the Dutch Republic, which, he believed, was in similar peril, and whose peril meant much more to him than any threat to the liberties or privileges of Englishmen. He too took an enormous risk. He left the Netherlands exposed to foreign attack and sailed, with his invading force, the whole length of the Channel, past that strong English fleet on which James II had bestowed such care. There was no comforting precedent for success either in such an invasion or in such a rebellion. Monmouth had failed. Argyll had failed. He was attempting what Philip II of Spain had attempted exactly a hundred years ago; and Philip II had failed too. Even if his army, unlike that of Philip, should succeed in landing, what guarantee had he of success? James II's standing army – it was one of the charges against him – was very different from the militia of Elizabeth. And how could he rely on the cohesion of his English allies? He knew, only too well, the fickleness, the treachery of the English, including, especially, the English Whigs. He too was well aware that the last aristocratic rebellion against the Stuarts had led to a decade of 'blood and confusion'. Short of a quick and complete success (and how could he, or anyone, be sure of that?), he might well, as Louis XIV hoped, and indeed expected, be entangled for years in that incalculable island.

We know that in fact this did not happen. But who could have predicted the accidents which prevented it: the winds which bottled James's fleet in port and carried William's to land; the nervous collapse of James, who had always hitherto shown such resolution; his flight from London, which enabled his Whig and Tory opponents to sink their ideological differences in the imperatives of the hour? And if we cannot assume this, then we have to ask what force, what conviction, impelled the conspirators to take this fearful risk? Why did they believe – both the Englishmen for their reasons and the Dutchman for his – that they all stood on the razor's edge, that they must act decisively together, that it was now or never? I do not believe that the answer to such a question is to be sought in 'high politics', in personal 'petulance' or 'treachery', or in economic interest. Such slender motives cannot carry men through so huge a risk. The only force which can unite men of different, even opposite interests in desperate common action is overriding common fear. The men who acted together in 1688 believed that they were facing a fearful threat: that they were threatened – to use their own words – with 'popery and slavery'.

Popery and slavery are abstract terms. What, in 1688, did they mean? If we are to answer this question, we must, I believe, look at the Revolution, as they did, in a large context, in both time and space: in time, because men do not live in one moment only, their philosophy is formed by the accumulated experience of their lives and of those of their generation; in space, because England was not, except in a geographical sense, an island. It was, is, always has been, part of Europe.

Most of the Englishmen who took an active part in the Revolution of 1688 were middle-aged. Their minds had been formed in the middle years of the century: troubled years in Europe as in England. They were conscious that, throughout Europe, royal power was becoming 'absolute' – not absolute in a literal sense, not arbitrary, tyrannical (though they sometimes used these adjectives), but centralized, authoritarian, its authority buttressed by a subservient law. This process they ascribed not to the objective momentum of politics but to the machiavellian policy of power-hungry rulers. They also observed that those rulers who were most successful in building up and preserving such power were Roman Catholics: indeed, that Counter-Reformation Catholicism was a kind of magic ointment, warranted to preserve such a monarchy, once established, against disintegration or reform. This view was held by monarchs too. It was indeed a truism of the time.

One of those who held it was the Catholic Queen of Charles I, Henrietta Maria. She considered that her husband had made a great mistake in seeking to set an authoritarian monarchy on the fragile basis of the Anglican Church, which, not being a true Church, lacked the essential preservative ingredients and, in consequence, had both failed him and itself dissolved in ruin. Why could he not have learned the lesson that her father, Henri IV, had so usefully learned? These views she pressed, in her widowed exile in the 1650s, on her two sons, who found them plausible, and who both, after the Restoration, in their different ways – the one indolent and astute, the other a conscientious bigot – sought to realize them. The opportunity to do so came after 1667, with the fall of Clarendon, who had made the Restoration on the old Anglican base. It was then that Charles II, for the first time, felt that he was really King. Being really King, he could embark on a personal policy, and in his astute, indolent way, he did.

The crucial years were 1670–2. In 1670, by the secret Treaty of Dover, Charles II promised Louis XIV, against payment of £200,000 to be made at a convenient time, to declare himself a Roman Catholic and to import a French army to assist in the conversion of England. In 1672 he prepared the way by publishing, on his own authority, a 'Declaration of Indulgence', i.e. a general toleration for Dissenters from the established Church. Such a toleration would have many practical advantages. It would weaken the established Church and engage the support of the Protestant Dissenters. It would also remove the disabilities of the Roman Catholic Dissenters and enable them, with the help of royal patronage and the 6,000 French troops, to play their part in the great design.

This personal policy of 1670–2 had its foreign dimension, for by the same Treaty of Dover Charles II also committed himself to a war against the Netherlands in collusion with Louis XIV. Such a war would not necessarily be unpopular in England. If successful, it would be profitable to English mercantile interests, which would thus be won over, and their increased profits would in turn, through the increased revenue from customs, improve the finances, and therefore the independence, of the Crown. Meanwhile the French subsidy would help. So a coherent policy was devised: toleration of Dissent, Catholic as well as Protestant; mercantile support; royal affluence. This much was avowed. The other element in the plan, the catholicization of England, was secret.

This coherent personal policy of Charles II soon foundered, and it foundered first of all in the Netherlands. When the French armies invaded the Netherlands, a popular revolt swept the old 'appeasing' rulers aside and brought the young William of Orange to the power from which he had hitherto been carefully excluded. Thanks to him, the invasion was halted. In that great national crisis, when the Dutch Republic was nearly extinguished by French power, William's life acquired its purpose. The Republic, he resolved, must never again be exposed to such peril. European coalitions must be organized to protect its independence, not now from Spain – that danger was over – but from France. Above all, England must not fall into dependence on France. That combination could be fatal to the

Netherlands – as it would have been, had the policy of Louis XIV and Charles II succeeded. In fact, on this occasion, thanks to the Orangist *coup d'état* of 1672, it had not succeeded. The Netherlands had been saved. With the failure of the French attack, and the prolongation of the war, Charles II's coherent policy began to crumble. England pulled out of an expensive and indecisive war. The policy of religious toleration failed too. The Anglican Church, having so narrowly survived, would not so easily jettison its protective monopoly. Charles II found himself obliged to withdraw the Declaration of Indulgence. Finally, his secret treaty became less secret. Instead of granting toleration to Roman Catholics, he was forced to accept a Test Act excluding them from office, and his cabinet – half accomplices, half dupes – disintegrated in disarray. He did not declare himself a Catholic. He never would.

Thus already in 1670–2 we see, as it were, a dress-rehearsal for the drama of 1687–8. Some of the actors would change in the interim, but one, William of Orange, would not. Nor would the plot of the play. Weaving his coalitions from The Hague, William, himself half-English, and from 1677 married to the heiress presumptive to the English Crown, watched its progress. Charles II had indeed been forced to draw back from his great design; but was that design abandoned, or merely suspended? In particular, would it be revived if or when the King's Catholic brother should succeed him? In the later 1670s the men who would be called Whigs were convinced that it would, and so they mounted a determined attempt to exclude that brother from the succession, unscrupulously exploiting for their purpose the canard of the Popish Plot. That attempt ultimately failed, broken on the resistance of the 'Tories' who, whatever their apprehensions, clung to that lifeline of the monarchy, divine hereditary right. When it had failed, Charles II, exploiting its failure, resumed his old policy. But after those traumatic experiences he resumed it more cautiously. Whatever his own religious preferences, he would not now meddle with popery. That was too dangerous a subject for public policy: a powder-keg which had nearly blown him up. Instead, he would build up his power with the aid of the new Tory party which had proved its worth and strength in the days of crisis, and he would rest it, ideologically, at least for the time being, as his father had done, on the Anglican Church, now greatly strengthened, since Laudian times, by lay support. Half a loaf was better than no bread. Louis XIV would understand, and pay. Perhaps, when royal power had been secured, Charles II could use it to complete the policy which, in 1672, he had been forced to suspend.

Perhaps, perhaps not: or at least not yet. In his last years, when he had dismissed his last Parliament, broken the organization of his enemies, and remodelled the institutions which they had used against him, Charles II felt that he was as absolute a King as any of his predecessors. He had also learned an important lesson. Popery might be the preservative of monarchy, but only if carefully and correctly applied by a qualified physician. The dose had to be adjusted to the patient, for it could encounter dangerous allergies or cause dangerous side-effects. England, he knew, was a difficult patient. He also knew that his brother was not a careful physician. Might he, if he were put in charge, apply the medicine too rashly and risk disaster? In his last days, when he realized that his brother would in fact be put in charge, Charles II seems to have had doubts and to have contemplated a complete reversal of recent policy, or at least tactics. He would declare his own Protestant son, the Duke of Monmouth, legitimate and thus disinherit his Catholic brother. But death forestalled him. 'Ah, cruel Fate!' Monmouth wrote in his diary on hearing that his hopes, so recently raised, had been so suddenly dashed.[7] If the report was true, it means that Charles II believed that the time for an open Catholic policy had not yet come; that the monarchy needed to be still further strengthened on its present Anglican base before the perilous leap could be risked; that meanwhile it was essential to move slowly; and that his brother could not be trusted to go slow. If so, he was dead right.

Here we must leave historical detail and face two more general but important questions. First, could royal 'absolutism' have been built up, by a continuation of Charles II's methods, on a Protestant base? Second, what was the real significance of the violent, even paranoid hatred of popery in England: a hatred which had been unscrupulously mobilized in the attempt to exclude James from the succession in the 1670s and which, in the end, would bring him down?

To these questions, in this brief space, I can offer only tentative answers. To the first I would simply say that a radical transformation of government – a change from the co-operation of monarch and estates to institutionalized, centralized monarchical rule – was not impossible, even in England. It had happened in several countries in contemporary Europe, and history had shown that it could happen, and the process be completed, within a very short time. Power, once established, is a magnet and soon exercises its attractive force. How easily the princes of Italy had taken over the old communes! Particular interests soon adjust themselves to new realities. Merchants are not necessarily hostile to central power, which is also patronage, especially in a mercantilist age. By 1685, in England, many old Whigs had made their peace with the government; those who were obstinate were in exile, and had resorted – a sure sign of despair – to attempted assassination. If Charles II had lived longer, or if James II had continued his methods, as indeed he did until 1687, it is difficult to argue that those policies would necessarily have failed. The crux was finance; but that problem now seemed soluble: increase of trade and of customs on trade could meet foreseeable peacetime needs. War indeed made a difference: Charles I might have succeeded but for the cost of the Scottish war, so skilfully forced upon him; but Charles II had secured himself against that danger. No latterday Pym or Hampden was capable of mobilizing an invasion, or a Parliament, against him. Shaftesbury had risked all and had failed. Even when James II had succeeded to the throne, but while he was still continuing his brother's methods, his Parliament supported him and the invasions mounted by his exiled enemies were easily repelled. We do an injustice to the men of 1688, and indeed to their precursors, if we suggest that the threat which faced them was unreal, either then or half a century before.

That the threat was independent of religion, that slavery could have been imposed without popery – indeed could even have been introduced more smoothly without it, although popery might be added when it was secure, as its final fixative – was recognized by contemporaries. In 1694, Robert Molesworth, who had been ambassador in Denmark, published *An Account of Denmark*, in which he described how, in 1660, that kingdom had 'in four days' time been changed from an estate little different from aristocracy to as absolute a monarchy as any is at present in the world'; and he argued that Charles II, in his last years, had almost achieved this in England, and that James II could have achieved it, 'had he left the business of religion untouched'.[8] For it was the change of policy in 1687, the precipitate attempt to substitute a Roman Catholic for an Anglican base, which, by alienating the Tory party and the established Church, had begun the ruin of the Stuart monarchy.

So we come to the second general question: what was the real significance of the paranoid anti-popery which the opponents of James II were able to mobilize against him? The answer, I believe, lies at two levels, one rational, the other irrational. On a rational level, the politicians who opposed the Stuart kings were convinced that Roman Catholicism, though allowable as a personal religion, was, in politics, inseparable from the absolutism which they feared. Therefore it could be tolerated only in private. This view was held by most literate Protestant Englishmen. Milton, who advocated universal toleration of all forms of Christianity, excepted Roman Catholics – although he had good personal relations with his own Catholic kinsmen – on the ground that Catholicism was not Christian at all.[9] Archbishop Ussher, Oliver Cromwell, Andrew Marvell were equally ambivalent. John Locke, who wrote explicitly in favour of the natural right to toleration of all religions, equally explicitly denied that right to Catholics, on the same grounds. For this rational and limited political anti-popery of the educated classes there was ample justification in contemporary Europe. It did not provide a reason for persecuting papists, only for excluding them from political activity.

The irrational anti-popery of the common people was quite different. It was, I suggest, a form of popular hysteria comparable with the persecution of supposed witches at that time or with anti-semitism at all times. Like them, it had a rationalized justification, but it was essentially irrational, an expression of popular psychology, of a *grande peur*. Moreover, having once been formulated and used for public purposes, it had acquired a momentum of its own: a dangerous momentum which was both increased and prolonged by periodic deliberate exploitation: for in certain circumstances it was a means, perhaps the only means, of mobilizing popular violence, if that were judged necessary, against a government which had a monopoly of legitimate, organized force. In 1641 it had been exploited against Charles I and Archbishop Laud. Since both men were firm Anglicans, it was then rationally indefensible, but it was used unscrupulously and defended cynically as a political necessity. Its use during the Exclusion crisis, in the agitation against the 'Popish Plot', was rationally more defensible in that there were some shreds of evidence for such a plot and the heir to the throne who was to be excluded was an avowed Catholic. In 1688 it needed no justification.[10]

Of course the high Tories, the Jacobites, the non-jurors denied this. They persuaded themselves that James II, when he offered toleration to Roman Catholics, intended no more than he said: that he was simply seeking equal rights for all his subjects. He would be a Catholic King of a Protestant country, just as the Elector of Brandenburg was a Calvinist ruler of a Lutheran country. No doubt this would bring some incidental advantage to his fellow-Catholics, but it would not alter the constitution of Church or State. This argument was of course necessary to Protestant Jacobites, as the only solution of the dilemma in which they found themselves: how else could they defend their double loyalty, to Church and King? It is amusing to hear it advanced today by their modern successors, who thus find themselves commending, in James II, a design to dismantle 'the confessional State' and replace it by 'a plural society' – precisely the policy which they condemn so severely in the Liberals of the 1820s and 1830s, when Catholicism was really ceasing to be committed to a particular political form. But let that pass. The more politically minded Tories of the time did not entertain such views. Forced to decide whether to be consistent with their own past actions – their resolute and successful championship of James's inalienable right to succeed – or to face the unmistakeable implications of his present policy, their minds were marvellously concentrated. They swallowed their pride and, with some face-saving formulae, joined their former adversaries and kicked him out.

Indeed, it was their kick which was decisive. The point is important and needs to be emphasized. Without Tory support in the country and in Parliament, neither the Revolution nor the subsequent settlement would have been achieved, at least in its actual form, and some respect is due to the men who were prepared, in effect, to admit that their hard-fought battle, so fresh in memory, had been a mistake and their hard-won victory vain, for their opponents had been right. It cannot have been an easy admission. Naturally enough, they did what they could to save their faces, and their former adversaries helped them to do so. Thus the abuses of power which were cited to justify William's invasion, and which would be set out in the Bill of Rights, did not include those practised in the last years of Charles II, when the victorious Tories had been in power. The whole burden of guilt was laid upon James II. This concentration of blame narrowed the context and abridged the pedigree of the Revolution. Historically it was inexact. But it served its immediate practical purpose: it enabled the Tories to make common front with the Whigs rather than be caught in the dilemma, or resort to the weak arguments, of the non-jurors and Protestant Jacobites.

It is difficult to argue that they were wrong. William Penn, the Quaker, like some other Dissenters, swallowed the bait of the Declaration of Indulgence. From an opponent of Charles II he became an election agent of James II, an active supporter of his policies. He evidently believed that, thanks to his personal influence with the King, the Quakers would be safe, and he preferred the promise of Catholic protection to the reality of Anglican persecution. But what if that personal link were snapped, as ultimately it must be? Could Quakers, or their Continental equivalents – Mennonites, Bohemian Brethren, Moravians – be found flourishing under any Catholic monarchy? And what of the Huguenots of France, granted legal toleration in 1598 and now, after their legal immunities had been withdrawn, their aristocratic protectors seduced by the court, and their numbers diminished by constant harassment, summarily ordered to conform or to be expelled from their country? This example of the King of France was quickly followed by his satellite, the Duke of Savoy. No doubt, once Roman Catholicism had become firmly entrenched in the English court, and the assets and the patronage of the established Church had been taken over (for that, clearly, was the end of the process of which the attack on the universities was the beginning), the same pressure and the same seduction would have been applied in England; and perhaps, in the end, the same force. So long as James II had no male heir, that argument could be countered, for the heir presumptive was his Protestant daughter, the wife of William of Orange himself. But the birth of the Prince of Wales changed all that. No wonder his adversaries decided that the time had come for desperate measures: to play the anti-popish card. The myth of the warming-pan was the new version of the Popish Plot: factually false, unscrupulously used, but, in a desperate situation, judged to be politically necessary.

The warning example of the French Huguenots must have been particularly obvious to the subjects of James II. Once again, it is necessary to recall the context, in time and space, in which the men of 1688 had lived, the memories they had inherited. The fortunes of the French Huguenots had been closely followed in England ever since the reign of Elizabeth. English governments, until the personal rule of Charles I, had supported successive Huguenot enterprises,

even *prises d'armes*, in France. A great Huguenot leader, the duc de
Rohan, had been godfather to Charles I, and English aristocrats –
an Earl of Southampton, an Earl of Derby – had married into great
Huguenot houses. In those days the Huguenots had still been a
power in France. But in the 1620s this had changed. As the French
monarchy became more 'absolute', the Huguenot nobility had been
reduced to impotence. Then, gradually but steadily, the pressure
had been increased. The process had been visible, obvious to all who
looked. Finally, in 1685, the very year in which James II had
succeeded to the British throne, it reached its predictable culmination.* As the exiled Huguenots, including some unconvertible
noblemen, sought refuge in England, English Protestant noblemen
could hardly fail to draw the parallel and to foresee the fate of their
descendants under the 'absolute' rule of a Catholic house of Stuart.
The process which had now ended in France was about to begin in
England.

The same process could be observed, even more closely, from the
Netherlands. The original Revolt of the Netherlands had been
sustained, on the spot, by émigré French Huguenots. The daughters
of the house of Orange were married to great Huguenot leaders.
Huguenot noblemen and gentry served as officers in the army of the
Prince of Orange. After 1685 their numbers were greatly increased.
Holland was then, in the phrase of Pierre Bayle, the great Ark of the
refugees. The Prince welcomed them, for he needed their help. The
1680s, the years of apparent creeping absolutism in England, were
also the years when Louis XIV's power was being extended most
aggressively: the years of the Chambres de Réunion, the invasions
and annexations and interventions in Flanders and Germany:
Strasbourg, Luxembourg, Cologne, the Palatinate. With the King
of England apparently a paid satellite of France, the situation, seen
from the Netherlands, was ominously reminiscent of that of 1672.
Once again William was seeking to organize resistance, to persuade
the States General and the city of Amsterdam of the danger. The
arrival of the Huguenot refugees turned the scale. It silenced the
voice of dissent, and strengthened the Orangist party throughout

---

*Already in 1665 Gui Patin could report from Paris, 'On dit que pour miner les
huguenots, le roi veut supprimer les chambres de l'édit et abolir l'édit de Nantes. Ils ne sont plus en
état de se défendre comme jadis: ils n'ont plus de prince du sang de leur parti, ni de ville d'otage, ni
de Rochelle, ni de secours d'Espagne, ni d'Angleterre.' Lettres de Gui Patin, ed. J. H. Reveillé-
Parise (1846), III, p. 516.

the country. On their side, the Huguenots hailed William as their Joshua, the man chosen by God to restore their fortunes.'' So the army which he would bring to England and which would fight in Ireland was swollen with Huguenot volunteers. Louis XIV did nothing to hinder the expedition to England. He reckoned that his most formidable enemy was being removed from Europe. Instead, in a few years, he would become its arbiter.

Thus all the evidence, available then or now, in England or in Holland, political or personal, historical or analogical, suggests that James II's personal professions of moderation could not and should not have been taken literally. Even if he himself had sought to abide by them, the nature of political Catholicism would have made it impossible for him to do so; and his Catholic successors would anyway not have been bound by them. And what then would have been the consequences? In Europe, of course, they would have been immense. Louis XIV, guaranteed against English intervention, would have had a good chance to divide and destroy any coalition against him. Whether he would have succeeded, we cannot say: we cannot press history so hard; it is enough to state the probability.

But what of the consequences in England? The astonishing speed and completeness of the Revolution, which constituted part of its 'glory', ensured that, socially, its effects were limited. The great risk, once William had safely landed and thus survived the first hazard, was of civil war. If James II had not lost his nerve and fled, if he had stood firm until the cracks in the alliance had opened up, who can say that civil war would not have broken out? That, after all, was what had happened in the reign of his father, in the great crisis of 1641–2 which was ever present in men's minds. At that time future royalists, like Hyde and Falkland, and future parliamentarians, like Pym and Hampden, had worked together, just as Whigs and Tories would do in 1688–9: it was Charles I's refusal to yield, his conviction that God was on his side and that there were men who would fight his battles – if not in England, then in Scotland and Ireland – which broke up the parliamentary coalition and led to the long struggle for sovereignty. In the course of that struggle, which no one had wanted, radical ideas and radical social forces had emerged. In 1688–9 all these possibilities existed; but the collapse of James II and the presence of an agreed heir enabled a still undivided political nation to settle for a quick compromise. The compromise, in the circumstances, was bound to be conservative. Civil war was confined to Ireland and Scotland, and there isolated. The radicals, the heirs of the Levellers, the Republicans, the Commonwealthmen of the 1640s and 1650s, were given no chance to emerge. The Revolution was therefore, in their eyes, incomplete.

One of those who discovered this was the old republican, Edmund Ludlow. For twenty-nine years he had lived in exile in Switzerland, a centre of conspiracy against the hated house of Stuart. In 1689 he boldly returned to London, in order, as he said, to strengthen the hands of the English Gideon. At the request of the House of Commons the English Gideon promptly ordered his arrest on the old charge of high treason, and he hurried back to Switzerland. Another was John Locke, whom now, with Richard Ashcraft, we must see as a radical. In 1690 Locke would publish his *Two Treatises of Government* (originally written against the rule of Charles II), in order, as he said, 'to establish the throne of our great restorer, our present King William'. That was very sound Whig language: William was presented as the restorer of the ancient English 'mixed' constitution. But privately Locke deplored the compromises of 1689. Why, he asked, did a revolutionary convention concern itself with 'small matters', as if it were an ordinary, traditional Parliament, when it had a priceless but brief opportunity to mend 'the great frame of the government' and set up a new and lasting constitution 'for the security of civil rights and the liberty and property of all the subjects of the nation'? Like the Levellers forty years before, Locke wished not to amend the government but to 'melt it down and make all new'.[12] Though he would be captured by the eighteenth-century Whigs and made into their philosopher, he looks forward not to Burke and Macaulay but to Tom Paine and the nineteenth-century utilitarians. Whether his new model of government, if established, would have lasted is another matter, and open to question.

The political system – if it can be so called – established by the Revolution did last. That indeed is its great merit. Some of it is with us still. Since it was essentially defensive, the product of determined resistance to innovation, it too was necessarily conservative. The framers of the Bill of Rights insisted that they were defending an ancient constitution: the institution of Parliament, the regularity of parliaments, the parliamentary control of finance, the independence of the judges, the rights of the established national Church. But even a conservative revolution can incidentally liberate new forces, and many of the consequences of the Revolution of 1688 were incidental, not intended. For every revolution must be defended against counter-revolution. The Revolution of 1688 was quickly over in England, but its defence involved it, as it had involved the more protracted and bloody revolution of the 1640s, in war in Scotland and Ireland, ending in an oppressive reconquest of Ireland and a parliamentary union with Scotland: here, as in other respects, the completion of the Cromwellian settlement, at less cost, and more durably, but without its radical social content. It also led to a foreign war, which in turn entailed a financial revolution: the founding of the Bank of England, the creation of the National Debt. At the same time it brought continued discrimination against Roman Catholic and indeed – in theory at least – Protestant Dissenters for another 150 years. William III, who has become the tribal hero of the most intolerant sectarianism in the British Isles, would have relieved both Catholics and Protestants, but was prevented. The disastrous attempt of James II to impose both 'popery and slavery' on his country, and even, after his failure, to set up a separate kingdom of Ireland under French protection, rebounded terribly on those whom he had claimed to serve. But what, we must ask, would have been the consequences of his victory: if William's fleet had been destroyed at sea or if his enterprise had foundered in civil war? At once we are lost in vain speculation. One thing we can perhaps venture to say. If James had succeeded in his plans, the English Parliament would not have survived in a recognizably continuous form and thus a vital organ of peaceful change would have been reduced to impotence. Whatever modifications we may make to the classical Whig interpretation, in the end it is difficult to contest Macaulay's thesis, that the English Revolution of 1688 saved England from a different kind of revolution a century later.

13

Our First Whig Historian:
Paul de Rapin-Thoyras

Anyone who studies the historical writing of the eighteenth century soon becomes aware of the great contribution – great at least in bulk – of émigré Huguenot scholars, the victims of the Revocation of the Edict of Nantes in 1685. Driven out of France, dissidents from the established culture of the *grand siècle*, and yet, at the same time, self-consciously French, refusing – at least for so long as they might hope to return with dignity to France – to be assimilated into the society of their host-countries, they became the representatives of an alternative France, the intermediaries between the two cultures of Europe: the firm classical–Catholic–Cartesian synthesis of the France of Louis XIV and the critical diversity of Protestant Europe.[1]

If we ask what was the general intellectual characteristic of the Huguenot diaspora, the answer, I think, must be that it was essentially critical, not constructive. The Huguenots had always rejected the Catholic synthesis, the grand scheme of history set out by the greatest of their persecutors, Bishop Bossuet; but in exile they also escaped from their own. As long as they had been a depressed minority in France, they had been dominated by their clergy, preaching doctrines of self-defence: fundamentalist, prophetic, apocalyptic – the expression of a siege-mentality. But in exile the situation changed. Some of their pastors, like Pierre Jurieu, 'the Grand Inquisitor of the *Refuge*', tried hard, by anathemas and persecution, to keep their flocks faithful to the old doctrines and discipline; but that was now difficult. In the new open pastures to which they had escaped, many of the sheep – and some of the pastors themselves – ran riot. They faced the necessity, or discovered the luxury, of doubt.

The two most famous of the émigrés, Pierre Bayle and Jean Leclerc,* adversaries in almost everything else, agreed in one thing: that there was no certainty, no possible system, in history. Of Bayle's great *Dictionnaire Historique et Critique*, 'there is not a single page', says Voltaire, 'which does not lead the reader to doubt, and often to disbelief',[2] but he would also add that it was 'the first work of this kind from which one can learn to think';[3] and Leclerc, attempting to formulate the rules of history, concluded that it was so difficult to arrive at historical truth, which was nevertheless so important, that very few persons should be allowed to write it: for to get it wrong could be fatal. On this his fellow Huguenot Henri Basnage de Beauval commented that 'his reflexions tend to fortify historical Pyrrhonism'.[4]

'Historical Pyrrhonism', scepticism, distrust of all great schemes of history – that was the chief contribution of the Huguenots to the study of history in the half-century after the Revocation. Because they had not been assimilated into French culture, and because they refused, for that time, to be assimilated into the culture of their host-countries, they became a distinct, coherent 'third force' dissolving the certainties of the previous century. Thereby they gave a new character to historical philosophy: 'Pyrrhonism' was to be its chief characteristic throughout that period – a period in which the great systems of the past were dismantled in preparation for the new synthesis of the Enlightenment.

However, the work of the Huguenot historians was not entirely destructive. They responded to their own challenge. For if the historical systems of the past were inadmissible, and had to be disintegrated, how was the historian to begin again? Obviously he must go back to first principles, re-examine the sources, collect and test the facts, eliminate the conjectures and prejudices, and so provide a new basis on which, perhaps, a more accurate system could afterwards be built. So the Huguenot scholars took to the

---

*At the conference, Madame Elisabeth Labrousse objected to my inclusion of Leclerc among the Huguenots on the ground that he was an Arminian who left Calvinist Geneva because of its intolerance. However, exactly the same could be said of Isaac Casaubon a century before; and we generally regard him as a Huguenot. The Huguenot diaspora, for me, consists of all those French Protestants who were forced, or preferred, to live outside France.

study of detailed, factual, objective history with the same scrupulous technical exactitude which their more practical co-religionists devoted to jewellery, enamelling, clock-making, and other delicate mechanical crafts. Serious-minded, industrious collectors and compilers, pedestrian writers, critical not constructive, judicious not elegant or vivacious, they compiled great 'lexicons', edited huge collections of documents. Their enemies complained that thereby they smothered all thought and drove men, through despair, even deeper into Pyrrhonism. But stronger minds knew how to use their labours, and today we can still detect their relics pickled in the footnotes of Gibbon or half-dissolved in the easily flowing prose of Voltaire.

I have spoken of the Huguenot historians as a coherent 'third force' in the intellectual world. Their cohesion came from the French language, which they insisted on using, and from their ubiquitous international journalism. Bayle's *Nouvelles de la République des Lettres*, Leclerc's *Bibliothèque Universelle et Historique* with its successors – both of them the single-handed work of their editors – were but the most famous of a whole series of international periodicals which disseminated the critical scholarship of the Huguenot diaspora throughout Europe. There was also Henri Basnage de Beauval's *Histoire des Ouvrages des Savants* and the *Journal Littéraire de la Haye*. There was the *Bibliothèque Germanique* through which the Huguenot circle in Berlin – a very active circle, thanks to the patronage of Queen Sophia Charlotte and then of Frederick the Great – sought to make the literature of Northern Europe (and of course their own works) known throughout Europe. There was the *Bibliothèque Anglaise* which did the same for English literature, and its successor the *Journal Britannique* of Matthew Maty, the friend, incidentally, of the young Gibbon, whose own short-lived periodical, *Mémoires Littéraires de la Grande Bretagne*, is a late entrant in the competition. Nearly all these periodicals were published in Holland – in Rotterdam, Amsterdam or The Hague. Holland remained to the end their intellectual and publishing centre, the place where, since the last years of Charles II, English Whigs had taken refuge and English ideas were translated into French by exiled Huguenots and thus supplied to the European Republic of Letters.

This conference is concerned with the Huguenots and Great Britain, and having thus prepared the ground, I shall devote the rest of this lecture to the Huguenot writer who did most to explain

English history and the English political system to Europe. In so doing, he had a considerable influence both in England and in Europe; for in England he provided the first systematic 'Whig interpretation' of its history and in France he gave ideas to Montesquieu and Voltaire. I refer to Paul de Rapin de Thoyras, generally known as Rapin-Thoyras, or simply as Rapin: a writer described by Erich Haase as the only Huguenot historian 'who knew how to combine the objective collection of facts with a clear opinion of his own'.[5]

Paul Rapin came of a Savoyard family which, having been converted to Protestantism, had emigrated to France in the reign of François I and had settled in Huguenot Languedoc.[6] His father, Jacques Rapin, sieur de Thoyras, was a lawyer at Castres and later at Toulouse; his mother, Jeanne de Pelisson, also came of a Huguenot legal family and was the sister of that Paul Pelisson who, having been converted to Catholicism and put in charge of the notorious *caisse de conversions*, played a significant, not to say sinister, part in the conversion of his co-religionists before the Revocation of the Edict. Paul Rapin studied at the Huguenot academy of Puylaurens, where Pierre Bayle had been before him, and then at the more liberal academy of Saumur, where Leclerc had studied. He was destined for the law, but in 1679 the suppression of the *Chambres de l'Edit*, in which his father pleaded, closed that prospect, and he was pressed by his now famous uncle to change his religion in order to open another. This he did not do, and in 1686, a year after the Revocation, his father being now dead, he left France and, with his younger brother Salomon, went to England.

Rapin had personal reasons to choose England; but once there, he soon found that the England of James II was not much more comfortable, for an obstinate Huguenot, than the France of Louis XIV. There too the *convertisseurs* were now at work, and Rapin discovered that he had escaped the attentions of his uncle Pelisson only to incur those of the French ambassador Paul Barillon and his chaplain the abbé de Denbeck. He therefore moved on to the Netherlands where his cousin, Daniel de Rapin, commanded a company of French – that is, Huguenot – volunteers. Rapin enlisted in this company, and it was as an officer of the Prince of Orange that he found himself returning to England to take part in the great adventure of 1688.

Rapin landed with William at Torbay, served him in England

throughout the revolution there, and then accompanied him on his expedition to reconquer Ireland. There he fought in the battle of the Boyne, was wounded in the assault on Limerick, and took part in the capture of the supposedly impregnable citadel of Athlone. Then he was stationed at Kinsale. William's governor of Kinsale was James Waller, a son of the regicide Sir Hardress Waller, and it was he (as Rapin would afterwards write) who first turned his thoughts towards the historical significance of these events in English as well as in European history. It was in Kinsale that he first entertained the idea of studying the history of this mysterious island, which had suddenly become so important, and explaining it, as only a Huguenot was qualified to do, to the inquisitive but baffled observers in Europe.

They had good reason to be baffled by recent events. In 1686, when Rapin had first visited England, Louis XIV was at the height of his power, the master, it seemed of Europe, and James II, having defeated all attempts to prevent his succession or challenge his authority, seemed securely established as his willing puppet. When Rapin moved on to Holland, that impression could only be confirmed. Holland – '*la grande Arche des fugitifs*' as Bayle called it – had welcomed not only Huguenots driven from France but also English Whig statesmen and thinkers who, since 1680, had found it prudent to escape from England. Among them had been famous names – Shaftesbury, Sidney, Burnet, Locke. By 1688 all such refugees, French and English alike, pinned their hopes on the half-English *stadhouder* William of Orange. To the Huguenots, he was the only leader of European resistance to their oppressor, Louis XIV, the only man who might secure their return to France. To the English Whigs he was the only practical alternative to James II as King of England. But how chimerical these hopes must have seemed in face of such securely established power! Then suddenly, less than two years later, the Revolution in England changed everything. By 1691 that Revolution was complete. William of Orange was effective ruler of all three kingdoms, ready to throw their resources into the war against France. Seen from Kinsale, after the collapse of resistance in Ireland, the Revolution in England might well prove to be a turning-point in European history.

However, first things first. If Rapin were to pursue his historical studies, he must exchange his accidental military career for some more scholarly employment. Luckily, in 1693, while he was still at

Kinsale, an opportunity presented itself. William's Dutch friend, Hans Willem Bentinck, Earl of Portland, needed a tutor for his eldest son, Lord Woodstock, then eleven years old. William's Huguenot general in Ireland, the Marquis de Ruvigny, recommended Rapin, praising him not only for his intellectual gifts but also for '*un certain air du beau monde et ces manières nobles et aisées qu'on n'attrape qu'avec gens de qualité*'. William urged Rapin to accept the post; and he accepted it.* For the next thirteen years Rapin was employed by Portland, living sometimes in England but mainly, it seems, in the Bentinck house at The Hague. He does not seem to have written much, if anything, in these years. No doubt he was reading; but the time of a tutor in a great nobleman's house was not his own, and it was liable to inconvenient interruptions.

One such interruption occurred in 1698, after the Treaty of Ryswick, which ended the War of the Grand Alliance, begun in 1689. By this treaty Louis XIV was forced to concede failure and to recognize William III as King of England. William thereupon sent Portland as his ambassador to Paris. It was a very splendid embassy, and the envoy of so formidable a ruler was treated with great deference: Louis XIV himself, according to Saint-Simon, welcomed Portland '*comme une espèce de divinité*'. Rapin accompanied Portland to Paris and, in the two years that he spent there, could observe the new interest in England and in the mysterious strength which it had drawn from revolution. Then, in 1700, with the resumption of the war, the embassy ceased; Portland returned to Holland, taking Rapin with him; and next year Rapin was required to complete his service by accompanying his pupil, now eighteen years old, on a Grand Tour. Because of the war, France was excluded from the itinerary, which was confined to allied or neutral countries: Germany, Austria and parts of Italy. The letters in which Rapin reported to Portland on the plans and progress of the tour do not suggest that he enjoyed it much.[7] He was not, I think, a man given to enjoyment. But they are interesting as showing, among other things, his attitude towards England, the country whose history he undertook to interpret to Europe.

Ever since the Reformation, the Huguenot exiles in England had been ambivalent towards their host-country. On the one hand, as

*This is stated by Jean Rou, who no doubt had it from Rapin: '*c'estoit sa Majesté même, le grand Guillaume, qui l'avoit obligé de se charger de cette commission*'. (Jean Rou, *Mémoires inédits et opuscules*, ed. F. Waddington (Paris 1857), II, p. 226).

Protestants and victims of oppression, they admired its Protestantism and its liberty. On the other hand, as Frenchmen, and rather
priggish Frenchmen too, they looked down on its lack of civilization.
When planning the tour, Rapin urged Portland on no account to
yield to his son's desire to begin it in England. At present, he
explained, Lord Woodstock was docile; but if he were to start a
European tour in a country 'where he will see so many bad
examples', all would be over: 'the air and manners of *les jeunes
seigneurs anglais*', their shocking conversation and barbarous behaviour, were only too catching, and they would undoubtedly incite him
'to shake off the yoke of an inconvenient tutor'.[8] These observations
were, alas, only too true, as Mr Graham C. Gibbs has shown in the
case of the unfortunate Huguenot tutor of Lord Wharton.[9]

However, it may be some consolation to our national pride that
during the tour (which did not include England) Rapin found
almost all other peoples just as disagreeable. The Austrians, he
observed, are insufferably proud and stuffy, the Germans
unsociable, pompous and ignorant; Italians look down on all other
nations as stupid and easy to cheat and treat them with contemptuous *insouciance*: cardinals, for instance, who had been liberal
enough with their invitations in the freedom and safety of the
carnival at Venice, forgot all about them when back in their palaces
in Rome; etc., etc. Rapin also complained that everything everywhere was very expensive; that Lord Woodstock's valet, undermin-
ing his careful tutor, encouraged him to wasteful largesse; that Lord
Woodstock himself preferred the company of flighty girls to that of
grave elderly statesmen; and that Italy, in this time of war, was not
at all safe for any of them: if Lord Woodstock should be captured by
brigands, he would be very expensive to ransom. It was all very
trying, and by the end of the tour Rapin was regretting that he had
ever accepted his present position: if he had stayed in the army, he
wrote, he would have been a major by now.

From these exasperating travels Rapin returned with relief to The
Hague. He was back before the end of 1702, and remained for
another two years in the Portland household. Then, in 1704, Lord
Woodstock married and established himself in England: his wife
was English, and he became a Member of Parliament – Whig of
course – for Southampton. Rapin's employment by the family
therefore came to an end: now at least he was his own master; and
being now married – to a Huguenot lady of course, who, we are told

was '*jeune, riche et surtout vertueuse*' – he could please himself and settle down to a life of scholarship and literature.

Rapin's life in The Hague, in these years, was agreeable enough. He had the stimulus of learned and congenial – that is, other Huguenot – society: for in Holland, as in England, he lived, as most of the émigrés lived, in a small Huguenot circle. He was in touch with Leclerc, whom he had known in Saumur, and through him with the Huguenot Republic of Letters. His closest friends in The Hague were Abel Rotolp, sieur de la Devèze, the author of an *Apologie pour les Refugiés*, and Jean Rou, a scholarly lawyer whose splendid and costly compilation of chronological and genealogical tables had been seized in proof and burnt in Paris at the instigation of Bossuet. The Bishop, it seems, had detected in it some whiff of heresy. Rou was now – thanks to the patronage of William III and the greffier Francis Fagel – official interpreter to the States General. Rapin had introduced him to the Portland family to teach Lord Woodstock law, and did his best to have Rou's *Tables Chronologiques* published in Holland; but the Dutch printers boggled at the cost. Rou, in turn, helped Rapin with his historical studies, which, from now on, were his main preoccupation: it was in 1705, on his release from his employment in the Portland family, that he began at last to write his *History of England*.[10]

Rotolp de la Devèze and Rou were founder-members of a scholarly Huguenot club which met every week for learned discussion. This '*petite académie*', as Rou called it, had been founded when Rapin was abroad; but when he returned, they made him a member of it. Others who were co-opted into it were Henri Basnage de Beauval, the author of the *Histoire des Ouvrages des Savants*, and his brother, the clerical statesman Jacques Basnage. At first, having seven members, this club was called *la Pléïade*; afterwards, having increased its numbers, it became *la Féauté*. After Rapin had joined it, it met regularly in his elegant house in The Hague.[11]

Alas, this idyllic existence did not last long. Life at The Hague was expensive. Rapin's own means, now that he was no longer maintained by Lord Portland, were limited. The pension somewhat belatedly granted to him by William III had expired with the King in 1702 and was not renewed by the States General. His wife's income was evidently inadequate to maintain their accustomed style; so, in 1707 he moved to Wesel in the Duchy of Cleves. Since Cleves was now under Prussian rule, he was still in approved

Huguenot territory, and could communicate easily with the Huguenot scholars in Berlin. He spent the rest of his life at Wesel concentrating on his literary work.

For several years Rapin kept his work secret. Only Rou, it seems, knew of his plans; and Rapin insisted that Rou was to mention them to nobody: any publicity on this subject, he said, could only damage him.[12] Why he was so secretive, we do not know. Perhaps it was a personal trait, perhaps merely the suspiciousness of an émigré. Perhaps also it was through fear of competition. For there was a competitor in the field. This was Isaac de Larrey.

Isaac de Larrey, seigneur de Grandchamp et de Commesnil, was a Huguenot from Normandy who, like Rapin, had been trained as a lawyer. After the Revocation he had left France for Berlin, where he had been patronized by Queen Sophia Charlotte, and found employment as counsellor to the Prussian embassy at The Hague. There he had become aware of the demand for a history of England, and in spite of discouragement from British friends, who doubted his capacity, he set to work, and in 1697–8 – the time of the peace of Ryswick – he published, at Rotterdam, two huge volumes covering the period 1485–1625. Two more volumes, he announced, would cover the medieval period and the period 1625–88. The third – the most modern – volume in fact appeared in 1707. Fortunately for Rapin, the work of his rival, after initial applause, sank to its true level, and by the time the last volume – the medieval – was published in 1713, it was clear that the great gap was still unfilled.[13] Then Rapin came out of his secret closet. In 1714 the Huguenot *Journal Littéraire* of The Hague, deploring the absence of any good history of England, announced, '*en passant*', that such a work was at last in preparation, that it would be far more exact than anything published hitherto, and that the author was 'a very able man who has been working on it for several years'. This very able man was Rapin, to whose slow and secret work, first in The Hague, then in Wesel, we may now turn.

Rapin's plan of work was not consistent.[14] At first, he tells us, he had planned to begin with the Norman Conquest, but then, seeking for causes and origins, he moved back to the Anglo-Saxons. Soon he was in love with the Anglo-Saxons. This, of course, was a sound Whig romance: English Whigs saw the Anglo-Saxons as the inventors of Parliament, and even Tories like Clarendon accepted the view that William the Conqueror had not subverted but continued the good old Anglo-Saxon constitution. It was also, *mutatis mutandis*, a sound Huguenot doctrine: the sixteenth-century Huguenot publicist François Hotman had similarly insisted that the Germanic Franks had brought into Roman Gaul the free institutions which later French kings, with their revived Roman ideas, had subverted. Having fallen for the Anglo-Saxons, Rapin decided to stay with them and to go no further forward than the reign of Henry II, in whose reign the Norman Conquest was rounded off by the conquest of Ireland. This would have been an elegant close to a study inspired by Rapin's own part in the reconquest of Ireland by William III.

It seems that this decision was inspired partly by mere fatigue: that Rapin's original impetus was failing. For clearly he was becoming bored in Wesel. Life there might be cheap but it was also very dull. As he wrote to his fellow Huguenot in Berlin, Paul-Emile de Mauclerc, one of the editors of the *Bibliothèque Germanique*, he was starved of intelligent conversation and had no one who could encourage him or criticize his work. If only he were back in The Hague, he sighed, or even in Berlin! But in Wesel he met only soldiers, talking endlessly of war . . . However, just as he was about to give up, a fresh wind from England filled his sagging sails. It was like that timely 'Protestant wind' which had carried William of Orange into Torbay. Now it carried Rapin forward to the completion of his work. This timely assistance was the arrival on the Continent of Rymer's *Foedera*.

Rymer's *Foedera* is a massive compilation of all the treaties entered into by the Crown of England since the Norman Conquest. It had been commissioned by Charles Montagu, Earl of Halifax, the Whig minister of William III, in imitation of Leibniz's *Corpus Juris Gentium Diplomaticum*. The chosen editor, Thomas Rymer, was a sturdy Whig whose father had been hanged for treason under Charles II. The work began to appear in 1704. By then William III was dead and had been succeeded by the Tory Queen Anne, who hated his memory and could not bear to hear his name; but this little dynastic accident, which might have disconcerted a more sensitive editor, had no effect on the hardy bigot Rymer. Indeed it only stimulated his Whig zeal. In an unctuous dedication of his fourth volume to the Queen he drew her attention to the interesting parallel between the reign of her father James II and that of another deposed King, Edward II. In particular he invited her to rejoice that during that 'most unprosperous and disastrous administration . . . amidst the greatest confusion and dismal jumble of affairs', Almighty Providence had sanctioned an alliance with 'William III, surnamed the Good, Count of Holland . . . whereby those measures were concerted which, in the next succeeding reign carried English arms victorious into France'. Luckily Queen Anne is unlikely to have read this insolent dedication.

In order to promote Rymer's work abroad, Halifax had copies of it sent to Leclerc in Rotterdam, for review in his *Biblothèque Choisie*. Leclerc duly published an abstract of the first volume in 1708; but then, 'having so many other important engagements in the Republic of Literature', passed on the remaining volumes, as they came in, to 'a gentleman of merit who is working on the history of England'. This gentleman was of course Rapin, now bored beyond endurance by the conversation of colonels in Wesel.

The arrival of Rymer's *Foedera* restored the drooping spirits of Rapin. He made abstracts of each volume as it arrived – fifteen volumes had been published when Rymer died in 1713 and the sixteenth was in the press – and these abstracts were duly published by Leclerc. They were so admired that the Grand Pensionary Heinsius caused them to be collected together and printed as an official document for the use of the States General. For this edition Rapin also wrote an abstract of the first volume to replace the more superficial review by Leclerc. This volume was afterwards translated into English and published in England as *Acta Regia*.

Rymer's *Foedera*, with its original documents, reanimated Rapin's *History*, offering it a firm and continuous spinal cord. He now worked on both concurrently, abstracting the one and composing the other, in order, as he wrote, 'to show the relation which the documents bear to the events which we meet in his *History* and to illustrate the one by the other'. It was an application of the new historical method of Mabillon and Leibniz. But it was also more than that. For Rapin also had a thesis: a thesis which he derived from his Huguenot predecessors of the sixteenth century and which had been fortified by his contact with the English Whigs. This thesis he was enabled to ventilate, even before he had completed any part of his book, by a fortunate incident in 1714.

For in 1714 Queen Anne died. Her last government – the high Tory government of Lord Bolingbroke – had just ended the war against France by the Treaty of Utrecht. That treaty marked the

final frustration of Louis XIV's grandiose ambitions and left Great
Britain the arbiter of Europe; but it was also regarded by the
English Whigs and their Dutch and Huguenot allies as a betrayal: a
'shameful precipitate peace', Rapin would call it, 'which has filled
all Europe with amazement and indignation'.[15] Now the Queen's
death brought a sudden and welcome reversal. The new German
dynasty came in; the Tories were removed from power; and the old
Whigs came back. Naturally all Europe was excited by this sudden
change – excited but also perplexed: what, men asked, did it mean?

At Wesel, at the house of the Prussian governor of Cleves, Field
Marshal Count von Lottum, the conversation one day was all about
these extraordinary English parties: what on earth were Whigs and
Tories? Rapin was there, but did not think, from what he heard, that
those present 'had a very distinct knowledge of those two parties'.
So, to clarify his own ideas, he wrote a paper on the subject. Some
time afterwards he was visited at Wesel by a courtly Whig virtuoso,
Sir Andrew Fountaine, to whom he showed the paper. Sir Andrew
was greatly impressed by it and urged that it be published. It was
published at The Hague in 1717, in French, as *Dissertation sur les
Whigs et les Torys*.

This pamphlet was a huge success in Europe. Translated into
English, Dutch, Danish, Spanish and German, it was frequently
reprinted. Of the French version alone there were ten editions in the
next hundred years. This journalistic triumph was well deserved, for
it was a lucid, temperate, sensible explanation, by means of history,
of otherwise unintelligible politics. Whether that history was correct
is another matter, which we can leave for the moment. The essential
fact was that it became 'the standard textbook on the subject,
accepted as authoritative even in England'.[16] 'These few pages', says
a Swiss historian, 'place their author in the forefront of modern
publicists.'[17]

Meanwhile Rapin pressed on with his *History*. By 1722 he had
reached 1640 and there he thought that he would stop; for how, he
asked, could he compete with 'milord Clarendon', whose classic
account of the Great Rebellion had now been published? Nor were
the years after 1660 any easier: 'in view of the present state of parties
in England', he doubted whether he could handle *'un morceau si délicat
et si difficile'*.[18] However, pressed by his friends in Berlin and
Rotterdam, he overcame his doubts and persevered until 1649, the
execution of Charles I. Then at last he broke covert. In 1723, having

whetted the appetite of his readers by extracts published in the *Bibliothèque Germanique* and in Leclerc's *Bibliothèque Ancienne et Moderne*, he published the whole work so far written. It was published at The Hague in eight volumes, fulsomely dedicated to the new King of Great Britain, the client and patron of the Whigs, George I.

It was the right moment, for just at that time the English Whigs were taking steps to recover the historiographical initiative, lost to the Tories in the reign of Anne. Next year they established the regius chairs of history in the British universities: an act prompted by the Whig Bishop of London, Edmund Gibson, and hailed with absurd rapture by the pushing young Whig clergyman William Warburton.[19] In the same year the first volume of Bishop Burnet's posthumous *History of his own Time* was published, giving a sound Whig account of the reigns of Charles II and James II. This last work was particularly timely: it spurred Rapin to further efforts, and when he died, in 1725, he left the manuscript of two more volumes which carried his *History* down to the coronation of William and Mary in 1689. These last two volumes were prepared for the press by his fellow Huguenot David Durand, a minister first in The Hague, then in London, and were published in 1727. Simultaneously an English translation was published in London.

'*1723, voilà une date vraiment importante dans l'histoire des idées*', exclaims Joseph Dedieu: Rapin has captured French public opinion and from now on he will be, for Frenchmen, the teacher of English history, the interpreter of English liberty.[20] That, of course, was what he set out to be: it was the function of the Huguenot scholars. But he also did more than this. He captured the Protestant world too. In particular he captured England itself.

For the next generation Rapin's work was the standard history of England. It was accepted as a classic throughout Europe. Catholic and Protestant, English and French, Whig and Tory vied to praise it. Even the Jesuits of Trevoux printed an edition of this Huguenot work, adjusting the text where expedient. In England it was praised, even by Tories, for its judiciousness. Bolingbroke was a subscriber to it. Six editions of the French text, five of the English translation, were printed in the next thirty years. An English historical catechism based on it ran through twenty-four editions in the remainder of the eighteenth century. It was, men said, the only impartial history of England.

That indeed was Rapin's own claim. Being quite independent of English parties or English patrons, and writing only for foreigners, he was, he said, rather smugly, 'free from all party passion and prejudice'. (The same claim had been made by the unfortunate Isaac de Larrey, but he was now quite forgotten.) Rapin's claim was endorsed by Voltaire, who wrote that his was the only complete and impartial history *'d'un pays où l'on n'écrivait que par esprit de parti'*, the nearest thing to a perfect history in all Europe. And Voltaire's praise was echoed by the editor of the sixth French edition, who explained that he had republished the work of this Frenchman because the English themselves, owing to their party spirit, were incapable of historical impartiality.

Rapin was certainly different from the English writers of his time. He was certainly judicious, cautious, temperate. But was he in fact impartial? Of course he was not. How could he be when his life had been spent – in so far as it was spent among Englishmen – entirely among Whigs? For neither Rapin nor any other Huguenot historian was able to transcend the limits of their situation. They were intermediaries, interpreters, critics, not thinkers. If they contributed to the thought of Europe, it was by demolition, not construction. Rapin tried to construct, but as he had no originality of mind, as he was essentially a journalist, not a thinker, he only interpreted and systematized the Huguenot history that he had read in France and the Whig theories that he had heard in England. So he produced, just as the Whig Ascendancy was being consolidated in England, the classic exposition of the Whig – the 'old Whig' – interpretation of history.

It was the doctrine of the ancient English constitution, with its guarantee of liberty through the separation of powers. Such a constitution (said Rapin, following Hotman) had once been common to all the Germanic nations, but in all the other nations it had succumbed to royal usurpation. Only in England had it been preserved intact. So English history became the history of its preservation, and Rapin described in turn the German origins of the parliamentary constitution, its introduction into England by the invading Saxons, the absorption of the Norman Conquest, the Whig principles of the medieval barons, the constitutional propriety of the Lancastrians and Tudors, the Stuart betrayal. It was a story of aristocratic virtue, of conservatism, of continuity: the English nobility, the ancestors of the grandees who had called William of

Orange and the Hanoverians to the throne, had been the guardians of their constitution (how different from the domesticated Catholic nobility of France who had betrayed theirs!): 'more Kings since the Conquest have mounted the throne by virtue of Acts of Parliament, or some other means' (he prudently adds) 'than by hereditary right'; and the four English kings who, with the support of the high Tories of their time, had attempted to break the constitution – Edward II, Richard II, Charles I and James II – had all come, deservedly, to sticky ends.

Such was the historical philosophy which a Huguenot historian, uniting the theories of sixteenth-century French Huguenots and seventeenth-century English Whigs, presented to eighteenth-century Europe. It was a philosophy of idealist conservatism. There is no suggestion in it that change has occurred or should occur in history, no reference to economic life or to ideas. The English constitution vindicated in 1688 was, according to Rapin, the identical constitution which the Anglo-Saxons had brought with them from Germany. In 1729, when Montesquieu came to England and was bowled over by his experience of English liberty, Rapin's work was the classic explanation of it; and he swallowed it. We have only to read that splendid work, the *Germania* of Tacitus, he wrote, to see that there lies the source of the English government: '*ce beau systeme a été trouvé dans les bois*'.[21] Voltaire, who came a few years later, was less certain: '*la Chambre de Pairs et des Communes, la cour d'Equité, trouvées dans les bois!*' he exclaimed, '*on ne l'aurait pas deviné*'.[22]

Of course there were dissenting voices in England too, especially from Tories and Jacobites, who were particularly enraged that a foreigner should take it upon himself to interpret their history. The Tories were now the national party, defenders of true-born Englishmen against interloping Dutchmen and Germans; and French Huguenots, they thought, were no better. The Jacobite Thomas Rawlinson even approved of the Whig regius chairs at the universities since at least they would save the sons of English noblemen from being taught history and languages by 'ignorant French Huguenots and Scotch pedlars'.[23] So Samuel Jebb, a non-juror, accused Rapin of 'all imaginable want of accuracy and judgment' in whatever concerned Mary Queen of Scots,[24] and the Jacobite antiquary Thomas Carte (who described himself provocatively, on his title-page, as 'an Englishman') found him 'utterly unacquainted with our constitution, laws and customs', having picked up his meagre knowledge of them in 'coffee-houses, the common habitation of his countrymen in this city'. Carte particularly disapproved of Rapin's thesis that the national constitution of England was the 'Whig' system brought in by the Anglo-Saxons. The Anglo-Saxons, to him, were unwelcome foreign invaders from Germany, like the Hanoverians, and their constitution was an improper German innovation. The true national constitution (he said) was that of the ancient Britons; and that was high Tory and clerical, having been devised for them by their clergy, the divinely ordained and universally respected Druids, who had 'their ordinary abode in colleges, retired from the world'.[25]

The Jacobites, the Tories, the modern Druids in their Oxford colleges, were unable to dethrone Rapin. Just as the Whig ascendancy itself was beginning to crumble, he was dethroned by a far greater man who, unlike him, was capable of original thought and could base his historical writing on radically new ideas – in short, by a man of genius: David Hume. Though Hume never cites Rapin's work in his *History of England*, it is clear that he had it continuously in his eye; and indeed, our considerable pleasure in reading Hume's *History* is increased if we are aware of the unspoken controversy which lurks behind it: if we recognize the sacred cows of Rapin's Whig orthodoxy – the virtuous Anglo-Saxons, the early Parliament, the medieval barons, Magna Carta, Simon de Montfort, the Reformers, the Scotch Covenanters, the Whig patriots – tumbling one by one to that exquisite marksmanship. To Hume the whole idea of history as the defence of a static system through the centuries was absurd. History, to him, was historical change, the transformation of the economy, the sophistication of manners, the improvement of life and thought, not the stubborn defence of an unchanging inheritance from the Dark Ages. His view of his predecessor, implicit in his *History*, emerges openly from the private letters which he wrote while at work on it. 'You know', he wrote, while engaged on his first volume, 'that there is no post of honour in the English Parnassus more vacant than that of History. Style, judgement, impartiality – everything is wanting to our historians, and even Rapin, during this later period' – for Hume began his work with the Stuarts – 'is extremely deficient'. A little later, he would express himself more strongly:

the more I advance in my undertaking, the more I am convinced that the History of England has never yet been written, not only for style, which is notorious to all the world, but also for matter; such is the ignorance and partiality of all our historians. Rapin, whom I had an esteem for, is totally worthless.[26]

Nearly a century later, when Macaulay set out to restore Whig history it was Hume whom he set out to dethrone; but he did so by accepting the essence of his thought – the central concept of material progress – and changing its political implications. He did not attempt to restore the obsolete Whig conservatism of Rapin.

Nevertheless, at a less sophisticated level, Rapin's thesis, detached from his name, survived. Englishmen have generally been proud of their history and like to emphasize its continuity, and that sense of continuity, which Hume had temporarily disintegrated, was strengthened in the nineteenth century. Then the middle classes took over the aristocratic institutions of the past and, while transforming their substance, gave their forms a new lease of life. The Romantic movement, the Gothic Revival, the rebuilding of the Palace of Westminster, and its decoration with frescos and statues commemorating – sometimes very inappropriately – the continuous history of Parliament, all supported the old Whig thesis, which at one level, the level of forms, is real enough. It is agreeable to think that the classic and most extreme version of that patriotic thesis was expressed not for Englishmen or by an Englishman but for foreigners by an author who had no great love for the English: by a French Huguenot who, having come over with Dutch William and served him in Ireland, afterwards retired to Germany and wrote in French, for publication in Holland, the first complete history of England.

14

Religious Toleration after 1688

One of the great achievements of the Revolution of 1688, at least
according to Whig historians, was religious toleration, secured at
last by statute, by the so-called Toleration Act of May 1689.
Macaulay, in his essay on Sir James Mackintosh's *History of the
Revolution*, was lyrical in its praise. While admitting that, as seen in
1834, it had many defects,

> we question [he wrote], whether in the whole of that vast mass of
> legislation, from the Great Charter downwards, there be a single
> law which has so much diminished the sum of human unhappi-
> ness, which has done so much to allay bad passions, which has
> put an end to so much petty tyranny and vexation, which has
> brought gladness, peace and security to so many private dwel-
> lings . . . etc. etc.

Fourteen years later, in his *History of England*, in rather more
measured terms, he repeated this judgment. The Toleration Act, he
then wrote, while illustrating the peculiar vices, also showed the
peculiar excellence of English legislation: imperfect though it was, it
secured uninterrupted progress towards the completer toleration
attained in his own time, and therefore could be described as
approaching 'very near to the idea of a great English law'.

Macaulay wrote as a statesman, well aware that politics is the art
of the possible. Academic historians, who are exempt from such
responsibility, have been more critical of the Toleration Act. It was,
they say, 'most unsatisfactory', 'freakish', 'incomplete', 'accidental

and temporary'; and some of them are pleased to point out that the toleration offered by the later Stuart kings, and in particular the second Declaration of James II, which provoked the Revolution, was more complete than that granted by the Act of William III. Macaulay was well aware of these objections, but he judged them unrealistic. To him the Toleration Act, incomplete and defective though it was – it was, after all, like the Revolution itself, a compromise, dependent on parliamentary consensus – was as much as could be obtained at that time, and the most that could be relied on to last. As for the argument that the Stuart Declarations granted a greater freedom, that would have received from him short shrift. Those Declarations, he insisted, were 'hypocritical': indeed they gave the very concept of toleration a bad name – or rather, an even worse name than before. For toleration was not, in itself, a virtue in the seventeenth century. In England it had been the watchword of the Independents, the sectaries of the Interregnum. Then it had become the engine of machiavellian kings seeking thereby to introduce an intolerant Catholic despotism. No monarchy in Europe, in 1685, was without an established Church; and, although there might be reasons of State for toleration of particular minorities, no established Church even considered a legal grant of equal toleration to Churches which dissented from it.

However, by 1688 the situation had changed. The policy of toleration for both Catholic and Protestant Dissenters – the policy from which Charles II had been forced to recede in 1672 – had been firmly, and indeed, it seemed, successfully, applied by James II. The adversaries of the established Church, to right and to left, Catholics and Non-conformists, were mobilized against it. Whigs and Papists, old Cromwellians and new Roman converts, Quakers and Jesuits, were being brought together by royal patronage. Meanwhile the Church itself was being subverted from within, at its heart, in its essential seminaries, the universities. To the defenders of the Anglican Establishment the danger was clear and real; and even the most rigid of Tory statesmen were prepared to oppose the Crown in order to break that unholy alliance. To do so they must expose its secret purpose and outbid the Crown by offering perhaps a more limited but certainly a more real and durable toleration to the Protestant Dissenters only.

The most rigid of Tory statesmen was Daniel Finch, Earl of Nottingham. After the flight of James II he introduced in the

Convention Parliament the two bills which were designed to realize that offer: the Comprehension Bill, which was to ease the way of tender consciences into the established Church, and, for those whose consciences were too tender for that, the bill 'for exempting Their Majesties' Protestant subjects, dissenting from the Church of England, from the penalties of certain laws'. The former bill died in embryo; the latter was passed and became known as the Toleration Act.

It was, as stiff churchmen were quick to point out, a misnomer. Dr Sacheverell, for instance, in his inflammatory sermons, would insist that there was no law tolerating Dissent. Strictly speaking, he was right, for the Act abolished none of the laws against Dissenters. Legally, all those discriminatory statutes remained in force. Only the penalties imposed by some of them were suspended for the benefit of some Dissenters, provided that they declared their allegiance to William and Mary. Roman Catholics and those who, in preaching or writing, denied the doctrine of the blessed Trinity – that is, Arians and Socinians, or, as they were now to be called, Unitarians – were explicitly denied any benefit from the Act. Even those who benefited from it remained subject to the Test and Corporation Acts, which excluded them from political or municipal office; and the university statutes continued to bar them from the universities.

Such was the limited and conditional toleration granted to Protestant Dissenters by the Act of 1689. It was the most that the patrons of Dissent could obtain, the most that the champions of the established Church would concede. Among those who would have granted more was William himself. During the debate he had proposed, from the throne, the repeal of the Test and Corporation Acts. That was a grave tactical error and contributed to the loss of the Comprehension Bill. Even as it was, the Act was disliked by the high-Church party as an improper concession. That party would have liked to make it temporary only – there was a proposal, in Parliament, to limit its validity to seven years. The extremists of the party, who opposed the Revolution itself, or at least its unforeseen consequences, would seek, for many years, to repeal or circumvent it.[1]

So long as William reigned, they had little hope of success. William was himself a Calvinist by upbringing, but, as a layman, a Dutchman, and a statesman, he was tolerant in practice: tolerant even of Roman Catholics. Though he was seen as an almost messianic saviour by the most intolerant preachers of the Calvinist diaspora in Europe, he had Catholic allies against France, including the Emperor and (discreetly) the Pope. He had Catholic officers in his own army. How ironical that he should have become, after his death, and should remain three centuries later, the patron saint of the most bigoted of British Protestants! After his initial rebuff over the proposed repeal of the Test and Corporation Acts, he left Church matters to churchmen, under the patronage of his wife. After her death in 1694 his own influence was direct, and there was no possibility of reaction. But on 8 March 1702 he died, and at once the high Anglicans raised their heads and their voices.

In particular there was Dr Sacheverell. To Sacheverell the day of King William's death was 'the most joyful day he had seen in thirteen years' – meaning since the flight of King James; and he was quick to show it. It was in May 1702, only two months after William's death, that Sacheverell began his open campaign against the toleration of Dissent. He began it in Oxford with his famous sermon urging his congregation not to 'strike sail to a party which is an open and avowed enemy of our communion' – that is, the Whig party, the political patrons of Dissent – but rather to 'hang out the bloody flag and banner of defiance'. This was the sermon which would provoke Defoe's famous satire, *The Shortest Way with the Dissenters* (1702). It was seen as an incitement to high Tory revolt, a call for the repeal of the Toleration Act and, in consequence, the overthrow of the recently passed Act of Settlement.[2]

Sacheverell's sermon was timed to support the first parliamentary campaign against Occasional Conformity – that device whereby Dissenters evaded the provisions of the Corporation Acts: by a single ritual and purely tactical act of Anglican communion, they qualified themselves for municipal office. This in turn had political consequences, for it could lead to the capture of marginal borough seats by Whig candidates. Three bills against Occasional Conformity were introduced into Parliament in 1702–4 and passed by Tory majorities in the Commons, only to be defeated in the Lords, where the episcopal bench, thanks to the exclusion of Non-jurors and the presence of Williamite bishops, was sound. The bishops hoped that Occasional Conformity would lead gradually to Comprehension; the high-Churchmen hoped, if they could stop it, to proceed to the repeal of the Toleration Act: they could then return to Laudian intolerance.

In 1705 Sacheverell preached another, even more aggressive sermon at Oxford, on the text 'in perils among false brethren'. It was the same sermon which, when preached again four years later, before a Tory and Jacobite Lord Mayor, would lead to the *cause célèbre* of his impeachment. These were the years – the hopeful years of Queen Anne – when another high-Church firebrand, Francis Atterbury, was turning the Lower House of the restored Convocation of Canterbury into a high-Church pressure-group, and banners inscribed with the device 'No Moderation!' were carried to the hustings during parliamentary elections. Throughout the reign of Anne, Dissenters had good reason to fear that the limited toleration which they had enjoyed under the Act would be withdrawn if the Tories should be in power.

In Queen Anne's last years the Tories were in power and the fears of the Dissenters were realized. In 1711 a bill against Occasional Conformity was at last passed. The Earl of Nottingham, the Tory champion of the Church, had bought the votes of the Whigs in exchange for a promise of support against the Treaty of Utrecht. It was a shocking betrayal of 'revolution principles' for opportunist purposes, and was denounced as such by the Dissenters. But worse was to come. Three years later, as part of his campaign to ditch his party leader and capture power for the intransigent Tories before the Queen should die, Bolingbroke pushed through the Schism Act. This Act was designed to destroy the Dissenting Academies, which were regarded with intense dislike by high-Churchmen. Had it been effective, Oxford and Cambridge, the two protected centres of intolerant Anglicanism, would once again have closed their monopoly. And had Bolingbroke succeeded in his plans, further infractions of the Toleration Act would no doubt have followed. Perhaps the Act itself would have been replaced. The Counter-Revolution then would be on its way.

In fact Bolingbroke failed. The death of Queen Anne spoiled all his plans. With the Hanoverian succession the Whigs returned to power and the dreams of the high-Churchmen evaporated. In 1719 Bolingbroke's two most notorious Acts, the Act against Occasional Conformity and the Schism Act, were repealed. Thereby the legal position established by the Toleration Act was restored. It might, therefore, be supposed that the Whigs, being now secure in power, would make use of their ascendancy to complete the work and move on from the compromises of 1689. In particular, they might be expected to improve the admittedly incomplete and, in some respects, irrational Toleration Act. In fact, they made no such move. They did not even re-enact the Act of General Naturalization of 1709, which the Tories had repealed in 1711. This Act had granted naturalization to Lutheran and Calvinist refugees who took the Oath of Allegiance and received the sacraments in a Protestant church. But the Whigs who were now in power were a new generation of men, who had not been engaged in the desperate struggles of the 1670s and 1680s and were more concerned to consolidate than to complete the Revolution. Their chief concern was defensive: to prevent the return of the Stuarts to the throne, of Bolingbroke to government, or of the heirs of Sacheverell and Atterbury to prominence in the Church. So Crown patronage must be used to ensure the appointment of sound bishops: men who would govern the Church, preserve its peace by keeping the high-Church party quiet, and support the administration in the House of Lords; and the task of those bishops in their dioceses must not be made more difficult by any material concessions to Dissent. Such concessions would only exasperate the lower clergy and cause trouble. Therefore, for the sake of social stability, the Dissenters must remain content with the limited gains of 1689.

On the whole they were content – at least for the time being. The Dissenters were now a dwindling body. Not many of them sought such office as was denied to them by the Test Act; and the Corporation Act, once the device of Occasional Conformity had been restored to them, could be legally evaded. Many made use of that device; others, who stickled at such hypocrisy, would find that they could rely on the indulgence or connivance of authority and so step quietly into the municipal office from which they were legally debarred. Thus *de facto* tolerance supplied the defect of *de jure* toleration.[3] Finally, if the Whig politicians were not prepared to make further concessions, what could the Dissenters do? Since the Whigs were their only patrons, they could hardly hope to gain from any political change. That could only be for the worse. In such a situation, those of them who were still dissatisfied could proceed only by very moderate courses: by petition or persuasion, by exciting sympathy, and by discreet pressure through organized bodies at times of parliamentary elections: times which, after the Septennial Act of 1716, were less frequent than before.

The growth of such pressure-groups is one of the interesting developments of eighteenth-century politics, the beginning of a new, extra-parliamentary force, and it began, like so much else in the politics of the time, with the religious sects. Deprived, by the failure of the Puritan Revolution, of direct political influence, disappointed, under the restored monarchy, in their hopes of royal patronage, and now blocked by the new conservatism and the apparent stability of the Whig government, these sects turned their attention to Parliament. They sought to influence elections, to win over individual members, to cultivate and persuade powerful ministers. It was a sign that the *locus* of sovereignty had changed.[4]

The first to recognize this were those Protestant Dissenters whose hopes had been most severely dashed by the Revolution of 1688: the Quakers. From their beginning, in the time of Cromwell, the Quakers, persecuted in the country, had looked for protection to the court: first to the court of the Lord Protector, then to that of Charles II. After 1675 they had looked also to Parliament, involving themselves in elections and pressing sympathetic members to support bills for their relief. Then, under James II, they had returned to the older method. Through William Penn and Robert Barclay they had a hot line to the throne, and they were not too fastidious in the methods by which they kept it open and warm. The Revolution, which brusquely severed that line, was a blow to them; but it was a blow from which they soon recovered. They had already, by this time, a well-organized system which was used to collect evidence of their 'sufferings' throughout the country and to put it, as occasion served, before their political patrons. From the moment when the Toleration Act was passed, they used this system to extend, or attempt to extend, their statutory protection.

The Toleration Act had made considerable concessions to the Quakers. It not only gave them the same freedom of public worship which it gave to other Protestant Dissenters: it also relieved them from subscription to any of the Thirty-Nine Articles of the Church, allowing them instead to subscribe to a general declaration, and it respected their conscientious refusal to swear oaths, allowing them to make a simple declaration of loyalty to the new monarchs instead of swearing the Oaths of Supremacy and Allegiance. However, the Act did not exempt them from the other oaths which had to be sworn before magistrates in civil affairs. To remedy this defect, the Quakers mobilized their well-tried machinery, the Meeting for Sufferings, or central committee of London Friends, and through it lobbied Parliament and made interest with the new King. Thanks largely to the favour of the King, they secured most of what they wanted in the Affirmation Act of 1696. Similar agitation secured the renewal of the Act in 1702 and its modification in their favour in 1722.

Another defect of the Toleration Act, in the eyes of the Quakers, was its insistence on the payment of tithes for the support of the established Church. Quakers not only, like everyone else, disliked paying tithes; they also had conscientious objections to them. But then they also insisted on obeying the laws of the country. So what were they to do? To get round the difficulty, they wished to be, or to seem to be, forced by the process of law. But they wished to be forced cheaply, and this could not be guaranteed. So they agitated for a law to guarantee it. For this purpose, in the 1730s, the well-established machinery was again mobilized, evidence was collected, 'sufferings' were exaggerated, and a tithe bill – not to abolish tithes but to simplify the procedure and reduce the cost of the face-saving device of enforcement – was drawn up. There was then much waiting on 'the proper person in power', the all-powerful minister Sir Robert Walpole.

Walpole handled the business with his usual cynical skill. He was eager to pose as the friend of the Dissenters, but he was equally eager not to give any opportunity for trouble from the high-Church party. So he sought to satisfy the Quakers with fair words and vague promises. He assured them, in general terms, of his sympathy, asked them for longer and longer supporting documents, but in the end, when these tactics had been exhausted, he advised them to defer any action till the next session of Parliament, when circumstances would be more favourable. The other Dissenters, he explained, were likely to agitate for a repeal of the Test and Corporation Acts, which would be 'troublesome to the state, if not dangerous'; the old high-Tory cry of 'the Church in danger' was always likely to break out; and he feared that the bishops might prove unsound in the Lords. By these and such methods, the Quakers were kept at bay as long as possible.

However, they could not be kept at bay permanently. In 1736 their patience ran out and they resolved to act. They distributed propaganda, mobilized all their forces, organized pressure on members of Parliament from their constituencies, lobbied them at Westminster. These activities predictably roused the country clergy, and anti-Quaker petitions flowed in. But, thanks to the effective Quaker machine and the expressed support of Walpole, these efforts failed to stop the bill in the Commons. There it was passed, 'greatly to the satisfaction of your Committee', as the Quaker committee reported, 'as well as the Meeting' – that is, the Meeting for Sufferings in London. But the satisfaction was short-lived. When the bill came to the Lords, it was defeated by fifty-four votes to thirty-five. Fifteen bishops voted against it. So did the Lord Chancellor and the Lord Chief Justice. Walpole, it seems, had seen the danger signal and found it prudent to yield.[5]

So ended the attempt of the Quakers to improve the legal toleration which they enjoyed. Meanwhile, what of the other Dissenters – the Presbyterians, Independents, and Baptists – whose demand for repeal of the Test and Corporation Acts had seemed to Walpole so dangerous? They, too, had begun to organize, though not so early or so efficiently as the Quakers. Having been tempted with the ample toleration offered them by James II, they naturally regarded the limited toleration granted to them by Parliament as insufficient; and, once the danger of Tory reaction was over, they said so. When an address of congratulation to the government on the defeat of the Jacobite rising of 1715 was being considered, some of them wished to 'speak plainly of the hardships the Dissenters lay under, and of the little regard that was had to them, notwithstanding their steadfast loyalty to His Majesty'. That was a time when Walpole had refused to consider the repeal of the Occasional Conformity and Schism Acts. It is true, an Act of Indemnity for those who had taken office in breach of the Corporation Act had been passed in 1714, but it was for one year only and had not been renewed: it would not be repeated till the last year of George I's reign, 1727.

In such circumstances the Dissenters might well feel betrayed, and it was in the same year, 1715, that a club of lay Dissenters was formed, explicitly in imitation of the Quaker system, to work for a larger toleration. However, it was not until 1732, when the Quakers were pressing for their Tithe Bill, that the other Dissenters made their serious attempt to secure the repeal of the Test and Corporation Acts. They were encouraged to do so by particular provocations in London and Liverpool and by the knowledge that Walpole was at that time planning to relieve Irish Dissenters of sacramental tests. Their model, once again, was provided by the Quakers, who, as their committee observed, with much smaller numbers and far smaller resources, 'have been more considered, and have received favours of greater difficulty to be obtained than anything we have to ask'.[6]

For ten years the Dissenters, through their 'Deputies', agitated for repeal of the Test and Corporation Acts. Walpole treated them much as he treated the Quakers. He received their successive leaders, assured them of his favour, reminded them of his immediate difficulties, urged them not to rock the boat, warned them of perils ahead if they pressed too hard, and, when they did go ahead in 1736, saw to it that they were defeated. This time he made no pretence of support. Lip-service might be paid to a small sect requesting limited concessions, but the Test and Corporation Acts were essential bulwarks of the Anglican monopoly. So, when the Dissenters' bill was brought to the House of Commons, he professed himself 'a sincere member of the Church of England' and voted against it. The bill was slaughtered. A new campaign mounted in 1739 fared no better; after which the attempt was given up. The Toleration Act, that hastily drafted and imperfect compromise, remained in force, its impact merely mitigated by growing indifference and now annual Acts of Indemnity.

If such was the fate of the Protestant Dissenters whom the Toleration Act of 1689 was designed to favour and reward, what improvement in their lot could be expected by those who were specifically excluded from its benefits: the Papists and the anti-Trinitarians? The Revolution had been made against the former, and naturally they now paid the penalty for the favour which they had enjoyed and the insolence which some of them had shown, under James II. For them the Revolution settlement was an emphatic defeat and the toleration previously granted by royal prerogative was explicitly withdrawn by the victorious Parliament. No Catholic, it was now ruled, could ever be King of England. If the old statutes which were now relaxed against other Dissenters were modified in respect of Roman Catholics, it was merely in order to make them more enforceable; and after each Jacobite plot, or alleged plot – 1696, 1700, 1706, 1715, 1722 – vexatious new measures were introduced: increased fines, licences, restrictions, a double land tax, a special levy, compulsory registration. Between these new pressures and the old restriction of their opportunities by the tests which excluded them from university degrees, Parliament, public office, and service in the armed forces, and thus severed them from Protestants of their class, it is not surprising that Catholicism among the aristocracy and gentry – its chief patrons hitherto – declined, and that by 1780 one of the spokesmen for that class (he was chaplain to the Duke of Norfolk) could plead for their relief on the grounds that they were an inoffensive and dwindling minority which no longer had the means or the will to disturb the Protestant Establishment.[7]

In Ireland, of course, it was quite different. There the Catholics were not a minority – far from it; they were not sheltered by their own aristocracy – that had been largely destroyed; and, though at present cowed, they were not inoffensive. How could the Whig ascendancy forget the events of the seventeenth century; the Irish massacre of 23 October 1641, whose history, vastly exaggerated in the lurid account by Sir John Temple, was regularly recalled in annual commemorative sermons and would long remain an essential part of official Protestant mythology; the Catholic Confederacy, which offered the Crown of Ireland to the Pope; and finally James II's attempt to sever Ireland from England and make it a separate kingdom under the protection of France? That would have been a social as well as a political revolution, and it was inevitable that the English settlers in Ireland would react after the Williamite as they had previously reacted after the Cromwellian reconquest. But Irish Catholicism, as yet, had no influence on the Catholics of England, whose Catholicism was of a very different and far less dangerous kind.

Even so, the English Catholics suffered greater legal disabilities than before the Revolution. But once again, reality was milder than the law, and for them too, as for the Protestant Dissenters, tolerance *de facto* mitigated intolerance *de jure*. English Catholics might be Jacobites at heart, as were many English Tories, but they no more allowed the right of the Pope to decide the matter for them than any of their fellow countrymen. Consequently there was no desire to persecute them. The laws against their priests were not enforced. Their aristocracy and gentry might be diminished by conversion, but at a lower social level their numbers apparently increased.[8] If they wished to send their sons to the university, they could do so:

they could not take degrees, but then neither did many of the Protestant laity. Degrees were for the clergy; for the laity the universities, in that century, were finishing schools. Educationally, they would not fare much worse at Douai. So they were reasonably content with their situation. They had learnt their lesson in the 1670s and 1680s and were not eager to put their practical sufferance at risk by pressing for legal toleration.

Very different was the position of the other group explicitly proscribed by the Toleration Act, the anti-Trinitarians. At first these were represented by the Socinians, 'the most rational of our Non-Conformists', as Francis Osborne described them in the 1650s. They were also – indeed always had been – the most thoroughgoing and systematic advocates of toleration. Consequently all other believers regarded them as intolerable. Because of their belief in the right of human reason to interpret Scripture, and their inability to discover in Scripture any evidence for the doctrine of the Trinity, anti-Trinitarianism was regarded as their distinguishing mark and the Toleration Act was framed to catch them. However, being educated men, and conscious of their numerical weakness, they preferred to evade rather than to challenge the Act, and they knew how to evade it. The most famous of them – and they included Locke and Newton – were careful not to publish their unorthodoxy, which had to be deduced from their resolute silence on the subject of the Trinity. In this they were wise in their generation. Newton's successor at Cambridge, William Whiston, who published his heresy, was deprived of his professorship and banished from the University. Less distinguished men could suffer worse fates. Thomas Emlyn, denounced as an Arian by the Presbyterians of Dublin, spent two years in prison. At a lower social level, the penalties could be worse still. The last heretics to be executed as such in England and Scotland – Edward Wightman burnt at Lichfield in 1612 and Thomas Aikenhead hanged at Glasgow in 1697 – were both condemned for denying the blessed Trinity.

By about 1710 Socinianism as such was on the wane: it was either subsumed into deism or concealed as an unavowed tendency within the established Church. This particularly exasperated the orthodox, who sought to flush it out by sending a pack of parsons into the theological thicket. The operation was not very successful. The famous Robert Boyle, who was an admirer of the Socinians and was himself liable to suspicion, had endowed a series of lectures to prove the existence of God by natural reason. They did not have this effect. As the deist Anthony Collins wrote, 'nobody doubted the existence of the deity until the Boyle lectures had undertaken to prove it'. Even more disastrous was the pious foundation of Lady Moyer, the widow of a rich Turkey merchant, who in 1721 endowed a course of eight lectures every year to prove the doctrine of the Trinity. In attempting this difficult task, the Trinitarians only succeeded in falling out among themselves, so their adversaries had only to sit back and enjoy the spectacle as charges of Tritheism, Sabellianism, and other arcane heresies flew about. The great champion of orthodoxy by this time was Daniel Waterland, Master of Magdalene College, Cambridge, 'our modern Athanasius' as he was called: for by now Arianism had taken over from Socinianism. Arius and Athanasius lived again in the reign of George I, and Waterland was indefatigable in declaring the importance of the doctrine of the Trinity as the necessary preservative against deism, atheism, etc. He provided briefs for the House of Lords in support of a bill 'for the more effectual suppression of blasphemy and profaneness', supported demands that heretics be prosecuted by law, pressed for the expulsion of crypto-Socinians from the Church, and persuaded his university to grant a doctorate to that paladin of orthodoxy, Lord Nottingham as 'a strenuous defender of the doctrine of the Trinity'.[9]

These theological controversies naturally settled nothing. The heretics were either too prudent to be caught or too distinguished to pursue, and the spirit of the age was anyway on their side. The Newtonian philosophy was compatible with a unitary God: it was not compatible with the bizarre *troika* of Athanasius. Like Socinianism before it, the Arianism of the eighteenth century tended to be absorbed into the established Church or to evaporate into deism. Legally it was not to be tolerated; but it was in vain that Charles Leslie, the Jacobite controversialist, hammered away at Socinianism or that the sound Hanoverian Waterland insisted on the importance of the Athanasian Creed, when one of those accused by Leslie was the Archbishop of Canterbury, and that Archbishop had himself declared of that Creed, 'I wish we were well rid of it.'

Thus by the time that George III came to the throne, no change had been made in the admittedly defective Toleration Act of 1689. The idea that there was a natural right to toleration was no more admitted in 1760 than in 1688. Such toleration as was enjoyed was a concession in return for peaceable behaviour, and could theoretically be withdrawn by the public authority which had conceded it. All that had been legally conceded was conditional exemption from the penalties which, legally, were still in force. However, the law, as so often, was behind the facts. Religious intolerance was now out of fashion. Ways had been found in which to evade the law where it was oppressive; and in such circumstances the demand for change needed an external impulse before it could be a serious challenge to the comfortable tolerance of the eighteenth century. That impulse came from the first great shock to post-1688 Whig complacency: the American Revolution.

In her important book, *The 18th Century Commonwealthman*, Caroline Robbins traced the ideas and the careers of the 'real Whigs', the men who considered themselves the true heirs of the Whig revolutionaries of the 1670s and 1680s, and who continued to advocate in the eighteenth century the pure Whig doctrines, as they understood them to be, of Russell and Sidney, Shaftesbury and Locke. These ideas, imperfectly realized in the compromise of 1689, and converted into mere ritual by the established Whig governments after 1714, continued to find expression, particularly in the less favoured countries or subordinate provinces of the British world; in Ireland – that is, in the educated members of the Anglo-Irish ascendancy, like Molesworth and Molyneux; in the Scotland of Andrew Fletcher; and in the America of Washington and Franklin. That 'real Whig' inheritance included the belief in toleration expressed by Milton and Locke – although it has to be admitted that neither Milton nor Locke, whatever their professions, believed in unqualified toleration, for neither of them allowed it to Roman Catholics.

The American Revolution, which split the ruling class in England, reactivated political thinking and gave the 'real Whigs' the opportunity to speak out and be heard. In Parliament, in the universities, and in the press, there were demands for repeal of the Test and Corporation Acts, modification of the Thirty-Nine Articles of the Church of England, abolition of religious tests in the universities, and complete legal toleration of all forms of Dissent. A leading part in this campaign was played by the Unitarians, to whom several 'liberal' clergymen now openly defected. The greatest defection was after the 'Feathers Petition' in 1772.[10] This petition (so named after the tavern in which it had been drawn up) had demanded relaxation of the Articles. After its rejection by Parliament, the struggle was continued in the universities. In Cambridge, thanks largely to the influence of Edmund Law, Master of Peterhouse (then a liberal college), there was a movement for the abolition of discriminatory tests for graduation. The most active agitator in this cause was Law's pupil John Jebb, Fellow of Peterhouse, who afterwards became a Unitarian.[11] Another pupil of Law at Peterhouse was the third Duke of Grafton, Prime Minister from 1767 to 1770 and Chancellor of the University, who was widely regarded as a Unitarian. In London, the centre of agitation was the new Unitarian Academy at Hackney, whose demands for general reform, including, of course, the religious reforms, found regular expression in the annual meetings of the Society for the Commemoration of the Glorious Revolution.[12] Thus powerfully expressed, it seemed that the extension of religious toleration could not long be delayed.

In fact, the one legal extension of toleration in the whole century after the Revolution was one for which no Whig and no Protestant Dissenter except the Unitarian Joseph Priestley had agitated. It is not mentioned by Caroline Robbins. It was indeed inspired by events in America, though in a somewhat oblique way. I refer to the Catholic Relief Act of 1778.

Like the American Revolution itself, this Act was a consequence of the British conquest of French Canada. That conquest led to the passing of the Quebec Act of 1774, guaranteeing, with some necessary reservations, the position and revenues of the Catholic Church.[13] This earliest Relief Act would afterwards lead on to others: first to Pitt's Act in 1791, and then, in the next century, to Catholic Emancipation and the whole train of events which would dismantle what it is now fashionable to call 'the confessional State'. But its immediate results were very different. When it had been passed in England, it was proposed that its operation be extended to Scotland, and a bill to extend it was prepared. In Scotland, however, as we are occasionally reminded, the Pope is still regarded, by the more rigid Presbyterians, as Antichrist. So a group of such stalwarts organized massive and menacing protests from presbyteries, burghs, and trade organizations throughout the country. Roman Catholics, and those who sought to protect them, were terrorized, their houses attacked. In the face of such opposition, the bill was dropped. But the organizers of opposition, having discovered their strength, decided to improve their victory.

'Having', as they boasted, 'by the blessing of Providence, intimidated the promoters of the Popish bill and forced them to desert their cause', they carried their crusade to the source from which the evil had flowed: to London. The result was the famous 'Gordon Riots', when the City was terrorized and ransacked for a week. Antipopery, the weapon that the Whigs had used so effectively in 1641, in 1679, and in 1688, had escaped from their control and been turned against them. That was a salutary, if expensive, warning against the danger of affronting vulgar prejudice by untimely gestures of liberalism.

Thus, except for one measure which was somewhat ironical, for it was certainly not envisaged or desired by any of the men who made the Revolution of 1688, the defective compromise of the Toleration Act remained unmodified, the intolerant Test and Corporation Acts unrepealed, for an entire century thereafter. And yet the main body of the Dissenters were not dissatisfied. They had sufficient practical toleration and a fair prospect of improvement in future. In 1788, the centenary year, on 4 November, King William's birthday and the eve of his landing in Torbay, the Rev. Andrew Kippis, a Unitarian tutor at the new Unitarian Academy at Hackney, preached, at Old Jewry, the customary sermon to the Society for the Commemoration of the Glorious Revolution. It was a very moderate, indeed, conservative sermon in praise of 'our great Deliverer and the blessings which by him were restored, confirmed and added to the British constitution'. The year 1688, he declared, marked 'the commencement of English freedom'. All that was needed was that the process be carried quietly forward.[14]

Exactly a year later, what a difference! The preacher then was Richard Price, another anti-Trinitarian tutor at the Hackney Academy, and his message was not conservative at all. It was radical, and lyrical in its radicalism. For now another revolution had broken out, and Price, who had already sung the praises of the American Revolution, hailed the Revolution in France as the dawn of a new day which left the English Revolution far behind. That Revolution, he said, had indeed defeated an odious tyranny, and by it 'the principles of toleration gained a triumph'; but we must not rest content with that: 'the toleration then obtained was imperfect'. What was now needed was the completion of that Revolution by imitation of 'a great neighbouring country'; and he went on to sing a paean in praise of a Revolution which was not tentative, pragmatic and limited but had established, all at once, a new system of perfect freedom.[15]

The sequel is well known. Price's sermon provoked the great tirade in which Edmund Burke castigated that 'hotbed of sedition', the Academy of Hackney, and all its preachers, denounced the French Revolution and all its works, and extolled the Revolution of 1688 – not as a stage in English progress but as a final settlement of the English constitution, the frame within which all future reform should be contained. Burke's tirade provoked in turn the manifesto of Tom Paine, repudiating the Revolution of 1688 as an inherently absurd and anyway outdated settlement of no modern relevance or validity. As for toleration, that, said Paine, was no longer even to be considered. The whole concept presupposed an established Church with the right to grant or withhold toleration: it was, therefore, inherent in the corrupt system which the Revolution of 1688 had continued, but which must now be destroyed altogether, as an affront to the natural rights of man. 'Toleration', said Paine, 'is not the opposite of intolerance but is the counterpart of it. Both are despotisms. The one assumes to itself the right of withholding liberty of conscience and the other of granting it. The one is the Pope armed with fire and faggot and the other the Pope selling and granting indulgencies.' So Paine advocated not reform but revolution, not a realization of the 'real Whig' programme which had inspired the supporters of the American Revolution, including Burke himself, but the complete dissolution of the old regime with its established Church, however tolerant. History was to be jettisoned in favour of philosophy, or logic.

The intellectual argument is insoluble, for the two positions rest on distinct foundations. But the practical result is clear. If the American Revolution stimulated the movement towards reform, the French Revolution arrested it altogether. In 1788 there were signs that the imperfections of the English Revolution of 1688 would be overcome. The old regime, which it had preserved and, in its basic structure, prolonged, was beginning to relax. But the French Revolution with its consequences, the Terror and the Napoleonic Wars, changed all that, and the abolition of tests and the extension of equal rights to Dissenters of all kinds, which had seemed so near in 1780, had to wait another half century. Once again we may note the irony of the situation. Just as the Catholic Relief Act of 1778 was the only legal modification of the Toleration Act in its first century,

so it was the Act of Catholic Emancipation in 1829 which precipitated the transformation of the English old regime and its replace-
ment, piecemeal and still incompletely, by a more plural society.
Both these legislative acts, being in favour of Roman Catholics, were
quite contrary to the aims of the reformers of 1688. Both were the
consequences of Empire: one of them a response to the conquest of
Canada, the other to the troubles of Ireland. But their effect was felt
in England in the removal of legal discrimination against all
Dissenters, Catholic, Protestant and Jewish alike.

When the final crunch came – when the reaction against the
French Revolution and the Napoleonic Wars had been digested –
the controversy between the two schools of reformers, between the
Whig Burke, appealing to history, and the radical Paine, appealing
to logic, was resumed. It found expression in the controversy
between the Whig Macaulay and the radical disciples of Bentham
and James Mill. In 1834 the unfinished history of the English
Revolution by Sir James Mackintosh was posthumously published.
Mackintosh was a disciple – a converted disciple – of Burke. Being
unfinished and posthumous, the book needed an editor. The editor,
Mr Wallace, was a radical; and as such he took upon himself to
reprove his author for his unenlightened Whiggish sentiments, his
celebration of the Revolution of 1688 as a glorious achievement of
liberty. Those achievements, said the editor, were really very
contemptible: why had the reformers stopped so short? Why had
they not gone forward to realize a truly radical programme of
complete liberty, general toleration, full rights for Dissenters,
Catholic emancipation?

Macaulay rounded on him and, as usual, did not spare his victim.
Yes, he admitted, the reforms achieved by the Revolution were
certainly incomplete. The old regime was not dismantled. The
Declaration of Right was indeed limited. The Toleration Act was
indeed defective. But what of that? Effective reform is essentially
limited by circumstances and leaves much to be done by later
generations. If the men of 1688 'had been fools enough' to seek to
make all things new,

> they might probably have been interrupted in a debate on
> Filmer's and Sidney's theories of government by the entrance of
> musketeers of Louis's household, and have been marched off,
> two and two, to frame imaginary monarchies and common-

wealths in the Tower. We have had in our own time abundant experience of the effects of such folly . . . This editor, apparently, would have had the English Revolution of 1688 end as the revolutions of Spain and Naples ended in our days. Thank God, our deliverers were men of a very different order from the Spanish and Neapolitan legislators.

Once again, the argument is insoluble. All we can say is that, of the alternatives on offer in 1688–9, there is no reason to suppose that James II's proposed toleration was sincere, or, even if it was, that it would have led to anything but either an intolerant Catholic monarchy or another civil war, while the limited toleration secured by the Act of 1689 was never effectively reduced and, as the Act was interpreted and applied, was effectively enlarged. Whether it could have been enlarged more widely or more rapidly is an open question. The Dissenters were not loved, and open concessions to them could be dangerous, as was shown by the successful opposition to the Quaker Tithe Bill in 1736, the riots which forced the withdrawal of Pelham's 'Jew Bill' in 1753, the Gordon Riots against Catholics in 1780, and the Church and King riots against Dissenters in 1791. Perhaps they achieved as much toleration, in that century, as was continuously practical. Complete toleration, at that time, was certainly impractical. Perhaps Macaulay, as so often, was irritatingly right.

15

The Anglo-Scottish Union

Great Britain was united, like France and Spain, in the seventeenth century. Unlike France and Spain, it is threatened with dissolution in the twentieth. Dissolution not through defeat in war – we have emerged victorious from two great wars – but in peace: as long a period of peace as Europe has ever known. Already we have seen the process begin. Ireland, a colony, conquered by England in the twelfth century, firmly subjected in the seventeenth, politically united in 1800, was detached after the First World War. That separation has been digested. The case of Scotland is quite different. Scotland has never been a colony. The Union of 1707, negotiated as between equal parties, has always been regarded as a political success. A few years ago the suggestion that Scotland might follow Ireland, that it, might reject the Union of 1707 as Ireland rejected the Union of 1800, would have been unthinkable. Today it is a possibility. Some people hope, some fear, that it will happen within a few years: that we shall soon see the end of Great Britain.

In these circumstances, having been invited to give the Rickman Godlee lecture on an academic, historical, but not too remote or untopical subject, I decided to speak about the Union of England and Scotland: that great, unique and irreversible act of statesmanship, as it has generally seemed, which for nearly three centuries has been taken for granted, but which now, quite suddenly, has been questioned and threatened with dissolution.

It is the suddenness, above all, which surprises us. For the Union was not suddenly made. It did not come from swift conquest, as in Ireland. When Edward I attempted conquest, he failed. The

Cromwellian conquest succeeded, but it dissolved with the conqueror. The Union which we know was a slow growth. The Union of Crowns of 1603, its first stage, had been foreseen, perhaps planned, for a century; the Union of Parliaments, of 1707, for half a century. The tempo of life, we all agree, has quickened in our time; but even so, there is something unnatural, something hectic, in the proposals for political dissolution of the Union after 1974, when we contrast them with its slow, almost organic growth.

The first chapter in the story of the Union is, admittedly, a story of mistakes. It is a story of attempted conquest and successful resistance. That attempted conquest broke the feudal interdependence of the two countries, which had been so obvious, and so productive, in the twelfth century. That successful resistance, which began as a baronial revolt – a revolt, as in eighteenth-century America, not of a people but of a planter class – ended by creating a nation, a national identity, a national myth. But modern colonial history shows that colonization can sometimes develop a country while independence can arrest its growth. The independence of Scotland arrested its development. Proud of their hard-won freedom, the Scots for three centuries jealously preserved themselves from corrupting contact with their immediate and more powerful neighbours. If they looked abroad, they looked to the enemies of England. So, when the War of Independence was followed by the Hundred Years War, they allowed themselves to be used as mercenaries of France: tribesmen available at call for diversionary raids. As Shakespeare's Bishop of Ely would put it, in a play demonstrably written before 1603 (for thereafter, of course, his tune would change),

> For once the eagle England being in prey,
> To her unguarded nest the weasel Scot
> Comes sneaking, and so sucks her princely eggs.

However, when that long war was over, men could look more objectively at the present relations, and remember the old interdependence, of the two countries. In the expanding internationalism of the early sixteenth century, a Scotchman in Paris – the most enlightened and interesting Scotchman of his time, John Mair – wrote that the future of Scotland lay in union with England. The union which he envisaged was a dynastic union, by royal marriage. Only thus, he argued, could two kingdoms, so long hostile to each other though contained in the same island, be brought together; 'and if it be said that the Scots would thereby lose their name and kingdom, so would the English, for the king of both would be called King of Britain'.

A century later, that dynastic Union was achieved, and Scotland, in theory at least, could look forward to a golden age of peace and civilization. James VI, having inherited the Crown of England and received the submission of Ireland, declared himself 'King of Great Britain', and looked forward to what he called a 'more perfect Union'. He wished to leave at his death, 'one worship to God, one kingdom entirely governed, one uniformity of laws'. In this ambition, he went beyond John Mair, for Mair – though as a pre-Reformation Catholic he assumed religious uniformity – assumed also the preservation of distinct laws. In fact, King James's ideal went beyond anything that would ever be realized even after 1707. And it went far beyond anything that would be achieved in his own century: that seventeenth century whose political pattern the modern Scottish nationalists wish to revive and which was in fact the darkest age of Scottish history.

That darkness was not the fault of James VI. In fact, throughout his reign, Scotland enjoyed peace, and his own absence in England was, at that time, a great advantage. The government of Scotland was more stable when its chief executive could no longer be kidnapped in the hunting field, seized in his palace, assassinated by noble factions, or 'rabbled' in the streets of Edinburgh by 'bangster Amazons' and insolent clergy. He could also use his English overdraft to bribe Scotch politicians. By the end of his reign, he could boast with justice that, for the first time in centuries, Scotland was under control: 'Here I sit and govern it with my pen – I write and it is done; and by a Clerk of the Council I govern Scotland now – which others could not do by the sword.'

Why then could it not last? We need not dwell on particular causes or occasions. The fact is that it did not. Immediately after the death of James VI, relations between the two countries went wrong. The King of Scotland used his new English resources against his discontented subjects in Scotland, and thereafter the organized parties of Scotland, having carried out a Scottish revolution with English help, intervened in English affairs. Having entered England, by English invitation, they assumed a right to dictate, in their own interests, the future form of its government. Their dictation became intolerable, and led, a few years later, to a terrible revenge. English nationalism was aroused and Scotland was conquered, as Cromwell put it, 'from the Tweed to the Orcades'. It was by conquest, not agreement – by 'our army at Newcastle' in 1646, by Scottish invasion in 1648 and 1651 – that the Scots had sought to impose their will on England, and it was by conquest, not agreement, that the 'more perfect union' which had been the ambition of King James and Francis Bacon was now imposed on Scotland by the army of the revolutionary English Republic.

Ironically, perhaps, this first 'perfect union', which entailed a union of Parliaments – the first Parliament of Great Britain met in London in 1653 – created, for a brief period, the second era of light in the general darkness of seventeenth-century Scotland. It is imprudent, as I know to my cost, to say this in a public lecture north of the Tweed; but in saying it I am only repeating what Scotchmen themselves have, however grudgingly, admitted. In 1706, on the eve of the successful union of Parliaments, a Scotchman who opposed the impending Union with all his eloquence – a man who, today, would rank as a left-wing SNP propagandist, for he advocated an independent, ideologically motivated Scottish republic – argued that the ideal form of government for such a republic would be what 'we had in the time of Cromwell's usurpation, which form and fabric was good, tho' we cannot approve of the usurper and usurpation in its exercise': so good, he added, 'that the praise and commendation thereof remains unto this day'.[1] A century later, a very different character, a Scotchman who believed in the Union but not in English domination or Cromwellian virtue, reached similar conclusions. 'Cromwell', wrote Sir Walter Scott, 'certainly did much to civilise Scotland.'[2] As Macaulay – another Scot – put it, fifty years later, Cromwell's rule 'had been propitious to the industry and to the physical well-being of the Scottish people. Hating him and cursing him, they could not help thriving under him, and often, during the administration of their legitimate princes, looked back with regret to the golden days of the Usurper.'[3] Perhaps the most telling illustration of that 'civilization', that brief *Pax Cromwelliana* in Scotland, is implicit in a work which records how, in those years, three Englishmen went on a peaceful tour of northern Scotland in order to fish.[4] It was the first time, I think, that Englishmen are recorded as taking fishing holidays in Scotland, and I doubt if the experiment was repeated in the following century.

Whatever its virtues, the *Pax Cromwelliana* lasted only a few years. Good government, toleration, civilization, could not compensate for conquest, national humiliation, forcible reforms. The organized parties of Scotland would not forgive that conquest. Nor, for that matter, would the English forgive the Scots for the attempted conquest of England which had provoked that fearful retribution. In the 1650s passions between English and Scots ran high, and in the 1660s exasperated nationalism expressed itself in the usual language of the time: that is, in religious antipathy. In the reign of King James, his three kingdoms had been tentatively united in a common religion: a cool, almost ecumenical, established Anglicanism which presided, not too uncomfortably, over the quiescent Scottish Kirk and the conformist Church of Ireland. By 1660 that loose and tolerant uniformity was a thing of the past. The three kingdoms might acknowledge a common sovereign, but embittered Counter-Reformation Catholicism in Ireland and embittered Covenanting Presbyterianism in Scotland were matched, in England, by the narrow resentful, persecuting Anglicanism of the so-called Clarendon Code.

In spite of this, the desire for a more perfect union continued. In 1667, seven years after the Restoration, the attempt was made again. Once again, as in 1603, the moving force came from Scotland. It was the Scots who, having enjoyed the full economic advantages of union under the late Usurper, sought to recover the same advantages by a treaty of union under their legitimate King. Once again, reference was made to the ideal set forth by 'His Majesty's royal grandfather, King James'. But this time the union was not to be quite so perfect. There was to be no amalgamation of Law or Church. Only the two Parliaments were to be united. The Scots, who always clung to their own law and their own Church, never showed any strong desire to keep their own Parliament. It was on this point that the English resisted. They objected to the proposed over-representation of the Scots at Westminster; and after three years the project was quietly killed.[5]

So Scotland resumed its independence, which lasted for another forty years. When the great Scotchmen of later times looked back to that period, the words which came naturally to their lips were 'barbarism' and 'slavery'. The feudal power of the nobility; the fanaticism of the clergy; the sterile feuds of the former; the intolerance of the latter; an arrested economy; politics without

public spirit; party labels without political ideas: such were the most
obvious features of Scotland in the later seventeenth century, the
years of Lauderdale and Dundee, the Cameronians and the Killing
Times. David Hume, writing in the 1750s of the political struggles of
the seventeenth century, could discover important principles at
stake in England. In Scotland he could find none. When the Earl of
Argyll landed in Scotland in 1685 to raise the country in support of
Monmouth, Protestantism and liberty, Hume's comment encapsu-
lates his judgment of the whole subject. 'It was in vain', he writes,
'that Argyll summoned a nation so lost to all sense of liberty, so
degraded by repeated iniquities, to rise in vindication of their
violated laws and privileges. The greater part of those who declared
for him were his own vassals: men who, if possible, were still more
sunk in slavery than the rest of the nation.'[6]

Economic arrest, political – and indeed, in certain classes
personal[7] – slavery . . . The primitive economy of Scotland was
emphasized at the end of the seventeenth century by the dreadful
famine years of the 1690s. And this economy, now more than ever,
depended on the English market. In an attempt to escape this
inescapable fact, nationally-minded Scots sought a new source of
prosperity in distant trade. The Darien Scheme, a plan for a Scottish
colony in the isthmus of Panama, like North Sea Oil today, offered
an alternative: a vision (or mirage) of independent wealth. When it
collapsed – through English wickedness, it was said – the moral was
obvious. The hard facts had to be faced. There was no alternative to
economic union with England. The Union of Crowns was not
enough. Indeed, it was now universally declared, the Union of
Crowns was itself a mistake. Separate governments under the same
Crown had only aggravated the disorders, and reduced the material
prosperity of Scotland.[8]

But if the Scots, in 1700, had an interest in economic union, the
English, as yet, did not. To England, Scotland was of interest only
for defence, for security. Always the enemies of England – France
first, then Spain – had sought to strike at England through Scotland.
Theoretically, that danger was now over; for by the Union of
Crowns, the King of England now controlled the defence of
Scotland. Only if that executive union should be threatened would
the English government take serious notice of Scotch politics, Scotch
demands. Already this had happened twice. In 1649 the Scots had
refused to follow the English in abolishing the monarchy, and

Cromwell had promptly invaded Scotland. In 1689 the English had similarly exerted themselves to ensure that William III would be accepted as King of Scotland; for otherwise the Revolution in England was in jeopardy. To England, whatever the internal political system of Scotland, the defence of Britain was an overriding necessity of State. If the Scots wished to force the attention of England to their grievances, the way to do so – a dangerous way but the only sure way – was to threaten a dissolution of the Union of Crowns. This was 'the tartan card' which, after 1700, on the death of Queen Anne's last surviving child, they could play.

In 1703 they played it. By their Act for the Security of the Kingdom, they declared their intention to dissolve the Union of Crowns on the death of Queen Anne. Unless their demands were met, they would not accept the House of Hanover as Kings of Scotland. Their demands, like their positive political plans, were unspecified, but everyone knew what was meant: economic union. The English saw the danger; but they knew also the strength of their own hand. Their response to the Scottish Act of Security was the English Aliens Act, which gave the Scots the choice of total independence, with all that that implied, or negotiation for a complete and permanent union: a union which would offer permanent economic advantages to the Scots in exchange for permanent political security to the English. The Scots did not take long to reflect. Their bluff had been called. They would not be allowed to have their cake and eat it. They at once offered to discuss the terms of Union.

So the negotiations began. The great question was, how could the Scots, while securing their economic advantages, preserve their essential institutions? In the end, the formula of the projected union of 1667–70 was preserved. The Church and the Law were untouched; the national Parliament was scrapped. These decisions showed the Scotch priorities. The lawcourts and the General Assembly of the Kirk were the real native institutions of Lowland Scotland, the guardians of its national identity. They were the Ark of its Covenant which it was profanity to touch or reform. Therefore they were untouched, at least for the time being. Ultimately, it was thought, time would gradually efface the differences which, at present, it was politic to respect. In fact, time did no such thing. Forty-seven years later, an English Lord Chancellor and a Scotch judge would lament together the slowness of the legal assimilation between the two countries which both thought desirable. 'Those great men who conceived and executed the plan of the Union, who felt *quantae molis erat Britannicam condere gentem*, wished', wrote Lord Hardwicke, to attain a uniformity of laws, 'but found it impracticable at the outset; but I have reason to think that they never imagined near half a century would have passed' without a remedy to that 'evil' which rendered 'an incorporating union . . . very defective'.[9] Over 200 years later, we happily accept that 'evil'.

Compared with the Law and the Church, those twin palladia of the Scottish nation, what was the Scottish Parliament? A formal gathering of 'barons' and burgh merchants, summoned simply to approve the acts of power, it had recently been emancipated from the effective control of the Crown exercised through the Lords of the Articles. But it had no deep roots, no historic rôle, no continuous identity. The Scots never lamented its loss under Cromwell. They had been ready to displace it to London under Charles II. Forty years later, their attitude was the same. The same radical writer whom I have already quoted, who dreaded the prospect of the Union as a threat to the nation, its independence, and its Church, had no wish to preserve its Parliament. Even in an independent Scottish republic, he would have abolished that secular institution, which only gave to the nobility an occasion 'for rumbling and rattling in coaches, spending and debauching their time, health, strength and estates in pride, prodigality, drinking and swearing and the like'.[10] If they could keep their Church and their Law, the Scots did not mind losing that costly and feeble Assembly.

Except, of course, the lesser nobility whose social theatre it was. Living frugally on their estates, afraid of the solvent power of money and of social mobility which would destroy their primitive economy, too poor to travel south to the new capital, or to 'rumble and rattle in their coaches' among the English nobility, it is not surprising that they were the last defenders of an independent Parliament, the most vocal opponents of a Union which threatened to dissolve their social power. When the Act of Union was debated in Scotland, what patriotic rhetoric was heard from the Scottish 'barons of Parliament'! When I was at school in Scotland, Lord Belhaven's pathetic lament for Scottish independence was held up to us as a model of classic eloquence. Demosthenes and Cicero were nothing to that preposterous bombast, which, when he printed it, had a great vogue among the shopkeepers and caddies of Edinburgh. Unfortunately, as delivered in the Parliament House, with a well-timed interval for a well-jerked tear, it had less effect. Not only was Lord Belhaven a somewhat ridiculous figure – 'a rough, fat, black, noisy man, more like a butcher than a lord'[11] – but, the votes being already fixed on party lines, not one of them could be shifted: a salutary lesson to anyone who hopes, by reason or eloquence, to sway a legislature.

More interesting, to a social historian, are the writings of that other great opponent of the Union, 'the patriot' *par excellence*, 'the Cato of Scotland', Andrew Fletcher of Saltoun. Saltoun was a travelled man, a scholar, a thinker, one of the 'Commonwealth-men' of the period, who believed in antique Roman virtue, the *virtù* of the 'civic humanists' of the Renaissance. And yet what was his solution to the problem of Scotland? In order to sustain its independence, he advocated the reintroduction of domestic slavery. Slave-labour, legally and forcibly immobilized, would, he believed, create the basis of new national wealth. It would also solve the servant problem for landlords. To make the system effective, it would – he admitted – have to be introduced secretly and cunningly; the Highlands would have to be conquered in order to close to runaway slaves that 'vast and unsearchable retreat'; and those who obstinately refused to submit to a servile condition should be dumped abroad: they should be presented as galley slaves to that other ruthless aristocratic republic, the Signory of Venice.[12] Thus Saltoun's patriotic alternative to union with England was an immobilized reactionary republic in which the 'freedom' of a Spartan nobility would be secured by the enslavement of a Helot peasantry. Such was the ideal of the last defenders of Scottish 'independence' against a union with England which seemed to them a dangerous social revolution.

In this at least they were right. To the English, the Union was an external matter, a matter of necessary defence, a means of securing an exposed coastline. When it was achieved, it changed English society not at all. Even the English Parliament was hardly affected by it. Forty-five Scotchmen, obediently following the Lord Advocate and voting solidly for the government, were not likely to disconcert an English legislature. In eighteenth-century parliamentary life, Scotland was – as to some extent it still is – a large and useful party fief. The impact of the Union on England was superficial; and because it was superficial there, its wider significance is too little studied by our Anglocentric students of history.

But to Scotland it was a far more fundamental change. Although it contained no explicit provisions for social reform – that Cromwellian mistake would not be repeated[13] – it was in fact the beginning of a radical and permanent change: the opening up of a closed society, a social transformation, a revolution.

The Act of Union should not be seen as the action of a few years only. It was the culmination of a century of frustration in both countries, and in Scotland the beginning of a century of rapid change. By it, in the next half-century, the old, introverted society of Scotland – the anarchical noble republic which Fletcher of Saltoun had hoped to pickle and preserve – was quietly dissolved. The independent 'Parliament' in Edinburgh was happily forgotten. Intelligent Scots were glad to be set free from sterile political faction and to concentrate on the new opportunities offered to them within the English empire, to which, by their energy, they gave a new substance, converting it, or parts of it, from an empire of commerce into an empire of settlement. By these methods, the wealth of Scotland increased. The mechanics of progress were studied. The age of 'improvement' had begun.

The process was not entirely painless. In 1745 the political danger which the English, by Union, had sought to avert suddenly reappeared. 'The Young Pretender' arrived from France and landed in the Western Highlands – that Celtic fringe which had always resisted government from Edinburgh, London or anywhere else. To politicians in London, the Highlands were a centre of Jacobitism: a political threat. That was too simple a view. The Highlands were not merely the headquarters, or the refuge, of a political party: they were a distinct society. Long before Jacobitism could exist, they had resented Lowland rule. Long after Jacobitism had ceased to exist, they retained their ancient jealousy. Jacobitism, to them, was a means, not an end: a temporary slogan under which the other clans could sometimes unite against the most aggressive of their number, the Campbells, and could even, at times, win over other, more civilized opponents of central rule. In 1745, the chief of clan Campbell, the Duke of Argyll, had long been 'manager' of Scotland. He represented the central government. Hatred of clan Campbell – the real political cement of Highland Jacobitism – coinciding with other resentments, overflowed to embrace the more solid society of Aberdeen. The episcopalians of Aberdeenshire, we are told, did more for the cause than all the Highlanders put together.[14] Thus fortified, the rebels were able by a sudden attack to seize the timorous city of Edinburgh, to carry their cause into England, and precipitate an unseemly panic in the still precarious Hanoverian government of London.

Today Jacobitism, as a cause, is dead, but its ghost sits crowned in its ancient, distinctive home. From the Western Highlands its heirs, by discovering a new opportunity and a new political slogan, have reached out towards Aberdeen. They look forward to a march on Edinburgh. They alarm, from afar, the precarious government in London. The prize that tempts them is not this time the patronage of the English Crown. It is the monopoly of North Sea Oil.

The defeat of the Jacobite Rebellion of 1745 marked the end of the long process of the Union. In the sixteenth and seventeenth centuries, those centuries of English expansion, the historic society of Lowland Scotland had been introverted and defensive, cramped between the power of England and the threat of the Highlands. Now all that was over. In 1707 it had been opened to the south, to England. In 1745 it was opened on its other side. Scotland was now an open society, freed from its past, its 'barbarism', its 'slavery', and like many other societies thus suddenly opened, it released astonishing energies. In the later eighteenth century Europe witnessed the efflorescence of a new culture in what had once been an unknown and primitive society. It was the Scottish Enlightenment: the phenomenon which redeemed the long centuries of darkness, and which is so disliked, if not positively hated, in some of the departments of Scottish history in modern Scotland.

It is interesting to compare Scotland and Ireland in the eighteenth century. Ireland had been ruled by the English Crown far longer than Scotland, but it still had, in the eighteenth century, its own Parliament, and even before 1782 that Parliament was the centre of a real political life. And yet, how little the Irish gained from that apparent independence! The Irish Parliament was not only as effectively controlled, until 1782, by Poyning's Act as the Scotch Parliament had been, until 1690, by the Lords of the Articles: it was even less representative of the country: for it was, after 1689, a Parliament of Protestants – that is, effectively, of English settlers only – the kind of Parliament, *mutatis mutandis*, which Fletcher of Saltoun would have welcomed in Scotland: for it guaranteed only the rights of the landlord class, who in Scotland were natives but in Ireland were foreign. Scotland, after 1707, had no Parliament; but thanks to the new opportunities opened by the Union, it enjoyed an economic and cultural renaissance which drew to it the admiration of the world. At the end of the eighteenth century, when the British government decided to contain Irish discontent by means of a parliamentary union, one of its first acts was to instruct the Keeper of the Records to publish all the documents concerning the Scottish Union, from 1603 to 1707.[15] But it was vain to hope that the union with Ireland of 1800 would have the same effect as the union with Scotland of 1707. Trees so radically different could not produce similar fruit.

For this reason, I believe, all comparisons between the present situation in Scotland and the recent situation in Ireland are invalid. It is possible to make superficial parallels between Irish Home Rule and Scotch Devolution, but as they have no depth, so they will bear no weight. Scotland was never 'planted' as Ireland was – though at one time, General Monck, the Cromwellian commander in Scotland, suggested in despair that it should be.[16] There was no systematic expropriation, no persecution, no disfranchisement. The result is apparent today in the attitude of the Scots abroad. The Irish outside Ireland have been the financial mainstay of Irish separatism, even of Irish terrorism. The Scots outside Scotland have no use for the SNP.

Perhaps it can be argued that the division which has been so fatal in Ireland is present in Scotland in a slightly different form. In each country there is a distinction betwen 'Saxon'* and Celt; Ulster against the rest of Ireland, the Lowlands against the Highlands of Scotland. But once again that division, inflamed by events in Ireland, has been reduced, almost eliminated in Scotland. The point was noticed and made, trenchantly, effectively, as always, by the historian who, above all others, understood the politics and the political history not only of England but of Great Britain: Lord Macaulay. Describing the two battles of Newton Butler and Killiecrankie, which were fought within a few days of each other in 1689 – the former a victory of Saxon over Celt in Ireland, the latter a victory of Celt over Saxon in Scotland – Macaulay remarked how unequally national memory has treated these two battles: the former forgotten in Ireland, the latter famous in Scotland. And he

---

*To forestall protests on behalf of Picts, Normans and Flemings, I hasten to say that I use the word 'Saxon' as a label for a cultural, not an ethnic identity.

gave the reason. 'The Anglo-Saxon and the Celt have been reconciled in Scotland and have never been reconciled in Ireland.' Whereas every victory in Ireland is remembered as a defeat by a large part of the population, 'in Scotland all the great actions of both races are thrown into a common stock and are considered as making up the glory which belongs to the whole country'. So when that great Scottish patriot, Sir Walter Scott, remembered Killiecrankie, 'he seemed utterly to forget that he was a Saxon', and 'his heart swelled with triumph when he related how his own kindred had fled like hares before a smaller number of warriors of a different breed and of a different tongue'.[17]

The creation of a Scottish national identity out of Celtic Highlanders and Saxon Lowlanders was the last, indirect, achievement of the Union of 1707, and it owed much to the mythopoeic powers of Sir Walter Scott. Before, and even after 1707, the Lowlanders looked on the Highlanders as barbarians. The Highlanders, James VI told his son, are 'barbarous', the Islanders 'utterly barbarous'. Half a century later, it was a crime never to be forgiven to Montrose that he had mobilized these barbarians against the settled towns of the Lowlands. Another half-century, and Fletcher of Saltoun was describing the Highlanders as wretched savages and beggars. Yet another, and David Hume would declaim against the 'bare-arsed Highlanders', 'the bravest but the most worthless' of British subjects, whose invasion in 1745 would threaten to overturn 'the most perfect system of government'. To all these men, and to their contemporaries, the Highlanders were lazy good-for-nothing rogues who lived by blackmail, wore Irish philibegs and spoke the Irish tongue. But once their distinctive way of life was broken – and after 1745, being already in decay, it was decisively broken – their character miraculously changed. From idle, illiterate, thieving rogues they became, in retrospect, romantic and picturesque. A Lancashire ironmonger devised for them a new garment, the tartan kilt;[18] and soon those kilts and tartans had been draped, not only over the bare arses of the Highlanders but, mystically, figuratively, over all Scotland from the Tweed to the Orcades. Once again, the magician who achieved this miracle was Sir Walter Scott. Once again, I appeal for descriptive words to that great historian who was himself by origin a Highlander, Macaulay. Describing the triumph of Highland romanticism over Lowland sense, Macaulay observes that:

the vulgar imagination was, by the early 19th century, so completely occupied by plaids, targets and claymores that, by most Englishmen, Scotchman and Highlander were regarded as synonymous words. Few people seemed to be aware that, at no remote period, a Macdonald or a Macgregor in his tartan was, to a citizen of Edinburgh or Glasgow, what an Indian hunter in his war-paint is to an inhabitant of Philadelphia or Boston. Artists and actors represented Bruce and Douglas in striped petticoats. They might as well have represented Washington brandishing a tomahawk and girt with a string of scalps. At length the fashion reached a point beyond which it is not easy to proceed. The last British king who held a court in Holyrood thought that he could not give a more striking proof of his respect for the usages which had prevailed in Scotland before the Union than by disguising himself in what, before the Union, was considered by nine Scotchmen out of ten as the dress of a thief.

Sir Walter Scott, who incidentally stage-managed this bizarre performance by King George IV, was a Unionist, a convinced Unionist – in retrospect. Had he lived at the time, he once wrote, he would have given his life to prevent the Union, but since it was 'done before my day, I am sensible [it] was a wise scheme',[19] and now he accepted and defended it. Indeed he thought it better for Scotland to be 'a subordinate species of Northumberland' than risk breaking the Union.[20] But within the Union which he thus accepted, he wished to see Scotland maintain its national identity, and he believed that, by his novels, by his romanticization of the old Scotland which events since 1745 had dissolved, he had given to his country a unifying, compensating national myth.[21] He wished, he wrote, to do for Scotland what Maria Edgeworth had done for Ireland: for her novels, 'had done more towards completing the Union than perhaps all the legislative enactments with which it has been followed up'. Scott's achievement was tied to his own generation. In an earlier generation – in the generation of David Hume or William Robertson – it would have been impossible. In those days Scotchmen were still ashamed of their 'barbarous' pre-Union past which they were busily seeking to undo. But now that, thanks to the Union, Scotland had overtaken England in Progress and Enlightenment, the badges of antique 'barbarism' acquired in retrospect, a nostalgic charm. So did the quaint habits of a defeated Celtic tribalism. Celtic colours could now be assumed, as harmless decoration, by the Saxon Lowlanders of Scotland as they could never be by the Lowland Scots of Ulster, surrounded and threatened by a far stronger Celtic society. The 'Irish' language which Johnson and Boswell heard spoken is now a curiosity, barely heard even in the farthest Hebrides, but today, in the Saxon Border town of Kelso the street-signs are written in bogus Irish characters. That would have amused Sir Walter Scott. It would have shocked another close neighbour, the son of the laird of Ninewells, David Hume.

Behind the mystical Celtic unity which is spread over it, how real is the internal unity of Scotland, how strong the cement which holds together its historically distinct parts? We cannot say. Perhaps it is firmly set; perhaps what seems cement is only veneer. If the SNP were to capture half the parliamentary seats and to declare UDI for the whole of Scotland, we would soon see. Perhaps this new Jacobite movement would then carry along with it the whole country, and the centre of its government would move from the Scots in Edinburgh and London to the Irish in Glasgow. Perhaps the unifying veneer would crack and we would see, as in 1745, as in Ireland since, a new civil war.

It is dangerous to presume upon our history. Hitherto that history has been remarkably smooth. But mistakes are sometimes more easily made than rectified. It is easy for enthusiastic nationalists to speak of simple solutions, a 'reformation without tarrying for any'. But history gives few examples of such easy changes. The new Jacobites, the heirs of the defeated party of 1707, may suppose that the Act of the Union, carried, as it was, against their spiritual ancestors, by an unrepresentative Scotch Parliament, can, nearly three centuries later, be as simply abrogated; for have not times changed and will not the Scottish economy find a firmer base on those speculative oil-rigs afloat and glimmering in the waters of the North Sea? If the Darien Scheme could not provide an alternative to Union with England, perhaps the North Sea Bubble will.

To this, all we can answer is, 'Possibly. Possibly not.' In this lecture I have tried to show that the Union of 1707 was not a simple political act: it was a stage – the most important legislative stage – in a long process. It was the consummation of a century of experiment, and, when it was made, the beginning of a social revolution in Scotland. After that social revolution, there can be no going back, as if it had not happened: no pretence that the last three centuries can be treated as a mere interruption of a history which can be resumed at will, by a mere act of revocation. Scotland and England have – to the great profit of both – become organically entwined and any attempt to divide them again would be not a political separation but the dissection of life. It would also create, of necessity, in the Rump Scotland north of the Border – for the real Scotland overflows its geographical bounds – another social revolution. What course that revolution would take, a historian cannot say. In times of revolution events often move faster than they can be controlled: faster even than they can be understood.

Sources

1 *A Spiritual Conquest? Matteo Ricci in China*

1 For a summary of these projects, see Joseph Needham, *Science and Civilisation in China* IV. iii (Cambridge 1971), p. 534.
2 On this see Needham, op. cit. III (1959), pp. 219ff, 437–50.
3 For the revival, by the Jesuits in China, for their purposes, of the discredited 'Hermetic' fantasies of the Renaissance, see D. P. Walker, *The Ancient Theology* (1972), ch. 6.
4 N. Trigault, *De Christiana Expeditione apud Sinas suscepta . . . ex Matthaei Riccii . . . commentariis libri V* (Augsburg 1615).
5 P. Tacchi-Venturi, *Opere Storiche del P. Matteo Ricci* (2 vols, Macerata 1911–13).
6 Pasquale M. d'Elia, *Fonti Ricciane . . .* (3 vols, Rome 1942–9).
7 Paolo Rossi, *Clavis Universalis* (Milan 1960); Frances Yates, *The Art of Memory* (1966).

2 *Sustaining an Empire: Two Spanish Imperial Statesmen*

1 Fernand Braudel, *La Méditerranée et le monde méditerranéen à l'époque de Philippe II* (Paris 1949), p. 517.
2 William S. Maltby, *Alba: A Biography of Fernando Alvarez de Toledo, Third Duke of Alba, 1507–1582* (Berkeley, Calif., 1984).
3 Gregorio Marañón, *El Conde-Duque de Olivares* (Buenos Aires and Mexico 1939).
4 J. H. Elliott and Jose F. de la Peña, *Memoriales y Cartas del Conde-Duque de Olivares, 1621–1645* (2 vols, Madrid 1978–80); Jonathan Brown and J. H. Elliott, *A Palace for a King: The Buen Retiro and the Court of Philip IV* (New Haven, Conn., 1980).
5 J. H. Elliott, *Richelieu and Olivares* (Cambridge 1984).

3 *Medicine at the Early Stuart Court*

1 Hist. MSS Comm. Cowper MSS II 291–5.
2 See Sir George Clark, *The Royal Society of Physicians in London* I (Oxford 1964),
 p. 196.
3 *Calendar of State Papers, Domestic, 1623–5*. pp. 330, 349.
4 *Works of Francis Bacon*, ed. James Spedding (1859–74), III, p. 373.
5 Ibid. XIV, p. 515.
6 See the account in W. R. Munk, *The Roll of the Royal College of Physicians in London* (1861), from Baldwin Hamey's MS, 'Bustorum Aliquot Reliquiae', in the Royal College of Physicians.
7 British Library MS Sloane 2072 fo. 2v. For other critical judgments of Harvey's therapy, see Sir Geoffrey Keynes, *The Life of William Harvey* (Oxford 1966), pp. 393–4.
8 BL MS Sloane 2069 fos. 65, 230.

4 *Hugo Grotius and England*

1 *Briefwisseling van Hugo Grotius*, ed. P. C. Moelhuysen (The Hague 1928–), Ep. no. 25. The twelve volumes of this great series so far published carry Grotius's correspondence up to the end of 1642. I therefore give references to it (as *BHG*) for that period, citing letters by their number. For the period 1643–5 I quote from the older collection published by Grotius's grandsons Huig and Jan de Groot, *Hugonis Grotii Espistolae* (Amsterdam 1687).
2 *BHG*, Epp. 1769, 1633.
3 *Parallelon Rerumpublicarum liber tertius* (Haarlem 1802), XXIV, pp. 34–5.
4 Hugo Grotius, *Meletius*, ed. Guillaume Posthumus-Meyjes (Leiden 1988).
5 *BHG*, Ep. 239.
6 *BHG*, Ep. 219.
7 *BHG*, Epp. 268, 271.
8 *BHG*, Epp. 259, 262, 265.
9 *Ordinum Hollandiae ac Westfrisiae Pietas* (1613).
10 *Defensio Fidei Catholicae de Satisfactione Christi adversus Faustum Socinum* (written ?1614, published 1617).
11 E.g. Bishop Bramhall. See *Bishop Bramhall's Vindication of himself and the episcopal clergy . . .* (1672), p. 18.
12 *Letters of John Chamberlain*, ed. J. C. McClure (Philadelphia 1939), II, p. 111.
13 *BHG*, Ep. 266.
14 *BHG*, Ep. 403.
15 *Hugonis Grotii Opera Theologica* (1679) III, p. 654.
16 *BHG*, Ep. 595.
17 The relations of Grotius with Dudley Carleton are documented in PRO State Papers, Holland, many of which are printed in *Letters from and to*

Sir Dudley Carleton from January 1615–6 to December 1620, ed. Philip Yorke, 2nd Earl of Hardwicke (1757). They are further illustrated by the private correspondence of Carleton with John Chamberlain. See *The Letters of John Chamberlain*, II, pp. 111, 138, 141; *Dudley Carleton to John Chamberlain 1603–24*, ed. Maurice Lee jr. (Rutgers University Press 1972), pp. 247, 250, 253. The letter to de Dominis is printed in *BHG*, Ep. 542. See also Noel Malcolm, *De Dominis (1560–1624), Venetian, Anglican, Ecumenist and Relapsed Heretic* (1984), pp. 58–60.

18 Carleton, *Letters*, p. 253.
19 *BHG*, Ep. 595.
20 *BHG*, Ep. 590.
21 *BHG*, Ep. 653.
22 *BHG*, Epp. 653, 662, 858. Grotius remained a firm supporter of de Dominis's ideas. He was 'a man of great judgment', he wrote in 1639, 'except for one thing: that he went to Rome' (*'magni vir iudicii, si unum excipias, quod Romam ivit'* (Ep. 4288).
23 *BHG*, Ep. 668.
24 *BHG*, Ep. 998. As Louis Aubéry du Maurier wrote, Richelieu drove a great man out of France to save 3,000 livres p.a. while spending 80,000 livres p.a. maintaining third-rate poets 'to praise him continually as a visible God' (*Mémoires pour servir à l'histoire de Hollande* (1680), p. 409).
25 *BHG*, Epp. 869, 874, 884.
26 *BHG*, Ep. 1864.
27 *BHG*, Epp. 965, 1460.
28 *BHG*, Epp. 782, 784, 788.
29 *BHG*, Epp. 1342, 1382.
30 Grotius's letter to Laud does not survive, but it is mentioned by Laud to Vossius on 7 Nov. 1631: '*Attulit secum* [Franciscus Junius] *litteras ab amplissimo viro Hugone Grotio ad me datas. Gratissimae illae . . . sed rescribendi otium non datur.*' (Laud, *Works* (1847–60) VI, p. 297). Since Junius left Grotius in Paris, the letter must have been written while Grotius was still there. For his uncertainty about his return as late as April 1631 see Grotius's letter to his brother from Paris, *BHG*, Ep. 1613.
31 *BHG*, Ep. 1737.
32 *G.J. Vossii et clarorum virorum ad eum Epistolae* (1690), Ep. clviii, and cf. ibid., Ep. clix.
33 ' . . . *sed et ab Anglia aliqua me aura afflavit. Deliberandum est diu quod faciendum est semel*'. *BHG*, Ep. 1745.
34 ' . . . *sed ut nunc res sunt apud nos, de ea re ne cogitandum quidem*'. Laud, *Works* (1847–60) VI, p. 299.
35 *Vossii Epistolae*, Ep. clxxxii.
36 *BHG*, Ep. 1745.
37 *BHG*, Epp. 1815, 1819, 1909, 1921.
38 *Vossii Epistolae*, Epp. cxcv, ccx.
39 *BHG*, Ep. 1907.
40 *BHG*, Epp. 1929, 1933, 1935; *Merici Casauboni . . . Epistolae*, p. 8, printed in *Isaaci Casauboni Epistolae*, 3rd edition (Rotterdam 1709).
41 *BHG*, Ep. 2011.

42 Louis Aubéry du Maurier, *Mémoires pour servir à l'histoire de Hollande* (1680), pp. 413–14.

43 Ibid.

44 Oxenstjerna's complaints were made by his son Bengt Oxenstjerna, who was Swedish ambassador at the Hague, to Grotius's brother-in-law Nicolas van Reigersberch, Letter of 6 Aug. 1644, cited in R. W. Lee, 'Grotius, the Last Phase', (*Transactions of the Grotius Society*, 1945).

45 As Grotius himself felt obliged to report to Oxenstjerna: *'ingratus sane Gallis hospes'*. *BHG*, Ep. 2734.

46 *'multusque mihi cum eo sermo'*. *BHG*, Ep. 2407.

47 Scudamore to Laud 2 Oct. 1637, cited in M. Gibson, *A View of the Churches of Door, Holme Lacy and Hempsted* (1737), pp. 78–81. Cf. *BHG*, Ep. 3355.

48 *BHG*, Epp. 3241–2, 3281, 4786.

49 For Laud's compliments to Grotius retailed by him to Oxenstjerna, see *BHG*, Epp. 3333, 3372.

50 G. H. Turnbull, *Hartlib, Dury and Comenius* (1947), pp. 159–60. Dury approached Grotius through Grotius's protégé Samson Johnson, then chaplain to the British ambassador to the German Princes, Sir Robert Anstruther. On Johnson, see below, pp. 71–2.

51 Turnbull, op. cit., p. 161.

52 For Laud's ambiguities, *BHG* 2207, 3372, 3416.

53 I have touched on this in my essay 'Laudianism and Political Power', in *Catholics, Anglicans and Puritans* (1987), pp. 106ff.

54 *BHG*, Epp. 514, 516, 539.

55 *BHG*, Ep. 660.

56 Laud to Goffe 30 Nov. 1638. *BHG*, Ep. 3869.

57 *BHG*, Epp. 2226, 2363, 2523. The States General employed another lawyer, Dirck Graswinckel, to answer Selden. Graswinckel was a former protégé of Grotius and submitted his drafts to him. Grotius sought to tone them down out of respect for Selden and Swedish interests. *BHG*, Epp. 2588, 2732, 2888.

58 For the affair of Samson Johnson see *BHG*, Epp. 2092, 2126, 3787, 3806, 3824, 4039, 4093, 4113, 4124, 4546, 5801; Laud, *Works* VII, pp. 555–7; *Cal. S.P. Dom. 1639*, pp. 76–7, *1639–40*, pp. 9–10, 305–6. Cheynell's charges are in his *The Rise and Growth of Socinianisme* (1643).

59 Laud, *Works*, VI, p. 297; *BHG*, Ep. 2126.

60 *BHG*, Ep. 4074.

61 Du Maurier, op. cit.

62 *BHG*, Ep. 4786.

63 *BHG*, Ep. 5331.

64 L. Twells, 'The Life of Dr. Edward Pococke' in *The Theological Works of the learned Dr. Pococke* (1740) I, pp. 18–20.

65 *BHG*, Epp. 4599, 4653, 4801, 5011, 5018, 5029, 5039, 5312.

66 *BHG*, Ep. 2907.

67 *BHG*, Epp. 4599, 5029.

68 *Hugonis Grotii Opera Theologica* (1679) III, pp. 672, 674.

69 *Grotii Epistolae* II, nos. 650, 674.

70 Johannes de Laet to Sir William Boswell, 9 May 1640. BL Add. MS 6395 fo. 59.

71 *Letters and Journals of Robert Baillie*, ed. D. Laing (Edinburgh 1841–2), III, p. 406.

72 *Lettres de Gui Patin*, ed. J. H. Reveillé-Parise (1846), I, pp. 352, 364. For Patin's personal devotion to Grotius see ibid. II, p. 536; IV, pp. 793–4.

73 '*Verum est bella ferme omnia seculi nostri per religionis dissidia nasci aut ali*'. *Grotii Epistolae* I, no. 1510.

74 *Grotii Opera Theologica* III, p. 684. Cf. *Grotii Epistolae* II, no. 686: '*status ille non malus, qualis fuerat post Licestrii tempora ad nostram captivitatem*'.

75 *Grotii Epistolae* I, no. 1753.

76 *Grotii Opera Theologica* III, p. 744.

77 Hans Bots and Pierre Leroy, 'Hugo Grotius et la Réunion des Chrétiens', *17ème Siècle* (1983).

78 *Opera Theologica* III, p. 744.

79 The clearest expression of Grotius's position in relation to Rome is in the moving letter which he wrote in 1623 to J. Hemelaer, a canon of Antwerp cathedral, who had helped him on his flight to France. *BHG*, Ep. 858.

80 *Grotii Epistolae* II, no. 739. The phrase '*qui* Χειρυθεσίαν *sumerent at Archiepiscopo Hiberno qui ibi est*' is ambiguous. '*Ibi*' could mean in Holland. In 1643 Ussher had contemplated emigrating to Holland and tried, through Dury, who was by then chaplain to the Queen of Bohemia at The Hague, to obtain a professorship at Leiden; but the attempt failed. In December 1644 he was still at Oxford – though still planning emigration.

81 *Grotii Epistolae* I, no. 1753.

82 See the evidence of Sir Richard Browne's chaplain cited by Francis Cholmondeley in 1707 and printed in Jean Leclerc's edition of *De Veritate Religionis Christianae* (Glasgow 1745).

83 The opinion was that of Jérôme Bignon, avocat-général in the Parlement of Paris, '*l'un des plus doctes sujets de ce siècle*', cited by du Maurier, op. cit., p. 393. Bignon encouraged Grotius to publish the Latin version of *De Veritate*, which is dedicated to him.

84 *Grotii Epistolae* I, no. 1597.

85 Grotius read Hobbes's *De Cive* (1640) but, predictably, disapproved of its philosophy (*Grotii Epistolae* II, no. 648).

86 P. Bayle, *Dictionnaire*, s.v. 'Grotius'.

87 Annie Barnes, *Jean Leclerc 1657–1736 et la République de Lettres* (Paris 1938), pp. 46, 145 etc.

88 *Hugonis Grotii Opera Theologica*, Preface. Pieter de Groot's letter to Sir Joseph Williamson seeking permission to dedicate the work to Charles II is printed in W. P. van Stockum, *La Librairie, l'Impression et la Presse* (The Hague 1910), nos. 85–8.

89 *Catholics, Anglicans and Puritans*, pp. 166–230, 'The Great Tew Circle'.

90 E.g. John Milton, who visited him, introduced by Scudamore, in 1638, and Gui Patin, who clearly saw him often: '*j'étois transporté de joie quand je*

l'avois entretenu' (*Lettres de Gui Patin*, ed. J. H. Reveillé-Parise (1846), II, p. 536).

91 *Christ's Passion, a Tragedie* (1640). Grotius was delighted with this translation and sent his thanks to both Sandys and Falkland through Meric Casaubon, who had sent him copies of the work. (*BHG*, Epp. 4405, 4416, 4458, 4543.)

92 Such a meeting is assumed by H. J. McLachlan, *Socinianism in Seventeenth Century England* (Oxford 1951), p. 69.

93 See my *Catholics, Anglicans and Puritans*, p. 218.

5 *The Church of England and the Greek Church in the Time of Charles I*

1 John Jewel, *A defence of the Apology for the Churche of Englande* (1567).

2 For its publishing history see Theodore K. Rabb, 'The Editions of Sir Edwin Sandys's *Relation of the State of Religion*', *Huntington Library Quarterly* 26 (1963).

3 George Sandys, *Relation of a Journey begun A.D. 1610* (1615), pp. 89, 105.

4 Grotius to Casaubon 7 Jan. 1612, in *Briefwisseling van Hugo Grotius*, ed. P. C. Moelhuysen (The Hague 1928–), I, p. 219.

5 Venier to Bailo of Venice, cited in R. J. Roberts, 'The Greek Press at Constantinople in 1627 and Its Antecedents', *Bibliographical Society* (1977).

6 Public Record Office MS SP 14/128. English version in R. Neile, *M. Ant. de Dñis Arch-bishop of Spalato, his shiftings in religion* (1624), pp. 85–8.

7 Cyril to Wtenbogaert 10 Cal Oct. 1613, in *Praestantium ac Eruditorum Virorum Epistolae Ecclesiasticae et Theologicae*, ed. Ph. Limborch (Amsterdam 1684), p. 314.

8 The earliest surviving letter is that of 1615 which I quote here from Bodl. MS Smith 36 fo. 13 (it is printed by Timotheus Themelis in Νέα Σιών 6 1909); but the previous interchange which it presupposes carries the correspondence back to 1612, when Cyril was in Constantinople as ἐπιγηρητής of the patriarchate, and Sir Paul Pindar reported his struggle against the Jesuits there (MS Smith 36 fo. 32).

9 See Savile's epistle to the Reader, in *S. Ioannis Chrysostomi Opera* (Eton 1610) I.

10 See Richard Simon, *La Créance de l'Eglise Orientale sur la Transsubstantiation* (Paris 1687).

11 *The Negotiations of Sir Thomas Roe in his Embassy to the Ottoman Porte 1621–8* (1740), pp. 36, 102.

12 Ibid., p. 146.

13 For Léger see Samuel Baud-Bovy, 'Antoine Léger, pasteur aux vallées vaudoises du Piémont et son séjour à Constantinople', in *Revue d'Histoire Suisse* 24 (1944).

14 Laud, *Works* (1847–60) II, pp. 27, 29, 385.

15 *Briefwisseling van Hugo Grotius* II, p. 240 (Franciscus Junius to Grotius, August 1622).

16 *Negotiations of Sir Thomas Roe*, p. 171.

17 Ibid., pp. 319, 334, 414, 442.

18 Ibid., pp. 459, 500, 618.

19 For the Greek press see especially the article by R. J. Roberts cited above, note 5.

20 Lucas Holstenius to Peiresc, cited in W. D. Macray, *Annals of the Bodleian Library* (1890), p. 73.

21 A. Wood, *Athenae Oxonienses*, ed. P. Bliss (Oxford 1813–20), III, p. 306.

22 For Pococke see L. Twells, 'The Life of Dr. Edward Pococke', prefixed to *The Theological Works of the learned Dr. Pococke* (1740); for Greaves, Thomas Smith, *Vita . . . Johannis Gravii* (1699), reprinted in his *Vitae Quorundam Eruditissimorum et Illustrium Virorum* (1707), and T. Birch, *Miscellaneous Works of John Greaves* (1737), preface.

6   *The Plunder of the Arts in the Seventeenth Century*

1 Albert Speer, *Erinnerungen* (Berlin 1969; Eng. tr. 1970); Cecil Gould, *Trophy of Conquest, the Musée Napoléon and the Creation of the Louvre* (1965).

2 It is the subject of an excellent work, to which I am indebted, J. von Schlosser, *Kunst und Wunderkammern der Spätrenaissance* (Leipzig 1908).

3 I take the phrase from Mr F. H. Taylor's book, *The Taste of Angels* (1948).

4 For Philip II's activity as a patron, see the pioneer essay of Carl Justi, 'Philipp II als Kunstfreund', in his *Miszellaneen aus drei Jahrhunderten Spanischen Kunstlebens* (Berlin 1908); also Pedro Beroquí, *Tiziano en el Prado* (Madrid 1927). According to Beroquí, Philip II '*es mas acreedor que ningún otro gubernante español, antiguo ni moderno, a la gratitud de los amantes de las bellas artes*' (p. 149). For the Familist connexions of Benito Arias Montano, Abraham Ortelius and Christopher Plantin, see (but cautiously) B. Rekers, *Benito Arias Montano 1527–1598* (Amsterdam 1962).

5 For the Habsburg collections in Austria and Bohemia see especially Alfons Lhotsky, *Die Geschichte der Sammlungen* (Vienna 1941–5).

6 Franz von Reber, 'Zur Geschichte des Bayrischen Gemäldeschatzes', in *Katalog der älteren Pinakothek* (Munich 1925). See also, for the Munich collections, M. G. Zimmermann, *Die Bildende Kunst am Hof Herzog Albrechts V von Bayern* (Strasbourg 1895); Franz von Reber, *Kurfürst Maximilian I von Bayern als Gemäldesammler* (Munich 1892).

7 For Antwerp as art-market see the two studies of Jan Denucé, *Inventare und Kunstsammlungen zu Antwerpen in den 16ten und 17ten Jahrhunderten* (Antwerp 1932) and *Kunstausfuhr Antwerpens in 17ten Jahrhundert, die Firma Forchoudt* (Antwerp 1931). Also J. A. Goris, *Études sur les colonies marchandes méridionales . . . à Anvers de 1488 à 1567* (Louvain 1925), pp. 280ff.

8 For this episode see Josef Svátek, *Die Rudolfinische Kunstkammer in Prag* (Vienna 1879), pp. 225ff; Lhotsky, op. cit.

9 The best account of the Palatine Library known to me is in H. Stevenson, sen., *Codices MSS Palatini Graeci Bibliothecae Vaticanae* (Rome 1885).

10 For the work of Baronius see H. Stevenson, sen., *Codices Palatini Latini Bibliothecae Vaticanae* (Rome 1886), pp. cxvii–cxix.

11 For Allatius see *Dizionario Biografico degli Italiani* II (Rome 1960), s.v. 'Allacci, Leone'.

12 For the history of the Mantuan collection and its sale see Alessandro Luzio, *La Galleria dei Gonzaga* (Milan 1913).

13 See Edmond Bonnaffée, *Recherches sur les collections des Richelieu* (Paris 1883).

14 Franz von Reber, *Kurfürst Maximilian I von Bayern* (see note 6).

15 For the Swedish collections before Queen Christina see Olof Granberg, *Svenska Konstsamlingarnas Historia* (Stockholm 1929) vol. I.

16 For Queen Christina's library see Friedrich Blum, *Iter Italicum* (Halle 1830) III, pp. 55–64; B. Dudik, *Iter Romanum* (Vienna 1855) I, pp. 123–80; H. Stevenson, sen., *Codices MSS Graeci Reginae Svecorum et Pii P.P. II Bibliothecae Vaticanae* (Rome 1888), pp. 123, 167; Sten G. Lindberg, 'Queen Christina of Sweden', *Documents and Studies*, ed. Magnus von Platen (Stockholm 1966), pp. 199–225.

17 That Queen Christina ordered the attack on Prague in order to secure the imperial collection was stated by Svátek, op. cit., in 1879. The point cannot be proved; but it seems the only reasonable explanation, and has been adopted by the two modern historians of the collection, Alfons Lhotsky, op. cit., and Jaromir Neumann, *The Picture Gallery of Prague Castle* (Prague 1967). As Neumann writes 'the fate of the Prague art treasures is rightly considered the greatest catastrophe that ever overtook any European art collection'. (Ibid., p. 22).

18 For Queen Christina's picture gallery and its later history see Olof Granberg, *Drottning Kristinas Tavelgalleri . . .* (Stockholm 1896). (Forty-five copies of a French translation of this work were published at Stockholm in 1897, as *La Galerie de Tableaux de la Reine Christine de Suède ayant appartenu à l'Empereur Rodolphe II, plus tard aux Ducs d'Orléans.*)

19 The earliest and best account of the sale of Queen Christina's pictures is the first-hand account by William Buchanan, *Memoirs of Painting* (London 1824) I. See also Granberg, op. cit., and Ellis Waterhouse, 'Queen Christina's Pictures in England', *Analecta Reginensia* I (Stockholm 1966), pp. 372–5.

20 The standard work on the sale of Charles I's pictures is Sir Claude Philips, *The Picture Gallery of Charles I* (1895). See also *Abraham van der Doort's Catalogue of the Collections of Charles I*, ed. Oliver Millar (Walpole Society, vol. XXXVII, 1958–60), and the same editor's *The Inventories and Valuations of the King's Goods 1649–1651* (Walpole Society, vol. XLIII, 1972). I am indebted to Sir Oliver Millar for much help on this subject. On some details of the Commonwealth sale see W. L. F. Nuttall, 'King Charles I's Pictures and the Commonwealth Sale', *Apollo* (Oct. 1965).

The quotation from Clarendon is from his *History of the Rebellion*, ed. W. D. Macray (Oxford 1888), IV, pp. 497–9. For Jabach see F. Grossman, 'Holbein, Flemish Painters and Everhard Jabach', *Burlington Magazine* (Jan. 1951).

8 *'Little Pope Regulus': Matthew Wren, Bishop of Norwich and Ely*

1 *Letters and Journals of Robert Baillie*, ed. D. Laing (Edinburgh 1841–2), III, p. 405.
2 Clarendon, *History of the Rebellion*, ed. W. D. Macray (Oxford 1888), I, pp. 137, 272.
3 On Andrewes as a patron of oriental studies, see Alastair Hamilton, *William Bedwell the Arabist 1563–1632* (Leiden 1985).
4 *The Correspondence of John Cosin . . .* ed. G. Ornsby (Surtees Society, Durham 1869–72), I, p. 44.
5 BL Add. MS 29587 fo. 41.
6 C. H. Cooper, *Memorials of Cambridge* (1860), p. 18.
7 Stephen Wren, *Parentalia . . .* (1750), p. 9.
8 A. Attwater, *Pembroke College, Cambridge, a Short History* (Cambridge 1936), pp. 65–6.
9 Elias Ashmole, *The Institutions, Laws and Ceremonies of the most Noble Order of the Garter* (1672), pp. 193, 201. Cited in *Parentalia*, p. 63; P. King, 'Matthew Wren . . .' (Ph.D thesis, Bristol University, 1969), pp. 61ff.
10 Richard Attwood, MS memoirs cited in *Parentalia*, p. 44.
11 Laud, *Works* V, p. 328.
12 Hist. MSS Commission, *Report* IX, part i, p. 261.
13 Clarendon, op. cit. II, p. 418. Cf. The articles of impeachment, art. 6.
14 Peter Heylyn, *A Brief and Moderate Answer to the seditious and scandalous challenge of Henry Burton . . .* (1636).
15 *The Autobiography . . . of Sir Simonds D'Ewes*, ed. J. O. Halliwell (1845), II, p. 114.
16 *Parentalia*, p. 10.
17 *The Journal of Sir Simonds D'Ewes*, ed. W. Notestein (New Haven, Conn., 1923), pp. 169–71, 178, etc.
18 J. Hacket, *Scrinia Reserata* (1693) I, p. 20.
19 The charge was most vigorously pressed by Francis Cheynell, *The Rise, Growth and Danger of Socinianisme* (1643).
20 N. Pocock, in *Theologian and Ecclesiastic* VII (1849), p. 292.
21 *Parentalia*, p. 34.
22 The correspondence between Clarendon and Barwick is preserved among the Clarendon MSS in the Bodleian Library. Many of the letters are printed in Peter Barwick, *Vita Johannis Barwick STP* (1721).
23 Cited in *Parentalia*, p. 44.
24 Ibid., p. 2.

9 *Edward Hyde, Earl of Clarendon*

1 See especially R. H. Popkin, *The History of Scepticism from Erasmus to Descartes* (Assen 1960).
2 For the fate of Falkland's books see H. J. McLachlan, *Socinianism in England* (Oxford 1951), pp. 121–5.
3 Bodl. MS Clarendon 126 fos. 53–62. 'Cursory and Occasional Con-

siderations, Castle Elizabeth'; fos. 64ff. 'Extravagancies. Jersey, February lst, 1646[−7]'.
4 It is printed, from Clarendon's own holograph MS, in *Essays Divine and Moral: A Collection of Several Tracts of the Rt. Hon. Edward Earl of Clarendon* (1727).
5 *Letters and Journals of Robert Baillie*, ed. D. Laing (Edinburgh 1841–2), III, pp. 387, 409.
6 Pepys, *Diary*, 27 Aug. and 11 Nov. 1667.
7 Hyde's (anonymous) reply to Cressy is his *Animadversions upon a Book entitled Fanaticism Fanatically imputed . . . by a Person of Honour* (1673).

10   *Prince Rupert, the Cavalier*

1 Eliot Warburton's *Memoirs of Prince Rupert and the Cavaliers* (1849) is still a valuable work, containing many documents the originals of which have since disappeared. A good modern biography is Patrick Morrah, *Prince Rupert of the Rhine* (1976).
2 The best study of Rupert's part in the Civil War is in Ronald Hutton, *The Royalist War Effort* (Oxford 1982).
3 *A Declaration of the Queen of Bohemia concerning her coming into England to both Houses of Parliament, wherein is declared the cause of her comming and what she intends to doe* (1641).
4 BL MS Sloane 555. The list is dated 1677.
5 BL MS Sloane 1990 ('*dictante et demonstrante principe Roberto Palatino*', 24 Maii 1637).
6 See Orovida C. Pissarro, *Prince Rupert and the Invention of Mezzotint*, Walpole Society vol. XXXVI (Glasgow 1956–8).

11   *The Continuity of the English Revolution*

1 The phrase in quotation marks is from J.C.D. Clark, *Revolution and Rebellion* (Cambridge 1986), p. 130. I hope I have not misrepresented the argument of this lively and stimulating book.
2 Roe to Queen of Bohemia, *Calendar of State Papers, Domestic, 1635*, p. 9.
3 I have dealt with this episode in *Catholics, Anglicans and Puritans* (1987), pp. 100–1.
4 *The Diary of Thomas Burton Esq.*, ed. J. T. Rutt (1828), II, pp. 214, 218–19, 227–31.
5 [Viscount Saye and Sele], *Vindiciae Veritatis* (1654), p. 33.
6 James Harrington, *Oceana*, in *Works*, ed. J. Toland (1700), pp. 129–30.
7 Clarendon, *History of the Rebellion*, ed. W. D. Macray (Oxford 1888), I, p. 93.
8 Ibid., p. 199.
9 Bedford's notes of his projects are among the MSS of the Duke of Bedford at Woburn, by whose courtesy I have seen them. His

discussions with Sir John Harrison are recorded in BL Stowe MS 326 fos. 71–7.

10 *Letters and Papers of Robert Baillie*, ed. D. Laing (Edinburgh 1841–2), I, p. 186.

11 Charles Webster, *The Great Instauration* (1975).

12 William Welles to John Dury 20 Sept. 1630, cited in G. H. Turnbull, *Hartlib, Dury and Comenius* (1947), p. 136.

13 *The Autobiography of Richard Baxter* (Everyman edition), pp. 71, 80.

14 For Bacon's plans of law reform see C. R. Niehans, 'The Issue of Law Reform in the Puritan Revolution' (Ph.D. thesis, Harvard 1957).

15 Bacon, *Works*, ed. J. A. Spedding (1857–74), XI, p. 252.

16 W. A. L. Vincent, *The State and School Education 1640–1660* (1950).

17 Webster, op. cit., pp. 232–42, Appendix II.

18 Locke's real radicalism and its relation to Leveller ideas is well brought out by Richard Ashcraft, *Revolutionary Politics and Locke's Two Treatises of Government* (Princeton 1989).

12   *The Glorious Revolution of 1688*

1 For an account of the celebrations in and before 1789, see *An Abstract of the History and Proceedings of the Revolution Society in London, to which is annexed a copy of the Bill of Rights* (1789). On the societies in general see E. C. Black, *The Association: British Extraparliamentary Political Organization 1769–93* (Cambridge, Mass., 1963), pp. 11, 29–30, 214–16, and cf. H. T. Dickinson, 'The 18th Century Debate on the Glorious Revolution', in *History* 61 (1976), pp. 28–45.

2 For the 'real Whigs', see Caroline Robbins, *The Eighteenth Century Commonwealthman* (Cambridge, Mass., 1961).

3 Richard Price, *A Discourse on the Love of Our Country* . . . (4 Nov. 1789).

4 T. Paine, *Rights of Man* (1791), pp. 13, 24, 44, 82.

5 The celebrations of 1888 are recorded in *The Times* (4 Dec. and 19 Dec. 1888). I am grateful for these references to Dr J. F. A. Mason.

6 J. C. D. Clark, *Revolution and Rebellion* (Cambridge 1986), p. 130.

7 James Welwood, *Memoirs* (7th ed., 1736), pp. 319–23. For a discussion of the evidence see Ronald Hutton, *Charles II* (Oxford 1989), pp. 441–2.

8 R. Molesworth, *An Account of Denmark as it was in the year 1692* (1694), pp. 43ff, 73, 259.

9 *Complete Prose Works of John Milton* VII (New Haven, Conn., 1974), p. 256.

10 I have developed this argument more fully in my *Catholics, Anglicans and Puritans* (1987), pp. 103–6.

11 Cf. Erich Haase, *Einführung in die Literatur des Refuge* (Berlin 1959), p. 119.

12 Richard Ashcraft, *Revolutionary Politics and Locke's Two Treatises of Government* (Princeton 1989), pp. 592–600.

13 *Our First Whig Historian: Paul de Rapin-Thoyras*

1 For the general character of Huguenot literature and scholarship, I am much indebted to the posthumously published work of Erich Haase, *Einführung in die Literatur des Refuge* (Berlin 1959).

2 Voltaire, *Le Siècle de Louis XIV (catalgue des écrivains)*.

3 Voltaire, *Oeuvres Complètes* (Paris 1825) XXXIV, pp. 326–8.

4 J. Leclerc, *Parrhasiana* (Amsterdam 1699–1701) I, p. 137, cited in Haase, op. cit., pp. 433–4.

5 Haase, op. cit., p. 400.

6 For Rapin's biography see Raoul de Cazenove, *Rapin-Thoyras, sa famille et ses oeuvres* (Paris 1866).

7 The originals of these letters, formerly the property of the Duke of Portland, are deposited in the Nottingham University Library. There are copies in the British Library (Egerton MS 1706).

8 Rapin to Portland 2 March 1701, in N. Japikse, *Correspondentie van Willem III en . . . Portland* (The Hague 1927–37) I, p. 529.

9 See Irene Scouloudi (ed.), *Huguenots in Britain and Their French Background 1550–1800* (1987), pp. 20–1.

10 This is clear from a reference in Leclerc's *Bibliothèque Ancienne et Moderne* (1722) XVIII, where Rapin is said to have been working on his *History* for seventeen years (quoted in Joseph Dedieu, *Montesquieu et la tradition politique anglaise en France*, Paris 1909, p. 87).

11 For an account of the life of Rapin in The Hague, and *la Féauté*, see Jean Rou, *Mémoires inédits et opuscules*, ed. F. Waddington (Paris 1857), II, pp. 258–9.

12 Ibid., p. 269.

13 On Larrey (apart from his own prefaces in his *Histoire d'Angleterre*) see Dedieu, op. cit., pp. 78–84.

14 Rapin's motivation and methods are documented partly in his correspondence (quoted by Rou and Cazenove), partly in the prefaces to his *Dissertation sur les Whigs et les Torys*, *Acta Regia*, and the successive volumes of his *History*.

15 'A Dissertation concerning the Whigs and Tories', in *Memoirs and Secret Negotiations of John Ker of Kersland, esq.* (1727) III, p. 120.

16 R. Shackleton, *Montesquieu* (Oxford 1961), p.292.

17 P. A. Sayous, *Le 18ᵉ siècle à l'étranger* (Paris 1861) I, p. 52.

18 Rapin to Mauclerc, quoted in Cazenove, op. cit.

19 See Warburton's effusion in *Tracts by Warburton and a Warburtonian*, ed. S. Parr (1789), pp. 138–9.

20 Dedieu, op. cit., p. 89.

21 Montesquieu, *De l'Esprit des Lois*, book XI, ch. vi. For Rapin's influence on Montesquieu see Dedieu, op. cit. Nelly Girard d'Albissin, *Un Précurseur de Montesquieu, Rapin-Thoyras* (Paris 1969), adds little to Dedieu.

22 Voltaire, *Dictionnaire Philosophique*, s.v. 'Lois'.

23 *Reliquiae Hearnianae*, ed. P. Bliss (1869), II, p. 311.

24 Samuel Jebb, *The History of the Life and Reign of Mary Queen of Scots* (1725).

25 *A Collection of Several Papers published by Mr Thomas Carte in relation to his History of England* (1744); *The General History of England by Thomas Carte, an Englishman* (1747–55); cf. *A Defence of English History against the Misrepresentations of M. De Rapin-Thoyras* (1734).

26 *The Letters of David Hume*, ed. D. Y. T. Greig (Oxford 1932), I.

14 Religious Toleration after 1688

1 See G. Holmes, *Politics, Religion, and Society in England, 1679–1742* (1986), p. 192.

2 G. Holmes, *The Trial of Doctor Sacheverell* (1973), p. 52; J.P. Kenyon, *Revolution Principles* (Cambridge 1977), p. 94.

3 N. C. Hunt, *Two Early Political Associations* (Oxford 1961), p. 127.

4 For what follows about the Quakers and the Dissenting Deputies, I have been guided by Hunt, op. cit.

5 See S. Taylor, 'Sir Robert Walpole, The Church of England and the Quaker Tithe Bill of 1736', *Historical Journal* 28 (1985), pp. 51–77.

6 Hunt, op. cit., pp. 117, 141.

7 J. Berington, *The State and Behaviour of the English Catholics from the Reformation to 1780* (Birmingham 1780), pt. 1.

8 See J. Bossy, *The English Catholic Community, 1570–1850* (1975), pp. 284, 324–7.

9 On Waterland and his campaign in defence of the Trinity, see the introduction to D. Waterland, *The Works of . . . D. Waterland . . . Now First Collected . . . To which is Prefixed, A Review of the Author's Life and Writings by W. Van Mildert* (Oxford 1823–8) I.

10 C. Robbins, *The 18th Century Commonwealthman* (Cambridge, Mass., 1959).

11 For the agitation in Cambridge, see D. A. Winstanley, *The University of Cambridge in the Eighteenth Century* (Cambridge 1922), and *Unreformed Cambridge: A Study of Certain Aspects of the University in the Eighteenth Century* (Cambridge 1935).

12 For this and other such pressure-groups, see E. C. Black, *The Association: British Extraparliamentary Political Organization, 1769–93* (Cambridge, Mass., 1963).

13 For further information about these events, see R. K. Donovan, 'The Military Origins of the Roman Catholic Relief Programme of 1778', *Historical Journal* 28 (1985), pp. 3–30; see also R. K. Donovan, 'Sir John Dalrymple and the Origins of Roman Catholic Relief, 1775–8', *Recusant History* 17 (1984), pp. 188–96.

14 A. Kippis, *A Sermon Preached at the Old Jewry on 4 Nov. 1788 . . .* (1788). On the Society, see *An Abstract of the History and Proceedings of the Revolution Society in London* (1789).

15 R. Price, *A Discourse on the Love of our Country . . . 4 Nov. 1789* (1789).

15   *The Anglo-Scottish Union*

1   Anon., *The Smoaking Flax Unquenchable* (n.p. 1706), p. 12.
2   *The Works of John Dryden*, ed. Walter Scott (Edinburgh 1809), notes to 'Heroic Stanzas on Oliver Cromwell'.
3   T. B. Macaulay, *History of England*, ch. xiii.
4   Richard Franck, *Northern Memoirs* (Edinburgh 1820).
5   For details see John Bruce (ed.), *Report on the Events and Circumstances which produced the Union of the Kingdoms of England and Scotland . . .* (1799) I, pp. 185–230.
6   D. Hume, *History of England* II (Edinburgh 1754), p. 390.
7   On the enslavement of the Scotch colliers and salters see T. C. Smout, *A History of the Scottish People 1560–1830* (1969), pp. 180–3.
8   See A. V. Dicey and A. S. Rait, *Thoughts on the Union between England and Scotland* (1920), p. 138.
9   Hardwicke to Kames in A. Tytler, *Life of Lord Kames* (1814) I, pp. 292–301.
10   *The Smoaking Flax Unquenchable*, p. 24.
11   G. M. Trevelyan, *England in the Reign of Queen Anne, Ramillies and the Union with Scotland* (1936), p. 274.
12   Andrew Fletcher, *Second Discourse on the Affairs of Scotland*, in *Works* (1749).
13   See Dicey and Rait, op. cit., pp. 249–50.
14   A. and M. Taylor, *Jacobites of Aberdeenshire and Banffshire in the Rising of 1715* (Edinburgh 1934), p. vii.
15   Bruce, ed., *Report . . .*, cited in note 5 above.
16   Monck to Thurloe 4 June 1657, *Thurloe State Papers* VI, p. 330.
17   Macaulay, op. cit., ch. xiii.
18   For the novelty of the kilt see my essay on 'The Highland Tradition of Scotland' in Eric Hobsbawm and Terence Ranger (ed.), *The Invention of Tradition* (Cambridge 1983).
19   *Familiar Letters of Sir Walter Scott*, ed. D. Douglas (Edinburgh 1894), II, pp. 311–12.
20   Walter Scott, *Miscellaneous Works* (Edinburgh 1869–71), XXI, p. 280.
21   General Introduction to *The Waverley Novels*.

Index